MYSTIC STORYTELLER

a Writer's Guide to Using the Tarot for Creative Inspiration

book and companion tarot by **Amanda Hughes**

art by **Roz Kazaz**

Cover and book design by Stacey Williams-Ng
Illustrations by Roz Kazaz
Body text set in Slippery by Eko Bimantara, and
Display text is set in American Typewriter by Joel Kaden and Tony Stan

For information, contact:
La Panthère Studio LLC
www.lapantherestudio.com

ISBN: 979-8-9887096-7-1
Library of Congress Data available upon request

For Pixie and Rachel.

I have heard it said that half the world has nothing to say. Perhaps the other half has, but it is afraid to speak. Banish fear, brace your courage, place your ideal high up with the sun, away from the dirt and squalor and ugliness around you and let that power that makes 'the roar of the high-power presses' enter into your work—energy—courage—life—love. Use your wits, use your eyes. Perhaps you use your physical eyes too much and only see the mask. Find eyes within, look for the door into the unknown country.

Pamela "Pixie" Colman Smith
Artist, Illustrator, and Author

To write about a subject for which you care passionately is a joy. To have other people read and appreciate it only increases that joy.

Rachel Pollack
Seventy-Eight Degrees of Wisdom, A Tarot Journey to Self-Awareness

Praise for Mystic Storyteller

As a writer, I'm always on the hunt for creative inspiration. As a tarot reader, I love looking at the cards in innovative ways. For me, writing is a spiritual practice, and tarot is a creative one—and vice versa. I channel information when I read tarot and do the same when writing. Even so, sometimes I need a little nudge.

In *Mystic Storyteller: A Writer's Guide to Using the Tarot for Creative Inspiration*, author Amanda Hughes ingeniously merges tarot and writing, guiding the reader to discover what she terms 'the intersection of intuition and creativity.' This meticulously researched book delves into the cards and the art of writing, offering a versatile toolkit to sharpen your writerly and tarot skills. With inspired spreads, personal anecdotes, and traditional tarot meanings, this book is adaptable to a variety of intuitive and creative processes, whether you're predicting the future or crafting your next literary masterpiece. From character and plot development to overcoming writer's block, this book is a comprehensive guide, beautifully illustrated with the *Mystic Storyteller Tarot*.

This book is like an MFA with a minor in tarot, the perfect companion for writers and readers alike. A must-have addition to every writer or tarot reader's bookshelf.

Theresa Reed, author of *The Cards You're Dealt - How To Deal When Life Gets Real: A Tarot Guidebook* and *The Uncommon Tarot*

. . .

I've never seen anything like this before, and I think every creative person could learn something using the *Mystic Storyteller* [book] and tarot deck.

From the first page, you're given a crash course on tarot. I've never seen it explained as clearly as this. The artwork on the deck is beautiful and inclusive. We also get a peek into Mandy's introduction to tarot. I believe we all discover our path for a reason. If you follow Mandy, you'll already know how special she is.

Mandy has created something incredible, with explanations of all the cards, examples of difference spreads and a more in-depth examination of the astrology behind the cards.

This is a detailed guide on how to use tarot cards in your creative endeavors, complete with activities, examples and understandable explanations. You don't need to have experience with tarot. You just need access to a deck of cards. There's no better cards than the ones that accompany the book.

Tarot, for me, is a guide to help me through life, so why wouldn't we use it to navigate through the creative parts, too?

Lisa Valentine, paranormal romance author and tarot enthusiast

• • •

Mystic Storyteller: A Writer's Guide to Using the Tarot for Creative Inspiration is a timeless resource for storytellers and tarot enthusiasts alike. Each chapter takes readers on a thoughtful journey guiding them in the practical and magical ways to use tarot to help develop characters, strengthen plotlines, and enhance creativity. Not only are the exercises fun and engaging, but they also encourage deep introspection - making this book a valuable resource for the writer and the seeker.

Mandy's passion for both storytelling and tarot is evident throughout this book - it's like having a best friend and a mentor available 24/7.

Shannon Knight, author of *Tarot & Self-Discovery* and host of "The Tarot Diagnosis"

• • •

The *Mystic Storyteller* tarot deck and book set is unique in the world of tarot offerings. It is a themed deck centered on creative writing, designed to inspire and support writers.

The author and creator, Amanda Hughes, is certainly not the first to create an oracle or book to help writers avail themselves of tarot's natural storytelling magic. Yet, I believe this to be the only tarot deck and book set to give such a broad understanding of tarot and the many ways tarot can be a writer's best friend.

While specifically targeted toward writers, the *Mystic Storyteller* book includes a remarkably comprehensive guide to tarot divination, appropriate for any tarot beginner or tarot enthusiast who wants to deepen their practice.

The *Mystic Storyteller Tarot* is very clearly designed in the Waite-Smith tradition, so most tarot enthusiasts will be able to read with this deck very quickly. The cards are borderless with reversible backs. The tarot characters are diverse and modern. Many card images include items such as typewriters, pens, pencils, notebooks, and laptops to reference creative writing. The artwork is simple, colorful, and appealing.

Although most of the Waite-Smith symbolism is present in the *Mystic Storyteller Tarot*, the traditionally nude characters are wearing clothes. The deck's fashion choices are interesting and often fun. I love that Death is a Goth woman and the Hanged One is wearing a tie-dye.

Amanda Hughes is a wonderful writer. She brings her own talent as a storyteller to the topic of tarot. The book is an excellent tarot tutorial and a creative writers' guide. There are moments when the book also feels a bit like a memoir. I loved learning about her grandfather, a pastor who wrote his sermons on yellow legal pads. My father, who was also a minister, used those same pads for his sermons.

Any writer interested in tarot, and any tarotist interested in writing, will love *Mystic Storyteller.* Tarot collectors, especially those working with the Waite-Smith tradition, and tarot students who want a thorough guidebook will also enjoy this deck and book set."

Christiana Gaudet, author of *Tarot Tour Guide: Tarot, The Four Elements, and Your Spiritual Journey* and host of "Your Tarot Fairy Godmother"

· · ·

Mystic Storyteller: A Writer's Guide to Using the Tarot for Creative Inspiration is more than just a book; it's a source of profound inspiration and empowerment. As a writer and creative professional passionate about discovering fresh ideas, I found *Mystic Storyteller* to be a treasure chest brimming with creative jewels waiting to be discovered.

The *Mystic Storyteller* companion tarot deck is an incredible tool that breathes life into the book's teachings, facilitating every step of your creative journey. The deck's vibrant artwork and innovative design make it an essential companion, enhancing the depth and effectiveness of the spreads and exercises.

The combination of rich historical context, clear and engaging instructions, stunning artwork, comprehensive card meanings, divination glossaries and keywords, deep symbolic interpretations, and versatile creative tools makes this book a must-have for anyone looking to enhance their creative journey through the magical lens of tarot. Whether you are aiming to craft your next bestselling book or the story of your life, this book is a powerful and beautiful instructive tool that reminds you of the magic you hold within.

Connie Diletti, writer, filmmaker, and executive producer of *Inside the Wooniverse* podcast with Colette Baron-Reid

For me, what makes *Mystic Storyteller* a stand-out—beyond the art—is the book: *Mystic Storyteller: A Writer's Guide to Using the Tarot for Creative Inspiration.* Coming in at more than 400 pages, the book guides readers through exercises, spreads, and writer-inspired solutions using every card in the deck.

Oh that I had this book back in the day!

There's so much good to say about this deck and book that I'm not sure where to even begin (or end). Let's just say that for those who don't know tarot and those who do, this is a must-have. The chapter on Symbols, alone, is worth every penny you spend to back the project. Not to mention the information on archetypes, intuitive tarot, practical magic, spreads, and intuitive writing.

It doesn't matter if you've always wanted to write or never wanted to write—you can learn so much with the *Mystic Storyteller* book in hand. And as gorgeous as the deck is, I was a Backer [on the crowdfunding campaign] for the book. The deck is yummy icing on the cake.

Nancy Hendrickson, author of *Ancestral Tarot, Ancestral Grimoire* **and the Ancestral Magick Oracle deck (edited for clarity and length from her original article on Substack)**

Also by the Author

Books by A. Lee Hughes

A Bright Light

Always Remember November

The Heartbreak Bucket List

The Missing Lamb

Only the Rocks That Float

The Scars We Choose, Books One and Two

By Mandy Lee

Searching for Signs

Choose Your Own Adventure

Part One: Let's Get Started 15
  Chapter 1 – Once Upon a Time 17
  Chapter 2 – Why I Wrote This Book....................................... 21
  Chapter 3 – What to Expect and How to Use This Book................ 23
  Chapter 4 – Working with This Book: What You Will (& Will Not) Need.... 25
  Chapter 5 – A Brief History of Tarot....................................... 27
  Chapter 6 – Practical Magic: Esoteric and Spiritual Language 29
  Practice Activity: Your Tarot Guideposts 32

Part Two: Mystic Storytelling.. 35
  Chapter 7 – Intuition + Creativity = Mystic Storyteller................. 37
  Chapter 8 – Why Tarot Cards?.. 41
  Chapter 9 – Tarot, Literally 43
  Chapter 10 – Pamela Colman Smith: The Mysterious "Pixie"........... 45
  Practice Activity: Gut Instincts 48

Part Three: Getting Acquainted with the Tarot 51
  Chapter 11 – Choosing Your Deck 53
  Chapter 12 –The Structure of the Mystic Storyteller Deck 55
  Chapter 13 – Handling the Cards.. 61
  Chapter 14 – Working with Tarot Spreads 64
  Chapter 15 – Reading the Cards Intuitively.............................. 69
  Chapter 16 – Intuiting Reversals 71
  Practice Activity: Tarot Stories 73

Part Four: The Tarot Files 75
  Chapter 17 – Major Arcana: The Big Picture............................. 77
  Key 0 – The Fool.. 80
  Key 1 or I – The Magician.. 88
  Key 2 or II– The High Priestess 96
  Key 3 or III – The Empress.. 104
  Key 4 or IV – The Emperor 112
  Key 5 or V – The Hierophant 120
  Key 6 or VI – The Lovers 126
  Key 7 or VII – The Chariot 134

Key 8 or VIII – Strength..142
Key 9 or IX – The Hermit..150
Key 10 or X – Wheel of Fortune................................158
Key 11 or XI – Justice..168
Key 12 or XII – The Hanged One...............................176
Key 13 or XIII – Death...184
Key 14 or XIV – Temperance......................................192
Key 15 or XV – The Devil..200
Key 16 or XVI – The Tower...208
Key 17 or XVII – The Star...216
Key 18 or XVIII – The Moon.......................................224
Key 19 or XIX – The Sun...232
Key 20 or XX – Judgement..240
Key 21 or XXI – The World..248
Chapter 18 – Minor Arcana: Everyday Stories...........259
Section 1 – The Suits: Elemental Correspondences.........261
Practice Activity: A Suitable Story...........................263
Section 2 – The Numbers: Numbered Correspondences.........264
Practice Activity: Write in the Numbers...................316
Section 3 – The Court Cards......................................319
Practice Activity: Courts of Personality....................348

Part Five: The Tarot Code..351
Chapter 19 – Symbolism in the Tarot........................353
Chapter 20 – The 3 X 7 Tarot Diagram......................387
Chapter 21 – Archetypes..389
Chapter 22 – Numerology: Tarot by the Numbers........395
Chapter 23 – Astrology and the Tarot........................405
Chapter 24 – Your Tarot Code.....................................419
Practice Activity: Similarities and Synchronicities.........429

Part Six: Writing from Within.......................................433
Chapter 25 – Intuitive Writing....................................435
Chapter 26 – Sensory Writing with the Tarot.............436
Practice Activity: Sensory Story-Showing with the Tarot.........439
Chapter 27 – Freewriting Using the Tarot..................442
Practice Activity: Freewriting with the Cards...........444
Chapter 28 – Poetry: Cards for Bards........................445
Practice Activity: Intuit a Haiku...............................447

Chapter 29 – Journaling with the Tarot 450
Practice Activity: Journaling for Joy 454
Chapter 30 – Memoir Writing with the Tarot 458
Practice Activity: Map Your Memoir 462
Chapter 31 – Shuffling Through Writer's Block 466
Practice Activity: The Foolish Trip 470
Chapter 32 – Plot Development: The Hero and The Fool 472
Practice Activity: Plotting The Fool's Journey 478
Chapter 33 - Character Development with the Tarot 480
Practice Activity: Tarot Story Starters 487

Part Seven: The Tarot Games 491
Chapter 34 – The Writer's Cross 493
Chapter 35 – Raiders of the Lost Story Arc 497
Chapter 36 – The Road Less Traveled 499
Chapter 37 – Royal Dialogue 501
Chapter 38 – Growing a Family Tree 502
Chapter 39 – Campfire Storytime 505

Part Eight: Footnotes & Sources 509

Acknowledgements 520

About the Author 522

Part One:

Let's Get Started

"The tarot is actually a book of wisdom that's disguised as a pack of cards... It's like having a sage as a wise friend right in your own pocket."

Ellen Goldberg
Author, Psychotherapist, and Palm Reader

"Celestial Pablum" by Remedios Vargos

Chapter 1: Once Upon a Time

. . . .

Many of my earliest memories include imagining stories I saw in pictures. In 1979, when I was not even three years old, my grandfather salvaged an old school desk from the neighborhood elementary school-turned gardening nursery. I remember sliding onto the wooden seat and opening my coloring books, pop-up fairy tale books, and Little Golden Books—all supplied by my Gran, who was a lifelong voracious reader. I would imagine the stories behind the pictures, often making them up as I wasn't yet able to read.

My favorite of those early books was *Snow White and the Seven Dwarfs*; there was something alluring about the Evil Queen. I loved the shape of her crown and cloak, and I wanted my own fancy mirror that could talk to me, too. I also remember being drawn to the primary colors of Snow White's gown and ribbon. They were the same colors on my circus-themed bedding and in those little colorful balls trapped inside my popper push toy.

As I grew older, the pop-up and Little Golden Books were replaced by picture book boxed sets. All the classics: *Heidi, Little Women, The Secret Garden,* and *Treasure Island*, to name a few. And in the mid-1980s, I discovered Garbage Pail Kids, those macabre, questionable, and hilarious trading cards that parodied the wildly popular Cabbage Patch Kids dolls. Over the span of a few years, I collected nearly the entire first and second series! I got a kick out of imagining the stories behind New Wave Dave and Weird Wendy, Jolly Roger and Phony Lisa.

All those early books and cards inspired me to create my own characters for my own stories, and as I colored and drew and painted my way through my childhood, I found stories everywhere and in everything. When I'd hear the opening tune for *Good Times* on our woodgrain boxed TV set—you know, the one with the broken knob and the foiled antennae— I would race to the living room just so I could watch Ernie Barnes' *Sugar Shack* scroll across the screen. Throughout high school, I wrote poetry, and I studied and created art. I imagined fictional stories behind paintings like Andrew Wyeth's *Christina's World*, Grant Wood's *American Gothic*, Van Gogh's *Starry Night*, *Nighthawks* by Edward Hopper, and all of Remedios Varo's works.

As a novelist, I've found inspiration in my travels and along nature walks. I imagined my very first novel, *The Decembers*, during walks at Fred Howard Park, a barrier island connected to the mainland by a causeway in Tarpon Springs, Florida. I'd made voice notes with my smartphone and eventually completed the book while sitting on the dock of the brackish lake right in our backyard. I wrote *A Bright Light* also while walking (that time at a park in Georgia), and I penned the outline for *The Heartbreak Bucket List* while on a business trip to Waco, Texas.

During my time spent in Tarpon Springs, characters from another book started appearing to me, as if in a vision. I remember the first time it happened as if it were yesterday. I was walking the causeway, surrounded by the Gulf of Mexico, the sun kissing my face, seagulls laughing above me, the wind in my hair. In my mind's eye a lady appeared: an older Black woman with watery eyes and a set of long, silver braids. Somehow, I knew her name was Pinkie Perideaux, but everyone called her "Ms. Pinkie." As the vision expanded, I could clearly see the woman sitting in a wheelchair on a porch. The ocean pulsed against the backyard beach behind her, and she faced a small table, a selection of tarot cards spread out before her.

The tarot is a mystical tool, and those who intuit stories from the cards are mystic storytellers.

Tarot cards? I thought, a shiver masking itself as a Gulf breeze scampering up my arms.

Days later, the scene stayed with me, details forming like clouds in a summer storm: Pinkie Perideaux, like the stone but French in spelling, an elderly woman, rich ebony skin, silver braids, the back porch of a bungalow nestled into a stretch of beach. Cobalt bottles. Wind chimes. Candles. Tarot cards.

She's magical, I said to myself. *A Seer, perhaps?*

That's when it occurred to me that in order to explore this story that was clearly unfolding on someone's back porch—someone wise and mystical and resolute—I needed to know a few things: 1) which cards were on that table, 2) what they meant, 3) who Ms. Pinkie was, and 4) the rest of her story. All of it.

And to know those things, I felt strongly that I needed to start with tarot.

I had to get my hands on a deck of cards. So, I did. After doing a little research to determine which deck included the images I'd seen on the old woman's table, I settled on a classic Rider-Waite-Smith. Flipping through the cards, drinking in every detail, felt like holding an art gallery in my hands. The illustrations—ink drawings with what reminded me of watercolor—seemed to tell a story, each story unique, yet each card its own slice of an overall plot.

Madness kindling a fire in my gut, I hammered out notes in the mornings, walking the beachside park in the evenings, and allowing that new, magical story to tell itself. My mind was opened in a way I'd never before experienced. I'd never imagined writing a story like that one. And using tarot cards? My Bible

Belt upbringing had taught me they were "of the devil" and I would "go to hell" if I dabbled with them. Ever the questioner of rules I don't understand, I began researching the cards and uncovered a wealth of information that was far from evil or "of the devil." I learned that the tarot was steeped in mystery, insights, stories to be discovered, and stories to be written. The cards served as a tool for sharpening my intuition, and through their inspiration I was able to complete Ms. Pinkie's story, my duology titled *The Scars We Choose*. After Pinkie Perideaux brought the tarot to me, I have used the cards to inspire my storytelling ever since.

As someone whose tarot education consisted of scary folklore and random sensationalized images fanned across the big and little screens, learning about the cards was like opening a magical treasure chest. I'd never seen or heard of anything like it, but I knew I had to explore everything inside. To my delight, what I discovered was an entirely new (to me) thought system with its own metaphysical vocabulary. Words like arcana and esoteric and mystic made themselves home in my creative dictionary, and I learned that occult does not, in fact, mean "somethin' that if ya mess with it'll send ya straight to hell." I learned that the pentagram is not satanic in nature but a symbol of life and our connection to the elements and Spirit that was also used centuries ago as a Christian symbol for Jesus Christ's five wounds. I learned that Spirit, with a capital S, is pretty much the same thing as God with a capital G. Most importantly, throughout my tarot education I uncovered an infinite link between mysticism and storytelling. I learned that each tarot card is a story, and when tethered together in a spread, these stories expand and evolve, incorporating applicable, real-life constructs such as relationships, home and work, critical thinking, and creativity.

After all those early months of study, I developed a keen realization of two distinct ideas: the tarot is a mystical tool, and those who intuit stories from the cards are *mystic storytellers*.

Like the pentagram, writers are connected with our stories, some-times   let's be honest, most of the time—investing blood, sweat, and tears during the process of bringing those stories to life. As such, like God, gods, goddesses, the Creator, the Universe, whatever your belief, writing is a divine endeavor. Stories are real, stories are magic... sometimes magick with a K, which manifests intentions to become reality. Therefore, writing is magick. Writers manifest lives and worlds and plots that feel real, well, because they are real. If you are a writer, you are reading this book, and any of this sounds and feels relatable to you, then you, my friend, are a mystic storyteller. I welcome you to join me at The Magician's desk. Every mystic storyteller is The Magician with a capital T, and I am honored to share with you all I've learned about the tools available for manifesting the stories beckoning to be written by you.

Chapter 2: Why I Wrote This Book

· · · · · · · · · · · · · · · · · · · ·

The tarot is a collection of stories, and *Mystic Storyteller* was designed to teach you how to use its stories to write your own. While crafting *Mystic Storyteller,* I blended my decades-long experience as an artist, writer, and instructional designer with my creative tarot practice. As such, from cover to cover this book was designed to function like a reference manual, workbook, and storybook all-in-one. However, the most important tool you will use while working through these pages is your sage intuition.

You are intuitive. You experience gut feelings about people, places, and situations. You somehow know you should turn right instead of turning left. As a writer, you have ideas that come to you, seemingly out of nowhere, and you pore over them until they coalesce into a story. Through your intuition, you can develop every character who first appears as a hint, you can figure out plotlines and build fictional worlds, and you can turn any idea that comes to you into a bestseller-worthy page-turner. The tarot is a vehicle that can help guide your creativity.

The tarot is also a tool that can help you unearth meaningful self-discoveries, shovel compelling ideas into plot holes, chisel away at writer's block, and even stake out an entire novel or fiction series.

Ultimately, I wrote *Mystic Storyteller* as a guide for using tarot cards to inspire and strengthen the craft of storytelling. As you work with this guide, you will uncover insights and instruction around employing the tarot to:

- Enhance your creativity.
- Strengthen your writer's intuition.
- Inspire storytelling ideas and composition.
- Improve your storytelling proficiency through building confidence and encouraging authenticity of voice and style.
- Nurture rich character- and world-building practices.
- Elevate your plot and scene development skills.
- Troubleshoot writer's block.
- Support self-discovery and wellness routines.
- Map out a memoir.
- ...and so much more.

The tarot offers an inclusive, comprehensive examination of the human experience. As such, through personal anecdotes, custom spreads, and stimulating activities, my greatest desire for *Mystic Storyteller* is that you find it supportive of your own.

Chapter 3: How to Use This Book

. . . .

Although *Mystic Storyteller* is arranged in consecutive parts, you are encouraged to use it as a resource, skipping ahead or going back as the instruction and/or practice is needed. No matter where you are in its pages, you will find activities and spreads designed for the practical application of what you've learned along your way. That said, here's an overview of what you can expect to uncover while reading this book.

Part One: Let's Get Started

You are here! In the pages that follow, I will share how to work with this book—what you will and most certainly will not need—along with a brief history of the tarot and some insight around language that might be new to you if you are just getting started with the cards. Finally, you will round out Part One with an activity that walks you through the entire tarot deck.

Part Two: Mystic Storytelling

Use the chapters in Part Two to learn about what awaits you at the intersection of intuition and creativity. In this section, you will learn how the cards can be helpful to your creative practice, as well as how other writers in history either used them or were inspired by them. Additionally, I will introduce you to the artist behind the most popular tarot illustrations to date, Pamela "Pixie" Colman Smith, and how her work inspired the illustrations of the *Mystic Storyteller Tarot* companion deck.

Part Three: Getting Acquainted with the Tarot

The chapters in Part Three cover practical details around handling the cards, working with spreads, reading tarot intuitively, and I will teach you all the ways in which I perceive the cards when they land upside-down, or reversed, in a spread.

Part Four: The Tarot Files

In Part Four, you will receive a thorough examination of the Major and Minor Arcana, including stories, insights, symbols, and word lists associated with the cards. The chapters in Part Four also include 22 spreads, one for each card in the Major Arcana, as well as three practice activities involving the suits, numbers, and Court cards within the Minor Arcana.

Part Five: The Tarot Code

As you venture through Part Five, be prepared to crack open a mystic treasure trove of intriguing facts and stories about the cards, including the symbolism, archetypes, numerology, and astrology interwoven throughout. Furthermore, during this exploration, you will uncover your own unique tarot correspondences: your tarot code.

Part Six: Writing from Within

In Part Six, I will share methods for infusing more mystic intuition into your storytelling practice. These techniques include sensory writing, freewriting, journaling with the tarot, using the cards to map a memoir, plotting and character development with the cards, and employing the tarot for working through writer's block.

Part Seven: The Tarot Games

Part Seven is entirely dedicated to practice activities and tarot spreads you can use for plot development, writing dialogue, and even fleshing out fictional family systems. I'm especially excited to introduce you to my very own "Writer's Cross," a creative version of the classic Celtic Cross spread, and "Campfire Storytime," a tarot game that is exactly what the title suggests.

Part Eight: Appendix

Throughout Mystic Storyteller, I've included references to sources and notes, which are archived in Part Eight.

Next up, I will share what you will and will not need in order to get the most out of working with this book.

Chapter 4: Working with This Book
What You Will (and Will Not) Need

. . . .

There is no right or wrong way to use this book; however, remember that it's a tool. As with any tool, before working with it you need to know how it works and other details around ensuring the tool functions as intended. Nevertheless, here's what you do need in order to work with this book.

What You Need:

The desire to write—and if you're a writer, then you can check this one off the top!

A tarot deck—My recommendation is to use the companion deck to this book, *Mystic Storyteller Tarot[1]*. Exclusively designed to accompany this text, the *Mystic Storyteller Tarot* is a modern, inclusive tarot deck inspired by Pamela Colman "Pixie" Smith's popular tarot designs and filled with new and unique stories to inspire your own.

Something to write with and on—pen/pencil and paper and/or your laptop, desktop, typewriter, or phone.

A quiet workspace—I recommend finding a spot where you have enough elbow room for working with your tarot cards and taking notes from this book's many activities. Ideas that come to mind are your desk (as long as there's enough space and the cat doesn't mind moving) the kitchen counter, a spot on your back porch, a table at the park, a table at your favorite coffee shop, or your bed.

Time—Allow yourself time to read the instruction provided within this book, as well as time to complete the activities. I advise writing when you are most inspired and when your schedule will allow. Like writing, finding inspiration in tarot cards requires the right headspace—when you aren't in the mood, step away. Timing and motivation are crucial to successful creative outcomes.

An open mind—While you don't have to agree with my own thoughts around tarot cards, at the very least I advise approaching the cards with an open mind around how to use their illustrations for practical writing and creative inspiration.

Minimal distractions—As you know, writing requires concentration with minimum interruptions and distractions; otherwise, factors like creativity and motivation are affected. Therefore, while working with your tarot cards, I wholly endorse un-plugging. Exit out of your social media apps and allow time and space for concentration. This means eliminating mental distractions. Can't get away from other people who are living and/or working nearby? Try headphones or earbuds.

What You Will NOT Need

You don't need any experience—Not only do you not need any experience working with the tarot cards to use this book, but you also don't need any writing experience. Whether you are a novice or a professional writer, this book is for you. If you're a seasoned tarot reader or if you have never even seen a tarot card, this book can work for you. Again, all you need is previously listed.

You don't need a finished manuscript or even a draft—If you are a writer but you don't yet have a finished piece, all you need is the desire to write and a willingness to learn new methods of elevating your storytelling experience. On the other hand, if you have a completed manuscript and/or a first draft of your own book, I encourage you to employ Mystic Storyteller for tips, considerations, and other information that might help polish your work before you're ready to move on with its next phase.

You don't need to be a spiritual and/or religious person or have a belief system—Although the tarot is a popular tool for mystical practices, such as divination and manifestation work, the cards can also be used for other purposes. The tarot functions just as effectively aside and separate from spiritual practices or belief systems. Whether you are agnostic, atheist, Christian, Pagan, or otherwise, you can certainly use the tarot for the practical and applicable purposes outlined within this book. (See also Chapter 8 – *Why Tarot Cards, What They Are, and What They Are NOT*)

Now that you know what you will and won't need while working with this book, I'd like to share a brief history of the tarot. I believe it's important, if only curiously satisfying, to know a little about any tool introduced into one's writing routine.

Chapter 5: A Brief History of Tarot

. . . .

Since the origin of human communication, people have shared stories. Even before written language, human beings utilized symbols, pictograms, and other illustrative means, such as cuneiform and hieroglyphics, to convey ideas. From cave drawings to myth and lore, from folk tales to fairy tales, oral tradition to the printing press, stories have informed, entertained, and inspired. Because the tarot is a book of wisdom, the practice of "reading" the cards is an act of storytelling in and of itself.

The tarot's history is as nebulous and mysterious as trying to exact the history of storytelling. Although many tarot scholars report the cards making their initial appearance in the fourteenth century Europe by way of Turkey,[2] other historians maintain that the tarot was brought to Pre-Renaissance Italy in the thirteenth century by a group from the Punjab region of northern India. At the time, because people were incredibly fascinated by the Ancient Egyptians, this group called themselves "gypsies."[3] Their cards, which were hand-painted and featured an array of archetypes and other rich imagery, were used as games for creating stories and writing poetry, and they were eventually employed as a tool for divination. In northern Italy, a version of these illustrated cards was used for a game called "tarocchi"[4] in Italian, which is believed to be where the French "tarot" was derived.

Prior to the early 20th century, the traditional format for tarot decks included fully illustrated and numbered Major Arcana cards, "key cards" that represented "Big Picture" ideas, and 56 Minor Arcana cards, which were called "pips" and conveyed day-to-day themes and ideas. These pip cards only contained symbols, one per suit—Cups, Pentacles (sometimes called "Coins" or "Discs"), Swords, and Wands (sometimes called "Rods")—but they were not fully illustrated. Think of a traditional pack of playing cards. The numbered cards (Five of Diamonds, Ace of Spades, Four of Clubs, etc.) featured symbols that represented the four suits.

In 1909, A. E. Waite commissioned Pamela Colman "Pixie" Smith to illustrate his new tarot deck, including the entire Minor Arcana, totaling 78 individually illustrated cards. This deck would go on to become the most popular and widely distributed deck in tarot history, as each pip was transformed into a fully illustrated scene, complete with setting, symbols, and in most cards, human figures.

You will learn more about Pixie in Chapter 10; however, for a comprehensive history of the tarot, I recommend researching the teachings of Ellen Goldberg, psychotherapist, mystic, and founder of School of Oracles.[5] Ms. Goldberg's lessons were instrumental in my own tarot education. Additionally, I also recommend listening to Theresa Reed's podcast *Tarot Bytes*. After all, she is The Tarot Lady, and her instruction was crucial to my understanding of how to read the cards. As for recommended reading, I wholeheartedly endorse Theresa Reed's *Tarot: No Questions Asked*, Mary K. Greer's *Tarot for Your Self*, and *Seventy-Eight Degrees of Wisdom, A Tarot Journey to Self-Awareness*, by the late, great Rachel Pollack.

In Chapter 6, I'll share with you a list of terms you will stumble upon while working with this book. These terms might not be familiar to you, so it might be helpful to bookmark the chapter.

Chapter 6: Practical Magic, Esoteric and Spiritual Language

. . . .

Sprinkled throughout *Mystic Storyteller*, you will discover terms that are esoteric and spiritual in etymology and relation. Because both the tarot and storytelling can be visceral, technical, and spiritual experiences, the research and musings within this book are imbued with spirituality, mysticism, and magical thinking. More importantly, however, this book is inclusive: everyone is invited to read and use it, no matter your spiritual beliefs or absence thereof. Using the tarot does not have to be a spiritual act or ritual. It can be practical. And this book was designed to be a resource for using the cards to inspire any writer's practice.

My hope is that *Mystic Storyteller*'s language feels accessible—an open pathway rather than a closed door. With that in mind, as you work with its pages, should you come across a term you are not familiar with, it's probably included in the following word list. Here, you can find definitions[6] of the esoteric and spiritual words used throughout this book.

Arcana | är-'kā-nə | (noun): mysterious or specialized knowledge, language, or information accessible only by the initiate. From Latin arcanus, meaning "secret."

Collective | kə -'lek-tiv | (noun): a collective body or group, as in a collective people, message, or experience.

Divination | di-və 'nā shən | (noun): 1) the art or practice that seeks to foresee or foretell future events or discover hidden knowledge usually by the interpretation of omens or by the aid of supernatural powers; 2) unusual insight: intuitive perception.

Energy | 'e-nər-jē | (noun): 1) dynamic quality; 2) a usually positive spiritual force.

Esoteric | e-sȯ-'ter-ik | (adjective): 1) requiring or exhibiting knowledge that is restricted to a small group; 2) difficult to understand; 3) limited to a small circle.

Ether | 'ē-thər | (noun): 1) the rarefied element formerly believed to fill the upper regions of space; 2) the upper regions of space: heavens.

Hermeticism | (,)hər-'me-tə-,si-zəm | (noun): 1) a system of ideas based on hermetic teachings; 2) adherence to or practice of hermetic doctrine.

Manifest |'ma-nə-,fest | (verb): to make evident or certain by showing or displaying.

Metaphysical | ,me-tə-'fi-zi-kəl | (adjective): 1) of or relating to metaphysics; 2) of or relating to the transcendent or to a reality beyond what is perceptible to the senses.

Mystical | 'mi-sti-kəl | (adjective): 1) having a spiritual meaning or reality that is neither apparent to the senses nor obvious to the intelligence; 2) involving or having the nature of an individual's direct subjective communion with God or ultimate reality.

Occult | ə-'kəlt | (noun): matters regarded as involving the action or influence of supernatural or supernormal powers or some secret knowledge of them.

Pagan | 'pā-gən | (noun): a person holding spiritual beliefs other than those of the main or recognized religions.

Pentacle | 'pen(t)ək(ə)l | (noun): a figure of a 5-pointed star usually made with alternate points connected by a continuous line and used as a magick or occult symbol. The circle represents completion and protection.

Pentagram | 'pen-tə-,gram | (noun): the Pagan symbol of the five elements: water, earth, air, fire, and spirit.

Polarity —as in "higher" and "lower," relates to the highest positive and lowest negative aspect, energy, or representation, respectively.

Self / Higher Self—relating to one's inner guidance separate from the personality.

Source | 'sȯrs | (noun): a point of origin or procurement.

Spirit Guides—relating to a spirit or spirits that act as one's protector or guardian.

Universe—relating to the cosmos and all its contents.

Universal consciousness—relating to the idea that there is an underlying source, essence, or universal awareness accessible to every individual in the universe.

Card Capitalization and Interpretation

As you venture through *Mystic Storyteller*, you will notice that the word "the" is capitalized when referencing cards that include it in their title. For example, I capitalize the T in The Fool, The Magician, The High Priestess, and so on. This capitalization is done intentionally, indicating a title and underscoring the idea that each figure within the cards is an actual character who plays a crucial part in their own stories, as well as within the collective. You know, a lot like reality.

No matter your ideals or belief systems, as you read and reference Mystic Storyteller, you are encouraged to adapt the instruction that feels right to you—use your intuition to decide for yourself how you might apply the information to your writing practice. Throughout this book, you are invited to use the cards purely for inspiration and creative insight. You are asked to look at the art—its figures, symbols, and colors—and then decide how you feel about what's happening in the card and how it might help amplify your storytelling. To do that, I'd like to introduce you to your first activity.

The Fool

The Magician

The High Priestess

Practice Activity: Your Tarot Guideposts

Your very first *Mystic Storyteller* activity will allow you the opportunity to uncover your tarot guideposts. Essentially, these "guideposts" will be your favorite cards—the cards that resonate most with you—and you will reference them often while working with this book.

What you need for this activity:

1. Your *Mystic Storyteller Tarot* deck.
2. A quiet space to write without distraction.
3. Tools for notetaking.
4. Your immediate instincts.

Part One:

Review each of the 78 tarot card images. Without thinking, set aside and list each card that speaks to you. These will be cards you find appealing, exciting, alluring—whatever the feeling. If it's a strong, positive feeling, set that card aside and note its title or number—with a simple description, if you are not yet familiar with the cards. After you have sorted through the entire deck, stack and put away the cards you did not select.

Part Two:

There's a reason the cards you selected caught your attention, and as you navigate this book, you will learn about aspects of the tarot and storytelling that can reveal more insight as to why these cards speak to you. For now, the cards you have selected in this activity will serve as guideposts along your journey through this book. However, before you set out to learn more about the images, numbers, and symbols on each card and how they can help season your writing, I'd like for you to take a moment and lay out the cards you selected so that you can see all of them together. Next, answer the following questions, capturing your answers in a notebook or journal.

- What similarities can you see in the cards you selected as your favorites?
- Are there any repeating colors, shapes, numbers, etc. in these cards?
- Do the individuals in the cards remind you of anyone in your life?
- Similarly, do the settings in the cards you selected remind you of somewhere you've been?

- Do any of these cards remind you of a memorable or favorite story or character(s)?
- How do the cards make you feel? Are there any that evoke an emotional response? Do they conjure a particular idea?
- How would you describe those feelings and thoughts?

Part Three: Activity Debrief

In this activity, you selected your personal tarot favorites. I refer to them as "guideposts" because they can serve as anchors for your writing practice. Moving forward, when one or more of these particular cards show up on your writers desk, you are encouraged to pay special attention. Why? Because I believe they can provide additional insight and/or encouragement to both your storytelling efforts and your personal routines. Your guidepost cards are the lights on a holiday tree, the syrup on a hot waffle, the perfect pair of shoes to compliment a great outfit. They are your unique connection to any tarot story.

For additional insight into the meaning of your tarot guidepost cards, Part Four: *The Tarot Files* includes a profile for each of the Major Arcana cards and each numbered set in the Minor Arcana. You can also reference the meaning of the various tarot card symbols and colors in Part Five: *The Tarot Code*.

What's next?

Throughout this book you will have the opportunity to practice using the cards with activities designed to help you incorporate them into your writing practice. As you will soon discover, application is one of the key points where writing and tarot converge. In Part Two, I'd like to introduce you to the intersection of the tarot and mystic storytelling.

· · ·  · · ·

Part Two:
Mystic Storytelling

"Writing is a divine art, and the more I write and read
the more I love it."

Virginia Woolf

Chapter 7: Intuition + Creativity = Mystic Storyteller

. . . .

You can find the mystic storyteller hanging out at the crossroads where intuition and creativity converge. As you are a mystic storyteller, full of magic and ideas and feelings and words that can create entire worlds, perhaps even changing our own, you can find yourself at this intersection.

As a writer, it's likely that you are incredibly creative. You possess the ability to transcend traditional ideas, rules, patterns, relationships, and the like, in order to create something innovative and unique. You are probably original in your thinking and can generate meaningful, new ideas, forms, methods, and interpretations out of seemingly nothing and/or nowhere. After all, creativity, by definition, is the synthesis of originality, progressiveness, and imagination.[7]

Additionally, if you are a creative writer, it's also likely that you experience gut instincts that flow from your fingers and onto the page. During these intuitive hits, I'm pretty sure you've sensed an inner knowing that you should write certain plotlines, give your characters specific attributes, and allow those characters to make various decisions. According to scientist and author Scott Barry Kaufman, creative people are more intuitive; they make decisions based on feelings[8]—on their intuition. In theory, intuition relates to one's inner compass, an inner voice, or a gentle nudging from somewhere or something unknown and unseen. Furthermore, the word intuition means "inner tutor,"[9] and many believe it's a muscle that requires exercise and movement in order to foster peak performance.

Writing is to be close to the Divine. To the creative writer and poet, the act is a spiritual one because we pour our heart, mind, body, and spirit into our work. We are mystics because we weave magic into words that evoke an emotional, mental, physical, and sometimes even spiritual response within both our individual selves and our readers. Mystic storytellers are intuitive. We write the ideas and characters that come to us seemingly from the heavens. Stories bubble to the surface from deep within our instinctive gut, and we cannot rest until they are written and shared.

Sometimes writing comes from the Divine, and thus we are bound to transcribe and share the message. As mentioned in this book's opening story, I am convinced that the fictional characters within my own creative works are not merely imaginings of my own. They appear to me whole and entirely unique to themselves, and a creative knowing moves over me: I am the writer they've chosen to share their stories.

This creative knowing is the best way I can articulate how it feels to find oneself at the intersection of intuition and creativity. The experience manifests itself as an intuitive hit, which sparks an idea, introduces me to a new project, and/or guides me through an existing one. Whenever I'm in the planning phase of novel-writing, my initial ideas that materialize are characters. Stepping forward one by one, I see their faces first, and then the scene unfolds around them, their bodies in motion, walking, standing, sitting, and/or interacting with other characters. Until I uncover the role they play within their stories, these muses seem to haunt me. They stay with me, rattling about, poking me, and pleading with me to give them a home. My story about Pinkie Perideaux is a perfect example (See Chapter 1 – *Once Upon a Time*). Ms. Pinkie wouldn't let up until I had written an entire fiction series around her.

Does this creative knowing resonate with you?

Mystic storytelling is certainly not unique to only me. Many writers have reported their stories appearing to them in either visions or dreams, and then waking from the experience knowing they had to write the people they saw as characters. Dracula first came to Bram Stoker in a dream. On March 8, 1890, Stoker noted in his journal[10] that he experienced a nightmare during which three women descended upon a young man to kiss him "not on the lips but throat." Six days later, after a second dream, Stoker wrote that a Count appeared, turning the women away. "This man belongs to me," the Count declared, becoming one of the most iconic quotes from the wildly successful novel, *Dracula*.

Speaking of vampires, Stephenie Meyer reported that her idea for *Twilight* came to her in a dream. In an appearance on The Oprah Winfrey Show in 2009,[11] the author said, "[The dream] was two people in kind of a little circular meadow with really bright sunlight, and one of them was a beautiful, sparkly boy and one was just a girl who was human and normal, and they were having this conversation. The boy was a vampire, which is so bizarre that I'd be dreaming about vampires, and he was trying to explain to her how much he cared about her and yet at the same time how much he wanted to kill her."

On a cross-country trip with his family in 1991, Stephen King drove through a small town in Nevada, which he said looked like a ghost town. His next thought was that everyone in the town was dead. In his daydreaming, he reported wondering who killed all the people, when what he referred to as his "inner voice" answered, "The sheriff killed them all."[12] That experience led King to penning his novel *Desperation*.

After more than three decades of writing, and even longer creating art, I've worked diligently at training my intuition. As such, my tool of choice for sharpening my inner tutor is the tarot. This book, for example, first appeared to me intuitively as a tool, and it's one that I hope will help you sharpen your intuition as well.

Anyone can use the tarot to spark or support inspiration. But why tarot cards? I will answer this question and more in Chapter 8.

detail of *La Chiromante* by Ettore Tito

Chapter 8: Why Tarot Cards?

. . . .

Why tarot cards? Because tarot is art, art imitates life, and life imitates art. Art is inspirational. Music is inspirational. Movies and theater and books are inspirational. Stories come from everywhere, and both a writer's lived and imagined experiences often inspire their writing. As such, the tarot is a collection of stories that outline the human experience. When using the tarot for creative inspiration, the illustrations can harvest thoughts from the subconscious mind, and as an intuitive storyteller, that's where all my greatest stories are sparked. Because the tarot and storytelling go together like time and the seasons, they can be an incredibly useful tool for intuiting characters, deciphering archetypes, building tropes, fleshing out goals, settling conflicts, understanding psychology and mysticism, and the list goes on.

So, What is the Tarot?

To answer this question, I would like for you to consider the magic of curiosity, learning, and the appreciation of diverse opinions. Synchronously, I ask that you also consider a few practical and quantifiable facts about the tarot. In the following list, I will share factual points about tarot cards, and I also debunk misaligned, preconceived notions and misconceptions about this inspiring tool.

1. The tarot is a set of 78 paper cards that, when arranged together, form a book. This book contains unlimited stories as each card includes infinite interpretations.

2. Each tarot card displays illustrations, which were/are typically designed with common, religious, numerological, and astrological symbolism. Although illustrations vary from deck to deck, this book references the Mystic Storyteller Tarot with custom-designed illustrations inspired by Pamela Colman "Pixie" Smith's traditional imagery. As you will learn in Chapter 10, the Smith-Waite Tarot was illustrated by Pixie in 1909, according to ideas written by mystic storyteller A. E. Waite.

3. The tarot contains two distinct sections—the Major Arcana (grand secrets), which consists of 22 big picture themes, and the Minor Arcana (lesser secrets), which involves 56 day-to-day situations found in everyday life stories. Major

Arcana cards are often referred to as "key cards," and as a collection, these keys are known as "The Fool's journey." The Minor Arcana cards include 16 Court cards (Pages, Knights, Queens, and Kings) as well as numbered cards Ace through 10, or "the pips." This book covers the tarot anatomy in its entirety in Part Three.

4. The tarot has many uses. The cards can be used for self-exploration, journaling, wellness, creative inspiration, storytelling, games, divination, cartomancy, manifestation work, and other practices. Because tarot cards are inanimate, paper cards, the intent with which they are used is most important. For example, my intention when using tarot cards is to learn more about myself and to enhance my storytelling skills. My intent for writing this book was to share that same learned experience with fellow writers like you.

5. The tarot is a comprehensive representation of universal archetypes. According to renowned psychologist Carl Jung, an archetype is a collectively inherited subconscious idea, pattern of thought, or image universally spanning the collective consciousness.[13] If you are a fiction writer, then you most likely know many an archetype: the hero or heroine, the warrior, the trickster, the queen, the mother, the father, the teacher, the lover, and so on. The tarot is full of archetypes, especially in the Major Arcana and the Court cards.

Long before you and I discovered the tarot and learned how the cards can serve our writing practice, other writers not only used them, but they also included the cards in their stories. In the next chapter, I will share a few examples of how the tarot has influenced the literary world.

Chapter 9: Tarot, Literally

. . . .

In this book's introduction, I shared my history of how using the tarot helped me write my fiction duology, *The Scars We Choose*. While my venture with the cards began with the uncovering of a single fictional character, and my subsequent exploration of the tarot cards she was reading, many writers before me have used the tarot for inspiring their own stories.

Historical examples date as far back as William Shakespeare, whose foolish characters were likely informed by The Fool card, the first card of the Major Arcana (See Part Four: *The Tarot Files*), which had been circulating for at least two centuries prior amongst the lineage of European aristocrats and alchemists who heavily supported his work.[14] Wildly regarded as one of his most famous fools, King Lear's trusted advocate takes on many qualities of the tarot's Fool: honesty, loyalty, wittiness, and irony.

Furthermore, when writing his final novel, *The Winter of Our Discontent* (1961), John Steinbeck was influenced by T. S. Elliot and other writers whose work the tarot had inspired.[15] Joseph Campbell's *The Hero with a Thousand Faces* (1973) outlines the Hero's Journey, the adventure model that directly informed A. E. Waite's "Fool's Journey," or the 22 cards of the Major Arcana. You'll learn all about these journeys in Chapter 32.

Tarot cards are also mentioned in *The Magus* (1965), by John Fowles, and in Italo Calvino's novel *The Castle of Crossed Destinies* (1979), his characters use the cards for storytelling purposes along their travels. Moreover, poet couple Sylvia Plath and Ted Hughes heavily relied upon the tarot and its overlapping Kabbalistic principles for many of their poems, essays, and fiction writings.

Stephen King's works such as *Danse Macabre* (1981) and *The Gunslinger* (1982), the first of eight novels in The Dark Tower series, suggest the horror author was familiar with and inspired by the tarot. In the former, King identifies what he refers to as "the three tarot cards of horror."[16] These archetypes, which he asserts are the basis for all monsters, are the Werewolf, the Vampire, and the Thing. Like the tarot, these three blood-thirsty archetypes have been interpreted in a myriad of ways throughout literature and folklore.

Although it's not confirmed whether Virginia Woolf used the tarot or was inspired by the cards when penning her many novels and themes, the celebrated author was directly connected to a web of artists and writers who were. To start, Woolf was a fan of William Butler Yeats, having reviewed his poetry collection,

The Tower (1927), which was deeply imbued with tarot symbolism. Additionally, she shared a 20-year friendship with T. S. Eliot, whose poem "The Waste Land" was published by her publishing company, Hogarth Press, in 1922. In the poem, Eliot mentions Madame Sosostris, "a famous clairvoyante... With a wicked pack of cards."[17] Moreover, Yeats, Eliot, and Woolf's friend, actress Ellen Terry, were all members of the Hermetic Order of the Golden Dawn, a secret society that devoted their time to studying and practicing subjects related to religious symbology, the occult, metaphysics, and the paranormal. Coincidentally, Ellen Terry was also a dear friend to Pamela Colman Smith, the artist behind the most popular tarot card images in the world. Terry even bestowed Smith with her nickname, "Pixie." In addition, writers A. E. Waite, Oscar Wilde, and Bram Stoker were all Golden Dawn members.[18]

It's impossible to know every writer or artist to have been inspired by the tarot. However, thanks to modern technology and diligent researchers, we know more now about the artist behind the most popular tarot images than ever before. In the Chapter 10, I will provide a concise overview of Pamela Colman Smith.

illustration by Pamela Colman Smith for *Annancy Stories* (1899)

Chapter 10: Pamela Colman Smith: The Mysterious "Pixie"

· · · · · · · · · · · · · · · · · · · ·

The *Mystic Storyteller Tarot*, and its illustrations featured throughout this book, were heavily inspired by the artwork of Pamela Colman "Pixie" Smith. As such, I couldn't have written this text or any of my novels her work inspired without recognizing her creative genius. Pixie has a history as sprawling and unique as her many names and creative ventures. A prolific illustrator, author, poet, folklorist, publisher, theater set designer, and psychic artist, Pixie spent most of her life painting, drawing, and writing in her own exceptional ways.

To share a biography about Pixie is to share with you a brand-new tarot deck and then encourage you to read, research, and decide for yourself what you believe. Opinions and theories about the artist's life, her psychic and occult practices, and especially her ethnicity are as varied as interpretations of her famous tarot illustrations. Research Smith's name and you won't find two stories about her that are the same. Gaze at her photos and compare them with those of her ancestral lineage, and, well, you're invited to believe what you will about her background—I know I have my own theories.

Corrine Pamela Mary Colman Smith was born on February 16, 1878, in London, the only child of upper-class Americans Charles Edward Smith and Corinne Colman Smith. The son of Brooklyn mayor and New York Senator Cyrus Porter Smith, Pixie's father was a decorator and developer, and her mother was from an affluent New England family of book publishers and artists. Her maternal uncle, Samuel Colman, was among the famed Hudson River School painters and his work hangs in the Smithsonian.

Because of her mother's love for London theater and her father's professional work in Jamaica, Pixie spent most of her formative years traveling between the two places. While in Jamaica, she was profoundly inspired by the culture and language, so she wrote and illustrated two works of Jamaican folklore, *Annancy Stories*[19] and *Chim-Chim, Folk Stories from Jamaica.*[20] Additionally, from 1893 to 1897, the artist lived in New York, studying at Brooklyn's Pratt Institute where her painting style was heavily inspired by Japanese watercolor techniques.

At the age of 21, after her parents had died, Pixie became actively involved in both the English and New York arts scenes. Right at the turn of the 20th century, when the arts were booming with unconventional ideas, and printing and publishing technology was advancing, Pixie surrounded herself with friends such as stage actress Ellen Terry (who gave her the nickname "Pixie" because of her small frame and impish spirit)[21] and her suffragette daughter Edy Craig. She illustrated projects for poet William Butler Yeats and his brother, artist Jack Yeats. Pixie also befriended stage actress Maude Adams, whose most popular role was Peter Pan, and she developed a fond connection with Bram Stoker, author of *Dracula*, whom she affectionately referred to as "Uncle Bramy."[22] In fact, she illustrated his final horror novel, *The Lair of the White Worm.*

In 1901, Pixie opened a studio space in London where she invited artists, authors, and actors to enjoy carefree evenings of arts and entertainment, as described in Arthur Ransome's book *Bohemia in London.*[23] Additionally, she wrote, illustrated, and published her own literary magazine, *The Green Sheaf,* with contributions from many of her aforementioned friends. After *The Green Sheaf*'s short-lived run of only 13 issues, Pixie established The Green Sheaf Press, which published novels, poetry, and folklore mostly by women writers.

Although earning very little for the project, in 1909 Pixie was commissioned by occultist scholar and poet A. E. Waite to create 80 paintings that would be used to illustrate the most popular tarot deck to date, the *Smith-Waite Tarot.* You may also know this deck as the *Rider-Waite-Smith* or the *Rider-Waite* deck, as William Rider and Son was its original publisher.

In the 2018 biography, *Pamela Colman Smith: The Untold Story*, authors Stuart Kaplan (founder of U.S. Games Systems, Inc., the first company to publish tarot decks in the United States), Mary K. Greer, Elizabeth Foley O'Connor, and Melinda Boyd Parsons note that A. E. Waite not only commissioned Smith to create his tarot images, but he encouraged her to take creative liberties with the Minor Arcana. As such, Pixie relied heavily upon her knowledge of religious and occult symbology as well as her own psychic abilities. A psychic artist, Pixie experienced a phenomenon known as synesthesia, a condition through which music and other sounds can be visualized as colors and shapes. In an interview by *The Strand* Magazine in 1908, Smith said, "[I paint] what I see when I hear music—thoughts loosened and set free by the spell of sound."[24]

Pamela Colman Smith's painting style and her creation of the original Smith-Waite Tarot illustrations are important to note because although her contributions to both tarot and the arts are vast and remarkable, she long went unrecognized. Speculation around her ethnicity and sexual orientation are believed to have motivated initial erasure from the tarot's credits; however, with the uncovering of information about the artist through books such as Pamela Colman Smith: The Untold Story, Pixie and her work are finally gaining the recognition they deserve.

While consulting on the design of the *Mystic Storyteller Tarot* card images, staying true to the classic *Smith-Waite* tarot illustrations was very important to me. Roz Kazaz's interpretation of Pixie's work modernizes the imagery while honoring her legacy.

Not only is Pixie's deck the most widely recognized and accessible, it has spanned many decades during which she was largely unappreciated—and even uncredited — for her contributions not only to tarot but to the arts. In the decades preceding her death on September 18, 1951, in Bude, Cornwall, Pixie faded into obscurity. Her name wouldn't become mentioned in most arts, literature, and tarot circles until Stuart Kaplan obtained the rights to publish the *Rider-Waite-Smith* deck in America in the early 1970s. Although her gravesite is unknown, Pixie's legacy lives on in the hearts and hands of those who admire her work.

Rider-Waite-Smith

Mystic Storyteller

Practice Activity: Gut Instincts

Regardless of how much experience you have with the tarot—and even if that experience is none at all—I'd like to show you how easy it can be to use the images to foster creativity with a simple, three-part activity.

What you need for this activity:

- Your favorite tools for notetaking or a journal.
- Your imagination.

Part One:

Below, you can see a single card: the Three of Wands. Without overthinking, write down your immediate thoughts about what's happening within the card's scene. Write the first thoughts to pop up in your mind, your initial feelings about the card, the first words to surface in your thoughts. Write down your gut instincts about the card.

Part Two:

Next, study the card. Ruminate on what's taking place in the scene. Who could this person be? What are they doing? Why are they doing it? If you were to write a short story about the image in this card, how might you tell it?

Part Three: Activity Debrief

In this activity, you used the Three of Wands card as an anchor for practicing freewriting, a technique especially helpful when using the tarot. I will cover this method in Chapter 27, but for now, what are your immediate thoughts about this Gut Instincts activity? Did you find it difficult to silence your inner-editor and write what came to mind while looking at the illustration? Did you find the act of crafting a story inspired by an image easy or difficult?

What's next?

Save your work! You will return to it in a future activity, and your thoughts around this card might even help uncover your own unique technique for intuiting card meanings. As an additional practice, you might decide to use what you've written about this card as the first entry of a tarot exploration journal. After all, daily journaling with the tarot (See also Chapter 29 – *Journaling with the Tarot*) is how many writers, including me, get acquainted with the cards. In Part Three of this book, I will help you do just that. However, if you are a tarot aficionado, and/or you consider yourself a seasoned card reader, you are encouraged to read through the instruction and determine if there is something new to discover and/or learn about the cards.

Part Three:

Getting Acquainted with the Tarot

"It will never be enough to simply note that a writer is neglected. Instead, scholars must show how a forgotten or understudied text helps challenge or advance the field."

Anne Fernald
Author and Psychologist

Chapter 11: Choosing Your Deck

. . . .

As previously mentioned in Part One, while there are likely thousands of tarot decks that include modern imagery, for the writer just getting familiar with the cards, and/or for those reading this book, the companion *Mystic Storyteller Tarot* is the optimal choice. Nonetheless, please choose the deck that most appeals to you.

My favorite tarot decks include Pamela Colman Smith's traditional illustrations, or, like the *Mystic Storyteller Tarot*, those inspired by them. In my experience, once you have become familiar with Pixie's imagery, you can feel increased confidence in learning how to work with more modern decks. After all, many contemporary tarot deck creators use the traditional Smith-Waite structure and imagery as the foundation for their designs.

A glaring issue with Pixie's traditional illustrations, however, is that the cards are not diverse with regard to ethnicity, and with the exception of a handful of cards they are limited to cisgender male and female figures. When choosing a deck, it's natural for one to desire a connection with the cards, to see oneself represented in the images. Ultimately, it's important to select one that includes people with whom you can identify. As such, the *Mystic Storyteller Tarot* reflects a diverse congregation of figures specifically designed to resonate with every creative. Roz Kazaz's artwork is inclusive of ethnicity, gender, sexual orientation, body types, and generational representation. It's also a deck that does a beautiful service of honoring the integrity of Smith-Waite structure and symbolism.

By and large, because intuitive tarot reading is unique to each individual, how you identify with the imagery is completely up to you. Take gender, for example: you get to define femininity, masculinity, androgyny, and otherwise, and how they show up in your life. Tarot cards are no exception—your intuition will tell the story it sees in the cards, no matter what anyone else believes.

With regard to the *Mystic Storyteller Tarot* and pronouns, throughout this book you will find that the pronouns used to describe the card images are aligned with how the figure is represented. For example, The Fool is a genderfluid individual, so I use pronouns they/them. The Queens, on the other hand, are represented by female figures, so I use pronouns she/her.

Additionally, if you desire to learn more about the tarot, you will likely cross paths with the superstition that you must be gifted your first tarot deck. The keyword in that sentence is superstition. No, you do not have to be gifted your first tarot deck; you can choose your own.

What about oracle decks? How are they different than tarot? Let's talk about that...

Oracle Decks

I'd like to mention oracle card decks and make the distinction between them and the tarot. While the tarot is a structured, 78-card deck, containing highly detailed imagery and nuanced symbolism, oracle cards are free-form. The number of cards in an oracle deck can vary, depending on the creator, and the content can include any theme or imagery. I own several oracle decks; I find them useful in my personal spiritual practice, and while writing my novel *Only the Rocks That Float*, I kept Stacey Williams-Ng's *Southern Gothic Oracle* close within reach. If you are just getting started with incorporating cards as part of your writing practice, however, I find the tarot is the best tool to help foster confidence. As for the use of this book and practical application of its activities, oracle cards are not recommended.

Next, let's dive deeper into the anatomy of the tarot with an examination of its structure.

Chapter 12: The Structure of the Mystic Storyteller Deck

· ·

When purchasing a new tarot deck, one of the first features you will become familiar with is what tarot readers refer to as "the little white book." They call the booklet that, because, well, that's what most early and/or discounted decks include: a small, chapbook-like booklet on white paper, stapled twice, and folded where the spine would normally be. When you acquire a copy of the *Mystic Storyteller Tarot*, the companion deck to this book, you will find it also includes a little white book.

So, what's inside the little white book? The average resource includes a brief history of the tarot, a list of the cards and their keywords, and a spread or two, one of which is typically the Celtic Cross spread.

You can learn more about the Celtic Cross in Chapter 34 – *The Writer's Cross*; however, this chapter provides an overview of the Smith-Waite deck structure, after which our *Mystic Storyteller Tarot* deck is patterned.

The Major Arcana: Keys to Unlocking the Big Picture

Starting with The Fool and concluding with The World, the tarot's 22 Major Arcana cards are the keys to unlocking "big picture" ideas and themes. These constructs include both the physical and psychological aspects of the human condition to include order, purpose, learning, motivation, morality, struggle, and success. Furthermore, each card, both in the Major and Minor Arcana, includes a Roman numeral at the bottom center just above the card's title. For those who might not be familiar with this numbering system, when referencing these cards throughout this book I offer both the Roman numeral and decimal system number. In Chapter 17 – *The Major Arcana: The Big Picture*, you can find a detailed profile of each Major Arcana card, complete with a story, traditional meanings, symbolism, and considerations from the writer's perspective.

Key 0	The Fool
Key 1 or I	The Magician
Key 2 or II	The High Priestess
Key 3 or III	The Empress
Key 4 or IV	The Emperor
Key 5 or V	The Hierophant
Key 6 or VI	The Lovers
Key 7 or VII	The Chariot
Key 8 or VIII	Strength
Key 9 or IX	The Hermit
Key 10 or X	Wheel of Fortune
Key 11 or XI	Justice
Key 12 or XII	The Hanged One
Key 13 or XIII	Death
Key 14 or XIV	Temperance
Key 15 or XV	The Devil
Key 16 or XVI	The Tower
Key 17 or XVII	The Star
Key 18 or XVIII	The Moon
Key 19 or XIX	The Sun
Key 20 or XX	Judgement
Key 21 or XXI	The World

The Major Arcana

The Fool

The Magician

The High Priestess

The Empress

The Hierophant

The Lovers

The Chariot

Strength

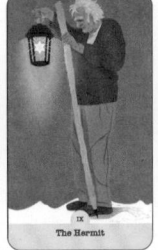

The Hermit

Wheel of Fortune

Justice

The Hanged One

Death

Temperance

The Devil

The Tower

The Star

The Moon

The Sun

Judgement

The World

Cups

Pentacles

Swords

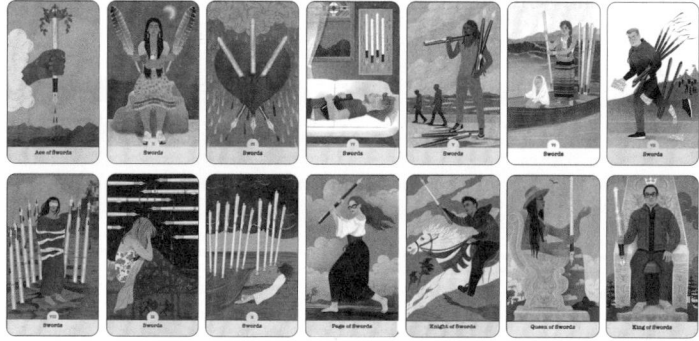

Wands

The Minor Arcana: Day-to-Day Stories

The 56 Minor Arcana cards represent aspects of day-to-day life that are influenced by emotions, feelings, home, work, material possessions, thoughts, change, conflict, passions, and spirituality. On each illustrated Minor Arcana card of the *Mystic Storyteller Tarot*, you will find the Roman numeral at the bottom just above its title. However, you will find that the Court Cards are titled but not numbered. The Minor Arcana consists of four different suits, the Cups, Pentacles, Swords, and Wands, and each suit contains 14 cards: an Ace card, cards Two through 10, a Page, a Knight, a Queen, and a King. In Chapter 18, you can find a more detailed assessment of the Minor Arcana and its elemental correspondences.

The Suits: Elemental Correspondences

Cups represent water, which relate to emotions, intuition, feelings, and relationships. In the *Mystic Storyteller Tarot*, this suit is populated with coffee cups, teacups, and other vessels that can often be found staggered about a writer's workspace.

Pentacles represent earth, which inform physical matters related to the body, home, and work. In the *Mystic Storyteller Tarot*, this suit includes physical tools a storyteller uses for their craft, such as books, typewriters, notepads, and electronic devices.

Swords represent air, which relates to conflict, intellect, and thought. In the *Mystic Storyteller Tarot*, this suit is populated with ink pens of all sorts and sizes. Personally, I've never met a writer who wasn't a pen hoarder.

Wands represent fire, which ignites the spirit of change, creativity, enterprise, and passion. In the *Mystic Storyteller Tarot*, this suit features candles and pencils, fire and wood to ignite a writer's inspiration.

The Numbers: Numerological Correspondences

- The Aces indicate new beginnings, new gifts or offerings, and planted seeds.
- The Twos denote choice, duality, and union.
- The Threes relate to creativity, expression, and growth.
- The Fours imply balance, security, steadiness, and structure.
- The Fives relate to change, conflict, and instability.

- The Sixes denote harmony, balance, and karma.
- The Sevens represent challenges, lessons learned, and struggles.
- The Eights relate to abundance, achievement, and manifestation.
- The Nines denote completions and endings.
- The Tens bring things full circle, informing completion, endings, and results.

Pages

Knights

Queens

Kings

Chapter 13: Handling the Cards

. . . .

Just like a deck of playing cards, your tarot cards should be kept in a moisture-free container and out of reach of children or furry familiars who might accidentally damage them. An equally effective method of storing your cards includes wrapping them in cloth and securing the bundle inside a drawstring bag. This is the storage method I prefer; however, you can store them in whichever manner feels right to you. As for shuffling the cards, you also have options.

Shuffling

There is no right way to shuffle a deck of cards. Really, the decision comes down to preference. However, you will want to make certain your tarot cards are shuffled well before using them. After all, a great deal of the magic in using the tarot happens when you pull cards from a randomly organized deck, and they resonate with you as profoundly as if you'd sorted through the stack and consciously selected each one.

When you become comfortable with your preferred method of shuffling, that practice might even grow to be part of your card-pulling routine. My own routine, for example, has evolved over the years and includes shuffling the cards casino-style (riffle shuffle) three times, followed by over-handed shuffling until the deck gives me the cards (through "jumpers," which are covered in this chapter) that I believe are meant for me at that moment. While these are my own beliefs, you are encouraged to adopt whatever methods and routines work best for you.

Riffle Shuffle

The riffle shuffle, also known as a "bridge" or "casino-style" technique, starts by splitting or "cutting" your tarot deck in half. Next, while positioning your thumbs on one end of the two stacks and fingers on the other, bend the edges upward so that they slip from your grasp and fold on top of one another. This movement causes the two card stacks to weave into a single deck. Finally, tap the edges of the deck until the stack is aligned and neat.

Overhand

Another style of shuffling is the overhand technique. This style involves placing the deck in one hand, and then releasing a portion of the cards into the palm of the other hand—some in front and others behind—allowing the cards to form a newly redistributed stack.

Scrambling

Also known as the "pile" shuffle, this style is probably the most fun method, and to some, it mixes up the cards most effectively. The scrambling technique harkens back to childhood, back to the days of finger-painting and playing 52 Pickup.[25] Because that's exactly what you do: Scatter your deck around your desk or tabletop (or any other flat surface) like a fun game (or prank) and then put the cards back together into a neat stack. In my experience, this method is highly effective for a random distribution of both upright and reversed cards.

Cutting the cards

"Cutting" the cards means setting the deck on your desk or tabletop, picking up half (or some sizeable chunk), and then restacking the two sections. You can also cut the deck into three or more stacks, putting the piles back together in random order.

Drawing or "Pulling" Cards

"Drawing" or "pulling cards" are terms used interchangeably and mean selecting your cards, which can be done in a few ways.

Consciously—You might want to deliberately select specific tarot cards, especially when working with a spread or activity that calls for pulling them in this manner.

Cutting and pulling from the top—Cut the deck and choose the card from the top. Easy-peasy.

Fanning—After shuffling, you can fan the cards in an arc and select the ones that "call" to you. This is a popular method used in TV and film. Plus, it looks cool.

Jumpers—Jumper cards are the cards that eject from your hands while shuffling. In my experience, jumpers happen more frequently while shuffling overhand. Take care not to shuffle sloppily, as this can damage your cards, and in my opinion, the cards that spring from sloppy shuffling are simply cards that have fallen out of the deck. They are not considered "jumpers," which happen at random. To me, when a card pops out of the deck, it has been given to me by the Universe, my Higher Self, or my Spirit Guides.

Whichever manner you choose for shuffling and selecting your cards, you are encouraged to practice with the method that feels right and works best for you. In the next chapter, I'd like to introduce you to tarot spreads and how to work with them.

Chapter 14: Working With Tarot Spreads

. . . .

A tarot spread is a type of layout or map, a predetermined format for pulling cards and then laying them down in a specific pattern or sequence. Spreads can be helpful in guiding one's quest for insight or clarity around a specific situation. While you don't have to use a spread when working with the cards for creative inspiration, working with a predetermined template often helps to build a framework for stimulating ideas.

Tarot spreads can range from a single card to laying out all 78 of them. A spread's goal and/or purpose is entirely up to you and the outcome you are trying to determine. Before working with tarot spreads, I recommend thinking of a question(s) in your mind that you'd like answering, and then using a notebook or journal to jot down your immediate, intuitive thoughts about the answer(s) the cards are displaying. In Chapter 15, you will find questions to ruminate on while considering individual cards and those arranged in spreads.

In addition to gleaning inspiration for my fiction stories, I use the tarot every morning for self-reflection. My favorite spread for this purpose is a three-card layout in which the first card represents a "theme" for my day ahead, the second (middle) card represents a potential "obstacle" (or opportunity, depending on my mood), and the third card represents a "blessing" to which I might look forward.

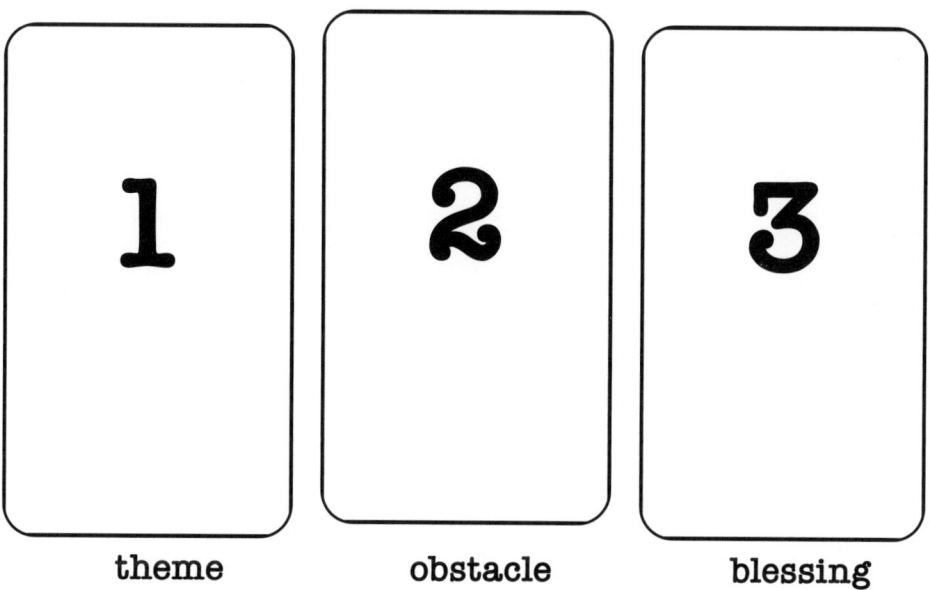

theme   obstacle   blessing

Spread Example: Theme / Obstacle / Blessing

theme   obstacle   blessing

Theme – The Fool: Keeping an adventurous spirit can open up all sorts of possibilities.

Obstacle – Queen of Swords, reversed: However, weakness might get the best of me, if I'm not careful, so remaining vigilant and aware when my defenses are lowered is important.

Blessing – The Chariot: Take advantage of the gorgeous weather! Get out of the house and stop being such a Hermit, Mandy.

Tarot spreads are designed in all numbers and layouts, from minimal to complex, and you are encouraged to design your own, if you choose. You can draw a single card for clarity around starting or finishing a story, one card as inspiration for a poem, or a card for daily insight into your writing practice. Whatever your desire, a spread can be as simple as one card. Although the following list includes a few examples of my favorite daily insight and writing spreads, you will find an assortment of spreads and activities peppered throughout this book.

One-Card Spread Ideas

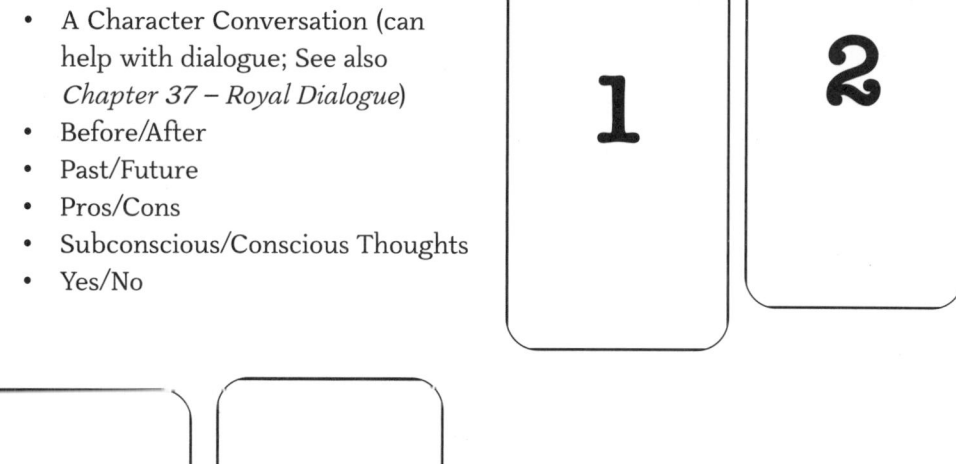

- Clarity on filling a plot hole
- Daily draw for insight
- Daily draw for writing inspiration
- Energy around the day/task/project
- Significator (a card that represents you; see the end of this chapter)
- Yes or No answers to a question(s)

Two-Card Spread Ideas

- A Character Conversation (can help with dialogue; See also *Chapter 37 – Royal Dialogue*)
- Before/After
- Past/Future
- Pros/Cons
- Subconscious/Conscious Thoughts
- Yes/No

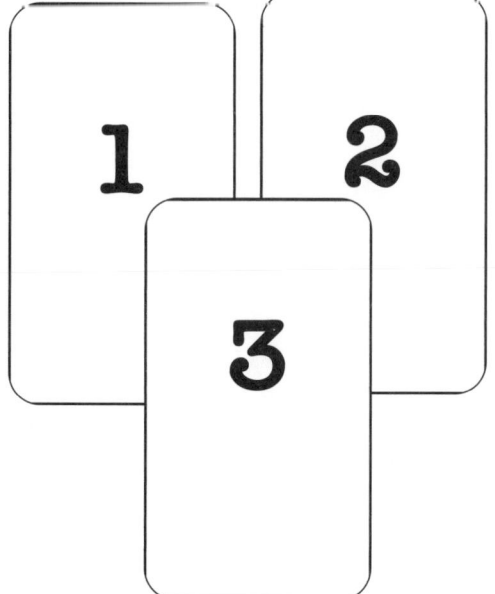

Multiple-Card Spreads

- Concern/Advice/Outcome
- Past/Present/Future
- Yes/Maybe/No—decision-making spreads
- Theme/Obstacle/Blessing
- The Writer's Cross – My version of the Celtic Cross, but for writers (Chapter 34)
- Dream up your own!

Significators and Clarifiers

Sometimes when working with the tarot you might want to pull a specific card to represent you, the writer, a card that represents a specific character, or a card that embodies the energy with which you wish to work. These cards are known as *significators*. For example, while working with spreads that require me to choose a card to represent myself, I often choose The Magician, The Hermit, or the Nine of Pentacles, as they are personal favorites of mine.

Some tarot spreads include a position specifically for a significator. Many of the activities throughout this book include spreads with a space designated for a specific card. Those cards are examples of significators.

When choosing a significator to represent you or your character(s) in a spread or writing exercise, the card chosen can reveal what could be informing choices and behaviors. On the other hand, it might also represent you or your character so that you can see yourself or them as an active participant in the spread. Significators can also be seen as anchors, helping to keep you and/or your character(s) centered or aligned.

When you need additional insight around what a card or a spread means, you can pull another card and lay it beside the original. These additionally selected cards are known as clarifiers, and they can help provide understanding and depth.

Now that you know the basics around handling your cards and working with tarot spreads, let's explore considerations for intuitive card reading.

Chapter 15: Reading the Cards Intuitively

. . . .

When you are reading a book, an article, a poem, more than likely you are paying attention to the words and details and imagining the story in your mind. The same goes for watching a movie, television show, or stage performance; the setting, dialogue, movement, gestures, all of the details contribute to the storytelling.

Reading tarot cards is no different. You don't simply look at the TV or theatre stage, you read the room, you think about the story that's unfolding. Whether using a spread or pulling cards at random, when you look at your tarot cards displayed on the table or desk before you, you aren't simply looking at the illustrations. You are reading the story those illustrations are sharing. From the colors to the animals, people, and symbols, you are observing the details in the card(s) and gleaning information (i.e., a story) from them. This explains the terms "tarot reader" and "reading" the cards.

As for reading tarot cards intuitively, the method, process, and/or approach are completely up to you. When you consider the painting *The Starry Night* by Vincent Van Gogh, for example, what do you see? What's happening in the landscape? Where is that little town and who lives there? What's happening in the weather to cause the sky to swirl? There's a story in that and every painting, and there are stories to be read from the tarot.

How to Read Tarot

Simply put, when reading tarot, be a tourist. Tourists are known for looking up at buildings, examining the stores and landscapes of a place that the locals may not always pay attention to, or no longer pay attention to because they've lived in that area and/or seen those details day in and day out. When reading tarot cards, look at everything: color, animals, people, symbolism, every detail. And pay attention to how those details make you feel. What emotions or responses are you experiencing as a result of viewing the card(s)? Do the images spark a memory? Do they make you feel frightened? Happy? Intrigued?

No matter your experience with the tarot, reading intuitively asks you to be a tourist and look everywhere. Although it's helpful to know the traditional meanings and keywords of each card, reading intuitively means setting aside the collective meanings that don't resonate with you and your purpose for using the cards and gleaning your own interpretations. Examine the cards as you would if you were seeing them for the very first time. This curiosity is how you are going to ignite your intuition.

As you incorporate card-pulling and the use of tarot spreads to help inspire your storytelling, a good practice includes knowing which questions to consider while consulting the cards. Asking yourself the following 21 questions can help you consider the tarot intuitively, deciphering meaning and relevance that can season your project and amplify self-awareness.

- What is my immediate, gut response to the card(s)?
- How does the card make me feel?
- What's happening in the illustration(s)?
- Are there people? Animals?
- Who do they remind me of?
- What are they doing?
- What symbols do I see?
- What numbers are there?
- What colors stand out?
- What is the weather like in the scene?
- What's happening in the background?
- If this card were the main character of my work in progress (WIP), what's happening to them and why?
- Where are they going?
- How did they get there?
- What's happening next?
- What if the person/animal in the card was me?
- How do I see myself in this card?
- Why am I doing whatever is happening in the card?
- How did I get there?
- Where do I go next?
- What overarching message do I believe this card might be telling me?

While these questions can be helpful in determining the meaning of a card or spread, what happens when you pull a card and it's upside down? Cue shrieking music à la the shower scene in *Psycho*. Reversals offer an entirely new perspective on intuiting the cards.

Chapter 16: Intuiting Reversals

. . . .

What happens when a card flips upside down? Reading reversed cards is completely preferential. When you pull a card, or when one jumps from your deck while shuffling and lands upside down on your desk, you can either turn it right-side up or leave it as is.

Many prefer reading reversals because they provide an additional layer of insight into what's happening (or not happening) in their spread. Additionally, many folks, including me, believe reversed cards are meant to be—they must have flipped on their heads for a reason. As a writer, you might find that reversals can help with story development, especially plot twists.

Leaving the card in a reversed position can mean many things; however, the following approaches are what resonate with me the most from a writer's lens:

Antagonist

Specific to fiction writers, when a card lands reversed on your desk, it could be interpreted as something your story's antagonist is up to... or plotting. How much influence are they having on your plotline? Is a twist of fate needed or would such an event enhance the narrative? Should a turn of events happen where the story has otherwise become predictable or stagnant?

Blocked

Whatever meaning or energy your intuition tells you the card means upright becomes blocked or slowed down when reversed. For example, if I draw the Strength card (number 8 or VIII in the Major Arcana) reversed, I might interpret it to mean feeling stifled or restricted. I'm useless in taming, controlling, or charming whatever the lion symbolizes for me at that particular moment or for a specific project.

Gravity

In a literal sense, how might gravity affect the scene in your card(s)? If you pull the Ten of Swords, for example, you will see a seemingly unlucky person who has been impaled by ten swords. Many dread seeing this card in its upright position. When reversed, however, what do you imagine happening to the person if gravity were involved? Those swords would fall downward, and that individual would be released from their predicament.

Opposite

Employing the Strength card example again, the opposite of strength is weakness. The Sun card typically means joy and happiness. When reversed, its opposite is sadness and disappointment. On the other hand, The Devil card usually indicates oppression and/or being controlled by fear or addiction. When reversed, oppression becomes freedom, fear becomes courage, and addiction becomes recovery.

Rejection

Simply put, you, your story, and/or your fiction characters completely reject the ideas represented by the card in its upright state.

Shadow

This reversal interpretation is my personal preference, and in this book I often refer to the cards' shadow aspects as their "lower polarity" (See Chapter 6). What are the darker aspects of a card? Once you sense a card's upright meaning, next consider what fears, vulnerabilities, and obstacles are lurking in the shadows. Like the Antagonist approach, this method of interpretation can also be effective in informing plot twists and turns of events.

Surrender

Whatever your interpretation of the card in its upright position, let it go. Surrender to the possibilities of what could happen, how the story might unfold. Abandon expectation of what you believe the card means. Take a leap and trust where your story and/or characters are headed.

Practice Activity: Tarot Stories

In the Gut Instincts practice activity that concluded Part Two of this book, you may have jotted down your thoughts about a single card, the Three of Wands. In this activity, you are going to build on what you've learned to this point, and you can continue doing so throughout this book.

What you need for this activity:

- Your *Mystic Storyteller Tarot* deck.
- Your favorite tools for notetaking.
- Your intuition.

Part One:

1. Shuffle your tarot deck and then pull a single card.
2. Just as you did for the Gut Instincts activity, tell the story happening in this first card.

Part Two:

3. Next, pull another card. You can either pull the next card in the deck, or you can shuffle again.
4. Whichever you choose, after pulling a second card, look at the two cards together and tell the story happening between them. From left to right, right to left, what is the interaction between these cards? What's unfolding in the combination of the scenes or in the collaboration between the individuals featured therein?
5. Keep pulling cards to add to this narrative until you are satisfied that you have reached the end of your tarot story.

What's next?

Now that you have the hang of the tarot and how to read the cards, let's explore them. *Part Four: The Tarot Files* includes a profile for each of the 22 Major Arcana cards and an overview of the 56 Minor Arcana, grouped by suit as well as by number.

Part Four:
The Tarot Files

"When interpreting tarot cards, the interpretation is heavily influenced by our past experiences and the lens through which we view the world around us."

Shannon Knight, MS, LMHC
Psychotherapist and Host of *The Tarot Diagnosis* Podcast

Chapter 17: Major Arcana — The Big Picture

. . . .

Like most stories, the tarot includes both major and minor themes and characters. In this chapter, I'd like to introduce you to the Major Arcana, the first 22 cards of the tarot deck. For the purposes of this book, each card's meaning, as well as some of the keywords used in their corresponding word lists, include the original Smith-Waite ideas as well as my own intuitive thoughts from a writer's lens.

The etymology of the word arcana dates back to the mid-sixteenth century and combines the Latin word arcanus with the English word arcane to produce arcana, meaning "secrets or mysteries."[26] The Major Arcana cards represent familiar universal archetypes and big picture themes.

Relative to both you as a writer and your fictional characters, these cards can help navigate major lessons and life events such as aging/croning, caregiving, childhood, covert affairs, crises, death, gender exploration, identity, indoctrination, marriage, menopause, paradigm change, parenthood, pregnancy, puberty, retirement, significant loss, sexual exploration, and weight-loss.

Beginning with the number zero—where all things are possible—the Major Arcana is The Fool's Journey. The Fool represents the ether, the Spirit within each of us as we navigate life events, such as the aforementioned list. Examples of stories that follow The Hero / Fool's Journey include *Coco, The Count of Monte Cristo, Forrest Gump, Harry Potter, Lord of the Rings, Memoirs of a Geisha, Moana, Moonlight, Slumdog Millionaire, Star Wars,* and *The Wizard of Oz.* You will learn more about The Fool's Journey and The Hero's Journey in Chapter 32.

As for this chapter, for each of the Major Arcana cards, you can expect the following structure, features, and insights:

Summary / Story

For each card in the Major Arcana, I start with an anecdote—some quite personal—that relates to and/or was inspired by the card's theme. For example, the Wheel of Fortune card is a portent for change, and in that card's profile you'll learn about a series of events that initiated a significant shift in both my personal and professional life.

Connecting the Story

This section serves as a bridge designed to help connect you from each card's story to an expansion of related topics and details.

What's Happening in the Card?

This section of each card in the Major Arcana includes a summary of what's unfolding within the card's illustration. As some figures and symbols might be new to you, understanding what you're looking at can help you get better acquainted with each card.

A Deep Dive

Here's where I demonstrate the convergence of intuition and creativity. For each card, this section includes an amalgamation of my intuitive thoughts along with in-depth research around the card's meaning(s).

The Card Reversed: The Shadow

In this part, I will share my thoughts around "the shadow" aspect of each card. By "shadow," I am referring to the lower polarity, or the meaning and/or insights which are not seen as clearly as when the card is turned right-side up. Remember, when the cards land upturned on your desk you are invited to intuit your own interpretations. (See also Chapter 16 – *Intuiting Reversals*.)

Notable Symbols

This part of each tarot profile includes research-based information around the astrological, elemental, and other symbolic correspondences depicted within the illustrations. Please note that "Spirit" appears on every Major Arcana profile. This is because the Major Arcana as a whole represents spirit in the tarot. As you investigate the cards, you can see that the tarot is full of symbolism, which I identify and define in greater detail in Part Five: The Tarot Code.

Numerological Associations

In this chapter, I introduce you to the numerological connections for each card of the Major Arcana, although you will learn more about the numbered associations across all 78 cards in Chapter 22.

The Card, Characterized

What if the figure in a particular tarot card represents the fictional character(s) you are writing? What if what's happening in the card and/or its symbolic meanings could directly affect a character's outcome? This part includes my insights around how the imagery might be characterized in a reading, spread, or storyline.

Notable Characters or Personas

This segment of each Major Arcana card includes a list of fictional characters, notable people, and/or personalities that come to mind when I consider the characteristics of the card's figure(s) and/or overall energy. My intention here is to provide you with a little more context around the cards' associations.

Spread / Practice Activity

For every card in the Major Arcana, I have designed a spread with a corresponding activity that directly relates to the card's energy. The instructions for each spread are listed in order of execution, and many spaces on the spreads are accompanied by questions. After following the instructions, ask yourself the questions, using your intuition to consider the answers. Many of these spreads are designed for you to work with them from your point of view as a storyteller. However, if you are a fiction writer, many spreads can be facilitated from the lens of your character(s), helping you to glean inspiration for plot design, scene development, and more.

Word List

To conclude each Major Arcana profile, I have provided a list of keywords—both traditional and my own insights—that can help inspire storytelling, spark creativity, and foster memorization of the card's meaning(s). However, because the cards will likely resonate with you in ways that are unique to your own intuitive hits, you are encouraged to build on the word lists, adding your own.

Like the individual in The Fool card, let's take a leap into the tarot's opening cards: the Major Arcana.

Key 0:
The Fool

The Fool

One of my favorite books is *The Heart is a Lonely Hunter*, by Carson McCullers. Without giving away the story's plot, the title tells it all: at times, the heart is a lonely hunter. I've spent many years of my life searching for—hunting—love, acceptance, stability, and a safe place to land. My childhood felt like being on a ship at sea, seldom finding the right port, and mostly being caught in storms. Figuring out how to navigate continuous change, never staying in one place long enough for roots to set or moss to grow, heavily informed my spirit. Infuse nomadic, unsteady beginnings with a natal chart dominated by Sagittarius and, well, as an adult I've spent many years on the hunt.

While Georgia will always be my first home, Florida remains the place for which I feel the most homesick. When I was seven, my paternal grandmother

(Gran) moved to Winter Haven, Florida where she married my Granddaddy Don and where I spent my summers. Since my first trip to Florida, the perpetual sunshine, the wide-open skies, the birds, the swaying palms, and the water, they all called to me. The experience was visceral; I could hear it and feel it. When I was a kid, and I'd gone down to visit my grandparents, they'd embraced me in warm hugs, and weeks later when I left for home they'd clung onto me not wanting to let me go. Leaving was a struggle. My heart wanted to stay behind. And there simply wasn't enough happiness to stretch between their home and mine. The tug-of-war was taxing. Happiness only went so far.

In 2013, an opportunity to move to the Sunshine State unfolded. The move had been a risk, as my husband and I were giving up the comforts of small-town living and the convenience of having family and friends just a few blocks away. The cost of living, we had discovered, would be higher, and our two middle school-aged boys dug in their heals at the prospect of leaving their friends. After a little research and LOTS of encouragement, we found a house on a lake not even a mile from the Gulf of Mexico.

Although most were happy for our opportunity, our friends and family weren't overly excited for our move, and many even said the decision to relocate was "foolish." Yet and still, we packed our things and made the leap.

Living in the sun, watching it rise while sipping my coffee on our backyard dock, taking walks to an island park after work, and walking our dog to the beach was pure joy. The experience fed my soul. My soul found its home and my writing found a calling. Purpose. While I had been a writer since I was four years old, I became a novelist in Florida. That's where I was inspired to write and publish my first novel, The Decembers. For me, the move played a massive role in summoning and inspiring creativity. Florida struck a match to an already smoldering urge to write the stories that I wanted to read. And I did—many, in fact.

Every story has its end, and unfortunately for us, our Florida adventure was no different. After learning that my Gran was unwell, and unable to live independently in her home—she had moved back to Georgia when my Granddaddy Don passed in '99—my husband and I moved our family back to Georgia where I could become her care partner. Doing so had been a struggle, and just like those childhood summers that tugged on my heart when they came to an end, I felt like I left a part of me in Florida.

Connecting the Story

In the tarot, The Fool card functions like an invisible, unbreakable thread. The Spirit of the tarot, The Fool pulses its energy into every card, its connection stringing together infinite opportunities for adventure, bravery, creative expression, and storytelling. As such, The Fool transcends labels—they can be anyone and anything. As a mystic storyteller, YOU can be and write anything your own unique spirit desires.

Like The Fool, love was the only sensation that helped my family recover from having to leave Florida. Happiness was nowhere to be found, and yet again, my heart had been pulled in two different directions. Eventually, love settled in, filling in the gaps, reminding me that our adventure, although brief, had been a blessing, and helped to maintain that visceral connection. At the time of writing this book, my heart is still a lonely hunter, always searching for the possibility of going back.

Let's review the first card in the Major Arcana for all its possibilities.

What's happening in The Fool card?

The Fool is young at heart and carefree. An androgynous spirit, both divine masculine and divine feminine, they are an adventurous bohemian, an initiator of adventure and change. In the card, The Fool seems to be on the start of a new journey. They've dressed in their favorite party vest, grabbed their favorite writing pen, and packed everything they need for their trip in their crossbody bag. The Fool's white rose is a symbol of innocence, youthfulness, and silence. They're silencing all the haters who've tried to stop their adventures—the ones who've told them they aren't good-smart-pretty-young-[you fill in the adjective] enough. With not a single cloud for miles, the sun above is white-hot, lighting and warming The Fool's way.

Just as our fearless Fool approaches the edge of what looks like a cliff, their little familiar companion—a white terrier—dances and yips. Is the dog excited to be accompanying The Fool on their journey? Or is it warning them of the potential dangers ahead? The little dog represents The Fool's subconscious mind, that voice of reasoning that whispers hints to keep us faithful to our cause, directed, and safe. In this scene, it looks as though The Fool isn't listening to reason; they're frolicking full steam ahead. Let's just hope the ground isn't too far down from the ledge over which they're about to wander.

The Fool: A Deep Dive

Why are they called a "Fool?" Because in the past (and perhaps even today, to some), people who were carefree and who did "silly" things such as taking chances and going against the grain—rejecting conformity—were often thought of as "foolish," lacking in judgment and good sense. The Fool as a concept is a threat to peaceful society, which promotes conformity, staying in one's lane, and doing what is expected. But conforming is a threat to spirituality, which encourages the seeking of one's own path and one's own way. What's right for one person might not always be right for everyone else.

The Fool is 2013 Mandy, the self-published author who thought that as soon as she published her very first book readers would easily find it and they would buy it and they would love it and they would review it with high remarks. But when those things didn't happen, as holds true for most newly self-published authors who don't have a sound grasp on book marketing, I hit the bottom of the ravine. Stunned by my failure, I looked back at where I'd started and wondered, *What in the hell happened?*

I didn't give up, though. I believed—and still believe—that I had everything it took to be a best-selling author. And so, I reached into my bag and unpacked all the tools I had collected—all of my tricks of the trade—and I used them to forge my way along the next leg of my writing journey.

If you are The Fool, be adventurous with your writing—take that chance. You don't have to be writing or doing or reading anything or everything other writers are writing-doing-reading. You do you. Be authentic. Carry along with you the things that feed your joy and propel you forward close to heart and mind. Be a risktaker, yes, but allow your voice of reasoning to be your compass. Be careful not to be so independent and willy-nilly that you aren't listening to your intuitive nudges around what is right for you and/or your project. Now is NOT the time to take a risk if your gut feels like it's pulling you in the opposite direction.

The Fool, Reversed: The Shadow

When reversed, The Fool can be held back and bound. Unable to make a step forward, they suffer from FOMO (Fear Of Missing Out) and they're reminded by even their little yippy dog that they're not good enough. They struggle with imposter syndrome, fatigue, and self-doubt. They're stuck in one place, suffering from cabin fever, or indecisive on an important decision and tentative to make one at all. The Fool reversed is the energy of The Man holding you back; it's allowing critics to decide your worth. It is also analysis paralysis, the inability to make a decision for the anxiety of mulling over all the options.

Notable Symbols in The Fool Card

Astrology—Uranus
Element—Spirit / Air

Other Symbols

Bag—The Fool's bag represents worldly possessions and the experiences they're carrying along with them. Theirs is a lot like Mary Poppins' and Hermione Granger's bags: full of possibilities. The Fool carries the tools they received from The Magician—a cup, pentacle, sword, and wand. These are the same tools we see again in the Aces.

Dog—The little white dog represents faith and the subconscious mind.

White Rose—The white rose stands for innocence, youthfulness, and silence.

Numerological Associations with The Fool

The Fool is many things, both separately and all at once—Spirit, ether, and the pure essence of life. Numerologically, zero is a non-number, yet it is every number. It's infinite and present in everything and everywhere. Zero is the cosmic egg from which everything in the universe is born. The number represents ether, God, life, Spirit, Source, and Universe. As such, The Fool is a pliable energy that transitions us from one life event to the next, one tarot card to the next, and like an invisible thread, this energy connects every card.

The Fool, Characterized

If The Fool is your fictional character, they are at the precipice of a new beginning. Nothing and nobody is holding them back. They have their eyes on something new, somewhere else. This individual is a nonconformist, nonchalant, and authentic in their thinking and behaving. They are at the start of a journey, a trip, an adventure, a new job, a new relationship, or a new project or mission.

    The Fool is the life of the party—a traveler, a hippie, a bohemian, a hitchhiker, a vagabond, a dreamer. They're a person with wanderlust, carefree and sometimes even a little naïve. The Fool might also be a teenager, an actor, a dancer, an irresponsible person, a foolish person, a courageous person, or simply an extrovert.

Notable characters, people, or personas

Forrest Gump (a runnin' fool); Don Quixote; Candide; Dorothy Gale in *The Wizard of Oz*; Elizabeth Gilbert, author of *Eat, Pray, Love*; Will in *The Fresh Prince of Bel Air*; Marianne Dashwood in *Sense and Sensibility*; and Michael Scott when Jim left him at the gas station (*The Office*, Season 7: Episode 14).

Who would you add to this list?

Word List

aura	feral	innocence	soul
authentic	folly	intrepid	spirit
beginnings	foolish	naïveté	spontaneity
benevolence	footloose	new adventure	transient
birth	free-spirited	nonchalance	traveler
childlike	fresh start	originality	trusting
drifter	hippie	purpose	unencumbered
essence	holy spirit	reckless	untamed
extroverted	humorous	risky	wild
fancy-free	indiscretion	serendipity	youthful

Spread: Foolish Decisions

Do you or one of your characters have to make a decision, and fast? Are you feeling torn between moving forward in a situation or hanging back? Use the following spread and your intuition for swift decision-making.

1. Shuffle your tarot deck until you are satisfied that the cards are ready.
2. Next, thumb through the deck until you find The Fool, which represents you or your character(s) in this decision. Before pulling the card from the deck, note the cards before and after it. Now, lay The Fool on the space for Card 2.
3. The card in front of The Fool (Card 1) provides insight for taking the leap, and the card behind The Fool (Card 3) offers considerations for turning back.
4. Ask yourself the following questions, using your intuition to consider the answers. If you are using this spread from your character's point of view, imagine them asking themselves these questions.

Card 1: What is the insight for taking the leap?
Card 2: The Fool—You / Your Character(s)
Card 3: What is a consideration for turning back?

Key 1 or I:
The Magician

The Magician

In my lifelong journey as a creative person, I have encountered artists, authors, poets, and musicians whom I have considered "Magicians." People who were able to make magic through the stroke of a brush, the arrangement of words, and/or melodic manipulation have invoked and bewitched me. I've studied these Magicians, steeping myself in their magic and making them both muses and imaginary friends. John William Waterhouse and Jean-Michel Basquiat, Nicola Yoon and Sue Monk Kidd, Emily Dickinson and Langston Hughes, Luther Vandross and Jennifer Nettles. But the Magician who stands out most to me, whose words, music, and chemistry captured my ear and conjured my heart at a tender age, is Prince Rogers Nelson.

I first discovered the Purple One's music in 1984. I was seven years old and had been invited into the apartment of the lady who lived below us. Her name was Jody. She made papier-mâché earrings and when I'd complemented hers she offered me a pair. "Let me go grab my box," Jody said, and as I waited in her living room, admiring her chunky wood furniture and Grecian goddess rain lamp, a song played on a bookshelf turntable. The singer's voice didn't sound like a man or a woman's—it was delicious and sexy and felt like something my seven-year-old ears didn't have any business listening to. But I was neither scared nor ashamed. At that very moment, my Mama could've walked through Jody's front door, and I wouldn't have been able to pry my attention away from that music.

I. LOVED. IT.

When Jody returned with her box of earrings and saw me standing there spellbound, I remember her giggling. "Purple Rain," she commented, nudging her chin toward the record. "His new album. And I thought 1999 was good!" I walked away from Jody's apartment that day with a funky new pair of earrings and an obsession with Prince.

For those of you who also love Prince, I don't have to remind you how revolutionary (no pun intended) his music was or how transcendent his style. He was special. He serenaded all of my firsts. He's still special and when he died, I felt like I'd lost both a dear friend and my first lover.

I never imagined I'd ever share a story about Prince and my highly conservative and religious grandmother in the same context, but The Magician is a conduit for working wonders. As long as I can remember, my Gran used to always tell me, "Girl, there isn't anything you cannot do." When I was a child, this praise had typically followed me showing her a new drawing or painting I'd finished. After I became an adult, and subsequently her care partner, she would bless me with the compliment after I completed a difficult task, like when I balanced her checkbook after she'd made a major accounting mistake, or when I'd assembled her new furniture and rearranged her bedrooms by myself.

After telling Gran I'd finished writing my first novel, her face lit up and she gasped. Her eyes sparkling, she hung her hands on both of my shoulders and looked me square in the eye. "Girl, there isn't anything you cannot do."

Connecting the Story

The Magician is Prince, The Magician is me... No, really, <u>that's me</u> in the *Mystic Storyteller Taro*t illustration! And, my fellow writer, I'm here to remind you The Magician is YOU. The Magician is anyone whose magic changes lives, and when we gather the necessary tools, sharpening and honing them and organizing them before us, there is nothing we cannot do. There was no instrument Prince could not (and possibly did not) master. There is no story that cannot be written, no book that cannot be finished. As mystic storytellers, when we use the magic within us (i.e., our talent and creativity), we can achieve our every goal—we can manifest our wildest desires, drawing energy from the heavens and enriching people's lives here on Earth, sometimes even affecting profound change.

What's happening in The Magician card?

The first numbered card of the tarot, The Magician serves as a conduit between the spiritual and physical worlds, making magic happen through concentration, skill, willpower, and practice. As you can see, The Magician is standing before a table (her writing desk, perhaps?) where she has collected items from each of the tarot suits: a wand (pencil), a sword (ink pen), pentacles (book, phone, and typewriter), and a cup (steaming mug of coffee, dark roast the way I like it).

The Magician concentrates and focuses on what she's doing, the intention she's setting, directing energy from above—the heavens, the Universe, her own intuition—to the present, physical plane. One arm is raised and holding a taper candle wand while the other arm is pointed downward toward the ground. In making this stance, *she* is a magic wand, inviting energy to flow through her right from the heavens down to the Earth. The lemniscate (infinity symbol) above her head confirms an unlimited capacity for doing so. As Hermes Trismegistus, the mythological combination of the Greek god Hermes and the Egyptian god Thoth, said, "As above, so below."

Ruled by Mercury, the messenger of the gods, The Magician is The Fool on the other side of their leap of faith. The Fool gathered their tools, listened to their intuition, and proceeded with their plan. They made good on their intention to set out on a grand adventure, to satisfy that call of accomplishment and/or mission to complete an important goal. In The Fool's journey, The Magician represents The Fool's fiery consciousness, and she has every intention of making magic happen wherever she goes.

The Magician: A Deep Dive

YOU are the Magician. You have everything it takes and everything you need to spin magical stories that become bestselling books. Your writing desk is your table, your altar where the magic happens, and you have all the elements there: pens, paper, a laptop, coffee or tea, books to inspire you, and maybe even a furry familiar at your feet... or resting on the keyboard. You're ready to channel energy from both intuition and spirit, creating something spectacular. As above, so below.

Stephen King is The Magician. In his memoir, *On Writing*, he shares the story about sending out letters to literary agents for representation in publishing his stories. When he received his first rejection, he found a nail and hammered the letter onto his bedroom wall. When the rejection letters kept coming, he stabbed them over that nail. And when the nail filled, Stephen King didn't give up, he simply got a longer nail.

The Magician Stephen King harnessed all of his skill, directed his intentions on literary representation, and maintained his willpower and persistence. And just look at what happened for him! He stayed the course; he never gave up. Again, YOU are the Magician.

Make sure you add longer nails to that writing space of yours and you'll have everything it takes to become a bestselling author, successful journalist, booming blogger... over and over again.

The Magician, Reversed: The Shadow

When The Magician shows up reversed in a reading, her stance becomes redirected, her intent on channeling the opposite of infinite good. She becomes an antagonist, a ruthless Trickster, her energy scattered as she pulls it from what she or others are doing and disperses it out into the Universe. The reversed Magician confounds you and everyone around you, a façade, an oasis. She can't make a decision to save *her* life, let alone yours or the lives of your characters. She's a cunning Joker, an antagonist hellbent on mess and madness. The Magician reversed is Mercury retrograde, wreaking havoc on communication and technology.

Notable Symbols in The Magician

Astrology—Mercury
Element—Spirit/Air

Other Symbols

Colors—Red is the color of passion, yellow (the background) represents hunger, and white is the color of Spirit and hope. The Magician has harnessed all of these in order to manifest their desires.

Lemniscate—The lemniscate is the symbol for infinity, and as we can see in this card, this symbol hovers over The Magician's head. This symbol can also represent simplicity and balance. It serves as a reminder that infinite possibilities surround us every day.

Red Rose—The red rose is a symbol of beauty, hope, love, passion, and pleasure.

Roses and Lilies Combined—Together, these flowers symbolize life and death, "as above so below." Lush foliage also represents the manifestation of beautiful intent—magic blooming before one's eyes.

White Lily—The white lily by itself represents death, majesty, modesty, and purity.

Numerological Associations with The Magician

The first numbered card in the Major Arcana, The Magician is associated with the Aces. In each Ace card, the hand of God/ The Universe holds one of the tools present on The Magician's worktable. (See also Chapter 18, Section 2 – *The Aces.*)

In numerology, one is the number of birth, bravery, ego, gifts, inspiration, initiative, identity, independence, initiation, new beginnings, novel ideas, offers, opportunity, potential, and self-confidence. Since The Magician follows The Fool, she channels new ideas that radiate through The Fool's entire journey.

The Magician

Ace of Cups | Ace of Pentacles | Ace of Swords | Ace of Wands

The Magician, Characterized

When inspired by The Magician, your intentions MUST be to write a character as innovative as Shuri and as powerful as Gandalf. Characters written with this card in mind are no wallflowers... although they might start out that way before a radioactive spider or a Midwest twister comes along.

The character patterned after The Magician could be just that: a magician. Similarly, they could be a joker, a trickster, or a charismatic leader. This person might be conniving and manipulative. On the other hand, this character could be a great communicator, an orator, a witch or wizard, a funcle (fun uncle), an alchemist, a tech engineer, a doctor, a pharmacist, your eccentric neighbor, a grill master, an extrovert, a manipulator, or a con artist.

Notable characters, people, or personas

Prince; Beyoncé; Stephen King; Frederick Douglass; Jareth the Goblin King of *Labyrinth*; Stevie Nicks; Dolly Parton; Taylor Swift; sculptor Edmonia Lewis; Toni Morrison; you and me.

Who would you add to this list?

Word List

action	discipline	magnetism	power
acuity	elements	manifestation	rebirth
clever	energy	manipulation	resourcefulness
collaboration	focus	mastermind	self-control
conjurer	handy	mastery	skillful
concentration	harnessing	mental	spiritual
control	humility	mystery	trickery
creation	intent	opportunities	virtuoso
deception	intention	planning	will
desire	magic/k	potential	willpower

Spread: Gifts of the Magi

Being a writer can sometimes feel unrewarding, and I don't know about you, but sometimes I look around and wish-dream-hope-pray for a nod from the Universe to carry on. Sometimes my heart needs nurturing, my body needs nourishing, my mind needs clarity, and my spirit needs a little spark. A fellow writer and dynamic communicator ruled by Mercury, The Magician can offer gifts to help support your storyteller needs. Use the following spread to uncover how those gifts might serve you. You might also use this spread from the point of view of your fictional character(s).

1. Pull The Magician from your tarot deck and lay the card in the space for Card 1. See their table? The Magician has gifts for you.
2. Next, shuffle your deck until you are satisfied that the cards are ready, and then turn the deck facedown as if you were about to deal them.
3. From the top of the deck, start turning cards over and laying them in the space for Card 2. When your first Cups card lands on this space, stop and move on to the next space.
4. Repeat the process by turning over cards and laying them on the space for Card 3 until you arrive at your first Pentacles card.
5. Repeat again for Card 4 (Swords) and Card 5 (Wands).

Card 2: Cups / Heart—How can I nurture my heart right now?
Card 3: Pentacles / Body – What nourishment does my body need right now?
Card 4: Swords / Mind – How does my mind need clarity right now?
Card 5: Wands / Spirit – What inspirational spark does my spirit need right now?

The Magician

2

Cups

3

Pentacles

4

Swords

5

Wands

Key 2 or II:

The High Priestess

I'm told that the moment I could hold a crayon, I was drawing pictures and telling stories. Even when I couldn't yet write, my parents said I would "scribble stories," pointing at my abstract expressionistic doodles and interpreting them as epic adventures. Because my memory stretches back as far as my mesh playpen, I vividly recall dreaming up stories in my mind, and actually being able to see them. My creative ideas brought me so much joy, and it was even more fun to transfer what I saw with my imagination onto my drawing pad (or my bedroom walls).

This technique, of *seeing* an image and then bringing it to fruition, followed me throughout school, and I benefited greatly—I won every elementary school drawing contest and placed in every middle and high school art show. When given an assignment, I would see the finished piece with my mind's eye, and then work out the details around how to bring it to life. I'd ask myself questions like *What medium will I use? What type of paper or canvas do I need? What technique is best for executing the idea?*

As if magically, even before asking the questions I always knew the answers, that creative knowing I introduced in Chapter 7.

In my earliest days of novel-writing, I had just finished college and had been writing research papers for so long that writing fiction felt daunting. After several days of poring over the details around the story I was imagining in my mind, I reverted back to the technique I used to create art—I saw the characters first, and then the story started falling into place. Like riding a bicycle, I eased into the practice of creatively knowing the outcome, and then figuring out how to get there. I found inspiration through personal experience, observing others, taking nature walks, reading books, watching movies, and meandering through art museums. Stories lived everywhere and in everything.

Adding the tarot to this list was a gamechanger.

Exploring the cards' imagery sparked ideas in a much more intuitive way than by walking, observing, and reading alone. The illustrations were each their own story, and when gathered together, the stories grew and evolved. Working with the tarot while writing my novels has helped me to fill-in the blanks, making it easier to find my way to the conclusions of my characters' journeys.

Connecting the Story

In the tarot, The High Priestess represents the mind's eye that sees and knows our stories. She's the Higher Self, the voice in our heads, the gnawing in our gut, the slight nudge or hunch we feel when we know something to be true or are led to go somewhere or do something we cannot otherwise understand. The High Priestess accepts what we've learned and manifested from The Fool and The Magician and unveils hidden secrets that can amplify our creative awareness. Let's meet this fascinating figure and learn how she can help you sharpen your mystic storyteller intuition.

What's happening in The High Priestess card?

The High Priestess is a beautiful Black Queen resting in her favorite high back rattan chair between two columns of Solomon's Temple. Boaz, the pillar of mystery, is on her right and Jachin, the pillar of consciousness, is on her left. Her dress is watery shades of blues and greens, with a gold ribbon snaking through the fabric. This design is reminiscent of kintsugi, a Japanese method of sealing together the pieces of sacred vessels with a golden lacquer. The High Priestess sits upright, firm but poised. She wears a cross pendant and the scroll resting in her arms is inscribed with the letters T-O-R-A. Many tarot enthusiasts believe this scroll to be a copy of the Torah, the first five books of the Hebrew Bible. While The High Priestess' gilt crown bears a full moon symbol, at her feet rests a crescent moon. The moon is a symbol of mysticism, fertility, cycles, intuition, and female empowerment. In the earliest versions of the tarot, The High Priestess was known as the Papess. She was inspired by the Egyptian goddess Isis, the Christian Virgin Mary, and perhaps even the legendary Pope Joan, as posed by Rachel Pollack in *Seventy-Eight Degrees of Wisdom.*[27]

Behind The High Priestess' wicker throne and two pillars stand a pair of pomegranate trees, their branches forming a type of curtain. This curtain is thought to be a veil between consciousness and the subconscious, the pomegranate a symbol of life regeneration.

In Greek mythology, Persephone was believed to have eaten pomegranate seeds and was able to travel between this life and the underworld—consciousness and mystery. As such, The High Priestess uses her intuitive power to access the unknown. The vast stretch of water behind her perch and trees is calm and quiet, and her dress is believed to be the source of water that flows throughout the entire tarot. Water symbolizes emotion and the subconscious, so perhaps the trees' veiled effect, along with the columns, represent the gateway between our conscious and unconscious minds, with our liminal High Priestess ushering our passage between.

The High Priestess: A Deep Dive

The High Priestess reminds us of the famous Greek declaration inscribed on the Temple of Apollo at Delphi, "Know thyself." A wise and intuitive mystic, The High Priestess implores you to listen to and use your intuition—your gut—always choosing what feels right. What is your internal wisdom telling you about what you're writing? Don't listen to everyone else tell you how or what you should write. Listen to your heart-mind connection (your Higher Self). Go deeper in your writing and explore all the possibilities. You're only scratching the surface.

As a writer, how can you embody The High Priestess' energy? Learn. Always seek knowledge and understanding of the themes, ideas, concepts, people, worlds about which you're writing. Because, as you well know, writers enter the worlds about which we write. We become either our characters or an invisible, hovering entity watching them embark upon the lessons they'll learn throughout their stories.

The High Priestess, Reversed:

If The High Priestess card lands on your desk in the reversed position, it means that intuition is blocked. That pomegranate curtain is closed and there is no passage through from here to anywhere else. Perhaps this momentary stifling of The Fool along their adventure is for their own best interest. They are warned to turn back in this physical space and take a respite; they are invited to recharge their intuitive energy and let that cute little dog wash the mud off its paws.

Notable Symbols in The High Priestess

Astrology—Moon
Element—Spirit/Water

Other Symbols

Cross—The cross symbolizes a crossroads, a point between all four directions. Which way?

Moon—The moon is representative of manifestation, the full moon reminding us to remain thankful for our many blessings. The crescent or sickle moon, on the other hand, represents psychic power, fertility, life and death, and in witchcraft it represents the Divine Feminine.

Pomegranates—In Greek mythology, Persephone is abducted from her parents, Zeus and Demeter, by Hades, Zeus' brother. While in the Underworld, she eats "the fruit of the dead," pomegranates. As such, the pomegranate is a symbol of life, death, and rebirth, its red juice representing an elixir of youth.[28]

Water—Water is a symbol of intuition and the subconscious mind. Similarly, light blue is a color with calming effects, just like the water beyond The High Priestess' chair and also like the color haint blue in the Coastal South. The High Priestess' garment flows like water, the starting point of all the water found in the tarot. Every rain shower, stream, and body of water flows from her robes.

Numerological Associations with The High Priestess

In the tarot, The High Priestess is directly connected to the Twos (See also Chapter 18, Section 2 – *The Twos*). In numerology, two is the number of duality, choice, union, and decision. As you've learned so far about this card, there are two pillars, each representative of two separate realms of thought, their embellished curtain a passageway between life and death, here and after, up and down.

The High Priestess

Cups · Pentacles · Swords · Wands

The High Priestess, Characterized

If your fictional character embodies The High Priestess' energy, whoa doggie! She is a mysterious force, multifaceted, wise, and layered with backstory, foreshadowing, insight, and maybe even a little fantasy. The character patterned after The High Priestess is mystic, always listening to their inner wisdom, consulting the Higher Self before making a decision or counseling others. This character has knowledge to share, lessons to teach.

The High Priestess-inspired character could be a goddess, an introvert, a teacher, an oracle, a papess, a pastor, a prophet, a psychiatrist, a reiki practitioner, a saint, a seer, a spiritual guide, a wise elder, or a witch. She can be anything, really, but whatever she is, be prepared to write someone mystical and complex.

Notable characters, people, or personas

Pinkie Perideaux in *The Scars We Choose*; Cher; Angela Bassett; Shirley MacLaine; and performance artist Maria Abramovic.

Who would you add to this list?

Word List

arcane	intellectual	passage	spiritual
awareness	intuition	psyche	subconscious
choices	intuitive	receptivity	tranquility
connection	keen	sacred	transcendent
discernment	knowledge	secretive	truth
ethereal	mediumship	secrets	unconscious
fluid	memory	seer	understanding
honesty	mysterious	sensitivity	unknown
imagination	mystery	sojourn	water
inner truth	oracle	source	wisdom

Spread: What's On Your Mind?

Although The Magician delivers gifts to help with our holistic needs, The High Priestess offers intuitive discernment. As such, by using your mind's eye (intuition), and with a little help from The High Priestess herself, this spread can help you or one of your characters uncover repressed thoughts around a person, place, thing, or situation. You can use this spread for yourself or for your characters.

1. Think about the person, place, thing, or situation that is troubling or puzzling you or your character(s).
2. While considering the details, shuffle your tarot cards.
3. When you are satisfied that the cards are shuffled well, search the deck for The High Priestess.
4. Pull the card behind The High Priestess and lay it on the space for Card 1. This card represents what's on your subconscious mind.
5. Lay The High Priestess on the space for Card 2. She's the veil of discernment in this situation.
6. Finally, the card in front of The High Priestess informs what's on your conscious mind, supporting what you or your character(s) already know about these circumstances.

Card 1: What's on my subconscious mind?
Card 2: The High Priestess—for discernment
Card 3: What do I already know about these circumstances?

Key 3 or III:
The Empress

III

The Empress

My maternal grandmother, whom my cousins and I affectionately refer to as "Meme," (pron. Mee mee) was one of the strongest, kindest, and most creative souls I've ever known. Although she endured turbulent hardships throughout her childhood and adolescence—many events of which inspired my novel *Only the Rocks That Float*—she persevered, using her learned experiences to create a life rich with love and art.

As a young, married woman and mother back in the 1950s, Meme expressed her creativity through her kitchen. From brewing the most delicious pot of coffee you'd ever smelled or tasted, to delivering a four-course meal every evening for her family and extended relatives, Meme imbued what she produced with care and love. She was a gardener, planting, growing, and harvesting her own herbs and vegetables: spearmint, oregano, thyme, tomatoes, squash, okra, and the list grows. Fruit trees staggered about my grandparents' property—fig, peach, crabapple, and pomegranate—the harvest of which Meme used for jellies, preserves, cobblers, and pies. Muscadine and scuppernong vines twisted along the tops of their chain-link fencing, the fruits from which Meme used to concoct (and hide from PawPaw, who was a Pentecostal pastor) her own wines.

Meme's fruit-stained hands were white lightning at her sewing machine; she designed and produced clothing for her children, grandchildren, and herself. When I was a little girl, almost all of my clothes were Meme's creations; everything she made was perfected down to the detail. Oh, how I looked forward to Saturday afternoons spent picking out fabric and notions with her at the Piece Goods store!

Meme also enjoyed quilting and crafting, and in the 1980s she went through a period of creating the cutest (or most terrifying, depending on who you asked) clown dolls you'd ever seen in your life. Fashioned from fabric remnants, Styrofoam balls, woodblocks, old-fashioned clothespins, and a glue gun, the resulting posable clowns each had their own unique personality. They were the stuff of Stephen King books, yet she couldn't stitch them fast enough for those at the church and schools who'd collected them. Many of us grandkids were secretly relieved when the nineties rolled around, and Meme's glue gun shifted toward constructing wreaths from dried grapevines and faux flowers.

Apart from the creepy clowns, everything my grandmother was doing I also wanted to learn how to do. And so, from cooking to crafting to sewing, Meme taught me everything she knew. When I was a freshman in high school, however, the tables turned, and I was able to help her birth and nurture her greatest and most rewarding creative endeavor of her life: painting.

In the late 1980s, I started painting landscapes and seascapes in oils on canvas, selling them to save money to buy school clothes and supplies. In 1991, when Meme and PawPaw built a new home next door to my parents' house out in the country, Meme liked to walk through the woods and watch me paint. She'd bring sweetened iced tea ("sweet tea") and something to snack on, and she'd marvel at how I was able to capture the likeness of a pine tree with a few easy taps of my fan brush, or the way scraping a palette knife downward along the canvas would form the reflection of bushes and trees in the stream or lake below them. One day, while I was painting a lighthouse scene and Meme snacked on Chex Mix, she told me, "Mandy, when I turn sixty-five, I want you to teach me how to paint."

Three years later, Meme turned sixty-five. It was 1994 and, as promised, I showed her everything I knew. We set up two easels in my art room, we chose one of Bob Ross' paintings as inspiration, and I laid out our palettes with all the requisite colors—Titanium White, Alizarin Crimson, and Yellow Ochre, to name a few. From the very first stroke of her paintbrush, Meme's natural artistic talent bloomed across the canvas. More than six decades of creativity manifested on that canvas that day, and when our paintings were done, we both stared at each other wide-eyed before erupting into a fit of giggles. Her landscape was spectacular! It looked as though she'd been painting her entire life.

Since that day, Meme painted right up until just weeks before she passed. She was 91. Over the years, my family and I made sure Meme had all the painting supplies and every Bob Ross and William Alexander video tape and book she'd wanted. PawPaw and my uncle built a sunroom onto their home so that Meme could have a studio space. She filled it with artwork she either sold or donated, and for many years she opened her home to students who also wanted to learn how to paint. Today, her work can be found in homes and businesses all over the world, and when I see one hanging on the wall of doctors' offices or restaurants in my hometown, I smile and think of my talented Meme.

Connecting the Story

My grandmother took the risks of The Fool, the ingenuity of The Magician, and the intuitive insight of The High Priestess to birth generations of creative people, including me. Like The Empress, she harnessed her imagination and honed her skills, nurturing and harvesting a legacy of love and creativity... and a collection of artwork to rival the Louvre.

What's happening in The Empress card?

The Empress is the Divine Feminine, the ultimate creator of potential. Pregnant with possibilities—creative, joyful, and pleasurable, she's the epitome of beauty, growth, and sensuality. The giant golden pen that rests in the crook of her arm is her magic wand, and she uses it to bring about fertility of the mind, body, and spirit. She is the physical manifestation of The High Priestess' hidden knowledge and desires, resting on a soft, relaxing chaise-of-a-throne and shrouded in a comfortable, breathable gown—the yoga pants of gowns—printed with sliced pomegranates.

The Empress' crown is fashioned with twelve six-pointed stars—the Jewish Star of David—one for each sign of the zodiac, and her shield-shaped pillow is embroidered with the symbol for Venus, the Roman Goddess of Love. Its shape is reminiscent of a planchette, a tool for divining messages from the spirit world to the physical. The Empress is both: she's equally sacred and mortal. She's Mother Nature, the Great Mother, and a celestial goddess.

The Empress lounges about on her plush throne, red, the color of passion and longing. She basks in the warmth and abundance of a lush forest, a flowing river, and a golden field of grain, her magical harvest, manifested by intent and desire. She is all things abundant and fertile and plentiful.

The Empress: A Deep Dive

The Empress nurtures abundance, beauty, and growth. These things can be found within you, dear writer, just waiting for the world to read. Whatever you are writing, whatever your process or practice, stay with it. Keep nurturing it because it can grow and thrive, your efforts cultivating a plentiful harvest of freelance work, blog entries, essays, book reviews, and sales. When imbued with The Empress energy, everything you touch or work on can grow and thrive.

When you are feeling The Empress energy, you are encouraged to pen that first novel, finish that fifth novel, or research, gather, and ponder that project you've been flirting with. Harness The Fool's faith, The Magician's will, and The High Priestess' wisdom, and you have the beautiful combination of creativity, expression, and growth that is The Empress.

The Empress, Reversed: The Shadow

When The Empress lands on her head, she has trouble getting back on her feet. She's lazy and uncoordinated. She's needy and dependent on other people for help. She can't make a decision on her own and her energy is erratic and undependable. The reversed Empress is codependent and desolate, barren of thought and action. She's terrible with money and she needs constant reminders of her worth. She seeks love and acceptance in all the wrong places as her self-esteem and value have plummeted from her once thriving status.

Notable Symbols in The Empress

Astrology—Venus
Element—Spirit/Earth

Other Symbols

Female Symbol—Her planchette-shaped shield boasts the female symbol, an emblem of Venus, the Roman Goddess of Love.

Pomegranate Gown—She wears a gown embellished with sliced pomegranates, a symbol of life, birth, and rebirth.

Star Crown—There are twelve stars adorning The Empress' crown, one for each sign of the zodiac.

Wheat—The Empress has manifested a robust harvest of grains, a symbol of abundance.

Water—A plentiful river flows around her, a symbol for the subconscious. Again, heaven and earth, intellect and intuition.

Numerological Associations with The Empress

In the tarot, The Empress is directly connected to the Threes, which represent creativity, expression, and growth in numerology (See also Chapter 18, Section 2 – *The Threes*). The number three also represents the unity of the mind, body, and spirit; the Father, the Son, and the Holy Ghost; past, present, and future; the sun, the moon, and the stars.

The Empress, Characterized

If you are writing an Empress-worthy character, then you'd better make certain she is one bad mama jama. An Empress character is as voluptuous as Serena Williams and as creative and expressive as Pamela Colman Smith... and my Meme. As Theresa Reed, The Tarot Lady, likes to say, "She's large and in charge,"[29] and she rules without having to lift a finger or say a word. Her mere presence is enough to bring any gender to their knees (no dirty puns intended).

The Empress would make an excellent heroine—honest, brave, and poised—or a thoughtful and strong supporting character—like a grandmother or a favorite auntie. She might also represent an alluring and seductive antagonist, or even the irresistible other woman. The Empress is every woman, any effeminate person, a mother, a surrogate, a side chick-turned main chick, a beauty queen, a princess, a queen, a drag mother, the GOAT, or an icon.

Notable characters, people, or personas

Beyoncé; Lady Violet Bridgerton; Rupaul; Michelle Yeoh as Mameha in *Memoirs of a Geisha*; Angelina Jolie; Freida Kahlo; Angela Bassett (in anything, but especially as Queen Ramonda in *Black Panther: Wakanda Forever*); the Sibyls; Brigid, Celtic goddess of fertility, healing, the hearth, poetry, spring, et al.; Demeter, goddess of fertility and agriculture.

Who would you add to this list?

Word List

abundance	creator	harvest	opulence
actualization	effeminate	healing	passionate
agape	femininity	healthy	poised
artist	fertility	love	pregnancy
beauty	flow	manifestation	prosperity
birthing	fortify	maternal	sensual
community	generosity	Mother Earth	sexy
confident	goddess	motherhood	thriving
creation	grace	natural	voluptuous
creativity	growth	nurturing	welfare

Spread: Deepest Desire

Some of the greatest stories ever written were penned by writers who felt an innate desire to bring that story and its characters to life. As a mystic storyteller, what is your deepest desire? Because The Empress supports abundant growth and success, her energy can help nourish your writing project and/or practice. Use the following spread and your intuition to help uncover, grow, and manifest your deepest desires. You might also use this spread from your character(s) point of view.

1. Imagine your deepest desire for your writing project or practice.
2. While envisioning the most optimal outcome, shuffle your tarot cards.
3. When you are satisfied that the cards are shuffled well, search the deck for The Empress and lay the card on the space for Card 1.
4. Shuffle your cards once more and turn the deck facedown as if you were about to deal the cards.
5. Moving clockwise from the bottom left of your spread, turn over one card for Cards 2 – 5.

Card 2: What do I need to know about my deepest desire?
Card 3: What is my intention for manifesting this desire?
Card 4: Where are opportunities for nourishment and growth?
Card 5: How might I scale my efforts to yield abundant success?

3

4

2

5

Key 4 or IV:
The Emperor

IV

The Emperor

I've always been a rebel. With so much fire in my birth chart (more on that in Chapter 23 – *Astrology and the Tarot*), I've intrinsically and continually questioned authority and balked at being restricted from personal freedoms. I don't like feeling boxed-in, limited, being micromanaged, or restrained for the sake of someone else's comfort.

As a little girl, these things happened in the form of rules and outdated expectations set by family leaders. One of my grandparents was notorious for declaring, "Children should be seen and not heard!" And when questioning a parent about something that didn't make any sense to me or an idea that didn't resonate with what I knew in my heart was right, their answers wavered between "Because I said so" and "Because that's just the way it is."

And so, when I wasn't being heard, when I didn't get any answers to my questions, I sought them elsewhere—in other people, books, and experiences. When adolescence set in, my rebellion billowed with anger, resentment, and distrust. In the American South, there were still so many vile, ignorant aspects of the culture and history still being preserved, and many members of my family were among those perpetrating the, well, I will call it what it was: hate. Because my intrinsic values did not align, I stopped seeking guidance from many of the adults in my life and shifted my trust to empathetic teachers, both tangible and in the media.

Through growth and maturity, I soon realized that not everyone shares the same experiences with leadership or privilege with regard to questioning authority, and I have also come to understand that not all leaders are as restrictive and uncompromising as those of my youth. Yet and still, the earliest impressions during my formative years managed to leave a stain on my psyche, and I still bristle when made to feel unseen, unheard, and cancelled.

As you venture through the tarot, getting to know and learn the cards, in addition to discovering which cards are your favorites—your tarot guideposts—you will also encounter those that make you bristle or cringe (or both). For me, until The Emperor of the *Mystic Storyteller Tarot* came into fruition, this card was one such card.

When I was first learning the tarot, The Emperor's demeanor felt derisive and off-putting, and he evoked the construct of "The Man," the epitome of unhealthy Patriarchal ideals. Sitting high on his cold, stone throne, The Emperor conjured childhood memories of being made to feel like my thoughts, feelings, and even my gender weren't valuable. The figure in Pamela Colman Smith's card seemed abrasive, like a crotchety old man who placed status, politics, and God (in that order, although he would have corrected me and reversed it, I'm sure) above all else, ruling with an iron fist and a cruel, unforgiving heart.

After many years of working with the tarot and growing impatient with how The Emperor card consistently made me feel, I decided to change my outlook. Intentionally, and mustering great resolve, I reimagined how I viewed the card, thus reshaping my responses to it when it landed on my desk. Consulting with Roz, the illustrator of the *Mystic Storyteller Tarot*, helped tremendously with altering my perception of the card. In an attempt to shift my negative feelings associated with the imagery in a positive direction, I requested that The Emperor be inspired by someone I love dearly. As such, the *Mystic Storyteller Tarot* likeness is that of my husband. The outcome resulted in a great appreciation for the card, and alternative to my early, harmful leadership experiences, I realized that by associating my thoughts of The Emperor with my husband's bold, committed, and stalwart character, The Emperor became sturdy, grounding, and supportive.

Connecting the Story

The Emperor is dependable. He's disciplined, decisive, and reliable. He says what he means, and he means what he says, which informs his trustworthiness. The Emperor fixes things that are broken. He leads through action, order, and structure, unfazed by working just as hard as anyone else around him. When The Emperor card shows up on your desk, consider it an invitation to shift your focus toward order and structure. Let's take a deeper dive into this often-misunderstood authoritative figure.

What's happening in The Emperor card?

A middle-aged male, The Emperor's posture is stiff, his back as straight as his stone throne, void of detail apart from the skulls of four rams, the symbol of Aries (or Ares), Greek god of war. The Emperor's "armor" is his everyday streetwear: a fiery red athletic suit and metallic-colored sneakers. In similar fashion, The Emperor's "crown" is his ballcap, emblazoned with an emblem reminiscent of Basquiat's iconic flourished crown. In his right hand, The Emperor grasps a black marker with a golden Egyptian ankh printed up its side. In his left palm, he holds a vintage-style pocket watch, a nod to Father Time, perhaps? In the card's background, you can see an apricot sky with ochre-colored mountains rising high above a cerulean stream. Overall, the colors in this card are warm, much like its governing planet, Mars, which, like Aries, is the god of war in Roman mythology.

The Emperor: A Deep Dive

Following right after The Empress, the Divine Feminine who creates, The Emperor is the Divine Masculine who facilitates. Similarly, while the mother teaches love through the heart, the father teaches love through character. A fatherlike figure, in his highest polarity (most positive aspect) The Emperor demonstrates love through action. The ultimate Doer, this figure establishes trust, first and foremost, followed by structure and protective boundaries. He does so through realistic guidelines and expectations in the service of holistic development, and when needed, he can be a disciplinarian. Nevertheless, The Emperor's discipline occurs through love. A steadfast, fatherly archetype, The Emperor is capable of unconditional love through resolve and objective truth. As such, he teaches that only those who stand in strength and truth can be truly free.

In his lower polarity (lesser or shadow aspect), The Emperor is resistant to change. A traditionalist, he subscribes to privileged, old school "values," and his outlook is binary. His archaic expectations are exacted and framed by conventional, conservative rules and boundaries that discriminate and oppress. Since my intentional reimagining of The Emperor card, I've discovered that my disdain was, in fact, a response to its lowest polarity.

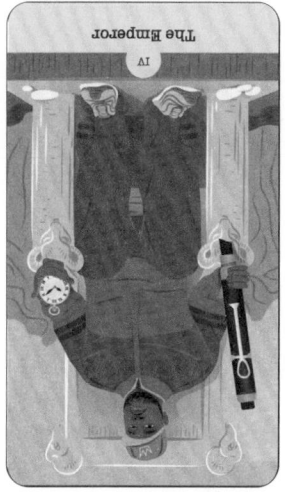

The Emperor, Reversed: Shadow

When reversed, The Emperor has fallen. He loses his grasp of his sword, and he is pinned to the ground beneath the weight of his crippling throne. This new structure provides a platform on which those he has oppressed might stand and deliver their grievances, forcing him to watch and listen.

Because it will take a village to move the throne and rescue him, The Emperor had better listen carefully and understand that once he is rescued things will NOT go back to the way they were. The situation is unsteady and insecure... just like those who have endured his punishments and cruelty. But not anymore. If he is to be freed, The Emperor is forced to step into the shoes of others. He must experience what it is like to be oppressed and stifled. He must know the fear of uncertainty and allow himself to be softened and humbled by his fall.

Notable Symbols in The Emperor

Astrology—Aries
Element—Spirit/Fire

Other Symbols

Ankh—The Egyptian symbol of life and immortality (See also Chapter 19 – *Symbolism in the Tarot/Ankh*).

Mountains—The mountain range behind The Emperor's throne represents a steady foundation, security, and structure.

Red Clothing—Scarlet fabric is a symbol of action, desire, and passion.

Numerological Associations with The Emperor

In numerology, the number four represents a steady foundation and security. As such, The Emperor card is associated with the Fours of the Minor Arcana (See also Chapter 18, Section 2 – *The Fours*).

  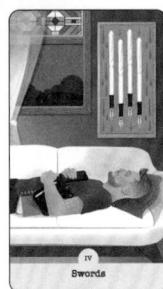 

The Emperor, Characterized

Depending on the story, The Emperor can represent one of many figures. These include, but are not limited to: a dictator, government official, harsh leader, king, masochist, mean neighbor, misogynist, an orator, old man, president, police officer, stern father, The Man, or a sheriff.

As you can tell from my story at the beginning of this card's profile, The Emperor can easily fill the role of a tyrannical antagonist. However, in his highest polarity, this individual would make a dependable Jack Pearson-type father figure.

Notable characters, people, or personas

Higher Polarity—Your father; your stern grandpa; your no-nonsense history teacher; your high school principal; Jake Sully in the movie Avatar; Santa Claus; Mufasa; John Amos as James Evans on Good Times; Samuel L. Jackson in, well, just about anything, but especially as Coach Carter in the movie of the same title.

Lower Polarity—Darth Vader; Charles Minor from *The Office* (Idris Elba's cringiest role, in my opinion); Genghis Khan, Lenin, Stalin, Putin, and other deplorable dictators; Louise Fletcher as both Nurse Ratched in *One Flew Over the Cuckoo's Nest* and as The Grandmother in *Flowers in the Attic*.

Who would you add to this list?

Word List

ambition	discipline	leader	permission
assertive	dominance	legacy	planning
austere	facilitator	majesty	power
authority	Father Time	management	protector
boundaries	fighter	masculine	rigid
conservativism	forceful	mastery	security
control	fostering	mighty	stability
dependable	fraternity	military	strategic
dictator	guide	nobility	structure
direct	inflexibility	order	The Man

Spread: Situational Leadership

Whether you like it or not, there will be times when you will have to step into a leadership role and coach, guide, and inspire others. Occasionally, you might even have to remove barriers in order to help those who depend on you to succeed. If you're a fiction writer, the same goes for your characters. As such, this Situational Leadership spread can serve as a contemplative method for channeling The Emperor's energy in order to coach, guide, inspire, and remove barriers for those who are depending on you or your character(s).

1. Find The Emperor in your tarot deck and lay the card in the space for Card This card is the significator for you or your character in this situation.
2. Shuffle your tarot deck until you are satisfied that the cards are ready, and then turn the deck facedown as if you were about to deal them.
3. Starting with the space for Card 2, count the fourth card from the top of the deck and lay it in that space.
4. Repeat for the rest of the spread, counting every fourth card, laying it down, and then moving on to the next space.

Card 2: What do I need in order to coach others through this situation?
Card 3: How can I guide others in this situation?
Card 4: How can I inspire others in this situation?
Card 5: What barriers need moving in order to help others succeed in this situation?

The Emperor

2　3　4　5

Key 5 or V:
The Hierophant

The motivation to write my first novel didn't surface until a couple of years after I finished my Master of Science in Psychology. For several years, I had only written academic research papers—211 to be exact—following the American Psychological Association (APA) Guidelines and checking for and correcting that troublesome passive voice. The structure and regulations were unwavering, and if I wanted to achieve my goal of graduating *summa cum laude*, there was no other choice than to comply.

When I set out to write that first book, however, I found myself unsteady with the creative freedom that many aspects of fictional writing allows. I felt like Ariel, standing and attempting to walk on her new human legs for the first time. Getting used to non-academic writing took getting used to loosening those robes and tossing aside that holy APA scepter. I had to learn to be The Hierophant reversed and today, writing my first nonfiction piece since college, I feel like that stiff ol' pontiff is hovering over my shoulder, watching for adherence to the writing rules and waiting to ding me over the head with his mace at the instance of passive voice.

Like their predecessor, The Hierophant is one such card I had to learn to appreciate. At first glance, the figure appears to be a leader of great distinction—the boss who calls the shots. They're stuffy and reserved, traditional in their way of thinking and teaching. As such, if you are ever feeling like The Hierophant, itching to loosen those robes and write without so much restraint, it might be time for a change. Consider doing research on writing methods or constructs you've never tried or that you once believed unorthodox. If you've never written poetry, try a stanza or a verse or two. Try haiku! Haiku was my gateway to becoming a serious writer, along with journaling, which is excellent for the preservation and development of ideas (See also Chapter 29 – *Journaling with the Tarot*).

Free association and automatic writing are examples of helpful freewriting exercises. Other examples are both the Gut Instincts and Tarot Stories activities in this book (the concluding activities in Parts Two and Three, respectively). In both of these exercises, you intuitively sketched out your free-flowing thoughts around a card or cards. Without thinking, you can silence that inner Hierophant critic and simply start jotting or typing your thoughts non-stop and see where they take you on the page.

Connecting the Story

Whatever the new avenue, my recommendation for shaking off the rules and developing one's own unique writing style is to start anywhere, start simple, quiet that inner critic, and lean in toward your intuitive thoughts. Let's explore the many ways of considering The Hierophant.

What's happening in The Hierophant card?

According to *Secrets of the Waite-Smith Tarot*, the word *hierophant* means "reveal the sacred."[30] Like The High Priestess, The Hierophant wears a fancy dress, a golden crown, and she's placed between two pillars. However, unlike Her Mystical Majesty, who conceals secrets, The Hierophant reveals them, sharing what is known to be irrevocably true (which some might refer to as "dogma") with those who would believe it. She stands at her chalkboard, pointing her staff at a collection of symbols: the keys to Heaven and Earth, green ivy, a cross, and a pair of acorns.

The Hierophant didn't find her position as an instructor available and take it, she was placed there by others, perhaps those who needed to be guided and taught. In the classroom before her, you can see two students. They listen eagerly to what The Hierophant has to say and are poised to conform as expected. At the tipping of her staff, these guys are off to spread what they've learned with others.

The Hierophant: A Deep Dive

The Hierophant is the keeper and deliverer of indoctrinated beliefs and rules, the revealer of sacred things.[31] She preaches adherence and compliance within the parameters of laws, but sometimes it can feel like she's chastising those who think and act outside of those guidelines.

In Greek mythology, hierophants were the chief priests of the Eleusinian Mysteries, an ancient Grecian rite which celebrated the Goddess Demeter's rescuing of her daughter Persephone from Hades, who had abducted her and taken her to the underworld.[32]

On the other side of mythology, religious dogma, and indoctrination, you can find cancel culture, or the modern ostracizing of a person or group by calling them out and/or expelling them from societal expectations and norms. In her lowest polarity, The Hierophant subscribes to these practices. In her highest polarity, however, The Hierophant teaches us that we can coexist quite peacefully alongside one another without having to agree. Dogs and cats do it all the time. Among her most constructive teachings, The Hierophant reminds us that cancelling a person or a thing because their beliefs oppose ours is in itself intolerant and oppressive. The solution? Asking questions, educating oneself and preventing feelings and religious or spiritual beliefs from informing how one treats others as human beings.

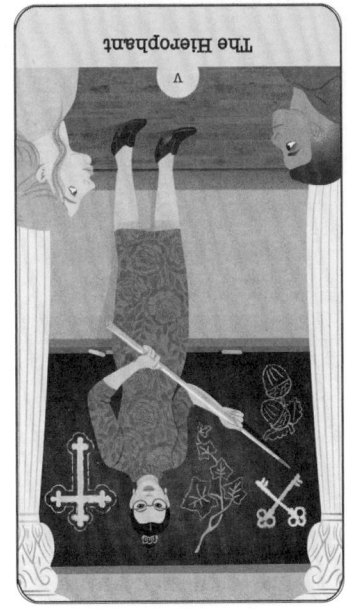

The Hierophant, Reversed

When reversed, the rules are broken, and the secrets are revealed in such a way as to allow you to decide for yourself what you believe in and how you wish to behave. The reversed Hierophant takes off her golden crown, loosens their high collar, and leans her staff against one of those columns. She's the Substitute Teacher who just wants you to do your work quietly while she reads her book with her feet propped up on your Everyday Teacher's desk. In some cases, a reversed Hierophant can be flippant and challenge the very authorities vested when she was upright on her feet.

Like the reversed Hierophant, I've never been a fan of being expected to conform. If you can also identify, then this reversal might be more along your speed of writerly practice. As such, when this card flips upside down on your writer's desk, ask yourself which doctrines, beliefs, or guidelines you're subscribing to that are no longer championing your creativity. Which processes and endeavors are snuffing your creative flame because of their stringent guidelines?

Notable Symbols in The Hierophant

Astrology—Taurus
Element—Spirit/Earth

Other Symbols

Acorns—A pair of acorns represents oak knowledge and wisdom.

Cross—The cross symbolizes a crossroads, a point between all four directions.

Crossed keys—These symbolize the keys to heaven held by Saint Peter.

Ivy—Ivy represents intellectual achievement.

Numerological Associations with The Hierophant

In the tarot, The Hierophant is directly connected to the Fives (See also Chapter 18, Section 2 – *The Fives*). In numerology, five relates to change, instability and conflict, which makes sense with regard to this card because so many writers are rebels who don't like conformity and who enjoy bending the rules in their stories. I am one such writer, as I enjoy dialect-heavy writing and forbidden romance tropes.

The Hierophant, Characterized

The Hierophant might be Saint Peter, the gatekeeper who holds the keys to heaven. She could also be the pastor of your church, a priest, a Pope, a church elder, a teacher, a babysitter, your micromanaging boss, a parent, a committee leader, your school's principal, the Dean, a judge, Congress, or anyone who implements rules and expects you to follow them.

Notable characters, people, or personas

The entire book of *Robert's Rules of Order* by Henry Martyn Robert; Professor Dolores Umbridge in *Harry Potter and the Order of the Phoenix*; and for a more pleasant example, Mary Poppins.

Word List

arcane	intellectual	passage	spiritual
awareness	intuition	psyche	subconscious
choices	intuitive	receptivity	tranquility
connection	keen	sacred	transcendent
discernment	knowledge	secretive	truth
ethereal	mediumship	secrets	unconscious
fluid	memory	seer	understanding
honesty	mysterious	sensitivity	unknown
imagination	mystery	sojourn	water
inner truth	oracle	source	wisdom

Spread: Silencing the Inner Critic

A dear friend of mine often reminds me, "We don't see ourselves as the world sees us." As a writer, I am willing to bet a thousand Schrute Bucks[33] that, like me, you also struggle against your own Hierophant inner critic. Inner critics can be loathsome and harsh, and if we allow them the power, they can suck the joy right out of storytelling. When you find yourself struggling against the opinions of your inner critic, use the following spread to swiftly silence them and invite creativity to flow freely and boundlessly. You might also use this spread from the point of view of your fictional character(s).

1. Shuffle your deck until you are satisfied that the cards are ready.
2. Next, find The Hierophant, which represents your inner critic. Lay the card down to be the center card.
3. Lay down the cards that were in the deck before and after The Hierophant on either side, to make a three-card spread.
4. Ask yourself the following question, using your intuition to consider all the possibilities. If you are using this spread from your character's point of view, imagine them asking themselves these questions:

Cards 1 and 3: How do I silence my inner critic?
Card 2: The Hierophant—your inner critic

Key 6 or VI:
The Lovers

VI

The Lovers

Some of my favorite songs are those which tell romantic—and often bittersweet—stories. From R&B to Country, Jazz to the Blues, I've always been drawn to songs that long for someone else, someplace else, and/or some other time. Songs like *A House Is Not a Home* (Luther Vandross), *At Last* (Etta James), and *Fall Into Me* (Sugarland) have burrowed deep under my skin and nestled into my bones. Like faithful lovers and old friends, they show up time and time again, reminding me of all the reasons why love is the best and most powerful drug.

My love for music was inspired by my mother, who always kept a record on the turntable, or the radio turned up loud. Her favorite singers were Karen Carpenter, Lionel Ritchie, and Dan Fogelberg. While her favorite songs were those that transported her from our impoverished life, mine were the ones that told stories about people in love. From a very early age, one Dan Fogelberg song stood out among the rest: *Same Old Lang Syne.*

The songs tells the story of a man running into his long-lost lover in the frozen foods aisle of a grocery store on Christmas Eve. He's a famous singer, longing for simpler times when he wasn't always traveling, she's married to a man who pays the bills but doesn't make her happy. The pair buy a six-pack of beer and drink it in her car while reminiscing on back when things were different—easier, perhaps—and they were in love with each other.

Every time *Same Old Lang Syne* would play, I remember Mama closing her eyes and swaying to the tinkling piano, somber lyrics, and Fogelberg's reminiscent crooning. Although the album featuring the song was released in summer of 1981, because the lyrics identify the setting as a snowy (and then rainy) Christmas Eve, it is a staple amongst the holiday playlists of those, like Mama and me, who love it. Over the years, I always wondered what had happened to those two people? How had they drifted apart? What was their backstory? Year after year, I ruminated on these questions, until the fall of 2020 when a creative spark ignited an idea.

In November of 2020, I decided for the first time to participate in NaNoWriMo.[34] NaNoWriMo, or National Novel Writing Month, is a creative writing challenge held every year in the month of November. In just thirty days, writers are tasked with penning the first draft of a novel. Although to "win" NaNoWriMo, one must complete 50,000 words, writers may set individual goals. In 2020, I set a modest and manageable goal of writing and publishing a novella by November 30. Inspired by the lovers in Dan Fogelberg's song, the story I imagined—*Always Remember November*—took me thirteen days to write, self-edit, and publish.

Unbeknownst to me at the time of writing *Always Remember November*, I have since learned that the song *Same Old Lang Syne* is autobiographical. It's based on a true story about Christmas Eve of 1975 when Dan Fogelberg ran to the store for whipped cream and his high school sweetheart, Jill Gruelich, popped in at the same store for more eggnog. Although the encounter on the frozen foods aisle actually happened, Fogelberg took creative liberties with sharing the details in order to make the lyrics rhyme and because he believed "in leaving a gentleman's silence."[35]

Connecting the Story

In the tarot, The Lovers card energy is of the sort that inspires songs like *Same Old Lang Syne.* While at first glance the card seemingly reflects binary, cisgender, carnal love, its energy encompasses a myriad of emotional and relational dynamics. Let's review this card's details and dissect all the ways it can inspire stories like those written as songs.

What's happening in The Lovers card?

At first glance, we see two people, a female on the left and a male on the right, each standing in front of a tree, each holding a notebook. The couple's eye contact is intense, as if they've only just met and we're witnessing the pull of their attraction drawing them closer. There is a mountain peak in the distance behind them, with the sun positioned high in the sky and shining down all around. An angel-like figure descends from the clouds above, their hands positioned in a gesture of blessings.

According to A. E. Waite, the couple is "unveiled before each other, as if Adam and Eve when they first occupied the paradise of the earthly body."[36] Many tarot historians, such as American occultist Paul Foster Case, who wrote many books on the tarot, believe the angel to be Raphael. His blessing comes to Adam and Eve after they have eaten from the Tree of Knowledge of Good and Evil, in front of which the female figure (Eve) stands. The male figure (Adam) stands before the Tree of Life, its golden leaves representative of fiery, carnal influences.

The Lovers: A Deep Dive

Iif you're anything like me, then by now you've taken some of the tarot cards' meanings quite literally... no pun intended. We are not wrong in this approach as we are often used to writing about people, places, and things exactly how we see them, whether physically or in our mind's eye.

The Lovers card is one such tarot card that, more often than not, will represent the concept of love rather than two specific people or a specific type of relationship (i.e., married folk, friends, lovers, partners, etc.). Now, should you work with a spread and The Lovers card lands on a space that signifies a particular person or persons, a more literal meaning might be considered. Sometimes, however, this card can indicate romantic love, and because of its placement in the Major Arcana, that love is tested, enduring, and profound. The meaning of The Lovers card can be simplified as a holy trinity of the love shared between two individuals connected by the Divine. Conversely, it can also represent the love between your body, your mind, and your spirit. Alternatively, The Lovers can suggest that love is a choice, and it offers guidance, partnership, an emotional and/or physical connection. As mentioned in my story about moving back to Georgia to care for my grandmother (See Chapter 17, *Key 0 – The Fool*), the decision to love her through her health struggles was a choice, one that proved quite costly on all accounts. As for me, however, real and true and lasting and BIG and all the adjectives-type-of-love is worth it. Always.

In addition, The Lovers card could mean intuitive guidance, the love resounding from one's Higher Self, lustful love, dedicated love, unconditional love, helpful love, self-love. While walking at the park one day, I heard someone in a podcast say, "We only value what we have a relationship with." Although I cannot recall who made the statement, nor can I locate a reference for that quote, the message deeply resonated with me, and it always harkens back to The Lovers card. As such, this card might mean anything with which one shares a relationship. Similarly, the card might also represent familial love, love for a pet(s), sibling love, twins, love for nature, parental love, or loving someone as if they were related by blood.

The Lovers, Reversed: The Shadow

When The Lovers card is reversed, well, the love is lost or blocked. This card positioning could reflect the inability to show and/or accept love. Similarly, the reversed Lovers could represent heartbreak, humiliation by a loved one, unrequited love, lost love, stubborn love, arguments, narcissism, a break-up, or even a divorce. When The Lovers card shows up reversed, it reflects energy similar to that of The Devil. The imagery is similar, too: Two people, one supernatural entity, a choice, and ultimately, oppression, dependence, obsession, and/or addiction.

Notable Symbols in The Lovers

Astrology—Gemini
Element—Spirit/Air

Other Symbols

Angel—The angel in this card is Raphael, known as the patron saint of healing, lovers, and travelers.

Clouds—Below Raphael, we see billowing clouds, which represent celestial messages and opportunities. They are symbolic of growth, production, and a brewing and churning storm.

Mountain—The mountain between the two figures and directly beneath Raphael represents the highest point on earth, the center of creation.

Snake—In Rachel Pollack's *Seventy-Eight Degrees of Wisdom*, the author writes that the snake is a magical creature representative of sexuality as "a force towards enlightenment."[37]

Sun—The sun represents warmth, hope, and blessings shining down upon the couple from the heavens above. The rays provide light and warmth for their bodies.

Numerological Associations with The Lovers

The Lovers card is the sixth card of the numbered cards in the Major Arcana (See also Chapter 18, Section 2 – *The Sixes*). In numerology, the number six denotes harmony, balance, karma, assistance, adjustment, alignment, healing, support, empathy, love, and compassion; therefore, The Lovers is associated with the Sixes.

The Lovers, Characterized

Because art imitates life, if The Lovers card represents your character(s), then their attributes are pretty similar to how the card might represent you, the writer. The Lovers might be a new couple, a married couple, two people dating, partners in an affair, fraternal twins, kissing cousins, life partners, best friends, caregiver to care receivers, or "Me, Myself, and I."

Notable characters, people, or personas

Adam and Eve; Jim and Pam; Barack and Michelle; Simon and Daphne; Jack Twist and Ennis Del Mar; Mr. Charles Bingley (with five-thousand a year) and Jane Bennett; Morticia and Gomez; Belly and Conrad; Belly and Jeremiah; Luke and Laura; Luke and Leia; Bert and Ernie; Siskel and Ebert; Laurel and Hardy; Mork and Mindy... and the list goes on.

Who would you add to this list?

Word List

Adam and Eve	commitment	friendship	partnership
adoration	compatibility	happiness	passion
agreement	connection	harmony	pros and cons
alignment	creation	health	relationship
appreciation	dating	intimacy	sexuality
assemble	decisions	karma	teamwork
attraction	dual	lovers	temptation
balance	ecstasy	matrimony	trinity
choice	emotional	morality	unity
collaboration	family	opposition	values

Spread: Romancing the Cards

The best relationships to read are those in which the characters experience and overcome significant struggles. Bonus points go to those who are extremely compatible, sometimes whether they like it or not, and other times to their detriment. Use this spread for inspiration with writing relationships, especially popular romance tropes like Friends-to-Lovers, Enemies-to-Lovers, Fake Dating, Forced Proximity, and Hidden Identity.

1. Shuffle your deck until you are satisfied that the cards are ready.
2. Next, find The Lovers, which represents your characters who are in (or will soon venture into) a relationship. Lay the card in the space for Card 4.
3. Pull the three cards in front of The Lovers card and place them in the spaces for Card 3, Card 2, and Card 1. These cards are associated with the individual on the left, whom we will call "Character Number One."
4. Pull the three cards that follow The Lovers card and place them in the spaces for Card 5, Card 6, and Card 7. These cards are associated with the individual on the right, whom we will call "Character Number Two."

Card 1: What (or who) is in Character Number One's past?
Card 2: What (or who) is Character Number One's weakness?
Card 3: What is Character Number One's best quality?
Card 4: The Lovers—Characters One and Two
Card 5: What is Character Number Two's best quality?
Card 6: What (or who) is Character Number Two's weakness?
Card 7: What (or who) is in Character Number Two's past?

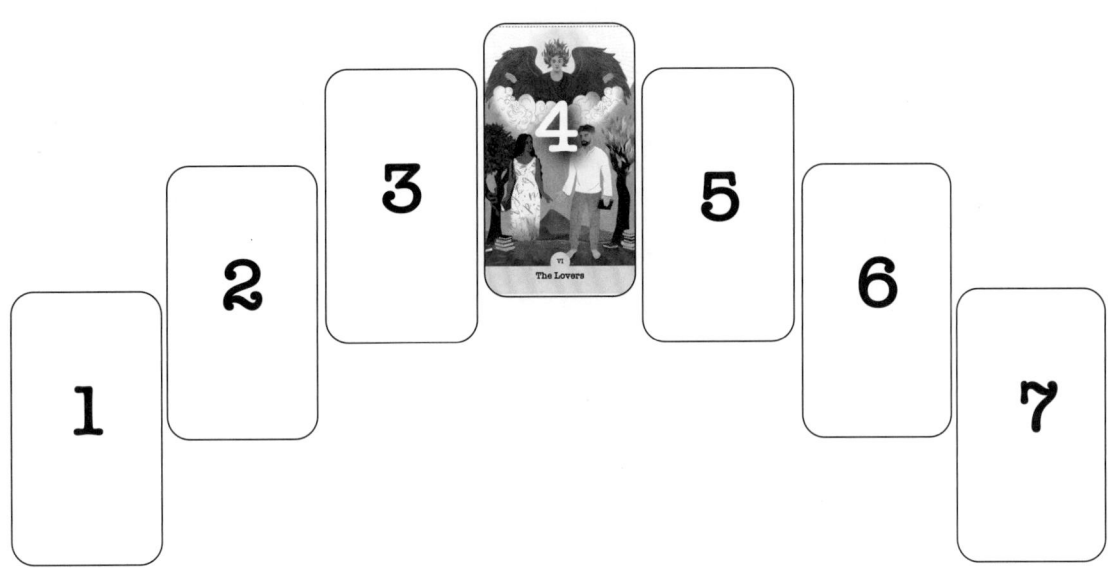

Key 7 or VII:
The Chariot

VII

The Chariot

Many of you reading this book are likely self-published authors or considering that option. I make this statement from experience—I began my publishing journey down the self-publishing path. As I've listened to the accounts of traditionally published authors, both those contracted with small presses and those working with larger publishing houses, I've come to understand that the differences between the traditionally published author and the self-published journey can be staggering. Support looks much different between the two publishing paths, and movement varies.

Until the publishing of this book, my experience with traditional publishing was limited to the literary agent querying process; however, I am aware that in order for authors to get their books into the hands of readers, reviewed, and (hopefully) elevated on the Best Seller ranks, they are supported by a team of dozens.

The self-published author's team looks quite... different. I started out as a self-published author, having self-published several dozen books both for myself and for other authors like me. As such, in order to even hope that readers discover our books, my fellow indie authors and I have to wear many, if not all of those aforementioned hats. The burden of book publishing can be heavy, and it's often impossible to coordinate and balance all the varying responsibilities at one time.

Like a symphony conductor, self-published authors must lead every functioning of the publishing process (with the exception of printing and distribution, which is typically handled through the self-publishing platform of the author's choosing) in order to produce a harmonious outcome. What does a "harmonious outcome" look like? I define it as capturing the attention of readers and gaining as many favorable reviews (four- and five-star) as possible in order to sell more books and, again, hopefully boost rankings on the Best Seller lists.

The self-published author's journey from learning to execution is often treacherous, without any road signs and no GPS. From the craft of writing to the tedious process of self-publishing, the majority of what one learns happens through reading, Googling, maybe taking some online coursework, watching videos, adopting and adapting what other writers are doing, and just going with what feels right. This has been the experience of numerous self-published authors I know, including me. And while the coordination of many of the responsibilities listed in the third paragraph of this profile can be done by the individual author, many folks need help. Some authors, while excellent writers, are not artists or illustrators, so cover and print design must be delegated to others—and these are not cheap investments.

When it comes to creating a self-published book, from cover to cover, I have worn all the hats. I have written the stories, self-edited—although I also depend on and highly recommend enlisting the keen eye of a copy, line, and development editor—designed and formatted my books' interiors, written the blurbs, and I designed my own book covers. As previously noted, I've also extended these services to multiple self-published authors helping them create works of fiction, nonfiction, and even children's books.

Effective book marketing is nearly impossible to do alone. If you know otherwise, please enlighten me. However, as for my experience with the task, marketing my self-published books has required the help of a village. From Beta and ARC (Advance Reader Copy) Readers and Reviewers to my Street Team (my most dedicated fans), I depend on the help of folks who would volunteer their time and energy to champion my work. This includes reading and reviewing my books, sharing them on social media, promoting them to book clubs, and simply helping create awareness in order to drive visibility and sales.

Connecting the Story

Inspiration is critical for writers, and the tarot has been my favorite tool for helping to guide my self-published author journey. Since 2014, I have used tarot cards to outline my stories, inspire characters, dissolve writer's block, and fill-in plot holes. During the entire experience of writing and publishing *Only the Rocks That Float*, I worked with the tarot to help inspire direction and amplify my imagination. Along this particular book journey, the card that jumped out of the deck and/or remained at the forefront of my mind the entire time was The Chariot. In the tarot, The Chariot is a trailblazing go-getter who maintains their trajectory and movement with the help of those supporting them—their faithful Street Team. Let's take a look at this card.

What's happening in The Chariot card?

A physically fit man stands over his bike, his helmet sporting an eight-pointed star. His athletic shirt is printed with a pair of crescent moons on the shoulders and a white square center of his chest. The "chariot," is this guy's bike, and a winged lingam and yoni symbol are featured front and center. Beside the biker stands a pair of large dogs—one with a white harness and leash and the other with a black collar and leash. Both also have stars to match. The biker and his canine companions rest on the grassy riverside, opposite of which rises a bustling city and a spangled blue sky.

The Chariot: A Deep Dive

The Chariot is a take-action card. It can mean leadership, drive, influence, momentum, motivation, rallying, organizing, taking the bull by its horns, making decisions, enjoying a victorious win, and doing so with utter self-control.

As a writer, when you see yourself as the individual in The Chariot, you most likely have a lot of drive and people are getting in line to support you on all sides. You are the driver of your storytelling vehicle, whether that be leading an existing project, a venture into an altogether new genre, or making a career in writing. Whatever your path, The Chariot confirms that your intuition and influence have never been greater. The card encourages you to take action and move forward. Your fans will champion you, for they have come along for the experience and of their own free will.

The Chariot, Reversed: The Shadow

The Chariot reversed warns of the lack of leadership and/or mismanagement. In a literal sense, the reversed Chariot could refer to transportation issues, dreaded car troubles, a missed bus, a broken bike chain, or when the Uber driver doesn't show up. A situation has fallen out of control, all willpower is lost. The reversed Chariot is a roadblock, a pothole, or anything in the way of or blocking progress and productivity.

Notable Symbols in The Chariot

Astrology—Cancer
Element—Spirit/Water

Other symbols

Crescent moon—The two crescent moons that flank the biker's shoulders are a callback to The High Priestess. Like our Intuitive One, The Chariot is armored with keen intuition, and they'll need it as the road ahead of them won't be easy.

Black and White Opposites—The canines' leads represent two opposing forces uniting and working together in support and victory.

Winged lingam and yoni—This is the symbol we see affixed front and center of The Chariot's bike. In the Hindu religion, the lingam and yoni together symbolize the union of the male and female principles and the totality of all existence, the eternal process of creation and regeneration. So, essentially, when humanity partners together, we succeed on a Universal, androgynous level.[38]

Numerological Associations with The Chariot

In the tarot, The Chariot is directly connected to the Sevens (See also Chapter 18, Section 2 – *The Sevens*). Seven, in numerology, refers to struggles, challenges, and lessons learned. Because this card is the first seven of the tarot, as it resides with the Major Arcana, The Chariot brings with them the first major lesson of The Fool on their journey.

The Chariot, Characterized

When inspired by The Chariot, if a character is a protagonist, then another ten Schrute Bucks the story is probably fantasy, sci-fi, romance, or suspense. These are perfect genres for such a gung-ho, advantageous lead. On the other hand, when writing a Chariot-inspired antagonist, that character is also victoriously effective, but at the expense of the followers who have either blindly signed up or have been bullied into doing their dirty work and bidding. The Chariot character is most definitely a leader, a warrior, and/or a mastermind.

While using the tarot, when this card shows up decisions are to be made and a clear path carved forward. The charioteer is brave and victorious in their efforts, having succeeded especially because of their faithful supporters.

The Chariot could be your Uber driver, your prom night chauffeur, a boisterous leader, a lively symphony conductor, a bartender on a busy Saturday night, a public speaker, a brash young person, a dog walker, a team leader, a self-published author, an entrepreneur, or a corporate CEO.

Notable characters, people, or personas

Higher Polarity—Buffy, Willow, and Xander (*Buffy the Vampire Slayer*); you and your faithful fans; and me while walking my dogs.

Lower Polarity—Draco Malfoy (with Crabbe and Goyle) in the *Harry Potter* series; that nasty Hilly Holbrook from *The Help*; and Lady Tremaine and her two daughters.

Word List

armored	direction	onward	self-starter
assertion	drive	overpower	steadfast
beginnings	elevation	persuasive	strategist
champion	focus	pioneer	success
confidence	guidance	possibilities	title
contemplating	journey	prepared	trailblazer
contradictions	leadership	progress	travel
control	mastery	purpose	triumph
decision-making	momentum	pursuit	warrior
determination	movement	self-confidence	willpower

Spread: Split Decisions

Has an opportunity presented itself that requires the weighing of options? Is there a decision that needs a little more time and attention to detail than what the Foolish Decision spread offers (See Chapter 17, Key 0 – The Fool)? If you have an important decision to make, but you need time to weigh your options, compare pros and cons, and decide on a direction for moving forward, The Chariot can be enlisted to help. If you are a fiction writer, you can also facilitate this spread from the lens of your character.

1. Pull The Chariot from your tarot deck and place the card in the space for Card 1. This represents you or your fictional character.
2. Next, deliberately select a card that most closely represents your ultimate goal and place it in the space for Card 2.
3. Shuffle your tarot deck until you are satisfied that the cards are ready, and then turn the deck facedown as if you were about to deal them.
4. Starting with the space for Card 3, count the seventh card from the top of the deck and lay it in that space.
5. Repeat for the rest of the spread, counting every seventh card, laying it down, and then moving on to the next space.

Card 1: The Chariot—You or Your Character
Card 2: The Goal—What information do I need to know about my goal?
Card 3: Dog (Left)—What does support look like should I venture in this direction?
Card 4: Dog (Right)—What does support look like should I venture down this path?
Card 5: What outcome is possible down this path?
Card 6: What outcome is possible down this path?
Card 7: What happens if I decide to go rogue and pave my own way?

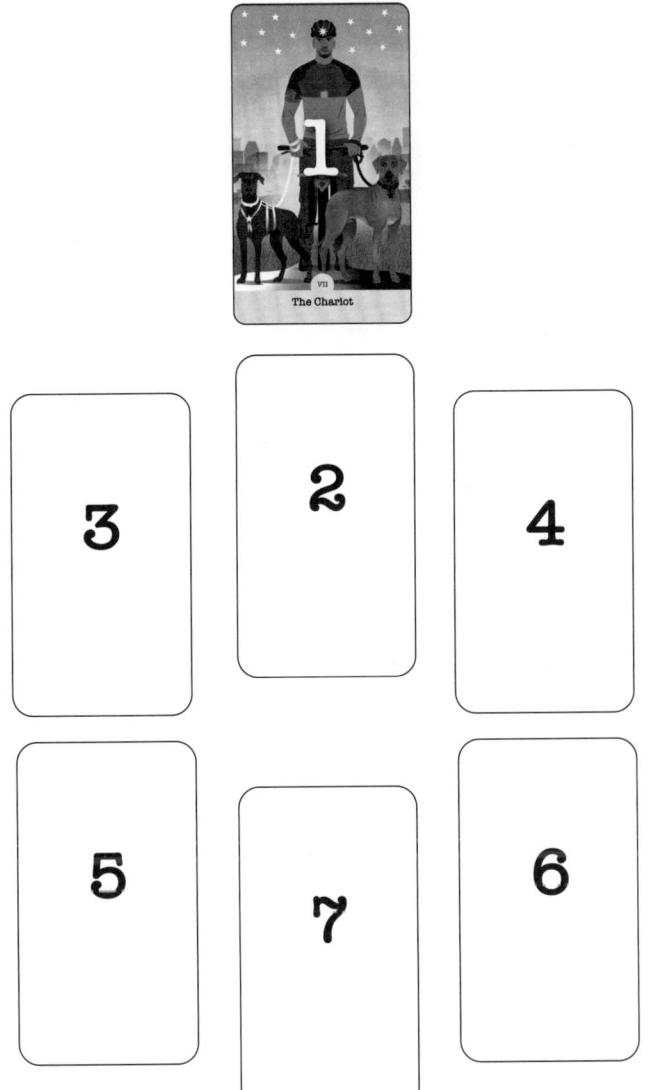

Key 8 or VIII:
Strength

VIII

Strength

When my youngest son graduated high school, and then left for college on a football scholarship the following month, a dark, threatening fear crept in. I'd known the day was coming; I'd felt it looming for quite some time. Yet and still, I'd pushed away the thought, imagining our home as always being filled with gaming laughter and pizza boxes, smelly gym socks and dirty jokes. Smiles and love and support. Our Team of Four.

Denial is easier. Safer. Less scary.

As Graduation Day approached, I was reminded of the time many years ago, after I had graduated high school and left home, when my Mama drove up to my little college town to visit me. Not long after settling into my dorm, I'd secured a job waiting tables at the local Pizza Hut. Mama walked in, as I had expected, but her eyes were swollen and wet. After hugging me tightly and looking me over, she sat in a booth on one of the restaurant's brick walls. As I brought her sweet tea to the table, I studied her. She looked small, tired, and her eyes were full of fear. When I assured her that I was smart and capable and independent, she cried into a napkin and said, "Yes, you are, but you'll never know this kind of fear until you're a mother."

Fast forward a couple of decades and there I was, helping my son pack for college, bawling and terrified. There weren't enough napkins in the world to catch my tears. What if my son was hurt on that football field? What if he made a stupid decision and lost his scholarship? What if he was caught in the wrong place at the wrong time? What if he never came home again?

And so, in the days leading up to our trip to drop him off at school, I hobbled around, crippled by fear. One morning, though, I experienced somewhat of a revelation. I was making my coffee and headed for my writing desk when a voice spoke clearly in my mind: What if you focused on how much bigger your strength is than your fear?

"Huh?" I remember saying aloud, stopping in my tracks, my coffee nearly spilling over my cup.

Once at my desk, I pondered the idea... What if I focused on my strength and what I KNOW I am capable of facing rather than the uncertainties and inconsistencies of fear and the unknown? Just what can I endure?

Just look at what you have already endured, that same voice whispered back. Look how strong you've already been.

Connecting the Story

I don't admit this often, but that day at the Pizza Hut my Mama was right. I had no idea how terrifying it was to watch your child move into the world until it happened to me. But I've also learned that strength is bigger than fear. It's steadfast, and as long as one believes it, infinite. In the tarot, the Strength card reminds us that we can silence the roaring beast that is fear. We can quiet our inner (and even outer) critics with fortitude and focus, and we can do so with grace and resilience—and sometimes a lot of napkins.

What's happening in the Strength card?

At first glance, the Strength card shows a tall, fair-skinned brunette and a roaring male lion with an impressive mane. Notice the lion's behavior; as he gazes up at the lady, he tilts his head and tucks his tail, both signs of submission. The woman is wearing a lacy, white dress with a white velvet top hat, a choker-style necklace, red gloves, a corset, fishnet stockings, and black combat boots. Like The Magician, a lemniscate hovers above her head. Stitched to her hat, it's a symbol for unlimited potential. While the hat is wreathed in red roses, a single rose adorns her choker. Our lady lion tamer holds a giant pencil staff with the confidence of someone who's completely conquered the beastly dilemma that is writer's block. She and her tamed counterpart appear as if they're waiting on the curtain call for their performance under the big top behind them. The day is a bright, sunny yellow with not a cloud in the sky.

Strength: A Deep Dive

The Strength card is one of the tarot's cards that needs very little analysis to surmise a meaning. Put simply, this card can represent calming the wild within, practicing restraint. It also serves as a reminder of the infinite courage (the lemniscate) and resolve one possesses within oneself (the woman) to overcome and/or accomplish the unthinkable (the lion). In relatable terms: you can do hard things.

If the Strength card lands on your desk during your daily card draw, or within a spot in your tarot spread that represents you, the writer, you are called to demonstrate gentleness and patience with yourself and your work. Your strength rests in your persistence for seeing things through by the detail. Your writing, the pressure to write, readers, your author platform are all roaring for your attention. Have courage and express strength through reserve and resolve. Courage is yours and is available to you at an unlimited capacity, and there are infinite possibilities for manifesting what many (including you) might deem impossible. These same characteristics apply when considering the card from your fictional character's point of view as well.

You may not feel like it at times, but you have Strength beyond what you think you can endure. As a writer, this includes conquering your worst fears: Fear of failure, self-doubt, fear of rejection, fear of criticism, fear of judgement, and even the fear of success. How can you draw upon your inner Strength when faced with one or more of these fears? How can you be the lion tamer of your life? This card is an invitation to work through your fears, not around them. Allow those feelings the space they need to run their course and then permit you to heal. Validate how you're feeling by doing what you do best: writing. Journal about how you're handling the situation and then pull a card or a few around how you can muster your Strength and move forward.

Strength, Reversed: The Shadow

When reversed, strength is lost or delayed. One becomes susceptible to doubt and the loss of self-confidence. Fear sets in, preventing good decision-making, and launching one into the dizzying turmoil of analysis paralysis. The lion turns on the woman, leaving her bootstraps slippery and illusive. Endeavors are stalled and constructs such as imposter syndrome and self-doubt can threaten to strike.

Notable Symbols in Strength

Astrology—Leo
Element—Spirit/Fire

Other Symbols

Boots—The lion tamer's boots are part of her armor, a symbol that she is capable of walking all over adversity.

Corset—These accessories are traditionally used to train one's waist or control one's curves. Our stately lion tamer is feminine and pretty, but make no mistake, she is equally strong and in total control.

Lemniscate—The lemniscate is the symbol for infinity, and as we can see in this card, this symbol hovers over the figure's head. This symbol can also represent simplicity and balance. It serves as a reminder that infinite possibilities surround us every day.

Lion—The "king of the beasts," the lion can symbolize majesty, strength, courage, power, royalty, pride, wisdom, protection.

Red Rose—The red rose is a symbol of beauty, hope, love, passion, and pleasure.

Numerological Associations with Strength

In the tarot, the Strength card is directly connected to the Eights (See also Chapter 18, Section 2 – *The Eights*). In numerology, the number eight can indicate accomplishment, achievement, action, control, goals, manifestation, mastery, movement, organization, power, strength, success, and work. The number relates to the eight spokes on the Wheel of the Year, with the corresponding eight Pagan Sabbats. Tip the number eight onto its side and it forms the lemniscate, the infinity symbol.

Strength, Characterized

When I was writing *A Bright Light*, a novelette about a single mother struggling to provide for her children around the holidays, I drew inspiration from the Strength card. I thought about the woman in the card and imagined her as my main character, Ashley. I considered the lion and thought about Ashley's struggles as a whole. Although she didn't realize it, she'd demonstrated incredible strength in past strife, and she had what it took to get through her current situation... with the help of a little magic, of course.

The woman in the Strength card can represent a heroine, a sister, a daughter, a friend, a mother, a witch, an angel, a zookeeper, a veterinarian, an animal whisperer, a caregiver, a lion tamer, or anyone who has had to demonstrate tremendous bravery and resolve.

Notable characters, people, or personas

Ashley in *A Bright Light*; Anne Frank; Nanisca in *The Woman King*; Helen Keller; Celie Johnson in *The Color Purple*; and John Coffey in *The Green Mile*.

Word List

acceptance	compassion	infinity	persuasion
accountability	courage	influence	potential
actualization	creation	instinctual	raw
atonement	desire	integration	resilience
attune	dominate	integrity	spellbound
authority	endeavors	maiden	strength
belief	feminine energy	motivation	understanding
bravery	fortitude	overcoming	vulnerability
caring	friendly	passion	wild
coercion	graceful	perseverance	willpower

Spread: Situational Leadership

Everyone is afraid of something, but if you can believe that your strength is bigger than your fears, you can start to overcome them. As a writer, I am afraid of a lot of things, including criticism, failure, FOMO (Fear Of Missing Out), judgment, rejection, self-doubt, and sometimes even success—I don't want anything or anyone to change who I am at my core. Using the tarot as an inspirational tool, however, helps remind me that I can overcome those fears. I can work through them.

I have designed the following spread to help writers channel the energy of the Strength card to identify and then conquer their fears. If you are a fiction writer, you can also facilitate this spread from the lens of your character.

1. Search your tarot deck for the Strength card and then lay it in the space for Card 1.
2. Next, shuffle your deck. While you are shuffling, think about your greatest fear related to being a writer. When you are satisfied that your cards are ready, turn the deck face-up.
3. Starting with the space for Card 2, sort through your tarot cards, stopping at the first card that evokes a fearful or uneasy reaction. This card should remind you of the fear you were ruminating on while shuffling. Lay the card in that space.
4. Repeat for Card 3, Card 4, and Card 5 searching the deck for cards that resonate with your fears, and then laying them in those spaces.
5. Shuffle your deck once again. When you are satisfied that the cards are ready, turn the deck facedown as if you were about to deal them.
6. Turn over the first four cards from the top of your tarot deck, laying them into the spaces for Card 6, Card 7, Card 8, and Card 9. These cards inform how you can overcome your fear.

Cards 2 through 5:

- What story does the top row of cards tell me about my fear?
- How are these cards an indication of what I need to stop doing in order to overcome that fear?

Cards 6 through 9:

- What story does the bottom row of cards tell me about my strength?
- How are these cards an indication of what I need to start doing in order to overcome that fear?
- Which card feels like a good place to start? (I recommend keeping this card on your writer's desk as a reminder of just how much bigger your strength is than your fear.)

Key 9 or IX:

The Hermit

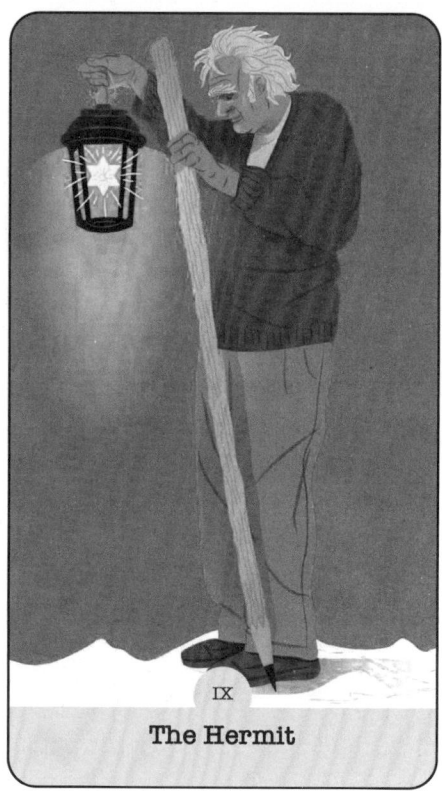

IX

The Hermit

For the entire duration of the winter season, I unplug from social media and nonessential email. I uninstall all the necessary apps from my phone, and I pause publishing blog posts. From the winter solstice to spring equinox, I cocoon myself into a winter hibernation, deliberately seeking solitude and turning inward. During this time, I intentionally listen to what my mind, body, heart, and spirit tell me they need. I endeavor to finish writing projects (such as this book during winter of 2022-2023), put a dent in my ceiling-high unread book stack, take daily walks in the park, adopt better eating habits, sleep more, and make short, inspiring road trips.

This unplugging is so effective, in fact, that at the time of writing this book, if the decision is left up to me, I plan on prioritizing a winter break for the rest of my life.

Since I was a little girl, every year right after Christmas, when the days become shorter and the nights longer, darker, and colder, I have struggled with what my Meme used to call "the winter blues." Today, I know the condition to be Seasonal Affective Disorder (SAD), also known as "seasonal depression," a type of depression that can take root as the seasons change, typically reoccurring around the same time every year. For me, SAD conjures mood swings and zaps energy, which severely informs my creativity. And when my energy is low and my motivation flat on the ground, social media can amplify feelings of inadequacy, envy, sadness, and worry. As such, for three full months I unplug... and the time away feels like a nourishing, holistic retreat.

Writing is hard work, and sometimes being an author can feel like being in a rat race. Physically, emotionally, psychologically, and at times even spiritually, writing requires motivation (first and foremost), discipline, inspiration, opportunity, physical materials—which, for me, looks like a hoard of notebooks and pens—and zero distractions. Sitting at the keyboard and letting my fingers work their magic is the easiest part. What happens after the writing is finished is what's so difficult. Laborious. Maddening. Exhausting.

In The Chariot profile, I wrote about the self-published author's experience with publishing and book marketing. From concept to execution, the process for getting one's book into the hands of readers can be a grueling race. But, what happens after a book launch? Days, weeks, months later when the author has done everything in their power to build a readership, what else is there to do? What happens when all the tedious and arduous work grinds to a halt before a rejection letter (or a hundred) and/or a deflating review (or a dozen)? What's next when one is exhausted—both physically and mentally—but the insatiable algorithm needs feeding in order to maintain relevance? And what about when productivity and results are high, yet the grind has threatened to unravel sleep patterns, priorities, and relationships? How does one prevent and/or rise from a plummeting energy spiral? How can one adjust to uncontrollable environmental changes?

Whether we want to or not, whether we like it or not, our minds-bodies-hearts-spirits must have a break from whatever hectic race we're running. Without rest, athletes run the risk of burnout, overexertion, and injury. These consequences can be the same for caregivers, hospitality workers, healthcare professionals, educators, the list goes on. In my experience as a creative person, not stepping back and prioritizing rest stifles my motivation to continue writing. Rest is necessary, otherwise an energy crash is inevitable. And for me, some crashes have felt impossible to overcome.

In the tarot, after The Chariot has encouraged you to endure the race, after Strength has gently reminded you of how much stronger you are than your fears, The Hermit taps his walking stick against your door and invites you to come along with him on a retreat. But this is no spring picnic—journeying with The Hermit means a deliberate, inward-focused period of solitude. The Hermit's withdrawal is a quest for personal truth, seeking guidance and/or answers. He endeavors to experience physical rest, mental clarity, and spiritual illumination, and if you join him, he can show you how to do the same.

Connecting the Story

Although working with The Hermit's energy comes naturally to me, as I am extremely introverted and his card is my Soul Card, I can appreciate another writer's hesitancy to answer the door when the old man comes calling. Might I remind you that retreat is not quitting. Taking a break from the algorithm does not mean you will be left behind and/or forgotten. And the solitude you are seeking is not intended for a prolonged state—The Hermit's retreats are just long enough that they are healing, nourishing, and enlightening. When you are ready, the hooded recluse can deliver you back to your writer's desk feeling renewed, inspired, and prepared to reenter the race.

In the event that you feel hesitant and/or anxiety around pausing from your grind, I have uncovered nine benefits of seeking solitude. Rachel Pollack, author of Seventy-Eight Degrees of Wisdom, wrote this about The Hermit, "By withdrawing from the outer world, we can awaken the inner self." My hope for you is that one of these benefits might resonate, supporting and encouraging you to deliberately pause and withdraw, thus fueling an intuitive and creative awakening.

9 Benefits of Seeking Solitude

- Gaining clarity in making an important decision.
- Re-energizing after a period of depletion.
- Soul-searching: understanding or unpacking a troubling or a perplexing situation.
- Setting and/or reestablishing goals.
- Allowing time and space to grieve.
- Focusing without distraction.
- Unwinding and rejuvenating.
- Winter hibernation: listening to nature's natural rhythm.
- Seeking spiritual connection and/or guidance.

What's happening in The Hermit card?

The Hermit is the last single-digit card in the Major Arcana. Appearing as an older male, he's dressed in muted gray tones and has a head of thick platinum gray hair. The Hermit grasps a lantern, holding it before him just far enough to light his next step. Inside the lantern glows a six-pointed star, the Star of David, which harkens back to The Empress card and abundance. Although the man can only see one step ahead, the light is enough to last his entire trek. The sky surrounding our Hermit is serene and beryl. Frozen and unstable, the ground is solid beneath The Hermit's feet. He moves slowly and precisely, inching along with his giant pencil staff to help write his way. It also assists him from slipping and falling. Nobody wants a broken hip, especially in the dead of winter.

The Hermit: A Deep Dive

Though The Hermit walks his path alone, he is not lonely. His trek is made in deliberate solitude. He has reflected inward, focusing on the next phase of his journey, which is nearing its end. He takes his time, though, putting his trust in only enough light to illuminate the next step along his way. The Hermit is a wise leader, but he's seeking the answers to the questions that have either intrigued or haunted him. If you were to join him along his walk, he'd most certainly take advantage of the quiet to listen to your stories, answer your own questions, if he can, and perhaps even teach you something profound about yourself and/or your life's path that you never before imagined.

The Hermit isn't privy to a lot of concrete information; he only knows what's here and now and maybe the next step. If The Hermit card finds its way to your writer's desk, you are invited to pause and ask yourself, What is there to learn by slowing down? What can I teach and to whom?

The great Buddha once said, "Make of yourself a light." Contrary to popular culture, you don't have to be doing everything that everyone else is doing in the same manner everyone else is doing them. Light your own path. Seek your own way and discover who you are as a writer, find your voice, your own unique writing style. Take time out. Embrace solitude. This card promotes seeking guidance from a teacher or a coach who can help you find your way.

The Hermit Reversed: The Shadow

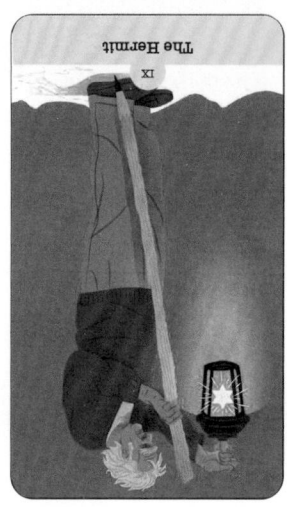

When reversed, The Hermit loses his way. He has succumbed to the ill effects of prolonged solitude. He's lonely and he forgets why he's headed in the direction he's going. He forgets his purpose and is doomed to make the same mistakes of his past, thus triggering a self-inflicted exile during which stagnancy curls its frigid hand around him and squeezes. When this happens, The Hermit lets go of everything he's learned, losing sight of his light. He slips and falls, and because of the frigid temperatures, he is unable to rise, frozen into the desolate tundra.

Notable Symbols in The Hermit Card

Astrology—Virgo
Element—Spirit / Earth

Other Symbols

Blue—Blue is the color of life, harmony, peace, and calmness.

Lantern—The Hermit's lamp represents inner light, knowledge, and truth.

Mountain—The mountain range in the distance implies structure and a steady foundation, security and protection.

Six-sided Star—This star is the Seal of Solomon, a symbol of wisdom.

Notable characters, people, or personas

Yoda; Maya Angelou; Professor John Keating of *Dead Poets Society*; Professor Dumbledore in *Harry Potter*; and William Forrester of *Finding Forrester*.

After learning more about The Hermit, who would you add to this list?

Numerological Associations with The Hermit

In numerology, nine is the number of completions and endings (See also Chapter 18, Section 2 – *The Nines*). It can represent attainment, contentment, fruition, fulfilment, leadership, philanthropy, protection, a spiritual awakening, and Universal energy. As the ninth numbered card in the Major Arcana, The Hermit aligns with the Nines in the Minor Arcana.

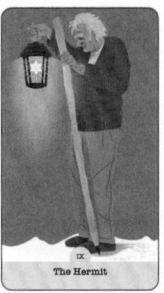

 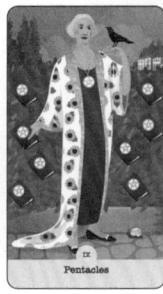  

The Hermit, Characterized

The Hermit is an excellent teacher, coach, and intelligent leader to whom other characters look for inspiration and guidance. Hermit-like characters are often written as the philosopher, wise elder, sage, or oracle. The Hermit is the reclusive neighbor with the stellar vinyl collection. The Hermit is a lone wolf, an introvert, a spiritual guide, a psychologist, or a mature person, having lived long enough to learn the importance of self-esteem and the benefits of occasionally seeking solitude.

Word List

alone	intellectual	prudence	solitude
authority	introspection	puritanism	soul-searching
considerate	introspection	reclusive	spiritualism
discretion	introverted	reflection	teacher
elder	isolation	sage	thinking
guidance	loneliness	scholar	truth
guiding	lonely	searching	tutoring
helping	mentor	seclusion	wisdom
humanitarianism	old soul	seeker	wise

3

2

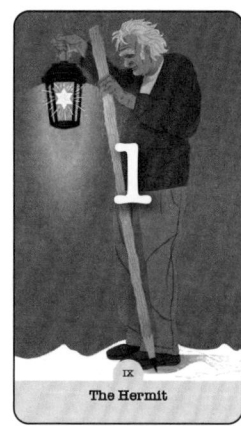

4

Spread: Introspection

When you find yourself in a position where retreating for a period of introspection feels like a necessary move, this spread can help explore the process. If you are a fiction writer, this spread can also help you work from the lens of your character in order to flesh out a scene or plotline.

1. Shuffle your deck until you are satisfied that the cards are ready.
2. Next, find The Hermit, which represents where you are right now. Lay the card in the space for Card 1.
3. Pull the card behind The Hermit and place it in the space for Card 4. This card represents what you're leaving behind.
4. Pull the two cards in front of The Hermit and place them consecutively in the spaces for Card 2 and Card 3. These cards inform where you are headed and considerations for the unknown, respectively.
5. Ask yourself the following questions, using your intuition to consider the answers. If you are using this spread from your character's point of view, imagine them asking themselves these questions.

Card 3: What are the considerations for the Unknown?
Card 2: Where am I headed?
Card 1: The Hermit—Where you are now.
Card 4: What's behind me?

Key 10 or X:
Wheel of Fortune

Wheel of Fortune

Kids are often asked, "What do you want to be when you grow up?" As far back as I can remember my answer to that question was, "An artist and a teacher. At the same time." Around the seventh grade, I decided that, more specifically, I wanted to be a graphic designer, but I also loved to write, and by high school I had it all figured out. I would be both a graphic designer and a writer—I would work for a media company, designing album covers and movie posters and penning marketing pitches—and then I'd retire as an art historian and instructor. I planned out my lifelong career goals, packing my college resume with art show awards and academic accolades, and I was set to win a scholarship to Savannah College of Art and Design (SCAD). All I had to do was get through graduation and I'd be home free.

Life—as it's either gloriously or notoriously known to do—took the reins, and after a decade of misdirection and mistakes, I found myself with one husband, two babies, and zero college degrees. I'd landed rock bottom behind the bar at an Olive Garden, assessing my life and regretting having never achieved my education and career goals. While I was the best beverage artist and cocktail counselor around, inside I felt lost. I felt like there was so much more I was supposed to be doing with my life—with my artistic talent, with my writing. I remember slow nights when the bar was dead, I would jot down book ideas on beverage napkins or draft character profiles on the backs of order pads. Don't get me wrong: bartending is a worthy profession, I just couldn't shake this voice that always seemed to be hovering over my shoulder and whispering, You are off-center. You are meant to do something else. As the years crept along, I felt myself fading from who I wanted to be. The voice grew louder. I needed redirection.

I love to walk. Specifically, walks in the park. And so, as per usual, one morning I went for a stroll. It was a Friday and I had to work that night. While I was walking, I thought about where I wanted to be in my life versus where I was, and I prayed for direction. I asked for help figuring out where in the world I was going and how in the world I might arrive at some sense of purpose. I needed help calculating how to introduce school back into my already wobbly work-life balance: toddler to toddler, paycheck to paycheck. I felt like I owed it to myself to reignite all that ambition I once had—I just didn't have that fire anymore. There was not a match in sight.

Depending on what you believe, God or the Universe or Lady Luck or fate intervened.

While on my walk, I saw a small passenger bus parked down by the park's small lake. A dozen or so senior citizens were strolling about, their grip secure on their walkers, arms looped with their caregivers, feeding ducks and looking out at the water. Displayed on the side of the bus was a company logo—green, the color of luck—that read Hickory Hills Alzheimer's Assisted Living.

Hickory Hills! I thought. That was the place where my grandmother (Meme) had taken my grandfather (whom I affectionately refer to with the very Southern epithet, "PawPaw") for adult daycare when they both needed a change of scenery. I nearly cried at the sight, stopping to catch my breath. In case you didn't know, you can't power walk and cry, or you might choke and die. At the time, my PawPaw had only been gone three short months. He'd lived with Alzheimer's disease for over 16 years. The experience had been a roller coaster. Having lived next door to my grandparents during the most trying years of his disease, I saw firsthand the impact Alzheimer's had on both the individual and their family.

The next night was a Saturday, one of the busiest days of the week in the service world, if not the busiest, and I was working behind the bar. I handed a couple their credit card receipt and a pen, and then turned to make a drink for another customer. When I returned to retrieve my signed copy of the receipt, my pen was gone, and a different pen was left behind. Hunter green with the squishy grip-thing toward the tip. Admiring the fact that the pen was nicer than the one I'd provided the couple, I turned it between my fingers. There was a gold logo. Hickory Hills Alzheimer's Assisted Living.

What a coincidence! I thought. A Hickory Hills pen! Of course, I kept it. I'm a pen hoarder!

After my walk the very next day, I stopped by the gas station where a blue newspaper box held up the wall beside the building's double doors. This particular box contained the weekly Career Builder, a newspaper version of LinkedIn and Indeed before those existed. I snagged a copy, went home, laid out the paper, and started circling job options. I was getting out of bartending if it killed me. I had to do something else. Halfway down the left side of the page, my eye tripped on a logo. Yep. You already know which logo: Hickory Hills Alzheimer's Assisted Living. And they were seeking an Activities Director.

All of the activities my PawPaw and I enjoyed raced through my mind: Scrabble and shelling on Mexico Beach and walks through the cemetery and rides through town and down Memory Lane.

I couldn't get to my computer fast enough.

That was Sunday. Before the sun set, I'd updated my resume and laid out the most professional outfit I could piece together. I would go to the assisted living building the next morning as soon as their office opened. I would fill out an application and submit my resume in person. And I did. On Monday morning, I received a clipboard and sat down in the assisted living's front lobby to complete the application. While writing, movement in my peripheral caught my attention. A man walked behind the receptionist a couple of times. He looked at me and smiled before leaning down and whispering something into her ear. After handing over the clipboard and thanking the lady, I was nervous when she got up from her chair and asked me if I had time to stay.

"I do," I said.

"Great," she chirped while leading me back to another room. "Our executive director wants to speak with you."

After a long, tearful conversation about how the executive director's parents had been connected with my grandparents—he had seen my grandfather's name mentioned in my cover letter—I walked out of Hickory Hills that day with the job as Activities Director.

While I worked at the assisted living, I was promoted within the company twice, developing activities programs for people living with dementia and training classes for their caregivers, both family and professional. I was recruited to work as a Regional Director of Programs and Services with the Alzheimer's Association, and I even went back to school. Because my path had changed, I changed my concentration of study from graphic design to psychology. In less than five years, I finished both undergraduate and graduate degrees in Psychology, and in 2013 my lifelong dream of becoming a designer and writer merged with my new career path. We moved to Florida where I accepted a role as Instructional Designer for a major hospital system in Clearwater. Not only did I have the pleasure of developing training content for caregivers spanning all of healthcare, but I got to write, design, and be creative every single day. Just as important, I developed a meaningful relationship with a group of women whom I affectionately refer to as my Soul Sisters. They are my people and moving to Florida led me to find them along my way.

Just what, exactly, happened with the series of Hickory Hills logo occurrences? Was the change of direction merely a coincidence or was it serendipity? Was it an answer to prayer? Was it manifestation? Did I attract the Activities Director position? Whatever it was, I'm convinced that what I experienced was a stroke of fortune. Those four consecutive days so many years ago plucked me from being off-center at rock bottom and redirected me onto a path I could have never imagined or predicted.

Connecting the Story

In the Major Arcana, there are three cards that inform varying types of change: Wheel of Fortune, Death, and The Tower. The type of change fostered by the Wheel of Fortune is resultant upon circumstances and unseen influences, which many believe to be God, the Universe, luck, or fortune. Today, I have the degrees, I have all those years' experience in training design and delivery, and I've written and published multiple novels. I design every single day, at my day job (my Muggle job) as well as creatively on the side, and I coach others around writing, publishing, brand design, and marketing. Because of redirection—a profound shift of the Wheel of Fortune—I am living my dream. I'm an artist and a teacher. At the same time.

What's happening in the Wheel of Fortune card?

The Wheel of Fortune card is one of the few cards in the tarot illustrated with mostly symbols, rather than a feasible scene. Like The World card, which you will learn about in Chapter 17, Key 21, there are four symbolic figures at each corner. Clockwise from top left, they are Aquarius (the angel), Scorpio (the eagle), Leo (the lion), and Taurus (the bull). An eight-spoke wheel floats in the direct center of the card. A sword-yielding sphinx perches at the top, while a serpent slithers along the left side and Anubis, the Egyptian god of the dead, rides the wheel on the right. Along four of the spokes, clockwise from the top, we can see the astrological and alchemical symbols for Mercury, sulfur, Aquarius, and the sun. We can also see the letters T-A-R-O, which rotate back to T, completing the word TAROT. Four colorful books form the shape of a cross around the wheel, a symbol for sacred knowledge.

Wheel of Fortune: A Deep Dive

At its best, the Wheel of Fortune card means Lady Luck is on your side. The planets are aligned, and your name is written in the stars! The Sphinx and Anubis have guided you to a place of contentment, achievement, and success. You are entirely supported in all four directions, with all four elements. However, all those things inform big changes about to happen. You are gaining momentum, and like my own story, the Universe is helping to direct you, moving you along a path that leads to favor. A turn of events is about to happen, and change is imminent.

The Wheel of Fortune is a metaphor for life. There are so many aspects of our unique experiences on this planet that are mysterious and inconsistent. If you've pulled this card in a position to represent you, the writer, it could mean that what you're preparing for pales in comparison with what is in store. You are manifesting results and momentum greater and faster than you ever imagined. The wheel has taken a swift spin in the right direction for your writing. Keep the pace. Maintain your grasp on the axis so that you can remain steady and poised for whatever direction the wheel turns.

The Wheel of Fortune is a lottery win, an inheritance, a new career, a new life plan, a change in direction, a major redirection. Numerologically, the card is directly connected to The Magician (1 + 0 = 1), whose efforts demonstrate the statement, "As above, so below." Similarly, the Wheel of Fortune reminds us that what goes up must come down. This statement applies especially if you're riding that wheel on the outside, grasping its edges and not securing your grip on the axis. On the other hand, once secure, the center of the wheel reveals a crossroads: you have a choice in the direction you'll take your writing. Which way will you go?

Notable Symbols in the Wheel of Fortune Card

Astrology—Jupiter
Element—Spirit/Fire

Wheel of Fortune, Reversed: The Shadow

At its lull, the Wheel of Fortune reminds us that change can be uneasy, and we might feel unsteady with how to navigate the varying directions our wheel is spinning. We might feel like a newborn deer attempting to stand. What rises fast falls fast. Feast or famine. Ebb and flow. Ups and downs. Change is one of the only consistencies in life. When this card lands topsy-turvy on your desktop, you might feel stuck in a rut, or like you've hit a speed bump or pothole in the road. Luck might be running out, or this reversed position could mean that you're testing your luck.

Other Symbols

Anubis—The original ancient Egyptian god of the dead (later replaced by Osiris), Anubis has the body of a man and the head of a jackal. The figure represents helplessness, death, and the afterlife.

Books—Books represent knowledge, learning, and wisdom. As they form the shape of a cross, they symbolize sacred knowledge, a key intention of the tarot.

Four Figures—The Lion, the Ox, the Man, and the Eagle—in each of the card's corners represent the four elements: fire, earth, air, and water. They also represent the Four Evangelists, Matthew, Mark, Luke, and John. In astrology, these creatures represent Leo, Taurus, Aquarius, and Scorpio.

Sphinx—The sphinx represents nobility and divine opportunity. It can also symbolize the sun, life, and the soul.

Wheel with Eight Spokes—In the tarot, the eight-spoked wheel can represent the Wheel of the Year, an annual cycle of eight Pagan festivals, or the Dharma Wheel, a traditional symbol in Buddhist teachings that advocates for moral order and enlightenment.[39]

Numerological Associations with Wheel of Fortune

In the tarot, the Wheel of Fortune is associated with The Magician, the Aces, and the Tens (See also Chapter 18, Section 2 – *The Tens*). Why The Magician and Ace cards? Because the Wheel of Fortune is number 10 (X) in the Major Arcana. In numerology, adding these numbers together yields the number one: 1 + 0 = 1. Furthermore, the number 10 can represent abundance, completion, coming full circle, end of cycle, final manifestations, moving on, a new beginning, renewal, results, and a return to center.

The Magician   Wheel of Fortune

Ace of Cups   Ace of Pentacles   Ace of Swords   Ace of Wands

Cups   Pentacles   Swords   Wands

Wheel of Fortune, Characterized

Rather than representing a person or character, the Wheel of Fortune denotes events, occurrences, situations, and above all else, change. However, if your character embodies attributes of this card, they can certainly be unsteady and unreliable. On the other hand, the character might be serendipitous and spontaneous, flaky and flippant.

Notable characters, people, or personas

Lady Luck; Fate; Destiny; Clarence Odbody in *It's a Wonderful Life*; the ghosts in Charles Dickens' *A Christmas Carol*; Carol Kane in *Scrooged*; Zoltar in *Big*; Professor Marvel in *The Wizard of Oz*; and Gloria Foster as The Oracle in *The Matrix*.

Word List

abundance	downturn	initiation	rewards
alternatives	ebb and flow	karma	risk
cause and effect	excess	luck	spinning
centered	flexibility	momentum	synchronicity
change	focus	movement	transformation
circumstantial	fortune	nuanced	transitioning
completion	imbalance	opportunity	turning point
culmination	impermanence	perseverance	up and down
cyclical	improvement	redirection	upswing
destiny	impulsive	resistance	wishing

Spread: Spin the Wheel of Fortune

Every person experiences ups and downs, ebbs and flow, upswings and downturns. No matter who or where we are, the Wheel of Fortune continues spinning, and we are challenged to hang on and persist. The sort of change fostered by the Wheel of Fortune is circumstantially influenced. However, we have agency over how we perceive this change and how we allow it to influence our lives.

I have designed the following spread to help you, the writer, navigate change holistically—heart, body, mind, and spirit—from a situational approach. With this in mind, heart refers to your feelings, body refers to your physical self, mind refers to your thoughts and cognition, and spirit refers to your internal Self or soul. If you are a fiction writer, you can also use this spread from the perspective of your character(s) in order to determine how they might manage change.

1. Think of a situation that requires you to face a significant change in your life, one that is beyond your control.
2. While ruminating on the situation, sort through your tarot deck and pull out the Wheel of Fortune. Place it in the center position for Card 1.
3. Shuffle your tarot deck until you are satisfied that the cards are ready, and then turn the deck facedown as if you were about to deal the cards.
4. Starting with the space for Card 2, turn over cards until you arrive at a Cups card and then move on to the space for Card 3.
5. Repeat the process, turning over cards until you get a card from the Pentacles suit (3), Swords (4), and Wands (5).
6. Next, shuffle your deck once more and then repeat the process for Cards 6 through 9, laying cards into those spaces which correspond with their suits.
7. Ask yourself the following questions, using your intuition to consider the answers. If you are using this spread from your character's point of view, imagine them asking themselves these questions.

Card 2: Heart (Cups) How might this situation influence my feelings?

Card 3: Body (Pentacles) What changes to my physical self are possible as a result of this situation?

Card 4: Mind (Swords) What about this situation might change the way I think or what I believe?

Card 5: Spirit (Wands) How might this situation affect my spirit? How can I change the way I perceive this change?

Card 6 supports Card 2.
Card 7 supports Card 3.
Card 8 supports Card 4.
Card 9 supports Card 5.

Key 11 or XI:

Justice

My maternal grandfather was a Pentecostal pastor. A charismatic man, PawPaw was an inspired, engaging communicator, and those who were in his presence always paused to listen to what he had to say. A few years ago, which was many years after his death, when my grandmother (Meme) wanted to redecorate her home, she called me and asked me if I wanted PawPaw's rolltop desk—the one that was off-limits to my cousins and me when we were grubby-handed little kids. "Are you kidding?!" I exclaimed. "Of course, I want it."

Before I arrived to pick it up, Meme had warned me that the desk was full of his old sermons and notes. She said I could keep anything of value that I found, and it was okay to just toss the rest of it.

I had been itching to poke around inside that rolltop desk since I was a child, and what I discovered within its drawers and nooks and crannies was exactly what my cousins and I had imagined: a treasure trove of trinkets and doodads, ephemeral odds and ends, money, both domestic and foreign, and notepads. As my grandfather often exclaimed, "Lord, have mercy!" There were A LOT of notepads.

After I brought the desk home, I spent almost an entire day sorting through the stacks upon stacks of yellow legal pads filled from front to back with sermons and the notes PawPaw had used to pen them. There were collections of photos, legal documents, lapel pins, cufflinks, rubber stamps, and fountain pens. Oh, the pens! And I thought I was a pen hoarder.

As I thumbed through the legal pads, sorting them by date, I noticed a distinct progression in PawPaw's handwriting. He had been diagnosed with Alzheimer's disease in 1988, and for many years after he retired from his professional career and the church, he faithfully studied his Bible and scripted weekly sermons. Comparing his earlier notes with the ones from more recent years, his handwriting evolved from boxy, slanted print, to deliberate, elongated and stiff characters. The words became spaced apart as if a young child had been practicing their alphabet.

On one of the earlier sermons, before his diagnosis, a series of emboldened, underlined sentences in red ink caught my attention: Grace is when we get what we don't deserve, Mercy is NOT getting what we deserve, and Justice is getting what we deserve.

Those words sat with me. Days, weeks after sorting through and cleaning out that desk, I went back to my own notepad where I'd scribbled my grandfather's message. There were so many lessons hidden within that sentence, so many ways of interpreting the three constructs. Eventually, one morning when I shuffled my tarot cards and asked Spirit to reveal to me what I needed to know about my life that very day, the Justice card jumped out. Immediately, my intuitive voice whispered, Justice is getting what we deserve. I thought about the notion in relation to me as a writer. The word "getting" stood out.

What if Justice isn't given but obtained? I thought. What if we are in control of the scales and we don't have to wait around for other forces to balance the [writing time, publishing efforts, marketing] scales for us? What would our writing practice look like if we actively seized every day? Carpe Diem.

As my thoughts are known to do, they immediately jumped to one of my favorite movies, *Dead Poets Society*, specifically to the scene when Mr. Keating asks his students to follow him out into the hallway and consider all the old photos in the trophy case. "Carpe Diem," he tells them. "Gather ye rosebuds while ye may..."

If justice is getting what we deserve, wouldn't we want to take the reins on securing whatever that looks like? Now, I don't believe my grandfather deserved Alzheimer's disease; that happened because of family genetics. His mother and all of his brothers and sisters developed that specific dementia. But what I do believe he deserved was a successful career and position within his church, both of which he'd worked so hard to secure and nurture. He also deserved a family who loved him, and in that regard, his scales were overflowing.

Connecting the Story

In the tarot, the Justice card seeks balance through what's fair and just. The card informs the seeking of harmony, making decisions, and finding middle ground. Let's explore this card.

What's happening in the Justice card?

Our *Mystic Storyteller* Justice is a woman in traditional Muslim dress. Strong and poised, she is capable of enduring and overcoming the turmoil and injustices she's experienced in her life, especially those directed toward women. Like both The Hierophant and The High Priestess, a crown hovers above Justice's head, a symbol for authority. Like her two commanding counterparts, she sits between two pillars; hers are white for purity. Like The Magician, she has one hand up and one hand down—as above, so below. In her right hand, she grasps a giant golden pen, symbolic of the Sword of Justice. In her left hand, she holds a set of scales which only balance what is deserving. Like Themis, the Greek goddess of wisdom and good counsel, this woman has taken her mission, knowledge, and experiences seriously and is leveling the scales.

Justice: A Deep Dive

The Justice card reminds us that the Universe will always make things right. There is a tedious balance to life, and we are only participants in helping to level the scales. This card is associated with Libra, which also teaches balance, and it informs fairness, education, and choice. Justice also implores us to adjust our karma, to center ourselves on what is best for us and what works in our highest favor. But both balance and favor differ for each individual. As such, if this card lands on your writer's desk, you are encouraged to intuit what those look like for you.

As a creative person, you deserve to pay justice to your work—to draw upon your intuition and your skills, balancing your creative scales and manifesting only the best outcomes for your endeavors. Write what you deserve, not what you think everyone else will want to read. Throughout this book, you will run across mentions and examples of the importance of—and empowerment in—writing authentically. If you've ever experienced injustices, hardships, marginalization, adversity, or just a terrible hand of cards, the Justice tarot card invites you to write with courage, seeking balance for what you went through.

If you are a fiction writer, allow justice for your characters and their muses. Create a horrible character after a horrible person. I know I did. Lorna Willoughby, the mother-in-law in *The Decembers*, my very first novel, was inspired by an individual I knew a long, long time ago who was unkind and bitter. She made the lives of everyone around her difficult and miserable. On the other hand, should you write a deplorable character, Justice reminds you to balance the scales. Consider providing a backstory that will shed light on that character's motives and origin of their antagonistic behaviors. What happened to them that caused them to be so nasty?

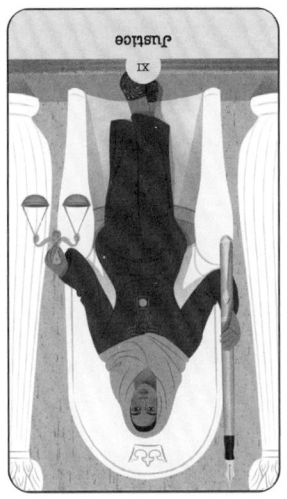

Justice, Reversed: The Shadow

When reversed, Justice's sword falls, and the scales are tipped. Nobody gets what they deserve. Injustice can cause disorder and discrimination. Misalignment. Turning the Justice figure on its head means the figure's robes fall over their face, shielding their vision and turning a blind eye on matters that need addressing and balancing. This looking away perpetuates systemic inequality, marginalization, turmoil, and confusion.

Notable Symbols in the Justice Card

Astrology—Libra
Element—Air /Spirit

Other Symbols

Columns—In the tarot, columns represent structure, balance, safety, security, and when appearing in a pair, they create a gateway.

Scales—The scales mean balance, measurement, and making things level, even.

Sword—The sword represents air, cutting through conflict and inspiring clear thought. In the tarot, swords also represent intellect, intuition, and wisdom.

Numerological Associations with the Justice Card

In the tarot and in numerology, the number 11 is easily seen as two ones, and when we add them together, we get two. Therefore, as previously mentioned, the Justice card embodies both the energies of The High Priestess and the Twos. Additionally, eleven is a master number, informing strength in trying times and helping one to cope during times of chaos and crisis. Eleven is a psychic number, a gateway to the subconscious, just like the pillars on both the Justice and The High Priestess cards.

Justice, Characterized

If your character is influenced by the Justice card, they are wise, careful, and fair. They likely move through your story with a mission to make things right and fair for all, not just for a select few, like your sinister antagonist and their wicked cronies. As such, a character with Justice card qualities is discerning and strong in their resolve. Many superheroes exude Justice qualities. Take Batman and Superman, for example. Both caped crusaders, while working individually, are part of the Justice League, a society of superheroes who help protect those around them from the sinister snares of their evil adversaries.

Notable characters, people, or personas

Malala Yousafzai, Martin Luther King, Jr.; Greta Thunberg; Atticus Finch of *To Kill a Mockingbird*; Eleven of *Stranger Things*; Michael Moore; Judge Judy; Ruth Bader Ginsburg; and Wapner (the way Dustin Hoffman pronounces it in *Rain Man*).

After learning more about the Justice card, who would you add to this list?

Word List

accountable	decisions	integrity	organization
advocacy	democracy	judicious	precision
alignment	diplomatic	justice	principles
balance	effort	karmic balance	rational
cerebral	equality	law	responsibility
civil	ethical	Law of Attraction	results
civilization	fairness	legal	rules
constraints	good news	level	scruples
courts	harmony	logical	service
decision-maker	honesty	mediation	truth

Spread: Balance the Scales

From the outside looking in, those who are not writers might think being a writer simply means sitting around for long periods of time thrashing at a keyboard, staring blankly at a computer screen or notebook, and consuming way too much caffeine in the process.

Did you just scoff or laugh?

Okay, perhaps the picture painted does actually happen, but in our defense, while writers are staring blankly at our tools, stories are being fleshed out, character interactions are being examined, and worlds are being built. Writers are storytellers, and storytellers create life, real or imagined. We entertain, inspire, and evoke emotional responses that can stay with our readers for the rest of their lives. Some books change lives entirely. Some books have even changed the world.

As I've stated before, writing is hard work. And oftentimes, in order to do our best work, writers need balance. As such, I have designed the following spread to glean insight around where you might need the most balance right now or in any given situation. Similarly, if you write fiction, you can use this spread from your character's point of view.

1. Shuffle your deck until you are satisfied that the cards are ready.
2. Next, find the Justice card, which represents you or your character(s) in this moment or situation. Lay the card on the space for Card 2.
3. The card behind the Justice card tells you where your life needs balance. Lay it in the space for Card 1.
4. What suit is Card 1? Cups, Pentacles, Swords, or Wands? Or is the card from the Major Arcana? Make a mental note and then reshuffle your deck. When you are satisfied that the cards are ready, turn the deck facedown as if you were about to deal them.
5. Turn over the card on the top of your deck and place it on the space for Card 3. Does the suit match that of Card 1? If yes, move on to the next step. If no, keep pulling cards from the top of your deck until the suits match—both Cups, Pentacles, etc. In the case of Card 1 being a Major Arcana, keep pulling cards until you get another Major for Card 3.
6. Using your intuition, consider the cards and answer the following questions. If you are using this spread from your character's point of view, imagine them asking themselves these questions.

Card 1: What aspect of my life needs balance right now?
Card 2: The Justice card—for leveling the scales.
Card 3: What or who is available to help support me?

Key 12 or XII:

The Hanged One

The Hanged One

I am a writer who has struggled with anxiety, depression, isolation, unhealthy self-conscious emotions, feelings of inadequacy, imposter syndrome, and chronic comparison. However, only one single aspect of my everyday life triggers every single one of these baneful responses: social media.

From the lens of a creative person, my experience with social media has been a bewildering paradox. On the one hand, the tool has been incredibly useful for staying connected with family and friends, building a sense of belonging and community among readers and fellow writers, gleaning inspiration, learning, and so many more worthwhile factors. When executed consistently, I've even experienced success in marketing my work. For all of social media's benefits, however, sometimes I simultaneously feel tethered to and/or obligated to interact with the notorious algorithm, which can dredge up the gray cloud of aforementioned responses.

Perplexed by this paradox of both enjoying and loathing social media, I engaged other creatives about their experiences; I wanted to determine if the paradox was unique to me or if others also shared similar feelings. During a survey[40] of my Instagram followers, many fellow writers reported maintaining their accounts as a necessity for staying connected to their writing communities, marketing their books, and growing their readership. Furthermore, the majority of those individuals also claimed they wouldn't be on social media at all were it not for the demands of marketing and engagement, citing negative reactions caused by scrolling disproportionate to positive responses. Most writers indicated that while they enjoyed connecting with friends, writing communities, and fun distractions like dog videos and silly memes, scrolling through their Instagram feed had sometimes caused an overwhelm of mental and emotional exhaustion, triggering feelings of envy, comparison, sadness, and worry. In her book *Trust Your Wings*, fellow writer and close friend Grisel Scarantino brought to my attention a construct known as doomscrolling,[41] the obsessive, self-perpetuated cycle of scrolling social media feeds only to spiral through feelings of dread and despair.

Satisfied that my experiences with the social media paradox were shared by other creatives, I started considering a solution. While scrolling social media, how much control did I have over my own emotions? How could I reframe those negative emotions so that I didn't succumb to the adverse effects of doomscrolling?

Here's my discovery: I have the autonomy to intentionally change the way I interpret my social media feed. I can choose to see things from a different angle. I can effectively reframe social media so that the benefits obliterate the burdens.

Connecting the Story

In the tarot, The Hanged One (often referred to as The Hanged Man) encourages making a conscious change in perspective, as well as becoming inspired to see and/or understand an idea or situation in a different, unique way. The card fosters surrender and enlightenment, two concepts that require a measure of awareness, acceptance, and self-control. As such, when it comes to doomscrolling, working with the energy of The Hanged One card can empower creatives to reframe how we understand social media's influence on our feelings in order to invoke positive mental, emotional, and even physical outcomes. The spread at the end of this profile can help. First, let's explore this card's details.

What's happening in The Hanged One card?

A blond man is pictured from an aerial view so that he appears to be upside-down on the card. He's wearing a blue tie-dyed T-shirt, red pants, and tan flip-flops. Although he seems to have found himself in a writer's predicament, what with a few balled up pieces of paper and a scribbled notepad resting on his blanket, his posture and facial expression indicate that he's rather contemplative. Rather than yelling and throwing those wads of paper, he has positioned his arms behind his back and his left leg is bent, his ankle behind his right thigh. This posture seems deliberate, symbolic. His dreadlocked hair mimics a glowing yellow aura, as if lying prostrate has fostered a magnificent idea, or even enlightenment. Could he have found inspiration in the clouds above? The tree printed on the man's blanket is shaped like the bottom portion of the Egyptian ankh, a symbol for life, and the blanket is surrounded by a peaceful, grassy lawn.

The Hanged One, Reversed

When The Hanged One is upright on his feet, he's still tethered, but now he's stifled. There is an inability to see or accept something in any way that is not negative or unproductive. There is a selfish refusal to surrender in the direction he's being pulled or led. Additionally, there is a fear of letting go. However, because he can now catch his footing and reach to untie those ropes, The Hanged One is in a position to free himself from his confinement... if he so chooses.

The Hanged One: A Deep Dive

The Hanged One can involve finding oneself in a situation requiring a surrender—letting go of preconceived notions, opinions, dogmatic teachings, and especially self-limiting perceptions. When this card lands on your writer's desk, you are encouraged to pause, meditating on a situation before making a decision, and/or surrendering to allowing circumstances to unfold organically. "Let it go" or "Let go and let God." You know the sayings. Furthermore, this card provides the opportunity for an awakening following the exploration of a challenge or conflict.

While The Hanged One is seemingly uncomfortable in his bound state, what with being suspended from a tree branch by only one foot, what if he's actually content? What if that enlightened glow around his face indicates a resignation to accept his circumstances and, in turn, learn valuable lessons from them?

Both can be true, a paradox of discomfort and pleasure.

Notable Symbols in The Hanged One Card

Astrology—Neptune
Element—Spirit/Water

Other Symbols

Egyptian ankh—The tree on The Hanged One's blanket is shaped like the Egyptian ankh, a symbol that represents the key to life, or eternal life. Therefore, we might conclude that The Hanged One is suspended from the Tree of Life.

Posture—The individual's legs form a cross and their crossed arms and head form a triangle shape. In alchemy, a cross above a triangle is the inversion of the symbol for sulfur, which means the completion of self-transmutation.[42]

Numerological Associations with The Hanged One

In the tarot, The Hanged One is associated with The Empress and the Threes. Numerologically, the number 12 represents the twelve signs in the zodiac, the months of the year, as well as the biblical twelve disciples. To the latter point, the card reflects self-sacrifice and martyrdom. Additionally, the number 12 can be reduced to the number 3, as 1 + 2 = 3. In numerology, three means creativity, expression, growth, celebration, longing, transition, drive, expansion, cooperation, results, communication, working, caring, and collaboration, such as indicated by the Holy Trinity and the Pagan Rule of Three.

(see the Three cards grouped, next page)

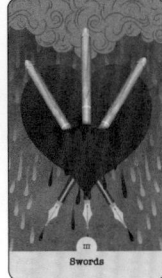

The Hanged One, Characterized:

When strung up by their ankle, a character inspired by The Hanged One has reversed their attitude and invited a spiritual awakening, an awakening of what their soul needs in order to be their best self. They have surrendered to the pull of the Universe and are patiently waiting for, listening for, and/or resting until they receive instructions regarding what happens next. This individual might be an enlightened person, a hippie, a teacher, a student, a patient, an acrobat, a dancer, a Buddha, or a monk.

Notable characters, people, or personas

Sir Francis Bacon; Benjamin Banneker; Buddha; the Dalai Lama; Rene Descartes; John Locke; Mr. Miyagi in *The Karate Kid*; Voltaire; and Phyllis Wheatley, among others.

After learning more about The Hanged One, who would you add to this list?

Word List

acceptance	pause	self-exploration	surrender
assessment	perseverance	self-sacrifice	thoughtful
breakthrough	personal growth	serenity	timeout
crossroads	perspective	shaman	topsy-turvy
delayed	relinquish	smitten	trapped
detachment	renouncement	stalemate	undecided
endurance	resistance	stalled	view
enlightenment	respite	stalling	visionary
intellectual	rest	standstill	waiting
patience	self-care	suffering	wonder

Spread: New Perspectives

Working with the energy of The Hanged One card can be extremely effective in helping to see a situation from a different viewpoint. Use the following spread to gain a new perspective on circumstances that are causing you a pause or discomfort. From the writer's lens, this spread can help you work through what's conflicting with your progress. On the other hand, if you are a writer of fiction, you can also use this spread from the lens of your character(s).

1. Consider an issue, problem, or conflict you have recently experienced that has affected your writing practice and/or your life.
2. Shuffle your tarot deck until you are ready to draw cards.
3. Search for The Hanged One card. Pull the three cards preceding The Hanged One card, pull The Hanged One card, and then pull the two cards following The Hanged One card. You will have a total of six cards.
4. Leading with Card 1, which is the first of the three cards preceding The Hanged One, lay the cards in the order indicated on the spread. Card 4 is The Hanged One card and Cards 5 and 6 should be the two cards that followed The Hanged One.
5. Ask yourself the following questions, using your intuition to consider the answers. If you are using this spread from your character's point of view, imagine them asking themselves these questions.

Card 1: The Situation—What is the origin or source of this issue, problem, or conflict?

Card 2: Your Feelings—What are my feelings about this experience?

Card 3: Reframe—How can I reframe how I feel about these circumstances?

Card 4: The Hanged One —Seeking a new perspective.

Card 5: Surrender—What am I being asked to surrender in this situation?

Card 6: Learn—What am I able to learn from this new perspective?

2	**1**	**3**

5

6

Key 13 or XIII:

Death

Death

The main character of the very first novel I wrote and published was a 30-some-thing-year-old woman who fell in love with (and commenced a torrid affair with) a 17-year-old boy. She was a therapist... and she was married.

As the story came to me, I was both appalled and fascinated by it. The rebellious freedom of writing authentically, without regard for who might read the words was, well, liberating. I felt fearless! That is, until I was finished with the novel, and my staunch Baptist grandmother told me she couldn't wait to read it.

I halted my publishing plan, set the novel aside, and floundered in terror. For several months I ruminated on whether I would even publish the book. All the excitement, adrenaline, and words (the thing had over 200,000 of them) I had put into the story weren't enough to rival the dread, the fear of being judged, criticized for publishing "filth," as Gran had warned me not to write.

But, in the end, I did it anyway. I published the book and advised Gran not to read it, a Death to my concern for her expectations. *The Decembers*, as mentioned in my story on The Fool card profile, is out of print now, but for a while I made it available, and the majority of those who read it liked it, but there were several who rated it poorly, citing that it had "too many storylines," "too much drama," and the obvious, "an inappropriate relationship." After several months of wallowing in my worry, I pulled myself upright, swallowed my fear, and pushed forward without regard for the opinions of others and despite probably being written out of Gran's will (I wasn't... She never read the book...), and I'm so glad I did. Unfavorable reviews or not, I have no regrets about publishing the book, and the experience inspired me to continue writing the stories I found most fascinating, no matter what others might think of them.

Writing fearlessly demands both authenticity and courage. It requires storytellers to change the way we think—about ourselves, about the craft of storytelling, and about the expectations of others—a death of the writer's ego, the sort of death necessary to initiate and endure a great transformation. When we write despite what others might think or say about our work, we make the difficult choice of relinquishing the control of others' opinions, embracing change that might result, and surrendering to what may come. I would like to make clear, however, that these encouragements are not an excuse for writing without regard for factors such as grammar, punctuation, and sensitivity. Prior to publishing, a sensitivity reader can help you identify and edit potentially harmful and offensive content, biases, and stereotyping.

Connecting the Story

In the tarot, the Death card informs change that is transformational. We are one person when Death comes calling, but afterwards we are left entirely different. More so than a literal death, the Death card represents the process of allowing aspects of oneself or a situation to die in order to promote change, growth, and/ or redirection. Let's examine this symbolism-rich card and its meanings.

What's happening in the Death card?

A woman—we'll call her "Death"—is dressed in a goth- or emo-esque style and is riding her white horse at her local Renaissance festival. She's carrying a rose-embellished black flag. Death brings a warning, not necessarily of literal death but of the promise of change. How we perceive this change, however, is completely up to us.

In the foreground, apart from the rider, we see three figures, and according to their posture and gesturing we can speculate how each chose to perceive Death's message of change. First, we see a bishop, most likely male, standing with praying hands. Is he pleading for Death to spare him from change? Or is he bowing to Death in acceptance? I'm reminded of a comment Carson, the butler of *Downton Abbey*, made around King George V's speech over the "wireless" radio. In Episode 2 of Season 5, he said, "Even kings must bow to pressure sometimes."[43]

The second figure in this card is a girl wearing a flower crown. From the way she's gathering her shoulders, perhaps she's a little afraid. The little boy sitting in front of her, however, gazes up at Death in naïve curiosity.

In the Death card's background, we see a small sailboat coasting along calm waters. A cliff rises above the water, and at the top we see a pair of pillars called "herms." Pay attention to the two herms, because you will see them again in The Moon card. In Greek mythology, these structures were boundary markers named after Hermes, messenger to the gods and the conductor of death for his fellow god, Hades. Beyond the herms, a bright sun either rises or sets against a serene sky, the promise of new days to come. What's on the other side of their gate? Well, what's on the other side of change? And what's on the other side of death? Until we know for sure, the answer is always: the unknown.

Death: A Deep Dive

Death is a harbinger of change. In her book *Seventy-Eight Degrees of Wisdom,* author and tarot expert Rachel Pollack suggests that Death invites one to "Give up your old masks and allow change to take place."[44] Thus, Death reminds writers that sometimes we must lean into a complete transformation, even if that means making changes to the way we write. If the Death card lands on your desk, it might be time to shed your old mask and try something new—new voice, setting, or even a new genre.

Death might also inform a necessary change within what you're writing. British writer Sir Arthur Quiller-Couch offered advice about self-editing to include "Murder your darlings." The Death card invites writers to submit to our intuition, editing objectively and without attachment to our well-crafted lines, and even walking away from stories and characters that don't resonate or belong. Why? Because doing so means following one's intuition. Even when your manuscript is polished and ready for submission to an agent, if you feel in your bones that you must scrap a paragraph, a page, a character, or even an entire chapter, it's worth considering.

Death, Reversed: The Shadow

When the Death card turns on its head, it informs an involuntary death or change. This change is the type that has not been invoked and is quite difficult to face and/or manage. Death reversed is "a living death," which tarot instructor and psychotherapist Ellen Goldberg identifies as boredom and/or lethargy. In her teachings, she notes that the fear of death is worse than an actual, physical death. "There is a kind of stunting of life that [happens to] people who fear death so that they are afraid to live. To make friends with death is to live more fully."[45]

Notable Symbols in the Death Card

Astrology—Scorpio
Element—Spirit / Water

Other Symbols

Black flag—The black flag is symbolic of death and the absence of light.

Pillars—Also called "herms," these pillars are a gate, welcoming or beckoning choices or decisions.

Skull—The skulls and bones on the horse's bridle are a reminder of what we leave behind after death, our most enduring part, and our very own hidden treasure.

Sun—The sun rises and sets with the promise of a new day.

Water—In this card, water means fluidity and intuition; The stream will always be water, yet water is always changing.

White horse—The white horse upon which Death rides represents spirit.

White rose—The white rose is symbolic of immortality, innocence, and purity.

Numerological Associations with the Death Card

In the tarot, the Death card is associated with The Emperor and the Fours. In numerology, the number 13 is reduced to the number 4. Four conveys steadiness, foundation, security, stability, structure, pause, planning, practicality, rigidity, focus, and preparation. In Death, however, these attributes occur after a significant change or transformation.

Death, Characterized

If Death shows up in a spread where the card represents your character, it could mean said character needs to undergo a significant transformation. Are you considering a plot twist for their storyline? Have you been toying with the idea of antagonist redemption? Does your character undergo a gradual transition spanning the length of your story? Is one of your minor characters a dark horse, riding along your plotline until they succeed suddenly and/or unexpectedly?

Other times, Death might represent you, dear writer. You are the one riding the horse and carrying the flag. And when this happens, consider giving yourself permission to explore what you really want to write—even if it's altogether opposite of what you are accustomed to creating. Author Joe R. Lansdale is credited with advising writers to "Write as if everyone you know is dead."[46] To me, this statement grants permission to write without regard for the opinions of others. Death to their expectations! Write for yourself. Write the book you want to read.[47] Apart from your own, no one else's opinion of your work matters, not even the reader's. If you love to read stories like what you're writing, there will be a market for readers like you. Write authentically, carving your own storytelling path, as opposed to continuing reluctantly down an unfulfilling path everyone else expects of you. Just be sure to keep in mind grammar, punctuation, and sensitivity.

Notable characters, people, or personas

Death can be the narrator of *The Book Thief*; Brad Pitt as Joe Black in *Meet Joe Black*; Frances Conroy as the Angel of Death, Shachath, in *American Horror Story: Asylum*; and the Ghost of Christmas Past in *Scrooged*. Death can also be the winds of change.

After learning more about the Death card, who or what would you add to this list?

Word List

anticipation	gloom	new beginnings	resolve
apathy	gradual	overcoming	rumination
barren	growth	posterity	severance
change	hedonism	process	shedding
clearing	immortality	razing	stagnation
destruction	improvement	realignment	surrendering
ending	invincibility	rebellion	termination
fear	liberation	refusal	transformation
fearless	loss	relinquish	transition
force	movement	remember	uncertainty

Spread: Inevitable Change

While the type of change brought on by the Wheel of Fortune is circumstantial, Death informs change that is transitional, shifting our way of thinking and behaving. Death's change is inevitable, and it cannot be avoided; however, just as swiftly as Death saunters into our lives, it strolls right on through and out. If you are faced with unavoidable change, this spread can help you explore the transition in order to understand how to respond. Likewise, if you are a writer of fiction, this spread can be used from the lens of your character(s) in order to determine how they might navigate a change in your storyline.

1. Search your tarot deck for the Death card and then lay it in the space for Card 1. This card represents an inevitable change.
2. Next, shuffle your deck. While you are shuffling, think about the change that is happening or will happen in your life. When you are satisfied that your cards are ready, turn the deck facedown as if you were about to deal them.
3. Turn over the first four cards from the top of your deck and lay them consecutively onto the four spaces for Cards 2 through 5.
4. Ask yourself the following questions, using your intuition to consider the answers. If you are using this spread from your character's point of view, imagine them asking themselves these questions.

Card 1: Death—An inevitable change.
Card 2: How am I fighting this change?
Card 3: What am I refusing to face about this change?
Card 4: What am I not seeing or realizing about this change?
Card 5: What am I being called to accept?

1

2   4   3   5

Key 14 or XIV:
Temperance

XIV

Temperance

Balancing my personal life and moments of creativity has been an interesting dance. As a rule, I've always separated the two, writing only when I'm alone and the house is quiet or when I don't have anything else on my mind that demands my attention, like packing for a family trip or preparing for a presentation at my Muggle job. I've tried to keep writing, creating art, and showing up in all of my life's roles separate from one another. But life-imitates-art-imitates-life, and sometimes life and art can occur simultaneously, the choreography of which can be tricky.

In the summer of 2021, both of my two sons moved out of the house. While I was helping them pack their things and then schlepping them off to their respective destinations (a first apartment and college), writing was set on the back burner. At the time, my novel *The Scars We Choose, Book Two* was in the works, the majority of Book One's readers patiently waiting to know what happened next in protagonist Scarlett Waverly's story. But as soon as I heard packing tape screeching from my eldest son's bedroom, the story had to wait. Focusing on anything other than our looming empty nest became nearly impossible.

Although I was dedicated to helping my sons with their moves, my mind often escaped to my desk where my book waited. For fleeting moments—especially when the waves of grief hit—I worried that I might never return to writing again. And then my sons were gone, the house was quieter than normal (although we do have two loud dogs), and my husband and I sat at the dinner table alone together for the first time in more than 20 years. Around those first few days, after I finished a nasty bout of ugly face-bawling, a message flitted through my mind, as gentle as a butterfly on a breeze: Creativity doesn't wait around on life to get out of the way before it steps in; it's always there, soaking up the events and storing memories that can be stitched into future stories.

Artists and writers often inject themselves into their work. I'm no different; Scarlett's story is partly my own. After our sons moved, it occurred to me that while I had been putting off the craft of storytelling until the moments when everything else in my life quieted down, I was simultaneously living and experiencing the life events that would more than likely inspire future writing. As a storyteller, I don't have to feel guilty for letting several days pass before my fingers touch the keyboard; the writing is happening inside my head and with my whole heart.

Connecting the Story

In the tarot, the Temperance card sweeps in directly after Death—after an intense transformation—to teach us how to reconcile the past with the present, how to heal old wounds and turn their scars into stories, and how to restore harmony and balance through moderation. Temperance reminds us that it's necessary to take time to heal, adjusting to new circumstances and pouring emotion and/or energy into new relationships, ideas, and endeavors. With one foot on land and one in the water, Temperance honors the balance of being in the here and now, while also imagining what may come.

My fellow writer, when life tilts you away from your keyboard, try to be easy on yourself and actively participate in what's going on. Consider the act of observation and immersion as not only an important aspect of living but an extraordinary benefit to your craft. Sometimes you'll have to pause your typing to experience the moments that will inspire you. This can be a tricky dance, but I think it's one worth learning.

What's happening in the Temperance card?

The Temperance card features an angel, thought to be one of two archangels: Gabriel or Michael. In the Bible, Gabriel is a messenger of God, and his messages are mostly concerned with time and the infusion of spirit with earthly matter. Michael, on the other hand, is an archangel of healing and protection.[48] The angel stands with one foot in a shallow pond and the other on the rocky embankment. He pours water from a pitcher into a glass, symbolic of filling one's cup. Violet irises grow along the waterside; they represent faith, hope, trust, valor, and wisdom. In the card's background, crawling from the water to the mountains, we see the path of spiritual attainment, its golden color underscoring the card's alchemical references. Who can recall another golden path on which its travelers sought individual attainment?[49] Also in the background, a bright sun hovers above the mountains. Like the glowing aura surrounding the angel's head, these are metaphors for crowning achievement.

Temperance: A Deep Dive

When the Temperance card lands on your desk, it might be time to refocus, practice balance, and/or seek healing. Focusing on the parts of your life that need attention can also help nurture your creative energy. A vacation, staycation, a walk, research, an act of self-care, reorganization of priorities, redistribution of need-to-haves and nice-to-haves might help you with the balance you're seeking both in your life and in your writing.

In his book *The 7 Habits of Highly Effective People*, author and educator Stephen Covey described a construct known as the emotional bank account.[50] Put simply, every relationship has an emotional bank account, which is balanced by deposits and withdrawals. The most fulfilling relationships thrive on aspects like trust, honesty, and commitment, and in order to establish and nurture these qualities, one must receive just as much as they are providing. There's a statement, credit for which is unknown, that says, "You can't pour from an empty cup." In the Temperance card, the angel's pitcher and glass appear balanced; they are pouring an equal amount from one vessel to the other. As writers, it's important that we seek a similar, nourishing balance. For me, this looks like living intentionally, observing and feeling and experiencing every aspect of my life so that when I sit down to write, I can pour from a full cup.

In the 14th century, the Temperance card used to be titled "The Alchemist." Rising in popularity during the Middle Ages, alchemy was a speculative practice that combined scientific and metaphysical theory. Preceding chemistry, alchemy's main initiatives were creating an anti-aging or immortality elixir and changing base metals (mainly lead) into gold. Why gold? Because, according to alchemists, gold symbolized human renewal and regeneration.[51] In the tarot, water represents these same virtues, and Temperance's angel uses the element for restoration and recovery following significant events or circumstances (i.e. the Death card).

Temperance, Reversed: The Shadow

When reversed, Temperance's angel teeters off-balance, their chalices fallen, and the path to attainment flooded. If this card lands reversed on your writer's desk, it could be an indicator that you and/or your character(s) are experiencing an unsteadiness, an upheaval of harmony, and a challenge to set things straight. Your lead isn't turning to gold and not even the philosopher's stone could help you achieve immortality. The reversal of this card conveys an adjustment after a great shift in equilibrium. Perhaps your life and/or your story has been disrupted and you or your characters are striving to manage your sea legs.

Notable Symbols in the Temperance Card

Astrology—Sagittarius
Element—Spirit / Fire

Other Symbols

Angel—An angel is a heavenly messenger or helper.

Glowing aura—This symbolizes crowning achievement or enlightenment.

Iris—This flower represents faith, hope, trust, valor, and wisdom.

Mountains—Mountains convey security, stability, and a steady foundation.

Path—The path is a metaphor for a journey.

Triangle inside a square—Featured on the figure's chest, the triangle represents God, Spirit, and humanity, while the square denotes the physical world.[52]

Two vessels—The glass and pitcher symbolize balance and harmony (See also Chapter 17, Key 17 – *The Star*).

Water—In the Temperance card, water is symbolic of intuition, healing, and rejuvenation.

Numerological Associations with Temperance

In the tarot, the Temperance card is associated with The Hierophant and the Fives. In numerology, the number 14 represents the expression of personal freedom, independence, self-determination, and lingering curiosity. When adding 1 + 4, we get 5, the number belonging to The Hierophant card. Because the number 5 lends to change, instability, and conflict, we can infer that Temperance's angel is working against these energies, encouraging balance, harmony, and moderation.

Temperance, Characterized

Temperance is an individual who seeks balance, compromise, and above all, harmony. They are a person of integrity, creative and insightful but not overly dramatic or emotional. This is an even-tempered person who might come across as a fence rider, someone who refuses to take sides. As a character, Temperance might be a bartender, a tightrope walker, a choreographer, a yogi, a chiropractor, a healer, or a therapist.

As a writer, during the moments when you are experiencing work-life balance and/or writing-life balance, you are demonstrating Temperance energy. Whatever it is that has afforded you the time to write apart from your other everyday roles, stay at it! Keep those creative juices flowing... from cup to cup.

Notable characters, people, or personas

Brian Flanagan in *Cocktail*; Nik Wallenda of *The Flying Wallendas*; choreographer, dancer, and actress Debbie Allen; Dolly Frasier in my novel *Only the Rocks That Float*; and Dr. Sean Maguire (played by the late, great Robin Williams) in *Good Will Hunting*.

After learning more about the Temperance card, who would you add to this list?

Word List

agreeable	compassion	intervention	quality
alchemy	compromise	merging	seeking
alignment	considerate	middle path	self-control
angel	control	moderation	self-help
balance	enlightened	patience	steadying
benevolence	forgiveness	peace	synergy
blending	harmony	perseverance	synthesis
calm	healing	precision	tempering
careful	helping	progress	understanding
chemistry	higher learning	purpose	vision

Spread: Balancing Act

Whenever there is significant change in our lives, our normal response is to gain our footing so we can return to stability. Oftentimes, however, stability requires giving and receiving. Like the Justice card, Temperance is a card that informs concentration in order to restore harmony.

Use the following spread for uncovering how you might invite harmony back into your life following a period of change. Similarly, if you are a fiction writer, you can use this spread to explore how your character(s) might restore harmony to their story.

1. Shuffle your deck until you are satisfied that the cards are ready.
2. Next, find the Temperance card, which represents you or your character(s) in this moment. Lay the card in the center space.
3. The card behind Temperance (Card 1) represents an invitation, and the card in front of Temperance (Card 3) indicates a release.
4. Ask yourself the following questions, using your intuition to consider the answers. If you are using this spread from your character's point of view, imagine them asking themselves these questions.

Card 1: What am I inviting more of into my life?
Card 2: Temperance—You / Your Character(s)
Card 3: What am I called to release after this change?

1

3

Key 15 or XV:
The Devil

XV

The Devil

As long as I can remember, I've been haunted. By words a child should never hear, by scrutinizing adults, by schoolyard bullies, by unhealthy decisions, by dishonesty, by regret, by relentless memories, by insatiable longing, and especially by the scales.

When I was in elementary school, I remember kids calling me "Miss Piggy" and being put on a diet because I was "chubby." I learned every exercise move and every word to every song on Jane Fonda's Workout Record, the one with her legs straight in the air, her ankles wrapped in maroon legwarmers. When my clothes didn't fit, I'd cry until my face looked like a red potato, and to "make it better" a family member would take me out for Mexican food and Swensen's ice cream. During a trip to the mall when I was around nine or ten, that same family member and one other made me step onto an oversized, vintage lollipop scale and weigh in front of everyone walking by. They'd each stepped upon the antique contraption, marveling at either how much weight they'd lost or how much they needed to lose. When it was my turn, I tried to refuse. I cried, begging them not to make me weigh in front of everyone, but I was threatened with a spanking if I didn't do as I was told. I was reminded that I was the child, and they were the adults. "You do as we say." When the needle flew past 150 pounds, one adult covered their mouth, laughing into their palm while the other turned and walked away, leaving me there on the scale. In middle school, I toppled two hundred pounds, and on the last day of my eighth-grade year, my P.E. teacher told me, "You know, you should really lose about twenty pounds or so this summer." Again, as per usual, I cried, and when I got home from school I drowned myself in a bowl of my grandmother's homemade peach cobbler and a buttered slab of her freshly baked sourdough bread.

Looking back, I'm not sure what was so special about what that teacher said to me or the typical way in which I nursed the scrutiny, but something inside me snapped. Maybe it was timing, the onset of puberty. Nevertheless, I'd had enough. I wasn't going to be The Fat Girl anymore. Over the next three months, I lost sixty-five pounds on SlimFast and MTV. My family raved at how great I looked, and the first day of my freshman year in high school, my friends didn't recognize me until the homeroom teacher called out my name. Everyone complimented me, everyone was proud of me, and the bullying was over. Finally, I felt free.

Since that first day of high school, I have struggled persistently with keeping off the weight. I've battled genetics, ravenous cravings, hormonal imbalances, binge eating, purging, peer pressure, social expectations, alcoholism, grief, anger, and shame. When people speak of their "demons," these are mine. My demons keep me up at night. They tell me I deserve the chocolate and then chant relentlessly about what a pitiful failure I am for indulging in it. Sometimes, they whisper even uglier, scarier thoughts. Until I learned how to set boundaries, my demons would appear in the form of the adults who were supposed to love me the most. The demons still show up; their favorite place to linger is my memories. At times, overcoming them can feel nearly impossible, their shackles weighing me down as they feed on my fears.

As a creative person, unpacking all the hurt my demons have caused was—is—made possible through art and fiction writing. For years, making art was enough to numb the pain—I'd earned the highest honors in every middle- and high school art show, and my work even earned a full scholarship—but channeling that pain through storytelling has proven an even more fulfilling and rewarding kind of therapy. These days, when grief, anger, and shame come calling, I renounce them, silencing them with a poem, journaling, or by writing a story. The latter is even more satisfying when I assign my pain to a character... and then kill them off.

Connecting the Story

In the Major Arcana, The Devil is a demon like no other; yet, although its presence can be startling the card is not always negative. It's informative, offering insights into influences over which we have complete control. Once we understand that we have full autonomy over our lives, we can walk away from our strongholds. Furthermore, The Devil card is one of a few tarot cards that when reversed shines light on its shadow. Let's review this card's seemingly frightening illustration and decipher what it might indicate for you, the writer, when it shows up on your desk.

What's happening in The Devil card?

In the *Mystic Storyteller Tarot*, The Devil is represented by an attractive, voluptuous woman with a sly smile, a sexy red dress, and a taloned manicure. Like Pixie's version, our Lady Devil is a half-human, half-goat deity representative of Baphomet, the Sabbatic Goat. Winged and boasting an inverted star on her forehead, our Devil hovers over a fiery plane, her scarlet dress fed by the flames. Chained and attached to each other are two human figures, our same couple from The Lovers card, seemingly under The Devil's spell. Similar in stance to The Magician, The Devil holds one arm upward and one pointing down. Her raised right hand makes the priestly blessing mudra, while her left hand points toward the fire below. While the man stands empty-handed, he is captivated by the woman, who holds a bunch of grapes. Both figures have sprouted small horns and although they are tethered to each other, their chains are loosened and might be easily lifted and removed. I don't see that happening anytime soon.

The Devil: A Deep Dive

The majority of writers I know—including me—and many famous storytellers have admitted to being tormented by "writer's demons." Such demons include bad reviews, blank page intimidation, criticism, dread, envy, greed, imposter syndrome, public speaking, reading aloud, rejection, self-doubt, worry, writer's block, and the list goes on. What's most important about our writer demons is how we manage them.

The woman featured in The Devil card would have you manage all of the aforementioned list through the bondage of obsession, through addiction, force, selfishness, and misaligned thinking. In this regard, The Devil is a false prophet and would rather you believe that you are not in control of removing those chains and saving yourself from the spiraling darkness that can accompany the pursuit of being a successful writer.

I don't have to tell you that recognizing and removing power from your demons is immensely important, but I will gently remind you that while those negative energies might sometimes hover over you, they're only as heavy and oppressive as you allow them to be. You are in control. Your shackles aren't always permanent; they are often quite relaxed. You can walk away from a blank page and return to it with a fresh perspective. You can write with clarity. You can overcome the fear of unsavory reviews. You have the power of recognizing what's killing your spirit and making the choice to eliminate the demon(s).

You are encouraged and supported in lifting those chains. Consider finding someone else who is also suffering and joining them in a support group, or even a writer's group. Therapy can also be extremely beneficial, as leaning on and/or confiding in others can help with healing. I know both have helped me. Before seeking treatment, however, please consult with your doctor.

At the conclusion of my scales story, I mentioned that The Devil card isn't always negative. Like many of the adults in my childhood, The Devil isn't always scrutinizing and abusive. On the contrary, this card can represent awareness, especially self-exploration and pleasure. Our Sexy Devil can inform human desires, particularly with regard to the material world, and her energy can spark passion, yearning, longing, and carnal craving. However, per what we understand about The Devil's propensity for spiraling us out of control, we might seek such human desires in moderation and with personal responsibility.

The Devil, Reversed: The Light

When The Devil is flipped on her head, she topples from the fire, the chains falling from the figures' bodies and the flames illuminating the darkness. You, your characters, and/or your writing in general are released from bondage and scrutiny. There has been a paradigm shift in consciousness, and you are thinking, believing, and writing with clarity and vigor.

Notable Symbols in The Devil Card

Astrology—Capricorn
Element—Spirit / Earth

Other Symbols

Arm pointing downward—The lowered left arm denotes bringing light into darkness.

Black (as seen in the background)—This color informs power, fear, mystery, the occult, strength, authority, and although problematic, it is a color often associated with darkness, grief, and shadow.

Inverted pentagram—Although the pentagram is the symbol of the five elements (air, earth, fire, spirit, and water), when inverted it represents the darker aspects of occultism and is sometimes associated with dark magic.

Fire and fruit—These details represent fire and desire, respectively (Rick James and Teena Marie, anyone?).

Goat horns (on our Lady Devil)—The goat is the symbol of Capricorn, which is the zodiac sign allocated to this card.

Horns (on the humans)—These imply the longer the individuals choose to stay chained, the more deeply they become entranced by The Devil's spell.

Loosened chains—The loosened chains around the humans' ankles are symbolic of bondage chosen and/or accepted.

The Priestly Blessing Mudra (hand gesture)   This gesture denotes the Hebrew letter shin. Fun fact: Leonard Nimoy, famous for his role as Spock in the iconic *Star Trek* series and films, intentionally adapted the mudra to mean "live long and prosper," a gesture he'd learned from his own Jewish upbringing.[53]

Vampire bat wings—These are symbolic of sucking the life out of one's prey.[54]

Numerological Associations with The Devil

In the tarot, The Devil card is associated with The Lovers and the Sixes. The Devil is card number 15 of the Major Arcana, but can you see the resemblance between The Devil card and The Lovers? When adding 1 + 5, we get 6. Easy math. If you recall from The Lovers card, six is the number of balance, karma, assistance, adjustment, alignment, and when reversed, The Devil reveals compassion, empathy, healing, love, and support.

The Devil, Characterized

The Devil is a ghoul, a haint, a poltergeist, an oppressor, an abuser, Depression with a capital D. The Devil's in the details and at the crossroads. It's anyone hellbent on wrongdoing, a trickster, a demon, a daemon, a monster, a masochist, a sadist, a cruel, evil individual. The Devil is also a sex symbol, lusty and seductive. She's a sexy siren, a *Devil in a Red Dress*. Where I am from in the American South, there's a common saying that claims, "The Devil is a liar!"

Notable characters, people, or personas

Baphomet; Beelzebub; Lucifer; Satan; Linda Blair as Regan MacNeil in *The Exorcist;* Glenn Close as Alex Forrest in *Fatal Attraction;* Al Pacino as John Milton in *The*

Devil's Advocate; Meryl Streep as Miranda Priestly in *The Devil Wears Prada*; *The Devil Went Down to Georgia* by Charlie Daniels; Beelzebub, Dracula, and in Greek mythology Pan, Persephone, and Pluto, among others.

After learning more about The Devil, who would you add to this list?

Spread: Strongholds

Although we are capable of conquering the strongholds that cause so much pain in our lives, doing so can be extremely difficult work. As such, I have designed this spread to surround The Devil in your life with a strategy to support defeating it. If you are a writer of fiction, this spread can be used to explore how to help your character(s) defeat their own demons from every direction.

1. Pull The Devil from your tarot deck and place the card in the center space for Card 1. This represents the stronghold or personal demon looming over you or your character(s) at this time.
2. Next, shuffle your tarot deck until you are satisfied that the cards are ready, and then turn the deck facedown as if you were about to deal them.
3. Starting with the space for Card 2, count the sixth card from the top of the deck and lay it in that space.
4. Moving clockwise, repeat for the rest of the spread, counting every sixth card, laying it down, and then advancing on to the next space until The Devil is surrounded by cards.
5. Ask yourself the following question, using your intuition to consider the answer. If you are using this spread from your character's point of view, imagine them asking themselves this questions.

What story are the four cards telling around how I can bind and defeat the stronghold in my life?

Word List

abhor	domination	lust	rotten
addiction	fear	maleficent	scared
adversity	fetish	malignant	self-doubt
afraid	grief	manipulation	sexuality
carnal	hate	masochistic	sinister
condescension	hindrance	misogyny	submission
despair	immoral	oppression	temptation
detachment	kink	perverse	terror
dishonesty	liar	racism	unholy
disillusion	limitations	restriction	weakness

Key 16 or XVI:
The Tower

Contrary to popular belief about human beings, I love change. I love trying new things, exploring new places, moving to new houses, and experimenting with new ideas. Change keeps me creative; going back to the drawing board and trying a different approach or revising an old idea keeps the act of writing and making art challenging, exciting, and fulfilling.

During the winter months, however, it's easy for me to slip into a depressive rut. At a certain point every year, when the sun shines less and the blue skies dull to gray, seasonal blues (which, in my opinion, should be called "seasonal grays") can cause a creative lull. Winter 2022 was no exception, and even when preparing to attend *Training* magazine's conference at Disney World's Coronado Springs resort in February of that year, my blood cooled, and the gray settled in.

It's hard to imagine being depressed while at "the most magical place on earth," but the location never matters. The dismal grays don't discriminate, and they certainly don't wait... but neither does the call of creativity.

During the first two days of that trip, when I wasn't in bed with a migraine, I strolled through the resort in dark shades, locating food and then getting back to my room. On the morning the conference started, I peeled myself from my pillow and went down to listen to the keynote speakers. After all, my boss had made an investment in allowing me to attend, and I was obligated to get the most out of the experience so I could share with my colleagues what I learned.

One of the conference keynotes was Pixar's Character Art Director, Deanna Marsigliese. A character in her own right, what with her mid-century lacquered coif and vintage circle skirt, Deanna described her method for becoming inspired—through intuition, curiosity, and meaning—and I removed my migraine shades and listened intently.

As I watched Ms. Marsigliese's video segments exploring her messy desk and workspaces, and while I listened to her backstory around the characters she'd designed for films such as *The Incredibles 2, Luca,* and *Soul,* I felt my headache slowly fade. My heart beat wildly as she shared a story about traveling to a tiny seaside Italian town, drilling into every detail, and making sketches that included her late grandparents (I do that, too—all of my work includes muses of my loved ones, including the *Mystic Storyteller Tarot*). Ms. Marsigliese's sketches would become the entire town in the movie *Luca.* I felt so inspired that I was sure I would dash right out of that conference hall and float back to my room to write.

My main takeaway from Ms. Marsigliese's lecture was a word of advice she gave her fellow creative souls, which I will paraphrase here: Tourists are always looking up, taking photos, and paying attention to detail. To stay inspired, you have to stay curious. Be a tourist, even in your own hometown. Look up, follow your intuition, take in every detail, ask questions, and discover meaning in the things you find most interesting.

By the conclusion of the conference's first day, my migraine was gone, and my magical surroundings blossomed around me as though I were seeing them for the first time. What Ms. Marsigliese's speech provided for me was an epiphany, a new way of thinking that shocked the gray, righting the skies back to blue. For the rest of that conference, I was led by my intuition, curious about each inspiring detail, and I found meaning in every experience. I returned home with Disney-like magic coursing through my bones, a renewed spirit, and an enlightened mind.

Connecting the Story

In the tarot, The Tower card is one that, for many, initially causes fear and anxiety.

In the Smith-Waite deck, for example, the imagery alone brings to mind calamity and destruction. However, when examining this card's details in a new way—and considering its position directly following The Devil—you might began looking forward to it popping up (or crashing down) on your writer's desk. In viewing The Tower through Ms. Marsigliese's lens of intuition, curiosity, and meaning, I hope I can help change your mind about this card when it strikes your writing efforts.

What's happening in The Tower card?

Destruction. A storm has settled over the area, causing the skies to turn black and looming gray clouds to settle in. Lightning has stricken the top of this Tower with such force that its crowned cap has been blasted off, and the structure is engulfed in fire. The strength of such an assault has not only toppled the roof, but it has jolted the folks inside the Tower with such force that they've been flung from its windows and are falling to the ground—or water; it's impossible to tell. From the expressions on their faces, this lightning strike was sudden, unexpected.

The Tower: A Deep Dive

While the Wheel of Fortune represents change experienced due to a turn of events, and the Death card informs impending, inevitable, and transformational change, The Tower brings about change that is swift and abrupt. This change occurs in the form of an upheaval, a violent move, and it can spark (pardon the pun) a sudden change of mind.

Associated with thought and intellect, the crown chakra is represented in The Tower's fallen crown. We might consider such a strike a wake-up call to one's subconscious, and for writers, such a revolution can ignite a creative awakening, a profound idea—an "Aha!" moment. Such a jolt implores us to ask What am I writing? Why am I writing it? and Is what I'm writing serving my creative needs or am I writing for others? If the latter, Tower energy demands us to pound that backspace and delete, snatch that paper from the typewriter, ball it up, and pitch it across the room. Scrap it and start over. Kill a darling or two and write what's inside you, possibly what's hiding just beneath the surface. What's been brewing within your mind and has now been provided a release? Write that. Write what haunts you, what frightens you; give it a character and then kill it. Write what clears the grays and brings you joyful blues.

The Tower denotes a paradigm shift in the way of thinking—an epiphany. When this card strikes, hierarchal systems are broken down and reimagined. After all, it's easy to stay in a hierarchy, to go with the flow, to not rock the boat, all the other idioms that indicate a chosen resistance to change and acceptance of the status quo. The Tower, however, changes the story, inviting such a storm that might level a manner of thinking and/or process for the sake of egalitarianism. Burn it all to the ground and start over.

Alternatively, The Tower might indicate a cultural transformation ignited by disaster, economy, education, invention, law, rights, and/or war. The card can denote intense movement and/or displacement resulting from gentrification, immigration, segregation, and urbanization.

The Tower, Reversed: The Shadow

When reversed, The Tower could uncover catastrophizing, automatically assuming the worst about a situation rather than imagining an opportunity for success and growth. A reversed Tower can indicate avoidance of a situation that results in a disastrous outcome. Denial of an obvious reformation. It can mean disaster averted or the calm before the storm. The Tower reversed indicates the fear of change, burying one's head in the dirt rather than standing upright and facing change head-on.

Notable Symbols in The Tower Card

Astrology—Mars
Element—Fire

Other Symbols

Crown—The falling crown symbolizes the ego, higher thinking, intellect, and wisdom.

Falling—The motion of falling indicates losing control.

Fire—In this card, fire is representative of cleansing through destruction.

Lightning—The lightning bolts represent a sudden clarity of mind and the eradication of ignorance. In the Bible, lightning represents God's power or wrath.[55]

Tower—The structure in this card represents the construction of ego, a false sense of security.

Numerological Associations with The Tower

In the tarot, The Tower is associated with The Chariot and the Sevens. In numerology, 16 represents intuitive power, inner wisdom, and confidence. It can indicate perfectionism, debate, and philosophy.[56] On the other hand, when we reduce the number by adding 1 + 6, we get seven, the number of struggles, challenges, and lessons learned.

The Tower, Characterized

The Tower is any element that brings about sudden change, such as a natural disaster, pandemic, war, or any major incident. It is also a radical thought that brings about immediate change within a story or poem. It's The Man, The System, or The Institution.

Notable characters, people, or personas

Pyornkrachzark, the Rock Biter in *The NeverEnding Story*; Lord Voldemort; Terminator; Thanos; Pennywise in It; *Back to the Future*'s Biff Tannen; and *Gone Girl*'s Amy Dunne.

After learning more about The Tower, who or what would you add to this list?

Word List

bankruptcy	emergency	redundancy	start over
blind-sided	enlightenment	renovation	stressful
catastrophe	failure	repossession	stricken
change	freedom	repurposing	suddenly
chaos	hindrance	resilience	terrified
crumbling	ideas	restoration	toppling
demolish	liberation	revelation	transformation
destruction	overboard	ruin	turbulence
disaster	overthrown	shaken	unexpected
divine intervention	radical change	shedding	upheaval

Spread: Revolutionary Idea

Unexpected change, as I've mentioned, isn't The Tower card's only meaning. Metaphorically, this card can also indicate the sudden strike of a revolutionary new idea. As you are well aware, a writer's greatest ideas often happen suddenly, arriving seemingly out of nowhere, and often without warning. A novel idea (pardon the pun) can happen in a flash, launching writers like you and me into a frenzied rush to open our phones or find a pen to make notes. Speaking from experience, when I think of a radical new idea for a book I'm working on, or an idea for a new story, I can hardly function until I've jotted it down so that I might explore it at my first chance of escaping to my computer.

The following spread is designed to help you intuit details about a startling new idea so that you might adapt it for quality storytelling.

1. Search your tarot deck for the card that most closely represents a likeness of your new idea and lay it on the space for Card 1.
2. Next, find The Tower and place it in the space for Card 2.
3. Shuffle your deck until you are satisfied that the cards are ready, and then turn the deck facedown as if you were about to deal them.
4. Starting with the space for Card 3, count the seventh card from the top of the deck and lay it in that space.
5. Repeat for the rest of the spread, counting every seventh card, laying it down, and then advancing on to the next space.
6. Ask yourself the following questions, using your intuition to consider the answers. If you are using this spread from your character's point of view, imagine them asking themselves these questions.

Card 1: This card represents your new idea.
Card 2: The Tower—Sudden jolt of inspiration.
Card 3: What is unknown to me about this new idea?
Card 4: What are my gut feelings around the new idea?
Card 5: What needs purging in order to bring this new idea into fruition?
Card 6: What needs purging in order to bring this new idea into fruition?
Card 7: What or who can I lean on for support in making this idea happen?

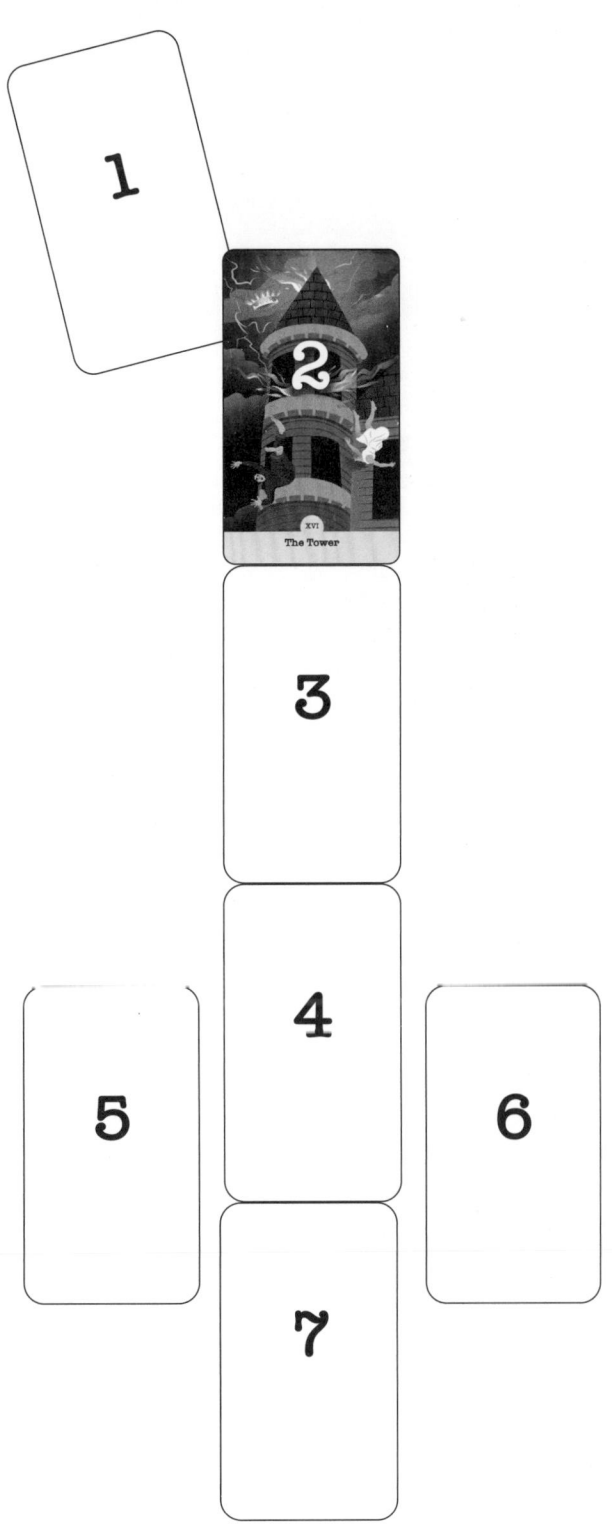

Key 17 or XVII:

The Star

My father was a tower of a man. Physically, emotionally, and intellectually. When he walked into a room, everyone noticed. Although he was a big ol' wallflower, his personality alone took up a lot of space, and whether he wanted to or not (mostly not), he attracted the attention of people. They wanted to know the gentle giant, to understand his quietness, they wanted to go fishing with him, hypothesize and philosophize with him, talk through movies with him (hey, there are things to discuss), and they wanted to include him in every gathering... no matter how loudly he yawped that he didn't like people and didn't want to go.

He liked people, in doses, but this detail is one of many examples of how his life experiences, genetic mental illness, and extreme introversion informed his isolation, especially after he suffered a work-related injury that upended and shortened his life.

My father's death crashed down around our family in a traumatic way. His suffering had been intense, his mental illness spiralic, and his last days lingered, as if suspended in time, like watching a tree fall into the ocean and sink all the way to the bottom. My mother's response to his death was a spiral of her own. She dealt with her grief by trying to erase the pain from her memory, denying her feelings around losing her partner of more than three decades, and gutting their entire house. She purged everything that reminded her of his "disability years:" she wrestled his favorite recliner to the dump, sold his boat and truck, gave away all his fishing tackle, blew his inheritance on clothes and food, and traded in their paid-for SUV for a brand-new sports car.

My response to my father's death was to rally around my mother when she needed support and get the hell out of her way when she didn't. My primary focus, however, hadn't been helping her to manage her grief, it had been helping my five- and seven-year-old boys understand their own. They'd just lost their Granddaddy, their most favorite person in the whole world. And so, I swooped in, scooping them up and helping them recover. I set aside my own recovery (as most caregivers do) until Mama was settled and the boys were asleep, and then I filled the loss with tequila and terrible choices.

Both my mother's and my response to my father's death were trauma responses, emotionally fueled stress reactions to a traumatic event. Both of our reactions were emotional and physical, and neither was healthy nor constructive. Our pain and loss took the shape of the hole my father had left in our lives, and for a while afterwards, it burned through my creativity and stifled my imagination.

Connecting the Story

In the tarot, The Star card follows The Tower for a reason. It provides counsel, guiding our response to trauma and grief, ushering us through recovery, and invoking a host of other RE-words around the sudden impact of significant change. The Star illuminates the construct of self-care, highlighting the fact that self-care is relative to the individual, and it's not always as accessible to some as it is for others. Alternatively, The Star is an invitation to artistic exploration, which, for writers, is a much-needed reprieve to the mess The Tower can make of your creativity. The Star asks you to pause, acclimate, and heal. Let's examine this bittersweet card.

What's happening in The Star card?

A woman wearing a white bathing suit kneels on a lush embankment beside a small pond. She holds a white mug in each of her hands, one pouring water out onto the land and the other pouring back into the pond. In the background, we can see two hills: a grassy one behind her upon which a tree has grown and a scarlet ibis perches, and the other a foothill or mountain. Above her head and all around the sky are eight eight-pointed stars, the largest of which is yellow and sparkles directly over the woman's body. The surrounding seven stars are white and scattered against a cloudless blue sky.

The Star: A Deep Dive

When the smoke clears and the dust settles around the fallen Tower, after you've experienced a significant change, a psychological and/or mental breakthrough, and you've worked intentionally at seeing something from a new/different perspective, The Star offers rest, reiterating (two of the RE-words) balance. It reminds you of the balance you've already learned from Temperance, right before The Devil interfered (or intervened, perhaps?) and The Tower came crashing down.

During this regaining process, The Star harkens back to Audre Lorde's thoughts around self-care and the difference between stretching oneself (via a healthy challenge) and overextending. "Caring for myself is not self-indulgence, it is self-preservation and that is an act of political warfare." Regarding self-care, if you're left picking up the pieces of you scattered by such abrupt change or overextension, The Star offers insight around what accessible self-care looks like for each individual. Although tequila and bad decisions were accessible to me after my father passed, they were not self-care. Eventually, my creativity returned, and I fully examined and healed from his passing through writing and publishing *The Scars We Choose, Book Two*, a novel in which I gave him a character with the happy ending he'd deserved.

To that point, when The Star shines on your writer's desk, it can encourage imagination and hope, empowering you to ladle creativity from every inspiring source—dreams, experiences, surroundings, everywhere. You are urged to collect as much inspiration as you can and apply it to your work. Like a current, allow your creativity to flow into you and through you, right out of your fingertips, and then share what you've crafted with the world.

The RE-words

The Star figure might not have any pockets, but she certainly carries with her plenty of RE-words: realization, reassessment, reconfigure, recovery, rediscovery, regaining, rehabilitation, reiteration, rejuvenation, reformation, relaxation, remembering, renewal, renovation, reparation, rescue, reset, rest, restoration, retrograde, retrospect, revelation, revitalization, revival, and rewilding. On a lower polarity (reversed), she might inform regurgitation, remorselessness, response (as in trauma response), restlessness, restriction, and retribution.

The Star, Reversed: The Shadow

When reversed, The Star can represent hopelessness, depression, illness, imposter syndrome, and as previously mentioned, overextension. The reversed Star is what my family and I experienced in my opening story: a trauma response to a stressful situation. It's anger, aggressive behavior, alcohol or drug abuse, guilt, Post-Traumatic Stress Disorder (PTSD), self-blame, self-harm, shame, or suicidal thoughts.

Similarly, The Star reversed uncovers all the Un-REs: unrequited feelings, unreal ideas, unresponsiveness, unreliability, unrealized potential, unrenewed vows, unrestored hope, unrevived dreams.

Notable Symbols in The Star Card

Astrology—Aquarius
Element—Spirit/Air

Other Symbols

Eight eight-pointed stars—The eight-pointed star is a symbol of balance and harmony, a reminder that all things are connected to the universe's natural rhythms.[57] This star is also representative of the four directions (north, south, east, west), intersected by the four elements (air, earth, fire, and water).

Grassy terrain with flowers—These features evoke newness, growth, blossoming, nurturing, and awakening.

Hill in the background—I believe the hill featured in the background of this card is where The Tower stood before it toppled. Additionally, hills and mountains in the tarot can denote security and stability.

Nakedness (nearly)—According to A. E. Waite, a nude figure in the tarot symbolizes unveiled Truth.[58] Nakedness also denotes bravery, freedom, naïveté, opening oneself to the possibilities, success, spiritual graduation, and vulnerability.

Scarlet ibis—The ibis is a sacred bird to both Hermes Trismegistus and Thoth, Egyptian god of wisdom. The bird perches in a treetop, a symbol of focus and concentration in order to welcome higher knowledge.[59]

Two vessels—The two water mugs represent balance and harmony (See also Chapter 17, Key 14 – *Temperance*).

Water—In this card, water represents intuition, healing, and rejuvenation.

Numerological Associations with The Star

The number 17 represents being on the right track spiritually and working hard to make one's dreams a reality.[60] When combined, 1 + 7 = 8, which is the number of achievement and manifestation. Therefore, in the tarot, The Star is associated with Strength and the Eights.

The Star, Characterized

The figure in The Star card can be lots of different people, I'm certain. However, I interpret her as being both you and me as writers or as caregivers. If the former, she represents tending to our own personal needs following an experience that brought great change into our lives and/or an event that changed us from the inside out. She is our Inner Self, our personal Truth, and her best interests are bringing balance, hope, and harmony back to our lives and our writing practice. She challenges and supports the stretches, and then intervenes when we've overextended ourselves. If The Star is a caregiver, then she is a person who makes our healing and wellbeing a priority; that individual might be a parent, a best friend, a spouse, a nurse, a doctor, a therapist, an acupuncturist, or your favorite Aunt Tillie whom everyone else in the family gossips about but wouldn't dare say those things to her face. Either way, Aunt Tillie doesn't care what anyone says. She loves you. You're her favorite.

Notable characters, people, or personas

Catherine Barkley from Hemingway's *A Farewell to Arms*; Hana from *The English Patient* by Michael Ondaatje; *Harry Potter*'s Madam Pomfrey; My editor and friend Grisel Scarantino; Harriet Tubman; Sojourner Truth; Florence Nightingale; Anne Sullivan; Mother Teresa; Princess Diana; and Eleanor Roosevelt.

After learning more about The Star, who would you add to this list?

Word List

astrology	healing	positivity	relief
blessings	heavenly	purpose	renewal
celestial	help	realignment	repair
clarity	hope	rebirth	rest
cleansing	illuminate	receptivity	revitalize
divination	inspiration	reconfigure	science
faith	nourishment	recovery	seeker
fulfillment	optimism	regeneration	spirituality
guidance	pause	rejuvenation	tranquility
happiness	peace	relaxation	visionary

Spread: RE-covery in the Aftermath

When you find yourself settling into the aftermath of an upheaval—a sudden, traumatic event—how can you heal, recover, and return to quality storytelling? If you are a fiction writer, how will your character(s) respond and recover after a traumatic event? Use this spread for the exploration of productive self-care and recovery, either from a personal lens or from your character's point of view.

1. Search your tarot deck until you find The Star card and place it in the center space for Card 1.
2. Shuffle your deck until you are satisfied that the cards are ready, and then turn the deck facedown as if you were about to deal them.
3. Starting with the space for Card 2, count the eighth card from the top of the deck and lay it in that space.
4. Repeat for the rest of the spread, counting every eighth card, laying it down, and then advancing on to the next space.
5. Ask yourself the following questions, using your intuition to consider the answers. If you are using this spread from your character's point of view, imagine them asking themselves these questions.

Card 2: Why have I been resisting self-care?
Card 3: How do I begin reorganizing my priorities in order to place myself first?
Card 4: How can I reframe what happened in order to recover?
Card 5: What support do I need in order to redirect and move forward?
Card 6: What does recovery look like?

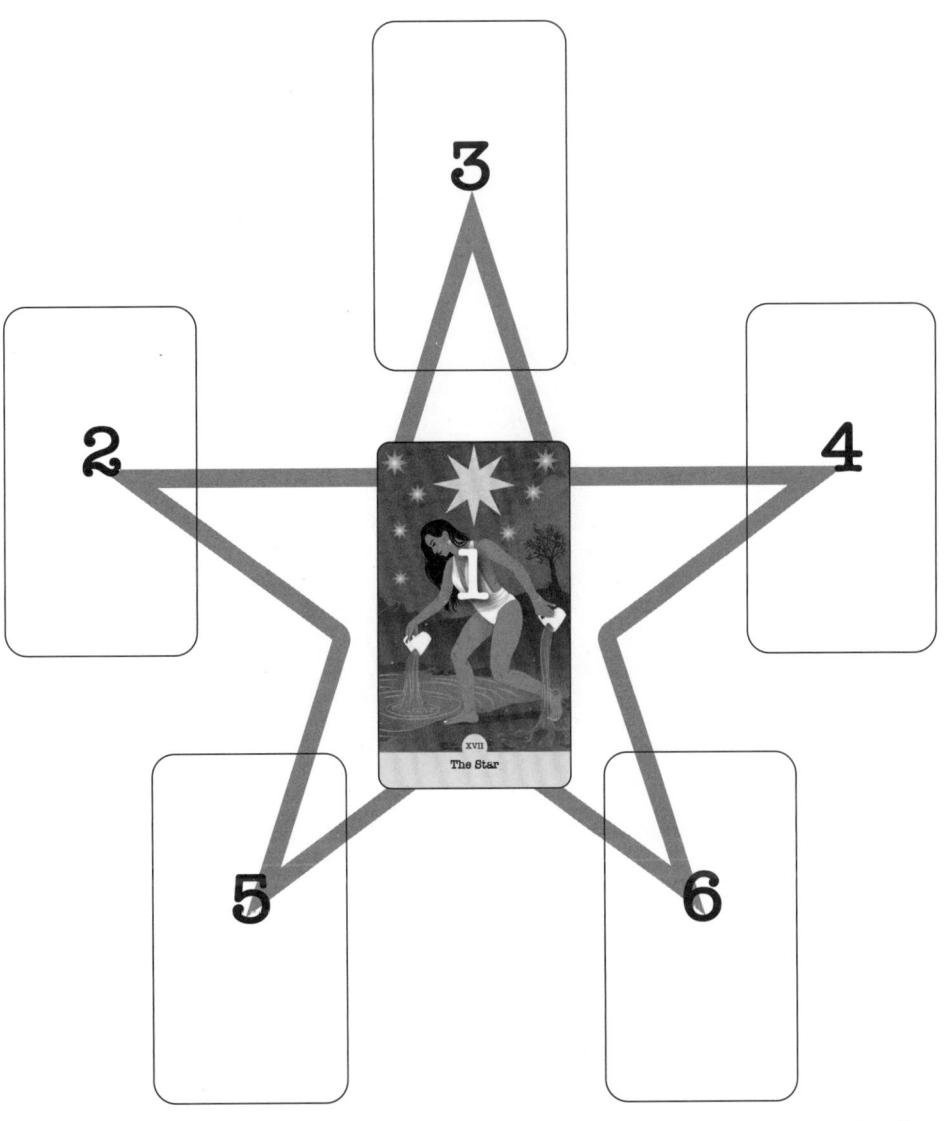

Key 18 or XVIII:
The Moon

The Moon

I don't believe it's a stretch to suppose that every writer knows there is mystery in the madness, as it were, of storytelling. However mysterious and unknown, I do believe there is also method.

Famous for his studies of archetypes and personality, psychiatrist Carl Jung theorized that the human collective unconscious is a culmination of complex psychological occurrences such as instincts, feelings, repressed memories, and other internalized functions. Additionally, Jung's colleague and friend, Dr. Sigmund Freud, suggested three distinct levels of consciousness: the conscious (ego), the preconscious (superego), and the unconscious (id).

In order to better understand how the writer's mind works, I have simplified and applied both Jung and Freud's theories to uncover my own. As such, I believe the writer's mind is a collective, more specifically a trinity of thought centers—the conscious, the subconscious, and the shadow—each with its own voice, which can influence every aspect of storytelling.

The conscious mind is what we know, what's in front of us. Details and tasks. It holds us accountable for the work of actually sitting down to write. Fiction writers, for example, are conscious of outlines, plotting (or "pantsing," perhaps), character development, world-building, and tons of other details. Many of us are directly connected to and affected by our writer's workspaces, rituals, and schedules. All of these details inform our conscious voice, which sounds like this, "Mandy, you know you really should be writing and not scrolling through Instagram."

The writer's subconscious mind is more mysterious, but (thankfully) it has a voice that provides us with warnings. It's intuitive, offering nudges around decisions to make, things to be on the lookout for, darlings to murder, and feelings about certain people and situations. Our subconscious mind is that little voice that guides us. It's our Higher Self, Inner Voice, Spirit, the Universe, God, whatever you connect with most. In reference to the tarot, I think it's safe to say our subconscious mind is The Fool inside our brains.

Lastly, every writer I know has struggled once or a thousand times with what I refer to as "the shadow." The shadow is a voice that can plague a writer's thoughts, taking up more space than necessary and causing more harm than should be reasonably possible. Our shadow can be our inner critic, that nagging voice of self-doubt. Shadow can invoke imposter syndrome, causing us to question whether we even have the right to write. Shadow can be a liar, a cheat, and a thief. It uncovers shame, doubt, and vulnerability around bad reviews or other critical feedback, keeping harmful words and feelings reeling over and over again and ultimately stealing our joy. On the other hand, shadow can also be an inner, wounded, and vulnerable child—a part of us that needs holding, cherishing, and grace.

Connecting the Story

In the tarot, The Moon is just as mysterious and wondrous as the mystic story-teller's mind, and its components align perfectly to the trinity of the conscious, subconscious, and the shadow. The Moon reflects the sun, offering a light in the dark, a beacon for moving through the night. Let's consider this card's details and then dive deeper into its esoteric meanings.

What's happening in The Moon card?

The most obvious aspect of The Moon card is the actual moon, its combination of phases—full, crescent, and eclipse (that even includes the pareidolic "man in the moon")—positioned against an indigo night sky. Radiating down from the moon are several sparkles. These glimmers are a callback to the yod, which, as we learned in The Tower card profile (See Chapter 17, *Key 16 – The Tower*), is the Hebrew letter that represents a divine point of energy and God's presence among us. Prominently featured beneath the moon and erected at the top of a hilly range is a set of twin pillars; these are believed to be the same herms present in the background of the Death card. A path trudges between the herms, and an expanse of lawn stretches down to a body of water. On opposite sides of the path a pair of dogs howl at the moon, while a crustaceous creature (we'll call it a "crayfish") emerges from the water.

In the *Mystic Storyteller Tarot*, the muses for these two pups are my very own: Kirby (left) and Indigo (right). To me, there's no mystery in how writers are not only kept company by our furry familiars but find them to be a whimsical source of inspiration.

The Moon: A Deep Dive

When The Moon presents itself to you, you can bet that self-reflection and/or subconscious decision-making are on the rise. Whether The Moon's energy represents you, the writer, or your characters, someone is on the brink of internal revelation or struggle. Considering the latter, The Moon can illuminate misperceptions, veiling the truth and obscuring understanding. Similar to how The Hermit's lantern lights his path of wisdom and knowledge, the light of The Moon illuminates our triad of inner consciousness.

From a writer's perspective, The Moon card implies the need to pay attention to the distinct voices at work as you venture along your path: your conscious voice, represented by the dog on the left, your subconscious voice, represented by the dog on the right, and your shadow voice, represented by the crayfish. Whichever rises, you are encouraged to listen to it. However, which one will you allow the most space? Which voice is the most practical? Which is guiding you in the direction of what's best for you and your craft? Which is misleading you? Which is provoking fear? Is your intuition telling you to be on alert? Being ill-prepared to format your book for a specific self-publishing platform? As you move forward on your writer's journey, take a mental inventory of your intuitive concerns and fears, but also look outwardly. Glance around, to the left and right, yes, but also behind you. What needs your attention along your way?

The Moon, Reversed: The Shadow

When The Moon shows up in the reversed position, the path is clear. Your writer's brain can find rest on an evident decision; there is no trickery at play. Your characters are liberated, shaking off those pesky shoulder-surfing angel wolves and devil dogs and discovering for themselves exactly how they feel about a situation, the best ways to respond, and they can look forward to truth and understanding of interactions with other characters. There is no mystery, deceit, delusion, drama, haters, or smoke and mirrors. A reversed Moon indicates nothing but clear night skies with cloudless days to follow.

Notable Symbols in The Moon Card

Astrology—Pisces
Element—Spirit / Water

Other symbols

Crayfish—This creature represents emotions, water, and one's shadow voice.

Dog—Dogs are symbolic of loyalty, friendship, confidence, and the conscious voice.

Eclipse—An eclipse symbolizes an awakening, a shift in energy, and a transition.

Pillars—Also called "herms," these pillars are a gateway, welcoming or beckoning choices or decisions.

Water—In this card, water represents clarity, fluidity, healing, and intuition.

Numerological Associations with The Moon

In Numerology, the number 18 is formed by the numbers one and eight, one representing new beginnings and new ideas, and eight representing achievement and manifestation. When adding 1 + 8, we get 9, which means completions and endings. Therefore, in the tarot, The Moon is associated with The Hermit and the Nines.

The Moon, Characterized

Overall characteristics of The Moon include the proverbial dark night of the soul, deception, dreams, fear, good vs. evil, illusion, imagination, initiation, intuition, mysticism, mystery, night owls, reflection, the subconscious, and the unknown.

If The Moon represents the theme or attitudes of your character(s), there could be some sneaky, underhandedness on the horizon for your protagonist, while your antagonist slinks along in the cut, rearing on their haunches, and preparing to strike. The Moon might signify your antagonist's internal struggles and fears, those layers not immediately revealed. Could your story benefit from humanizing that character so the reader sees a glimpse of their vulnerabilities? Is it time to provide some backstory around why your antagonist has become such a jerk and the internal battles fueling their messiness? And what about your sweet, innocent, naïve protagonist? Has The Moon shone a side of them that has become ruthless as they face their fears?

Notable characters, people, or personas

The Moon can be a writer, a pack of dogs, a wolfpack, a zoo, a farm, two siblings, twins, triplets, or two siblings and their irritating cousin. It can be George Bailey of *It's a Wonderful Life*; Professor Lupin; Scott Howard, Scott McCall, Jacob Black and Sirius Black; Mr. Malcolm; and Mr. Wickham.

After learning more about The Moon, who would you add to this list?

Word List

astral	expansion	luminary	opaque
channeling	falsehood	lunar	psychic
complexity	hidden	magic/k	secrets
confusion	illusion	mediumship	subconscious
creativity	insecurity	misleading	translucent
deception	insight	misunderstanding	treasure
decisions	insomnia	mystery	trinity
dreams	intuition	mystical	uncertainty
eclipse	jaded	mysticism	unconscious
empathy	knowing	occult	veiled

Spread: Illuminating for Clarity

The Moon illuminates the dark, shining just enough light to see a situation for what it is. When we look deep enough, the moon's light can reveal aspects of the situation that were previously unknown or unrealized. As such, when you are faced with circumstances in which you need more clarity, this spread can help. If you are a writer of fiction, you can use this spread from your character's point of view in order to gain clarity around a scene or plotline.

1. Shuffle your deck until you are satisfied that the cards are ready, and then find The Moon card. Place it in the space for Card 1.
2. Next, find the card just before The Moon and lay it in the space for Card 2. This card represents what's on your conscious mind in this situation.
3. Now, find the two cards that followed The Moon and place them in the spaces for Card 3 and Card 4, respectively. These cards inform what's on your subconscious mind (Card 3) and the shadow voice (Card 4) misleading you in this situation.
4. Ask yourself the following questions, using your intuition to consider the answers. If you are using this spread from your character's point of view, imagine them asking themselves these questions.

Card 1: The Moon, illuminating the situation.
Card 2: The Conscious Mind – What do I know for certain about this situation?
Card 3: The Subconscious Mind – What do I need to pay more attention to in this situation?
Card 4: The Shadow – What is misleading me in this situation?

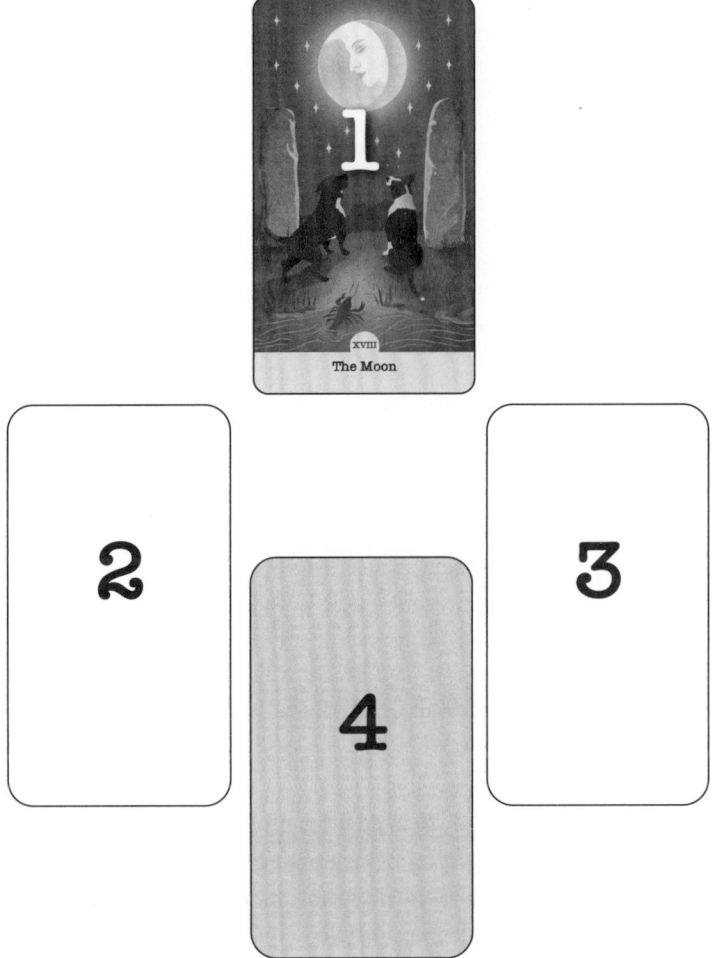

Key 19 or XIX:
The Sun

XIX

The Sun

Throughout my lifetime, I have dedicated a lot of thought to the concept of happiness. I've studied the idea from a psychological lens: through positive psychology, toxic positivity, and even addiction. I understand the varying definitions of happiness and I'm clear that it's a state of mind. On the other hand, I've wondered how and why people arrive at said state of mind. How do people, evoke happiness? Does it come from a place, a thing, a feeling, an activity? Why do people enjoy cosplay? Puppies? Seafood? Hunting Bigfoot? Watching those videos of people carving huts and swimming pools out of the middle of the dense jungle? And why, exactly, do rainbow sprinkles make me so unbelievably happy? We're talking bright-eyed, wide-smiled giddiness! After all, they're just cornstarch and food coloring. Even so, bring that container over here and pour those multicolored waxy bits all over my entire life, please.

Happiness. I'm convinced that I've dissected every aspect of the construct—from joy to satisfaction, contentment, well-being, and wonder. For many, happiness is a choice, and as I've grown older and wiser I've observed that in addition to all of the aforementioned themes, happiness is both relative and intentional.

Years ago, when I was working with the Alzheimer's Association, Georgia Chapter, I facilitated a family caregiver support group in a rural town almost an hour away from our office. One of the meeting's attendees was the husband of a person living with Alzheimer's. An older gentleman, at the very least an octogenarian, the man greeted me at the door, and I helped him step into the room. "How are you today?" I asked him. His response was both startling and puzzling, and it has stayed with me all these many years later. That man looked me square in the eye, smiled, and said, "I've never had so little and felt so good."

While that gentleman had every reason to be sad about his circumstances—visiting his wife, who had Alzheimer's disease, at a skilled nursing facility—his joy seemed intentional, as if given those circumstances happiness was the best option he had. While there were plenty of unavoidable negatives, the man chose to focus on the positive. What were the positives? In dissecting the meaning of his answer, I would venture a guess that despite watching his partner suffer, maybe he was carefree because visiting his wife at a nursing home was a much better option than visiting her at her grave. As such, perhaps he intended on making the most of the time he had remaining.

Connecting the Story

Like The Sun card's placement along The Fool's Journey, I am over The Moon to explore how it can cast its cheerful rays onto your storytelling practice. In continuing to contemplate happiness, joy, success, and all the feel-good words from a storyteller's point of view, let's examine this card and its possible meanings.

What's happening in The Sun card?

A large yellow sun shines bright above a field of sunflowers. The flowers peek over a stone or brick wall where a little girl is riding a white horse. The child wears a flowered crown, and in her grasp is a large red crayon, its color reminiscent of the clothing worn by several figures in the tarot. The little girl's golden T-shirt is printed with a pinwheel design, a symbol of fun, happiness, and childlike wonder. The girl extends her arms out, not holding onto her horse but embracing the thrill of riding into a shiny new day full of possibility and joyful blessings.

The Sun: A Deep Dive

The Sun shines light on our actions, dreams, reactions, and how we outwardly express our desires and urges, whether conscious or subconscious. Like my story about the elderly gentleman who chose to keep a positive outlook on his situation, this sunny revelation reminds me of something else I heard that I believe resonates with The Sun card.

In the recent past, I was listening to an episode of one of my favorite podcasts, The Tarot Diagnosis, when Shannon, podcast host and my dear friend, said, and I paraphrase, "Never forget about the time when you dreamed of having the things you have right now."

As a storyteller, I can relate profoundly to this message, because at the time of penning this book, happiness doesn't look the same as it did when I first started writing. Years ago, simply finishing the first draft of my very first novel was the goal I dreamed of most. Once that accomplishment was reached, the goal post moved, and writerly happiness moved with it; I found excitement and joy (initially) in seeking literary agent representation. After the newness of that process faded and the struggle of rejection wore me down, I changed course and endeavored to self-publish. That process brought so much fulfillment to my craft! From cover to cover, I was able to design every aspect of my work, an undertaking that was incredibly rewarding.

Today, as I write this book—while I'm still not a world-renowned novelist and my work hasn't yet won an Oscar or a Pulitzer—I haven't forgotten all the blood, sweat, and tears that brought me to where I am right at this very moment. I appreciate every experience, every lesson learned, and my writerly happiness has shifted to writing this book, researching for a Southern Gothic, magical realism series of novels, and dreaming of the moment when the accolades and honors start galloping into my life.

As I venture through the next phase of my storytelling journey, I'm choosing to keep The Sun card in my pocket, a reminder that I have achieved everything I once dreamed of accomplishing.

The Sun, Reversed: The Shadow

When The Sun is reversed, you and/or your characters could be dangerously close to being a "Pollyanna." First appearing in Eleanor H. Porter's novel by the same name, Pollyanna was an orphan who had an excessively positive attitude. Since the novel's publishing in 1913, the name Pollyanna has become a term synonymous with a person who is positive to the extent that it becomes unhealthy. People who display Pollyanna-ish attitudes tend to avoid negative thoughts entirely. Such an outlook leans toward toxic positivity, which can be detrimental to oneself and others.

Another interpretation of The Sun reversed is falling victim to or being taken advantage of by someone who portrays themselves as a positive, kind, and jovial person. Even the sun can burn you if you stay in it too long.

Notable Symbols in The Sun Card

Astrology—Sun
Element—Spirit / Fire

Other symbols

Absence of a saddle—Riding without a saddle indicates positive thinking and free will.

Flowered crown—Crowns represent ego, intellect, and higher thinking.

Red—The color red represents love, passion, and power.

Stone or brick wall—A wall represents safety and security.

Sun—In the tarot, the sun and/or its rays convey confidence, clarity, direction, energy, life, peace, positivity, and warmth.

Sunflowers—Sunflowers indicate adoration, fame, and fortune.

Yellow—Yellow is the color of joy, energy, happiness, honor, intellect, and loyalty.

White horse—White is symbolic of purity and horses in the tarot represent direction, movement, and progress.

Numerological Associations with The Sun

In the tarot, The Sun is associated with Wheel of Fortune, The Magician, and the Aces. In numerology, the number 19 is related to completions, success, honor, joy, and happiness. When combined, 1 + 9 = 10, which harkens back to The Wheel of Fortune. Tens in the tarot represent finality and/or a return to center. And when reduced again, 1 + 0 = 1, the number of new beginnings and new ideas. One is represented by The Magician in the Major Arcana and the Aces in the Minor.

The Sun, Characterized

What makes a writer happier than ____ ? You fill in the blank: quiet, free time, reading, people-watching, tea, coffee, notebooks. For me, it's writing. When The Sun card shines on your writer's desk, representing you, the storyteller, whatever you've been working on, however you've been writing it, stay the course. Your writing is a gift to this world. The Sun is both illuminating and enlightening, and it can bring clarity and awareness. As for the act of storytelling, that awareness looks like knowing exactly what you want to write, how to write it, and clarity in identifying an audience and market for it.

If The Sun card represents your character(s), that individual is most likely a happy person. Perhaps they're a baby, a young child, a person with good news, or someone with a proposal.

Notable characters, people, or personas

Sunny in J. D. Salinger's *The Catcher in the Rye*; people who live in Finland;[61] Pharrell Williams; Betty White; Leslie Allen Jordan; Soleil Moon Frye; Eddie Jaku; a happy baby or child; Tibetan Buddhist monk Matthieu Ricard who has been called "the world's happiest man."[62]

After learning more about The Sun, who would you add to this list?

Word List

abundance	childlike	happiness	Pollyanna
acceptance	confidence	honesty	positivity
achievement	endurance	innocence	radiance
ambitious	energy	intensity	reliable
attention-seeking	enlightenment	joy	success
beginnings	excited	life	sunny disposition
blessings	fame	manifestation	truth
celebration	fortunate	nourish	vacation
centering	fulfillment	opening	vitality
childhood	fun	optimism	warmth

Spread: The Sun is Also a Star

Each and every day we can be certain about three things: the sun will rise, the sun will set, and there is happiness to be found in the in-between. In that regard, I have designed this quick and simple spread to help you intentionally seek more happiness and joy in your day. Use this spread for daily inspiration, or if you are a fiction writer, you can use this spread to help your character, scene, story, or world to shine bright.

1. Shuffle your deck until you are satisfied that the cards are ready.
2. Next, find The Sun and lay it on the space for Card 2.
3. The card in front of The Sun (Card 1) indicates what you have to look forward to today, and the card behind The Sun (Card 3) shines light on unseen victories.
4. Ask yourself the following questions, using your intuition to consider the answers. If you are using this spread from your character's point of view, imagine them asking themselves these questions.

Card 1: What do I have to look forward to today?
Card 2: The Sun, shining bright on your day.
Card 3: What are the unseen victories in my day?

Key 20 or XX:

Judgement

To this point in my life, the construct of change has presented itself most frequently in the form of travel. And I absolutely love to travel. Wanderlust is one of my strongest motivators. From January through December of 2019, I traveled the entire year. The trips were mainly for work, but I also took a few personal excursions, all of them life-giving. They offered me an opportunity to grieve—the loss of my Gran that January, and the loss of who I used to be as a creative person before I became her caregiver. On the other hand, traveling also provided me with time to start planning my life again and I began asking myself questions that might help resurrect my creative purpose. What am I going to do with myself? What should I write next? To that point, I had published a total of six novels and none of them were selling. While I enjoyed writing and the process of book design and self-publishing, once my books had launched, they just kind of went nowhere.

What is the purpose of doing all the hard work to publish my novels if they aren't getting into the hands of readers who might enjoy them?

As fall of 2019 painted the trees and cooled summer's sting, I began skipping lunch during the weekdays and going down to the gym in the building where I worked. I put in my earbuds and watched *The Office* while walking on the treadmill. After several days and multiple episodes, my thoughts began straying to my books, and I found that I couldn't focus on what was happening at good ol' Dunder-Mifflin Paper Company. What should I do with my novels? How am I ever going to increase my sales? What is the purpose of even trying? Those were the questions that seemed to overpower even the inimitable Michael Scott.

One day in late September, I hopped on the treadmill and untangled my earbuds. What am I going to do with my books? There was the nagging thought again. As I walked, I considered what I had determined the root problem in my lack of book sales: marketing. I didn't market my work—at all—and I had no clue how and where to even start. On a whim, I opened YouTube and typed How to market... and true to YouTube's intuitive search mechanism (or God or the Universe or Lady Luck), the rest of the sentence populated: *How to market your book.*

I clicked on the words and an onslaught of videos resulted. The first one that caught my eye was the face of a young woman with kind eyes, a sweet smile, and the cutest little corgi pup. I clicked on her video and watched. And then I watched another and another and another until every day at lunch all I was watching while on the treadmill were young adult fantasy author Bethany Atazadeh's videos around writing and self-publishing.

While the first of Bethany's videos that I discovered was a checklist of the top things to consider when marketing one's book, the video that sparked an Aha! moment was one that provided insight around developing one's author platform. An author platform? I thought. Until that point, the notion hadn't been anywhere near my radar. I continued watching, listening to Bethany describe the importance of building a personal brand, engaging with social media, and providing value to readers and fans. The experience of learning entirely new-to-me practices around marketing books and developing real, quality relationships with other readers and writers was absolutely invaluable. What happened to me on the treadmill during that time was a revelation: I was called to do something more with my creative endeavors.

For the two months that followed stumbling upon that first *How to Market Your Book* video, the Aha! sparks ignited a creative inferno. By November, I had entirely reinvented myself as a storyteller; this included my own personal brand, an interactive website, an overhaul of my social media accounts, two separate pen names, all-new redesigned book covers, and a marketing plan. Those treadmill video sessions uncovered aspects of self-publishing I hadn't even known existed.

I was set ablaze! I was motivated, and for the first time in years I was excited about the direction my creative purpose was moving.

Purpose is an incredibly rewarding and transformative construct. In my opinion, without creative purpose, a void can swallow up a writer's joy, causing floundering, worry, anxiety, depression, and disappointment. For me, when I uncovered a new purpose for my storytelling endeavors, identifying goals, and then easing into a writing routine that actively supported those goals, my entire life changed.

Finding purpose in what I love doing has been a revelation, causing a ripple effect that has impacted how I feel about my physical self, how I view my surroundings, and how I manage my anxiety and depression. In the words of the gentleman from my profile on The Sun card, "I've never had so little [lack of purpose] and felt so good!"

Connecting the Story

In the tarot, the Judgement card is a calling. It beckons us to stand up, dust off the monotony of our lives, shake off the listlessness, and lean into the beckoning of something new, something more, and/or something bigger and different than our wildest imaginings. This type of purpose-driven change is invaluable to us, and quite often it happens on a whim, out of the blue, or directly from the Heavens above. Let's examine the Judgement card and uncover how it relates to purpose, among other constructs.

What's happening in the Judgement card?

Floating down from a cloud set against a clear, ice-blue sky, a winged, angelic figure showers writing tools down from the heavens. The angel's eyes rival the blue of both the sky and the water below, his locs swaying in his descent, scarlet wings splayed. Below his generous offering are four nude figures, their bodies frigid as if they've risen from the dead. As if reaching for a second chance at penning their stories, they raise their arms raised with eager hope. In the background of this card, we can see an ice-capped mountain range, and the foreground is covered in an indigo lake (with its undead occupants).

Judgement: A Deep Dive

In the tarot, the Judgement card is one that, like The Star, uncovers a few vital RE-words: revelation, resurrection, rediscovery, revitalization, and repurposing. When this card lands on your writer's desk, you can bet you are being called to a higher purpose, you are experiencing a revival of energy, a renewed motivation, and/or a dream realized. Yes, on Pixie's illustration of this card those are dead bodies rising from their watery grave; however, there is nothing to fear when working with Judgement. On the contrary, Judgement is a card of revelation— of mind, body, energy, and spirit—and because this card is part of the Major Arcana, you can expect said revelation to be significant.

Revelation of mind could look like an epiphany after experiencing an extended bout of writer's block. It's an interested literary agent after you've filled your nail to capacity with rejections (See Chapter 17, *Key 1 – The Magician*).[63] As a writer, sometimes a revelation can be a new story idea that comes to you seemingly out of nowhere and all at once. It's the kind of idea that halts you from whatever you are doing in that moment and demands that you start drafting notes. Another revelation might be a grand announcement you've been waiting for: the acceptance of your piece into a literary anthology, winning a writing contest, a publishing offer, or the pinnacle (to me), a Pulitzer Prize in literature.

Judgement can also present as a physical revelation in that our bodies have the propensity for demanding that we listen to them. When we are hungry, thirsty, exhausted, in love, grieving, injured, or stressed our bodies often respond by demanding that we listen and act. On the other hand, Judgement can be an energetic calling. Consider the moments when you are inspired to write, make art, give the house a deep cleaning, organize the garage, book a much-needed getaway, or do something to help someone in need.

Lastly, in my experience Judgement has proven a revelation of spirit. It's waking up one day (most days), making my coffee, switching on my desk lamp, sitting down at my computer, and realizing that I might never become a famous, bestselling author... but that doesn't mean I can't—or that I shouldn't—persist with consistent effort toward writing what brings me happiness and purpose. Revelation of spirit looks like persistence and consistency. It's the gnawing urge to stick with this writing venture, the calling to see a story to its completion... no matter what or how many stories are lined up and waiting to be written.

Judgement is being called to write this book—to share with my fellow storytellers how I use the tarot to get inspired and remain that way. Even though there's a queue line of characters like Pinkie Perideaux waiting patiently (and some naggingly) to be assigned their stories, I've been called to finish this book, which has provided profound purpose.

Judgement, Reversed: The Shadow

When Judgement turns up in a reversed position on your desk, you can expect everything to stop. There's a significant barrier, an error in judgment, or the grounding of your plane. You and/or your characters might find yourselves stuck, in gridlock, at an impasse, or completely defeated. Stale mate. Now is not the time to take action; it's a time of waiting. Moreover, Judgement reversed can inform being treated unfairly, being judged, ostracized, marginalized, banished, jilted, ignored, discarded, or abandoned.

Notable Symbols in the Judgement Card

Astrology—Pluto
Element—Spirit / Fire

Other Symbols

Angel—There are differing opinions around which Archangel is featured in the Judgement card. While many believe the figure in Pamela Colman Smith's illustration to be Gabriel, the angel announcer, herald of visions, and messenger to God, others think this angel is Michael,[64] the protector and healer of people. In the book of Revelation, Michael was the defender of God's realm against Satan. As for our *Mystic Storyteller Tarot's* Judgement angel, I'll let you decide his identity.

The Color Blue—There is a lot of blue in this card, the color of calmness, harmony, life, peace, and spirituality.

Mountain range—In the tarot, mountains indicate structure and a steady foundation, security and protection.

Naked bodies—These figures represent rebirth or renewal of purpose and/or spirit.

Water—In the Judgement card, water is a symbol of intuition, the subconscious mind, and washing away the old in order to rise toward the new.

Numerological Associations with Judgement Card

In the tarot, the Judgement card is associated with The High Priestess and the Twos. In Numerology, the number 20 denotes the preparation for a spiritual journey.[65] The number is a reminder to take care of your whole self: mind, body, energy, and spirit. When broken down, 2 + 0 = 2; therefore, the Judgement card directly relates to The High Priestess. As you will recall from reading The High Priestess card profile, two is the number of duality, choice, union, and decision.

Judgement, Characterized

Along their Journey, The Fool is experiencing a final transition, leaving behind who they were before—and perhaps even during—their venture. If the Judgement card arises for you, perhaps you are moving on to a new way of thinking, living, creating, or simply being. Characteristically, this card is an epiphany, a crossroads, or a decision. It's an event or action that requires you and/or your characters to drop what you're doing and respond. Judgement can be an awakening, a fork in the road, a gate, a door, a crusade, a portal, or a last call to make a decision. It can be a direct calling to make something extraordinary of what you are writing and/or yourself.

Notable characters, people, or personas

Rand al'Thor in *The Wheel of Time*; Kratos in *God of War*; Christof, played by Ed Harris in The Truman Show; Soul Reapers or Shinigami in *Bleach*; Archangel Michael; Jesus Christ; Anubis; a sphinx; Odin; and Zeus.

After learning more about the Judgement card, who or what would you add to this list?

Word List

acceptance	decision-making	realization	resurrection
accountability	endings	rebirth	revelation
announcement	higher	receiving	rite of passage
atonement	consciousness	reckoning	second chances
awakening	inner calling	redemption	signal
beckoning	memories	reflection	summoning
calling	moving on	reincarnation	threshold
choices	outcomes	renewal	transcendence
confidence	pivotal	reparations	transition
conviction	purpose	rescue	turning point

Spread: A New Calling

When you hear the calling of a new creative endeavor—when a story beckons to be written, when you feel in your gut that a character, essay, poem needs your attention and energy—this spread can help answer that call. With this spread, you can uncover what you are being called to embrace and what you are being asked to shed in order to heed this new calling.

1. Shuffle your deck until you are satisfied that the cards are ready.
2. Next, find the Judgement card and lay it on the space for Card 2.
3. The card in front of Judgement (Card 1) represents what you are being called to embrace, and the card behind Judgement (Card 3) reveals what you are being asked to shed.
4. Ask yourself the following questions, using your intuition to consider the answers. If you are using this spread from your character's point of view, imagine them asking themselves these questions.

Card 1: What am I being called to embrace?
Card 2: Judgement card—the calling.
Card 3: What am I being asked to shed?

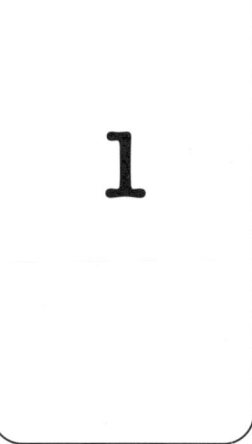

Key 21 or XXI:

The World

XXI

The World

In the mornings before work, while I'm "putting on my face," as we call it around these parts (AKA applying makeup), I love listening to podcasts.

One particular morning, while scrolling through Spotify in search of new podcasts to discover, researcher and storyteller Brené Brown's *Unlocking Us* climbed up my smartphone screen. I tapped on the icon, listened to an episode, and then found myself returning to the podcast again on my walk later that day, and then again in the car while driving to pick up dinner that evening. By the end of the week, I had binged a couple dozen episodes. I LOVED the show.

While I could go on and on about Brené's wisdom, my rabbit hole ventures through her research on shame and vulnerability, and her incredibly inspiring podcast guests, one of the greatest takeaways I've learned from *Unlocking Us* is a recurring theme across many episodes: the paradox of seeking joy in the midst of conflict.

In a conversation with her friend, author and activist Karen Walrond, Brené mentioned being "not okay" right now. At the time of the episode, "right now" was March 2022. Pandemic procedures were still in place, and the media was peppered with news about coronavirus variants, the prevalence of police brutality directed toward Black Americans, extremely upsetting laws being passed in both Karen and Brené's home state of Texas that demoralized trans children, and the war with Russia and Ukraine.

Despite being "not okay" with all of that fear, pain, and hardship, Karen reminded Brené of the importance of seeking joy.

How? I wondered. How can anyone seek joy in spite of all this heartbreak? In the podcast episode, Brené with Karen Walrond on *Accessing Joy and Finding Connection in the Midst of Struggle*, Karen reminds listeners that, and I paraphrase, "I am/we are responsible for accessing joy in order to remind ourselves of what's worth fighting for. No matter how small, you can hang hope onto joy and the intentional seeking of it."

I had to pause the podcast.

I returned my green-capped mascara wand back into its pink tube and opened my notes app on my phone. Immediately, I typed these words:

What's worth fighting for is worth living for is worth writing for.

I thought about the aforementioned situations that, like Brené, were also rendering me "not okay," and my mind drifted back into the past, recalling many struggles and hardships that had threatened to break me. They hadn't, though, and I remembered how far I had come despite them. Rather than ruin me, my experiences had inspired me to write about them, to wrangle the fear, pain, and difficulties and channel them into stories. I asked myself, How can I access joy in spite of the raging dumpster fires that threaten to steal it?

I can return to my core: I am an artist, advocate, and writer. Rather than continue to spiral beneath the horrors unfolding in my community and in the media, I can use what I've endured and make a difference in the lives of others. I can turn my struggles into stories.

Connecting the Story

In the tarot, The World card is The Fool's return—to home and/or to themselves—after their long, tedious, and sometimes heartbreaking journey. Like the adventurous Fool, you are also The World, and this card serves as a reminder that while you have endured struggle and suffering, despair and disappointment, you can always look around for reasons to seek joy, reasons to be grateful for how far you have come.

Storytellers spin our ideas and adventures into experiences that might make a difference in our life and in the lives of others. No matter what's going on in the world, in our communities, and/or in our day-to-day, there are always reasons for intentionally seeking joy. What's worth fighting for is worth living for is worth writing for. As I complete my own journey of writing each of the Major Arcana card profiles, I feel tremendous joy and accomplishment. Thank you for coming along this journey with me. Now, let's explore the meaning of The World card and all its festive and divine symbolism.

What's happening in The World card?

Immediately and prominently, we see a woman. She's older and wearing a gauzy white dress with a purple sash. In each of her hands, she holds a candle wand. Is she floating or is she dancing? Either way, she's seemingly satisfied with life and in total harmony with the four "fixed" signs of the zodiac, which are represented by the symbols in the card's four corners. The person at the top left corner represents Aquarius, an air sign; the eagle is Scorpio, a water sign; the lion represents Leo, a fire sign; and the ox is Taurus, an earth sign (You can find more on astrological correspondences in Chapter 23). Encircling the lady, we see a green oval-shaped wreath. It's wrapped at the top and bottom in red lemniscate ribbons. The shapes, symmetry, and symbolism of this card are similar to those found in the Wheel of Fortune.

The World: A Deep Dive

The World is completion, small and large. From the end of a week to the end of a life cycle, The World ushers in a return, either back to the start or onward to what comes next. The World is karmic fruition, the end of one journey and the start of something new.

The World is Saturday, the completion of the week. It's the day before an equinox or solstice. It's New Year's Eve. The World is a spiritual graduation, a coming of age, a return to center. From a writer's lens, The World marks the polishing of an outline, the end of a chapter, the finalization of a first draft, the conclusion of a project. You did it... and now you must do it even more.

If The World card lands on your desk, whatever it is that you are working on is in full alignment with the energy you've spent bringing it into fruition. You're right on track, most likely nearing an end, a conclusion, and you can anticipate the manifestation of all your efforts and consistency.

Along every phase of our creative journey, however, The World invites us to draw upon the four elements. Featured on the four corners of the card, clockwise from top left, we can see Air (Aquarius), Water (Scorpio), Fire (Leo), and Earth (Taurus). Air is a reminder that the sky is the limit—let those imaginations soar! Water endorses pouring one's all into our creative process... just don't forget to refill your cup. Fire is an invitation to set a fire in the soul, igniting creativity, and letting that energy imbue everything along its path. Finally, Earth cautions us to stay grounded when necessary and humbled always.

The World is a card of travel, especially long-distance, and exploration. Have you ever considered a writer's retreat? One of the most effective methods, for me, in helping to cultivate stories and develop characters has been immersing myself in their environments. For example, I have been planning a magical realism series that takes place in Central and Coastal Georgia and Florida. As such, when I've been able to, I've traveled to and spent a lot of time in Warm Springs, Savannah, and St. Augustine, my series' three main locations. For fantasy writers, however, you might venture somewhere reminiscent of your inspired world. Alternatively, if you are unable to travel, virtual immersion can be just as enlightening! Most of my inspiration is drawn from reading books within my project's genre and watching an abundance of movies that take place in similar settings.

No matter the approach, when it comes to inspiration, the sky's not even a limit, and The World card serves as a reminder of infinite opportunities to behold.

The World, Reversed: The Shadow

When The World is turned upside-down, everything pauses. Activities, travel, goals, they all hang in the balance. What's blocking your character from completing their journey? What's keeping you, the writer, from finishing that first draft? Something has been left undone and is waiting for action, either by you or your characters, whichever resonates. Decide what you can do in order to tie up those loose ends and set The World right again.

Notable Symbols in The World Card

Astrology—Saturn
Element—Spirit / Earth

Other Symbols

Four Figures—The Lion, the Ox, the Man, and the Eagle—in each of the card's corners represent the four elements: fire, earth, air, and water. They also represent the Four Evangelists, Matthew, Mark, Luke, and John. In astrology, these creatures represent Leo, Taurus, Aquarius, and Scorpio.

Eagle—This is the symbol for Scorpio, a water sign.

Lion—This is the symbol for Leo, a fire sign.

Head—This represents Aquarius, the water bearer, an air sign.

Ox—The oxen is the symbol for Taurus, an earth sign.

Purple sash—The color purple is associated with spirituality, enlightenment, and because the earliest purple fabric dyes were costly, only the wealthy could afford them. Therefore, the color came to be associated with royalty, luxury, and opulence.

Sky and clouds—Clouds represent higher thought, perspective, and elevated thinking.

Vesica Piscis—The shape made by the wreath is known as a Vesica Piscis, a geometric shape and sacred symbol formed by the intersection of two circles. Symbolically, this shape in The World card means the connecting of Heaven and Earth. The two circle halves are connected by a red lemniscate, the infinity symbol also found in The Magician and Strength cards. The Vesica Piscis represents divine femininity, fertility, the seed of life, and the Universal womb.[66]

White—This color symbolizes hope, peace, and purity. Historically, white has represented healing and protection, and in the tarot, it informs faith and innocence.

Wreath—In the tarot, wreaths symbolize accomplishment, achievement, success, triumph, and victory.

Numerological Associations with The World

In the tarot, The World is associated with The Empress and the Threes. In numerology, 21 denotes fulfillment and manifestation; however, when adding 2 + 1, the number reduces to three, which represents creativity, expression, growth, celebration, and longing.

The World, Characterized

The World is you and/or me after the completion of a journey. Because we are writers, that journey probably had something to do with a creative endeavor: a poem, book, memoir, blog post, short story, research paper, or any other writing project.

If The World represents your character(s), they have arrived at the completion of their own journey. Depending on where this card falls in the spread you are using, The World can mean that your character has completed a cycle and is ready to graduate on to something new. They are ready for what's to come next. The World is The Fool after their return home, the Divine Feminine, and Mother of the Universe. The person in this card might also be a cheerleader, an enlightened individual, a flight attendant, a hostess, a magician, a mother, and/or a witch.

Notable characters, people, or personas

Celie and Nettie as they reunite in *The Color Purple*; Mary, Mother of Jesus; Goddesses Aphrodite, Diana, Venus, and Hermaphroditus; The Earth Mother; Mother Nature; Tituba; Marie Laveau; Mother Shipton; Laurie Cabot; and/or Odysseus.

After learning more about The World, who would you add to this list?

Word List

abundance	elemental	infinity	relocation
accomplishment	encounter	integration	return
achievement	ending	intelligence	reunion
belonging	enlightenment	limitations	self-actualization
boundaries	eternity	nirvana	success
closure	exploration	outcomes	totality
completion	finality	performance	unity
conclusion	fulfillment	possibilities	universe
corral	harmony	profound	wholeness
culmination	homebound	realizations	world travel

my worlds collide.

Spread: Return to Self / Center

Alas, The Fool has returned from their journey, and you can bet they are affected (if not changed) from the inside out. Whether literal or metaphorical, this spread was designed for use after a long journey. After returning home from your experience, or upon arriving at your desired destination, use this spread to reveal all the ways in which your experience might have affected or changed you. For insight into a character you are writing, you might also use this spread from that characters' point of view.

1. Search your tarot deck for The World card and lay it on the center space for Card 1.
2. Next, shuffle your deck until you are satisfied that the cards are ready, and then turn the deck facedown as if you were about to deal them.
3. From the top of the deck, start turning cards over onto the space for Card 2. When the first Cups card lands on this space, move on to Card 3.
4. Repeat the process by turning over cards and laying them on the space for Card 3 until you arrive at your first Swords card.
5. Repeat again for Card 4 (Wands) and Card 5 (Pentacles).
6. Ask yourself the following questions, using your intuition to consider the answers. If you are using this spread from your character's point of view, imagine them asking themselves these questions.

Card 1: The World
Card 2: Aquarius / Water / Heart / Cups—How has this journey touched my heart?
Card 3: Scorpio / Air / Mind / Swords—What aspects of this journey have influenced my way of thinking?
Card 4: Leo / Fire / Spirit / Wands—How has this journey changed my spirit?
Card 5: Taurus / Earth / Body / Pentacles—What aspects of my body have been affected by this journey?

Spread: Return to Self / Center

Chapter 18: Minor Arcana — Everyday Stories

· · · · · · · · · · · · · · · · · · · ·

Meaning "lesser secrets," the Minor Arcana includes 56 cards that illustrate day-to-day themes such as emotions, relationships, home, work, change, thought, enterprise, desire, and conflict. Also referred to as "the pips," the Minor Arcana cards are organized by suit: Cups, Pentacles (sometimes called "Coins" or "Discs"), Swords, and Wands (sometimes called "Rods"). Additionally, the suits each represent an element: Cups are water, Pentacles are earth, Swords are air, and Wands are fire. There's a fifth element represented in the tarot: spirit, and it can be found in each and every card.

Within each Minor Arcana suit in the *Mystic Storyteller Tarot*, you will find 14 cards: 10 illustrated pips and four Court cards, or "Courts." Like face cards on a traditional playing card deck, the Courts include the Page, Knight, Queen, and King.

In the sections to follow, I have segmented the Minor Arcana into three groups: the suits and their elemental correspondences, the numbered groups (Aces, Twos, Threes, etc.), and the Court cards. Let's start reviewing the suits and their elemental associations.

· · ·  · · ·

cups	pentacles	swords	wands

water	earth	air	fire
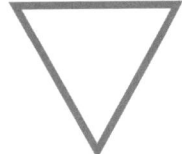	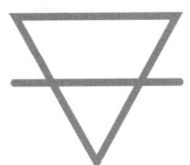		
heart	body	mind	spirit

Section 1 – The Suits: Elemental Correspondences

To expand on what you learned about the *Mystic Storyteller Tarot* in Chapter 12, the Minor Arcana's suits directly align with a given element. Moreover, each element directly informs a specific aspect of the human condition: the Cups reflect what's felt in the heart, the Pentacles suggest what's tangible to the body, the Swords offer a peek inside the mind, and the Wands spark intrigue from deep within one's spirit. In the four sections to follow, I provide an overview of the Minor Arcana suits as they relate to their assigned element.

The Cups

Ruled by water, the suit of Cups relates to the emotional, social, or relational aspects of our everyday lives. Cups cards are aligned with the heart, conveying human feelings and sentiment. Like water, the Cups can be deep or shallow, but they always find a way. They persevere, filling in the blanks and nourishing the heart. They express empathy, feelings, intuition, psychic energy, relationships, and spirituality. On their lower polarity, the Cups can be flooded with uncontrollable emotion, and they can also be emptied, giving all of themselves to serve the needs of others.

In the *Mystic Storyteller Tarot*, the Cups suit is stocked with coffee cups, teacups, and other vessels the writer's workspace often collects.

The Pentacles

The suit of Pentacles is ruled by the element of earth, which relates to everyday physical and material concerns, such as matters of the body, home, and work. Pentacles cards align with physical human needs, and they inform how we relate to money, possessions, and anything tangible in the material, practical world. Like earth, the Pentacles are sturdy, tangible, and foundational. They are predictable and promote growth and production. On their lower polarity, the Pentacles can be rigid, unforgiving, and heavily guarded. They can become too grounded, keeping one held down or "stuck in the mud."

In the *Mystic Storyteller Tarot*, the Pentacles suit includes physical tools a storyteller uses for their craft, such as books, typewriters, notepads, and electronic devices.

The Swords

Ruled by the element of air, the Swords suit relates to ambition, curiosity, intellect, thoughts, and conflicting aspects of our everyday lives. Swords cards are aligned with the mind, conveying communication, intuition, philosophy, and psychological aspects of being human. Like air, the Swords breathe life into the everyday. They circulate and transport thoughts, reasoning, and dreams. They can speak ideas into fruition, incite conflict, and cut through or sharpen motivation. On their lower polarity, Swords cards can be clouded, chilly, brisk, forceful, unpredictable, and unstable. If left untethered, they can float away and become lost or confused.

In the *Mystic Storyteller Tarot*, the Swords suit is populated with ink pens of all types and styles. After all, the pen is mightier than the sword.

The Wands

The suit of Wands is ruled by the element of fire, the energy of action, ambition, drive, and passion. Like the Pentacles cards, the Wands can relate to work and career; however, Wands energy originates from spirit. They inform the internal aspects of being human, such as inner growth and personal development. The Wands convey action and imagination, the fire within that ignites purpose, sparks creativity, and keeps our carnal motivators smoldering. They express creativity, desire, enterprise, ingenuity, and inspiration. On their lower polarity, and like fire, the Wands can be aggressive, out of control, and they can initiate permanent change.

In the *Mystic Storyteller Tarot*, the Wands suit features candles and pencils, fire and wood to ignite a writer's inspiration.

What's next?

You just learned about the Minor Arcana and their elemental correspondences. Next up, I will share with you how the Minors are distinguished by number. In the section to follow, you will learn about the Aces, Twos, Threes, and so on.

Practice Activity: A Suitable Story

This activity will give you the opportunity to select one of those suits—I recommend the one that resonates with you most profoundly—and practice mystic storytelling.

What you need for this activity:

- Your *Mystic Storyteller Tarot* deck.
- Your favorite tools for notetaking.
- Your intuition.

Part One:

1. Sort through your tarot deck and pull out all the cards in the suit of your choice—the Cups, Pentacles, Swords, or Wands— and then set aside the rest of your deck.
2. Next, lay the cards on their corresponding spaces, Ace through King.
3. Considering the cards from left to right, what story is unfolding across this suit? Use your intuition and draft the story you see the cards sharing.

Part Two:

4. Put your tarot deck back together in its entirety and shuffle the cards.
5. When you are satisfied that the cards are shuffled well, turn the deck facedown as if you were about to deal them.
6. Turn cards over onto the first space until you arrive at the first Ace, laying it on top.
7. Move to the space for the Two and repeat the process, turning cards over until you arrive at your first Two.
8. Do the same for spaces Three (III or 3) through King. At any point, if you run out of cards simply collect the cards beneath the previous spaces and reshuffle your deck, repeating the process until you have a single card turned over for each space.
9. From left to right, Ace to King, what story are these cards telling? Use your intuition and draft the story as it unfolds.

Section 2–
The Numbers: Numbered Correspondences

In Chapter 22 – *Numerology: Tarot by the Numbers*, I provide a brief overview of numerology and its influence on the tarot. This chapter, however, offers an introduction to the Minor Arcana's illustrated pip cards Ace through Ten (X or 10) and their various numerological associations. Additionally, similar to the Major Arcana card profiles, each numbered grouping includes details and considerations that can help spark intuition and inspire storytelling.

Regarding reversals, as you examine each Minor Arcana card, you are encouraged to intuit your own interpretations of its reversed state. Chapter 16 – *Intuiting Reversals* offers my own thoughts around what the card might represent when it appears upside-down on your desk.

Starting with the Aces and concluding with the Tens, here's what you can expect to find within each card grouping:

Summary and Possible Meanings

For every numbered group, I provide an overview of traditional meanings along with my own interpretations from a writer's point of view. I also offer information specifically relevant to the writer as a person and how one might relate to the individual and/or constructs within the numbered groups.

Everyday Constructs

Within this part of each card, I have included considerations for how the scenario unfolding within the card might represent one or more everyday constructs. These insights might be especially helpful to the fiction writer. However, as mentioned in the Major Arcana, you are encouraged to explore how the cards resonate with you in ways that are unique to your own intuitive insights.

Questions

Each Minor Arcana numbered group includes a selection of questions you can ask if the cards are among your tarot guideposts (See *Practice Activity: Your Tarot Guideposts*, following Chapter 6), and/or if the cards appear in a spread. These questions are crafted to amplify intuition, and they can be asked from the perspective of a fictional character, if desired.

Word List

To conclude each Minor Arcana numbered group, I have provided a list of keywords that can help inspire storytelling, spark creativity, and foster memorization of the cards' meaning(s). However, you are encouraged to build on the keyword lists, adding your own words. From here, let's start with the Aces.

Minor Arcana
The Aces

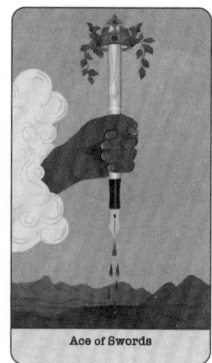

Ace of Cups   Ace of Pentacles   Ace of Swords   Ace of Wands

The Magician

Although not numbered, the Aces are considered by many the first card of the Minor Arcana suits. Corresponding with The Magician, the first numbered card of the Major Arcana, I look at the hand plunging through the clouds on each Ace card as that of The Magician offering up their sacred tools. Alternatively, perhaps we are witnessing the hand of God providing unexpected gifts at the very moment of need. The Aces are the initiator of each suit, seeds planted to encourage growth of each Cup, Pentacle, Sword, and Wand to follow. Aces can represent birth, bravery, ego, gifts, inspiration, initiative, identity, independence, initiation, new beginnings, novel ideas, offers, opportunity, potential, and self-confidence.

Ace of Cups: Everyday Constructs

The Ace of Cups is a gift from the heart. It's pure emotion, enough to fill every cup in the suit. This Ace is a direct connection to the gods, whose gifts are abundant. If this card lands on your desk, you can expect an overwhelm of emotions. Perhaps your feelings around what you are writing right now are in overdrive. Use these feelings, as they are a gift. Journal about them. Jot a rudimentary outline for your next project. Wrap up your current story. Either way, the Universe is allowing you to experience such an abundance of emotion for a reason. Accept and apply it. Pour it into the cracks and let it help you find a way.

As the Aces are initiators, the Ace of Cups can inform the occurrence of a new connection or relationship. Because the details haven't yet been revealed, you are encouraged to take a communion of faith and hope. Have faith that what you're experiencing is serving your best interests, even if you don't yet understand the details. In addition to investing in hope, this card could mean the birth of a new baby, publishing a book, or a deluge of emotion initiated by an event of a comparable emotional caliber.

Ace of Pentacles: Everyday Constructs

The Ace of Pentacles is the seed from which all material blessings originate for the body, home, or career. It's a gift substantial enough to suffice every coin in the suit. Whether this card applies to you, the writer, or to your fictional characters, an opportunity is being offered. Perhaps it concerns what you're writing or what's happening to your character at present? Is a publishing contract on the horizon? Are you being commissioned to write a book forward for another author? Are you to expect an abundance of book sales? Is a business partnership underway? No matter the blessing, when this card shows up, you can bet that either you or your character(s) are about to reap the rewards of all your diligence and hard work.

At its core, the Ace of Pentacles can represent any new gain: a business deal, an inheritance, a lottery win, a monetary gift, any unexpected wealth, a raise or promotion, a new home or appliance for the home, a new car, or a new work assignment that will bring about financial gains.

Ace of Swords: Everyday Constructs

The Ace of Swords is the clearest thought, sharpest idea, and the keenest intuition in the Minor Arcana. An intellectual gift, this Ace is The Magician's brightest idea, passed along for you to carry out. This card reveals an opportunity for an exciting new endeavor, a thought wielded into fruition. Consider the opportunity; however, be sure not to hang up your hat on your other endeavors. This card is an invitation to fight shiny object syndrome. Being presented with new ideas can be exciting and fruitful, but just be sure to complete what you're working on first. The Ace of Swords is a reminder to maintain a sharp focus on the details and timeline, and it can also suggest a new challenge or conflict. Depending on how you or your fictional characters respond to such an initiation will reveal whether the event was a learning opportunity, a risk, or a headwind.

Ace of Wands: Everyday Constructs

The first spark of fire from The Magician's wand, the Ace of Wands is a gift of inspiration. From this initiating spark, the rest of the suit is ignited. Every Wand throughout the suit is a shard splintered from this Ace. At its core, this card can represent a new passion, self-esteem, internal fire, inner wildness, and the flame of spirit. The Ace of Wands expresses ambition, creative energy, drive, passion, a new project, a new beginning, and willpower.

For the writer, the Ace of Wands incites all the fiery idioms, adding fuel to the fire, lighting a fire under [whatever or whomever)], but where there's smoke, there's fire, so be careful not to jump from the frying pan into the fire. If this card lands on your desk, it can be received as a creative gift; however, on its lower polarity, this card is a warning. After all, fire can easily spread out of control; understand that when you grasp this wand, you are accepting full responsibility for whatever magic (or mayhem) it conjures.

Questions

When the Aces land on your desk, ask yourself the following questions, answering them intuitively by recording your immediate thoughts. These questions can also be asked from the fictional character's perspective.

- **Ace of Cups:** How can I express and share my heart without pouring too much from my cup?
- **Ace of Pentacles:** How will this gift foster growth and prosperity that are in my best interest?
- **Ace of Swords:** What new idea, concept, or conflict needs my attention right now?
- **Ace of Wands:** What is at the core of my wildest desire?

Word List

cups	pentacles	swords	wands
abundance	beginnings	breath	ambition
birth	budgeting	clairvoyance	desire
bliss	energy	clarity	endeavor
creativity	fortunate	communication	enterprise
emotion	found money	conflict	expression
energy	gift	courage	fire
expression	goal-setting	decision	gift
feeling	greed	defeat	ignite
flooded	investment	discipline	impotence
gift	manifestation	focus	inspiration
happiness	materialistic	forceful	invention
love	monetary gift	gift	motivation
new baby	new job	goal	new venture
new love	new money	idea	opportunity
opportunities	opportunities	illusion	optimism
overflowing	planning	inspiration	passion
overjoyed	potential	intuition	pessimism
overwhelmed	poverty	invention	potential
pleasure	promotion	logic	power
potential	prosperity	mental	powerlessness
proposal	raise	strategy	spark
rebirth	rebirth	success	spirit
receptive	seed	thinking	unruly
sensitivity	success	truth	wild
spirituality	valuable	vision	willpower

Minor Arcana
The Twos

In the Minor Arcana, the Twos often reveal agreements, balance, choice, compromise, contract, cooperation, decisions, diplomacy, duality, harmony, opposition, partnership, tranquility, and union. They serve as a reminder that there are at least two sides to every story. The Twos align with The High Priestess, the keeper of what's known and unknown. They receive knowledge and instruction from The High Priestess, and then decide on a direction for pushing forward.

When writing fiction, the Twos can help with factors such as choice, decision-making, dialogue, and direction (east or west, left or right, etc.). On their lower polarity, the Twos can express fickleness, indifference, and uncertainty.

Two of Cups: Everyday Constructs

When the Two of Cups lands on your desk, you can expect to find yourself entering into a creative partnership, or maybe you've been considering a proposal to work on a project with someone else—an editor or cover designer, perhaps? For the writer, this card can indicate an agreement or conversation with others. Are you the gal on the left receiving a proposal? Or are you the fellow on the right making the first move? What relationships are drawing themselves to you? What requests have you received lately? Listen to them. Look into the one that feels right and fills your cup, not necessarily the first proposition that seems to reach out to you.

In fiction writing, while the Two of Cups can indicate agreements made between two people, it can also inform duality. The two figures in the card might be a pair of lovers, a couple having an affair, or a person making the first move or an attempt at a relationship. They could also be a married couple, a toasting couple, best friends, work colleagues (who may or may not be getting too friendly after the office party), or any partnership. At its lower polarity, this card can indicate an argument, fighting, or feeling coerced.

Two of Pentacles: Everyday Constructs

If the Two of Pentacles has shown up on your desk, you or your character(s) have a choice to make that will affect your security, finances, home, or work. Have you received an offer that will change your writing routine? Have you planned two initiatives that fall right on top of one another and now you have to pick which one to work on and which one to table for later?

At its core, the Two of Pentacles epitomizes the never-ending balance of home and work. It expresses the coordination of physical and material responsibilities, weighing of options, and managing two projects at one time. Because the Two of Pentacles is one of the tarot's stage cards (See Chapter 19 – *Symbolism in the Tarot / Stage Cards*), its energy might sometimes feel performative or theatrical. It can also indicate the tendency to make everything look easy while struggling under the weight of those responsibilities. Layer on a social media audience and you and/or your character(s) can be stuck in a continuous cycle of feeding the algorithm of expectation. This performance, this "show," will go on and on until you and/or your character(s) buckle under the pressure, or worse, capsize.

Two of Swords: Everyday Constructs

At its foundation, the Two of Swords represents internal decisions, intuitive insights, blind trust, and choosing one's battles. Pay close attention to your thoughts on both sides of a decision, blinding yourself to outside influences and distractions so that you can "see" clearly. Regarding conflict, this card invites you to listen to your intuition to understand which conflict is worth paying attention to—time management is a good example—and which isn't worth your energy. A bad editor is an even better example. Don't argue with terrible editors, don't chase after them if they consistently fail to deliver your work in the agreed upon timeframe. Part ways with them and move on to someone more capable and professional.

On its lower polarity, the Two of Swords might symbolize an enemy, an ex, or someone judgmental. Conversely, the figure in this card might be an oracle, like her counterpart The High Priestess, or a judge, like her colleague on the Justice card.

Two of Wands: Everyday Constructs

The Two of Wands serves as a reminder to remain faithful to your internal spirit and confident in your own abilities, finding your own place in the world. You can achieve all the success and status available to you, but beware: you may still be unsatisfied and discontented. You can have every possibility at your grasp—the whole world in your hand—and yet, if they aren't feeding and nourishing your spirit, you will keep searching outward.

If the person on this card is you, the writer, you are encouraged to look around. The view from where you stand is one of success and abundance. You've worked so hard. You've written important stories and people love them. Your reader audience grows daily. Enjoy the view from the top but don't get too comfortable. There is still more work to be done, more stories to tell. Take a moment from staring out at all that you don't have and appreciate all that you have accomplished. Be mindful of staying original—success is relative, so your view may not look like others, and that is okay! You're manifesting your wildest dreams, and those may not necessarily look like the dreams of your colleagues or peers. Stay strong-minded and confident, continue to grow, and set goals for achievement.

If the individual in this card represents your character(s), they may be trying to find their place in the world. There are decisions that have been made to elevate this person to the heights which they have reached, yet more decisions are to come. This person should remain careful, however, not to covet the achievements of others and/or to become bored and dissatisfied with their own.

Questions

- **Two of Cups:** Is a certain relationship, partnership, or agreement filling my cup, or is it asking too much of me?
- **Two of Pentacles:** How can I maintain a healthy work-life balance right now?
- **Two of Swords:** What decision needs my undivided attention at this time? How can I clear my mind so that I can respond wisely?
- **Two of Wands:** What goals are on my horizon and what resources are within my grasp for accomplishing them?

Word List

cups	pentacles	swords	wands
a toast	adaptability	avoidance	choice
advancement	balance	blinded	decisions
agreement	capsize	choices	desires
alignment	commitment	clarity	direction
arrangement	cooperation	closed off	dreamer
attraction	coordination	considering	exchange
beginnings	cycle	decision-making	expectations
coercion	decisions	decisions	goals
cohesiveness	distributive	difficulties	goal-setting
conversation	exchange	energy	greed
cooperation	falter	exchange	harmony
decisions	handling	harmony	horizons
dialogue	harmony	impasse	opposition
exchange	juggling	indecision	outlook
harmony	managing	intuitive	perspective
invitation	never-ending	opportunities	planning
mutual	opposition	opposition	possibilities
opposition	organization	potential	power
partnership	performance	protection	privilege
proposal	priorities	rebirth	relationship
proposition	relationship	resistance	reluctance
relationship	repetitive	seeing	stance
selflessness	tension	stalemate	tension
tension	theatrics	tension	vision
trust	wishy-washy	thinking	wanting

Minor Arcana
The Threes

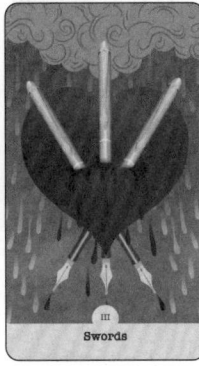

Associated with The Empress, the Threes offer the first opportunity for stability in the Minor Arcana. They take the decisions, connections, and partnerships established by the Twos and nurture their outcomes. Threes foster growth, expansion, and harvest—reaping the rewards and/or consequences of the Twos' choices. Depending on their suit, the Threes cultivate stability of the heart, body, mind, and spirit.

When writing fiction, the Threes can help with themes including celebration, collaboration, communication, compassion, cooperation, creativity, drive, expansion, expression, growth, longing, mystery, results, teamwork, and transition.

Three of Cups: Everyday Constructs

When the Three of Cups lands on your writer's desk, it's a call for creative celebration! Are you planning a book launch? Are you meeting with a writing group? Or maybe it's been a long week, and you're stoked about a Girls' Night Out. Who's in your circle of support? Gather with them today and marvel at your accomplishments. Today is a day to celebrate YOU and your incredible contributions to storytelling. Whether the Three of Cups resonates with you or your fictional character(s), expect to channel the energy of the Three Graces, or the Charites, who were Greek mythological goddesses of Charisma, representing beauty, nature, fertility, and creativity. On the other hand, you might also channel the Sanderson Sisters, the sisters from Charmed (both the old- and new-school versions), the Three Musketeers, the Party Planning Committee, the Holy Trinity, or any triad whose energy you'd like to invite into your life and/or your storytelling practice.

Alternatively, the Three of Cups could indicate a romantic celebration: a honeymoon, a tryst, a sapphic threesome, or any kind of ménage à trois, for that matter. On their lower polarity, Three's company, or Three's a crowd, with one too many spoons stirring the pot or one too many irons in the fire. Insert your favorite idiom relating to an overkill, and you get my point.

Three of Pentacles: Everyday Constructs

If the Three of Pentacles pops up for you in a reading or in a spread, it could indicate that others are recognizing your skills. Back in my '90s heyday, we used to call this "Game recognize game." When other writers see you working successfully, for example, be prepared for them to ask you for advice or even assistance on a project. While helping others with their endeavors is noble, take care not to allow them to take advantage of your kindness and craftsmanship. On the other hand, you could be the writer who needs assistance. After all, few writers can pen a good article, book, essay, etc. exclusively on their own. There are editors, proofreaders, and cover designers to employ, folks who can help take what you've written and develop it from a horse into a unicorn. Therefore, seek insight from others to elevate the quality of your work, but don't rely on them to do the work for you.

If this card resonates with you and/or your fictional character(s), it could inform collaboration, teamwork, critique, consultative, or contracted work. Perhaps a complete renovation is underway, or a simple changing out of the lightbulb in your desk lamp.

Three of Swords: Everyday Constructs

At face value, the Three of Swords card looks a lot like heartbreak and betrayal. One of the scariest cards in the tarot, this Three can indicate pain caused by dishonesty, death, infidelity, grief, a change of heart, humiliation, and/or a painful ending. From a writer's lens, the Three of Swords can mean pure disappointment—pouring blood, sweat, and tears into something you've written and/or are passionate about to yield no outcome or a less than favorable result. This card is a metaphorical death of the writer's three minds: the conscious, the subconscious, and the shadow (See The Moon card profile in Chapter 17, *Key 18*). Furthermore, the Three of Swords might indicate a profound delay in creativity, expression, and/or growth, which can inspire taking action to guard against responses such as depression and anxiety.

If the suit of Swords represents thinking and intellect, and the number three represents creativity and expression, the Three of Swords encourages creative thinking as a means of rising above internal conflict. Writer's block and imposter syndrome come to mind. But how does one think creatively when creativity is the very thing being challenged? Writing strategies such as freewriting, brainstorming, word clouds, journaling, and outlining can help you work through those creative lulls.

Three of Wands Everyday Constructs

When the Three of Wands settles on your writer's desk, it could indicate the need for planning, goal-setting, and figuring out next steps. Like the individual looking out over a busy body of water, it's time to focus your outlook forward, rather than behind you. The Three of Wands employs the opportunities and resources provided by the Two of Wands and exacts a launch plan. But what are you launching? Have you written a collection of poetry or a novel and are preparing to query literary agents? Are you considering self-publishing avenues? Whatever the plan, this card invites you to pause and consider every detail involved. You have all the passion and desire to invite successful outcomes; now is the time to draft a plan on how to achieve them.

On its lower polarity, the Three of Wands could express feelings of doubt, uncertainty, or distractive wanderlust. If the individual in the card resonates with you or one of your fictional characters, what's fueling your fire? If not where you are, where would you rather be? What's keeping you from taking a step forward? What or who is the source of your apprehension?

Questions

- **Three of Cups:** What reason(s) can I find for celebration right now? Who is among my community of supporters?
- **Three of Pentacles:** Where are my skill sets needed at this moment? How can I help others? Who can assist me with my current task?
- **Three of Swords:** How are my thoughts wounding me right now? How can I work through what is troubling me the most?
- **Three of Wands:** What is my plan for moving forward?

Word List

cups	pentacles	swords	wands
actualization	activity	anxiety	apprehension
beauty	assistance	betrayal	assessment
celebration	collaboration	change of heart	comfortable
collaboration	community	creativity	considerations
community	consultant	death	desires
comradery	contract	depression	doubt
creativity	craftsmanship	disappointment	entrepreneurship
dance	doing	dishonesty	expansion
excitement	employment	endings	exploration
festivities	enterprise	grieving	forward
friendship	exacting	healing	future-focused
fun	group	heartache	goal-setting
group	harmony	heartbreak	growth
nature	helping	humiliation	launch
overkill	job	infidelity	observation
participation	learning	kill your darlings	opportunities
party	order-taking	loss	outlook
pleasure	organization	mind over matter	planning
sharing	quality	pain	preparedness
stimulation	renovation	painful ending	progress
threatened	resourcefulness	release	stuck
threesome	sharing	scorned	success
tribe	skill	sorrow	uncertainty
tryst	teamwork	strife	vision
	work	turmoil	wanderlust

Minor Arcana
The Fours

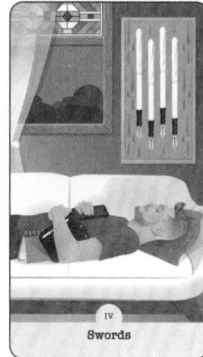

After the Threes have settled—the planning done, changes made, work finished, and the party quieted down—the Fours instill a steady foundation, stability, security, and structure. Directly supported by The Emperor, the Fours suggest day-to-day ideas around staying focused, pausing to rest, practicality, preparation, and eventually enjoying the fruits of one's labor. As such, when writing fiction, Fours can serve as excellent guideposts for planning and preparation, pause and plotting.

Four of Cups: Everyday Constructs

The ficklest of the Cups (and certainly the Fours), the individual in the Four of

Cups card plants himself against a tree and sulks. Even though the party's over, the Universe is presenting him with another gift—a fourth cup to complete his collection. And yet, the arm protruding from a small cloud hovering just in front of the guy's face doesn't even register. He's too busy pouting, probably upset that the Graces weren't so graceful with his original three cups. Apart from choice, decisions, indecision, and apathy, the Four of Cups represents cynicism and disbelief. Nothing can be as good as the other three cups (in their pre-party state), so why should this chap even bother looking at what's being offered him? If this person resonates with you and/or your character(s), what are you overlooking that might very well be a blessing for you? What is the root of your skepticism about what could potentially be a stabilizing missing link?

Four of Pentacles: Everyday Constructs

The Four of Pentacles can represent two sides of a coin, pun intended. On the one hand, the card serves as a reminder to hold onto every aspect of your writing practice: your available resources, project plans, methods, characters, storylines, and so on. Protect yourself and your craft from those who would see you fail. After all, like this stage card, if you are a published author, you might feel like you're on display for everyone to see your work. Others might assume that just because you've written and published a book you have the means to share—and that might be true, to some extent—however, you must protect the foundation you've worked so hard to build. On its lower polarity, this card can serve as a reminder that if you lose sight of what's important, paranoia, anxiety, and greed can sneak into your life and rock your core. There is a saying that pairs nicely here: "It's better to want what you have than to have what you want."

If you or your fictional character(s) can relate to the woman on the card, there are considerations for each of her four pentacle-embossed books. Collectively, these books represent a plan. The two beneath the woman's feet symbolize the resources invested to establish a foundation. Without a sturdy, safe place to start, she'll never arrive at her goals, represented by the sprawling city in the background. For the writer, this metaphor translates to investments such as a good laptop and a professional-looking website. Next, this woman holds a book closely to her bosom, indicating the importance of maintaining a savings, protected so that it remains untouched—by you and others. Lastly, the book hovering over the woman's head represents the portion of resources invested in her ideas. To the writer, this means money spent on research, supplementing time off from one's day job, and renting a space to write. For example, even though renowned poet and author Maya Angelou had a house, with an office, she regularly rented a hotel room just for writing without distraction.

Four of Swords: Everyday Constructs

Sometimes, it's necessary to take a timeout—a breather, a retreat, a respite, an unplugging from social media—whatever time away might look like for you. No matter how excellent you are as a writer, and no matter how successful you've become, it's necessary to rest for the sake of stabilizing your thoughts, gaining clarity, recharging your energy, and even inviting inspiration. As an artist, I've always been a dedicated advocate of resting my eye in order to return to a project and see the next steps. Like me, many painters stroke and spackle away at their canvases until they arrive at a point where they no longer see how the painting might look any better. Putting down those brushes and palette knives, walking away, and then allowing the eye and the mind to rest affords a bright, new perspective upon returning to the work. The same can be true for the writer and your own work.

Now, I understand that, to some, recommending time away from one's writing and/or unplugging from social media can generate a FOMO (Fear Of Missing Out) response. I get it. However, those dedicated fans and readers who are there for what you have to say will be there, waiting and ready, to hear your message and/or read your work upon your return.

Four of Wands: Everyday Constructs

The brightest, cheeriest of the Fours, the Four of Wands serves as a reminder that there can be stability, success, and even victory in what you're working on right now. A project you've spent a lot of time writing and editing can bring you creative security, and that's worth celebrating! Keep working with those who have supported and championed your growth, because the finish line is so close. What other reasons for celebration are there in your life? Apart from celebrating life itself, the Four of Wands represents a special occasion and/or event, such as a wedding, retirement party, going away party, birthday party, May Day, Midsummer, or any type of festivity.

If this card resonates with you as a writer, it can indicate the importance of celebrating your successes. After all, continuous work (Four of Pentacles) without taking breaks (Four of Swords) can lead to burnout. Celebration can look as simple as treating yourself to coffee and a new book. The Four of Wands is an invitation to surround yourself with people who love and appreciate you, and, if you can, immerse yourself in a beautiful, inspiring location. Enjoy all the many reasons to cherish this life and all you've done to manifest a fruitful harvest.

Questions

- **Four of Cups:** What gifts or blessings am I overlooking in this situation?
- **Four of Pentacles:** How can I establish, save, and invest what I earn in order to sustain and advance my writer practice?
- **Four of Swords:** What does taking a break look like to me? How can I take time away in order to recharge and gain clarity?
- **Four of Wands:** How might I celebrate how far I've come and how much I've grown?

Word List

cups	pentacles	swords	wands
apathy	accountant	banishment	balance
blessing	assets	burnout	bridesmaids
boredom	assurance	clarity	celebration
complacency	banker	contemplation	esbat
cynicism	boundaries	disconnect	events
discontentment	budgeting	exhaustion	festivities
disinterested	careful	exile	harmony
fickle	conservative	healing	joy
guarded	control	illness	marriage
introspection	desire	insomnia	midsummer
meditation	frugality	intuition	new home
missing link	greedy	isolation	newlyweds
overlooking	guarding	peace	party
overthinking	hoarding	preparation	progress
pouting	miser	recovery	retirement
questioning	planning	renewal	reunions
rigid	power	respite	rite
skepticism	preparations	rest	ritual
spoiled	protection	retreat	sabbat
stability	satisfaction	reward	security
stubborn	scarcity	sleeping	stability
sulking	security	slumber	success
unappreciative	stability	timeout	surprises
waiting	unyielding	truce	wedding
withdrawn	waiting	waking	welcoming

Minor Arcana
The Fives

In the Minor Arcana, the Fives are the first energetic lull, involving ideas around adaptability, challenges, change, conflict, flexibility, grief, instability, liberation, and loss. The Hierophant oversees what's happening in the Fives, initiating change and issuing challenges that might help their constituents (i.e. you, your writing practice, and/or your fictional character(s)) learn and grow. In The Hierophant card, the two learning figures walk away from the throne and distribute what they've learned throughout the Minor Arcana.

Five of Cups: Everyday Constructs

Throughout the tarot, the Fives bring about change. When the winds of change blow, and the Five of Cups slaps you in the eye, you can expect some sort of progress-stalling internal conflict on the brink. The Five of Cups brings to mind old wounds and upsetting memories. As such, if the figure in the card is you, the writer, then this card can represent second-guessing your efforts. At the moment, you might think your work is terrible, stupid, not special, already written, cliché, and/or that you should give up (Don't!). Maybe you've had a change of heart, or your reviewer or agent query has been rejected. Or perhaps you've been working on something so long that you're no longer seeing its full potential. If so, pull the Four of Swords and place it beside this card, for it might be time to rest your eyes, work on something else for a while, and then when you return to your current work, you can more easily recognize the direction you should take and appreciate all the progress you've already made. You can pick up those toppled cups (fears, sadness, disappointment), turn them upright, and continue on your journey. Who knows? Your story might be taking you and/or your character(s) away to an entirely different and unexpected place.

If the figure in the scene represents a fictional character, they could be mourning a loss, responding to feelings of betrayal, experiencing a change of heart or regret, or maybe they are simply not seeing opportunities that the reader sees. Maybe if this character would stop focusing on their glass as being half-empty, they might turn around and see the possibilities still remaining. And, like the Four of Cups, look how close those possibilities are—they're right at the woman's grasp. Alternatively, the bridge and stream in the background are an invitation to move on from the current situation. Be done with it, for it is "water under the bridge."

Five of Pentacles: Everyday Constructs

The Five of Pentacles is a card of hurdles and setbacks. It's not seeing the obvious or yearning for something out of reach. This is a writer's block card—ideas, inspiration, and momentum have left you feeling isolated and out in the cold. However, be mindful of depression settling in. The stained-glass windows are an invitation to look around for encouragement and inspiration. You might be walking right by them and not even recognizing them for your own dismal outlook.

On an even lower polarity, the Five of Pentacles can represent getting what one deserves, feeling helpless to change a situation, or waiting on someone else for rescue. The figures in the card could be homeless and/or in need of charity. They might be panhandling and have found themselves seeking shelter in extreme conditions.

When this card lands on your writer's desk, consider what's missing or lacking in your routine (or in your life), and then pause. Take a look around and try to see possibilities for healing and for rising above the difficulties.

Five of Swords: Everyday Constructs

Traditionally, the Five of Swords is one of the most unpopular and unsavory cards in the tarot. However, in our *Mystic Storyteller Tarot*, I'd like to frame it from alternating perspectives, considering both the cons and the pros. For the writer seeking notoriety, publishing contracts, and/or an established and thriving readership, here are the cons: If you aren't careful about how you manage your writer platform, you'll lose the interest of followers, subscribers, and readers. Yes, clicks, likes, views, reviews, and book sales can all be important, depending on the writer. However, no matter what your writing goals and successes look like, it's important to give back to your fans. Rather than always taking, consider what you have to offer in reciprocity. Are you able to create reader magnets? Have you considered hosting a giveaway? Are you reading and reviewing other writers' work? Are you allotting a specified amount of time for engaging with your fan base and fellow creatives on social media?

On an even lower polarity, the Five of Swords can represent constructs such as plagiarism and slander. If you are a writer of fiction, be careful about how you write another person, living or dead. Muses are incredibly helpful for developing rich, relatable, and nuanced fictional characters; however, take care not to share misinformation, project slander, or offend your readers with insensitive content, such as cultural stereotyping.

What about the pros? Are there any to be found if this card lands on your desk? Of course there are! Remember, perception is a key factor when reading tarot. Therefore, if this card pops up for you, it could be a motivation to overcome all of the aforementioned hurdles. You and/or your character(s) are the person in the foreground and the people who have wronged you are slinking away in defeat. Stand your ground. Stay true to what you know to be best for both you and your writing practice. Protect your mind from those habits or people who would bully you and champion your defeat.

Five of Wands: Everyday Constructs

The Five of Wands is an indication of creative competition, settling differences, drama, dysfunction, instability, and/or uncomfortable change. Creatively speaking, you might've found yourself at odds with others or even yourself. If the latter, this card is an invitation to pick and choose your internal battles—competition anxiety, imposter syndrome, sales and marketing struggles, writer's block. Decide for yourself what's worth fighting for and what to walk away from, leaving the overwhelm and its potential threats to your wellbeing behind you.

On the other hand, if external factors are causing your struggles, you still have a choice: fight or flight. You can choose to fight what's happening to and/or around you, or you can keep running from whatever the conflict you're experiencing. If you choose to "fight," that could look like standing your ground and powering through the difficulties by engaging in one or more constructive activities, such as journaling or blogging about those exact struggles. And, if you do so through social media or in your writer's group, I can guarantee with confidence there will be at least one other writer experiencing something very similar. However, as the saying goes, "Misery loves company," so be careful not to plunge yourself into a festival of whining and complaining; that's counterproductive and will only exacerbate matters.

At its best and most constructive, the Five of Wands represents advocacy, fighting for justice, defending yourself and/or others, healthy rivalry, positive creative battles, protecting one's spirit, good fun and games, or coming together to build something. At its lowest polarity, this card might also reflect anarchy, chaos, mayhem, a bunch of bumbling buffoons, a group of all workers and no leader, or too many cooks in the kitchen.

Questions

- **Five of Cups:** Are my cups half-empty or half-full? What am I missing that might help me overcome this difficult time?
- **Five of Pentacles:** What is available or who can I call on for help in this difficult moment?
- **Five of Swords:** When other people or situations threaten my peace of mind, how can I protect and defend my mental health?
- **Five of Wands:** What activities or methods can I employ to fight my creative battles? How can I protect my spirit from a threatening situation unfolding around me?

Word List

cups	pentacles	swords	wands
avoidance	ailments	betrayal	anarchy
betrayed	anxiety	bullying	arguing
bleak	depravity	challenging	challenges
change of heart	desperation	cheating	chaos
dark	destitute	conflict	competition
devastation	difficulties	conspiracy	conflict
disappointment	homeless	contrition	contest
disheartening	hopeless	defeat	conundrum
dismal	hospital	disagreement	crowded
doubt	illness	fight	disagreement
grief	impairment	guilt	disorder
hanging on	infirmary	misinformation	disorganization
hurting	isolation	penance	dysfunction
longing	loss	plagiarism	fighting
loss	misery	propaganda	frenzy
mournful	needy	resentment	frustration
neglect	poverty	slander	havoc
overlooking	sanctuary	sneaky	hullabaloo
pessimism	seeking	snitch	mayhem
pining	setbacks	stolen	overwhelmed
regret	sickly	struggle	pandemonium
rejection	struggle	theft	rivalry
sadness	unhealthy	threat	scattered
suspicious	wandering	unfair	teamwork
wounded	worry	upheaval	tension

At its lowest polarity, the 5 of Wands can mean anarchy, chaos, mayhem.

Minor Arcana
The Sixes

The Sixes spring back from the difficulties brought on by the Fives. They offer achievement, advocacy, assistance, balance, compassion, empathy, harmony, healing, karma, love, and support. As for Major Arcana alignment, the Sixes are associated with The Lovers card. After all, I believe, as many people do, that love conquers all. As such, when writing fiction, the Sixes can serve as guideposts for care, dedication, and devotion.

Six of Cups: Everyday Constructs

I like to imagine that the scene unfolding in the Six of Cups is what the person in the Five of Cups is witnessing after they've crossed that bridge and moved on to a new, happier place. After all, at its core, the Six of Cups is a card of friendship, protection, nostalgia, security, and welcoming. If the figures in the card resonate with you as a writer, and/or the characters you're creating, perhaps you're drawn to a sense of nostalgia and it's reflecting in the music you've been listening to, the conversations you're having, and/or the scenes you've been writing.

Alternatively, the Six of Cups serves as an invitation for turning inward, caring for, nurturing, and healing one's inner child. If you've experienced a period of disappointment or loss, as previously indicated by the Five of Cups, this card can indicate brighter days ahead. As for what you are writing, the Six of Cups conveys a feel-good approach. Be kind to yourself and allow yourself to feel secure about what you're working on. Additionally, this card serves as a calling for volunteer work. Perhaps someone around you might benefit from your help? Maybe you can "pay it forward," offering assistance to a fellow creative whose struggles appear all too familiar.

Six of Pentacles: Everyday Constructs

At its core, the Six of Pentacles represents advocacy, charity, karma, and providing assistance to others in need. Renowned tarot practitioner and scholar Rachel Pollack said, "Give people what they are able to receive."[67] For you, the writer, this serves as a reminder to give back to others but do so in a manner that serves their best interest, not yours. Give what you can—time, money, effort, kindness, resources, words of encouragement. Are you able to volunteer your time? Support someone on Patreon? Do you have time to write that review for that book you just read? Consider intentionally creating an opportunity to do something charitable and watch how good it feels. Then, watch how that warm feeling inspires your words.

Conversely, don't be afraid of accepting help from those who have it to offer. You are not alone in your struggles. Others have endured similar obstacles. Take a look around at the stories other writers are sharing around their difficulties. Sound familiar? If you pay attention, listening attentively and engaging with your fellow creative peers, you just might find support for your own troubles. And this can be inspiring!

At its lowest polarity, the Six of Pentacles can indicate help disguised as control. Therefore, check your motive(s). Are you offering to help someone else in order to manipulate the situation for your own benefit? If the answer is "yes," well, karma might have other plans.

Six of Swords: Everyday Constructs

If the Six of Swords sails into your writing space, it could represent the need for you and/or your fictional characters to press forward, moving on to a more settled situation, and seeking a calm environment. It's time to advance onward, leaving behind the pain and hurt caused by the Five of Swords. However, if conflict is the motivator for your move, just remember that if you carry that conflict with you, no matter what it looks like in the direction you're headed, once you get there, you'll have to unpack it and do something with it. What is the scene going to look like then? Will it be any different from where you've already been? Probably not, because those same conflicts will be waiting to be faced.

From a writer's perspective, the Six of Swords asks you to move on from unhealthy creative expectations—Rome wasn't built in a day, so your story is likely not going to write itself inside seven. Pace yourself, take your time, and move on from those unrealistic expectations you've somehow adapted. Your creative mind is listening. Now is their time to experience all those things. It's your time to write. Relieve your mind of the perception that you should be farther along than you are now. You are right where you are supposed to be; therefore, stop comparing your journey to others' and write where you are right now. With persistence and consistency, you'll get there, and then it will be your time to reap the rewards.

Six of Wands: Everyday Constructs

One of the tarot's celebration cards, the Six of Wands strides onto your writer's desk confidently and triumphant. Perhaps you and/or your fictional character(s) have been victorious in your pursuits. Maybe there's good news to share? Have you finished your first draft? Did your work capture the eye of an agent, magazine, or publishing house? Whatever the reason for your glory, this card is an invitation to celebrate your successes! After all, word on the street is that everyone who has read your work is singing your praises. The reviews are in, and they are glorious! If the individual in the card resonates with you, then despite the confetti and congratulations, be sure to remain humble and focused. Keep your attention resting directly ahead, over the crowds and beyond the echoing of cheers, not on your laurels but on your next goal.

As a fictional character, the Six of Wands might be a bringer of good news, a famous person, royalty, a soldier or Marine returning home, a victorious person, a winner, or a warrior. However, in its lower polarity, this card warns of egotism, fame having gone to one's head, sitting on one's high horse, or acting too big for one's britches.

Questions

- **Six of Cups:** How can feelings of nostalgia help season my writing? What aspects of my inner child need nurturing, and/or healing?
- **Six of Pentacles:** How can I be of service to others? What can I give?
- **Six of Swords:** What thoughts or mindsets do I need to move on from right now? What do I need to do in order to work through my internal conflicts and arrive at peace of mind?
- **Six of Wands:** After enjoying my recent successes, what's on the horizon? What creative goals am I ready to conquer next?

Word List

cups	pentacles	swords	wands
assistance	acceptance	advancement	achievement
babysitting	advocacy	change	adoration
caregiver	assistance	conflict	attention
childlike	balance	consistency	award
children	charity	daunting	confidence
child's play	control	destination	congratulations
darlings	donation	determination	conquest
forgiveness	eager	direction	egotism
friendship	enablement	escape	fame
gift-giving	generosity	evicted	focused
helping	giving	experience	glory
inner child	healing	fleeing	good news
innocence	helpful	journey	hero
joy	karma	leaving	praise
kids	kindness	moving on	progress
kindness	manipulate	outlook	publicity
memories	offering	persistence	pursuit
nostalgia	opportunity	reframing	recognition
play	payment	refugees	respect
precious	receiving	release	reward
protection	recovery	relocation	satisfaction
reunions	rescue	seeking	success
security	seeking	transition	triumphant
sweet	selflessness	view	victory
volunteer	support	voyage	winner

Minor Arcana
The Sevens

Although considered a lucky number to many, the Sevens are not always lucky in the Minor Arcana. These cards represent analysis, assessment, burden, challenges, conflict, faith, investigation, lessons, mystery, reflection, spirituality, struggles, and wisdom. The Sevens are directly connected to The Chariot in the Major Arcana, which supports decision-making, perseverance, and movement. However, the Sevens are transitory, bridging the gap between what came before (the Sixes) and what's next (the Eights).

Seven of Cups: Everyday Constructs

At face value, the Seven of Cups is a card of decision-making. It displays all the best options and then requires you to decide on the ones that feel right for you. From matters of the heart to being given the chance to have your wildest dreams come true, this card beckons for a choice. From the writer's perspective, if ever there were an anti-writer's block card, it's this one. If you are the type of person who struggles with making decisions, then the Seven of Cups invites you to assess your projects, plots, and/or characters from the lens of "need to haves" versus "nice to haves." Next, start with the process of elimination. Use your intuition and decide which project calls for most of your attention right now, which plotline falls flat, and/or which character(s) absolutely MUST be included in your storyline... and which won't contribute much and could be offed. As the saying goes, "Kill your darlings." Commit to what feels right in your gut, for that is always the best choice to make.

At its lowest polarity, the Seven of Cups is a card of analysis paralysis. You've pored over the details for so long that you have no idea what direction to take your writing (or your heart) and you have arrived at a point where you feel paralyzed to decide. Alternatively, this card offers everything you could ever want or need, leaving you feeling like a kid in a candy store. However, access to the heart's every desire can breed greed, entitlement, privilege, and addictive behaviors. Be careful what you wish for.

Seven of Pentacles: Everyday Constructs

If the Seven of Pentacles takes root on your writer's desk, it serves as a mirror of all your hard work. And although it offers a moment of rest now, it won't last long—there is so much more work to be done. The skies aren't always going to be clear, either. They could cloud over, and as the witty and wise Dolly Parton says, "The way I see it, if you want the rainbow, you gotta put up with the rain." To the writer, the Seven of Pentacles is a reminder to stay the course. Whether penning an essay or marketing a book, engaging in meaningful work will almost always lead to personal growth. The Struggle Bus won't stay parked on your desk for good. It moves on. And it will move on from yours, too. Keep plowing through that book you're writing or the feedback you've received from your editor—you have a lot of work to do, but the outcome can be quite fruitful if you'll just stay at it and put in the work.

When the Seven of Pentacles shows up in a spread where one of your characters is represented, that individual might be feeling disappointed with what's going on at home or with their finances, but trouble doesn't last always. Complacency, however, will keep the Struggle Bus outside of this person's house long after the meter runs out. What should your character do? Keep pressing on. Be patient. Productivity and prosperity take time, effort, and endurance. What can your character do while waiting for all their hard work to manifest? Who might come along and help this person so their investments will keep growing and remain fruitful?

Seven of Swords: Everyday Constructs

Like the Five of Swords, the Seven of Swords is one of the least popular cards in the tarot. At face value, it can look and feel like sneaky thievery. While that is partly true, there are also positive aspects to this card. As such, let's review its pros and cons.

I love to talk about the work I'm doing: the research I'm conducting for a new novel, what I'm learning, and especially what I'm writing. I love to talk about my WIP (Work In Progress). From my characters to my ideas for new and interesting settings, I enjoy sharing those ideas with those who show interest. However, as much as I want to yell my plans from the highest mountain, I have to be mindful not to share too much. At its lowest polarity, the Seven of Swords can represent a fellow writer who has come along and swiped the ideas, details, plot, and/or characters right off your desk. Writers seek knowledge and inspiration. You know this. This card flashes like a caution light, warning you NOT to let anyone steal yours. Instead, encourage your peers and inspire them to come up with their own ideas and plots.

At its best, the Seven of Swords indicates taking one's thoughts and ideas and running with them. Put those concepts into an outline and hammer away at that next writing project. Be cognizant, however, of shiny object syndrome, for this card can warn against moving on from one story to the next before it's complete. Press forward with your ideas, but don't look back. Also, running with scissors is dangerous, so looking ahead and being careful with how you're managing a tricky situation can prevent permanent injury.

Seven of Wands: Everyday Constructs

If the Seven of Wands resonates with you as a writer, you might be feeling like everything you're doing right now is being met with resistance, or perhaps even a full-on battle. You could be struggling to manage multiple creative endeavors as they come to you, not allowing them to slow your progress on what you're currently working. The good news is that while a torrent of inspiration is great, too much happening all at once can be a real challenge, and yet you are rising above the struggle. You're standing strong and are poised to keep everything else demanding your energy at bay while you focus on what's important right now.

On a lower polarity, the Seven of Wands is a reminder that adversity doesn't care how or when it strikes. From the writer's point of view, one of our greatest adversities is being interrupted and/or distracted while we are working. To quote author and inspirational speaker Robin Sharma, "An addiction to distraction is the death of creative production." Therefore, when distracted or interrupted, pay attention to what is happening and identify that event and/or behaviors as such. Resistance can also be a distractor—resistance to getting out of bed when the alarm sounds, wanting to hit the snooze button rather than tackling the day.

The Seven of Wands card can also represent being defensive. Against what or whom are you and/or your fictional character(s) guarding? If the individual in this card resonates with a character in your story, from what or whom are they protecting their spirit? What threat—real or perceived—is causing such defensiveness?

Questions

When the Sevens land on your desk, ask yourself the following questions, answering them intuitively by recording your immediate thoughts. These questions can also be asked from the fictional character's perspective.

- **Seven of Cups:** Of the options presented to me, which are "need to haves" and which are "nice to haves?" Which idea or project is worth investing my heart in right now?
- **Seven of Pentacles:** What more work needs to be done? How can I continue to yield the same positive results that I am experiencing?
- **Seven of Swords:** Which thoughts or ideas are worth running with, and which are best left behind?
- **Seven of Wands:** How can I protect my creativity from distraction? What or who is threatening my spirit and/or energy right now?

Word List

cups	pentacles	swords	wands
abundance	assessment	betrayal	adversity
addiction	disappointment	condescension	assault
analysis	discipline	conniving	battle
attention	effort	criminal	challenge
busy	endurance	deception	competition
choices	exertion	dishonesty	defend
commitment	focused	distracted	defender
confusion	giving up	evasion	defensiveness
daydream	growth	greedy	demanding
decisions	halting	hesitation	distraction
dreams	harvest	ideas	encounter
entitlement	impatient	impulsiveness	enduring
gifts	investment	inspired	exhausted
greed	lazy (low)	irresponsible	frustration
illusion	limbo	paranoia	giving up
misalignment	longing	reckless	interruption
opportunities	manifestation	research	overwhelmed
opulence	patience	runaway	perseverance
options	pause	seduction	prepared
overflow	perseverance	sneaky	problems
overwhelmed	progress	strategy	protection
paralysis	struggle	theft	resistance
privilege	time	thoughtless	stamina
temptation	vision	thrill	struggle
wishing	waiting	tricky	threatened

Be patient. Productivity and prosperity take time, effort, and endurance.

Minor Arcana
The Eights

After the Sevens evoke sometimes uneasy decision-making and change, the Eights follow with action and movement. Supported by the unwavering, limitless power of the Major Arcana's Strength card, the Eights make things happen. When writing fiction, Eights can serve as excellent guideposts for accomplishment, achievement, control, focus, mastery, and perseverance.

Eight of Cups: Everyday Constructs

When the Eight of Cups appears on your writer's desk, it's time for you or your fictional characters to walk away from matters of the heart. Perhaps you have spent a great deal of time and effort nurturing relationships and/or feelings that are no longer serving your best interest. This card can be one of unrequited love, of moving on from hurt, loss, and/or the painful memories that linger long after. The cups are stacked neatly and with care, indicating the incredible extent of emotion and effort exerted in their honor. The Eight of Cups invites you to put the needs of yourself—your Self—above others at this time. Your heart requires more than what has been offered; you deserve the same dignity and care shown for these eight vessels.

Before an airplane takes off, the cabin's attention is directed to a video or live demonstration instructing passengers on how to respond in the event of an emergency. Oxygen masks will lower from panels over each seat, and passengers are encouraged to put on their own masks first, before helping the person beside them. The Eight of Cups asks the same of you and/or your characters: put on your oxygen mask first. Make self-care a top priority, especially when that means walking away from emotional connections and relationships for the sake of self-respect, healing, dignity, and/or simply doing what is right.

Alternatively, the Eight of Cups is a card of travel. Perhaps the person in the illustration is only temporarily leaving behind their precious cups—for a vacation, respite, or a short errand. Or maybe they've experienced a great epiphany—as symbolized by the eclipse hovering in the sky above (See Chapter 19 – *Symbolism in the Tarot / Eclipse*)—and they're feeling called to a take a sabbatical. Either way, this individual is on the move and are clearly not taking all they've built along for the journey.

Eight of Pentacles: Everyday Constructs

The Eight of Pentacles is a card of employment, production, and persistence. If the woman sitting at her desk, hard at work, represents you, the writer, perhaps you've been so busy with your own endeavors that you haven't had the time to stop and examine your work and decide where to take it. While having loads of ideas, seemingly endless inspiration, and producing a lot of content is absolutely remarkable, stay cautious of your routines or tasks becoming monotonous. This can cause you to overlook errors, as symbolized by the coin lying on the floor. If there's an error in the process or an edit that needs making, you might need to pause production and correct the inconsistency before continuing with your endeavors.

Furthermore, this card can serve writers as a reminder of the importance of staying persistent and consistent with your work. Keep going and don't stop until you've achieved your goals. However, if you have too many unfinished projects sitting around on your desktop or in your hard drive, you might look up from your computer one day and realize what you actually have is a bunch of unfinished work you can't do anything with. As such, be sure to finish one project before starting the next.

If the person in the Eight of Pentacles resonates with a fictional character you are writing, they are certainly on a mission to build, produce, and establish something profound. Whatever the task, the demand for what they are creating is high, keeping them focused. This individual has no time for idle hands.

Eight of Swords: Everyday Constructs

At first glance, the Eight of Swords can seem chilling and threatening, what with the blindfolded and bound woman standing in the midst of all those ink pens posing as sharpened swords. But look at this woman's feet; they're not stuck. She is able to move about freely, and although she cannot see where she's walking, with careful planning she can free herself from her struggle. If this woman resonates with you, perhaps you are feeling blinded by a situation unfolding around you, and/or that your hands are tied, keeping you trapped and unable to escape. Or have you been blinding yourself? Have you unintentionally backed yourself into a corner? If so, keep walking and carefully inching forward. Maybe even lean against one of those swords to cut away those bindings and pull that blindfold from your eyes. What's more, you are strong. Whatever the conflict or troubling thoughts, this card is a reminder that you can overcome them even with your eyes shut—you just have to believe that you can.

Alternatively, the Eight of Swords can be calling you to intentionally blind and bind yourself: blind your outlook and bind your hands to tangible influences. In doing so, you might be able to turn your focus inward, blocking out ideas, thoughts, and actions that are not serving your best interests, and intuitively deciding the right moves for you. This card asks you to stop listening to the critics, the hecklers, and the folks in the cheap seats. Listen to your intuition and allow your gut to guide your thoughts and actions.

Eight of Wands: Everyday Constructs

When the Eight of Wands strikes your workspace, it can be calling you to attack your writing, your process, your project, whatever the idea or story, with passion and drive. Point all of your energy in the direction of what you want to write, that which is nagging to be written. What's more, this card is one of the few in the tarot without figures. In this case, the lack of people means the absence of opinions and influence—nobody is stopping you, not even you. Not today.

At its core, the Eight of Wands is intense action, energy, and movement.

However, it's not volatile, it's calculated. From a writer's perspective, when you direct all of your attention and effort toward your endeavors, you're not just tossing ideas at the wall to see which ones stick, you are aiming and releasing your efforts calculatedly. In doing so, you can maintain your trajectory and increase your chances of hitting your target.

If you are a writer of fiction, and this card resonates with a character, setting, or plot development, the eight wands could represent a group of people, busybodies, gossipmongers, travelers, nosy people, troublemakers, trolls, a micromanaging leader, a group of teenagers, a group of rambunctious children, a swarm/flock/herd/gaggle of animals.

In its lower polarity, the Eight of Wands is having too much going on, being swamped with tasks assigned to you, requests asked of you, and/or endeavors put into action. You might have found yourself overwhelmed by a wave of exciting news, or perhaps your efforts are culminating all at once. Whatever the case, things are moving along at a rapid rate, and you are challenged with hanging on and keeping up.

Questions

- **Eight of Cups**: How might a change of scenery fill my cup at this time? In what new direction are my endeavors being called?
- **Eight of Pentacles**: Are my efforts high quality or are they merely high quantity? What edits can I make along the way so that my project is consistent and polished?
- **Eight of Swords**: How can I shut out external influences so that I might focus on what's best for me in this situation? What threatening thoughts or conflicts are entrapping me?
- **Eight of Wands**: Where are my efforts aimed and how can I maintain the strength and energy to see them through?

Word List

cups	pentacles	swords	wands
abandonment	activity	blinded	action
avoidance	apprentice	bondage	advancement
closure	artisan	bound	aimful
disappearance	consistency	bravery	alignment
disappointment	content	conflict	busy
epiphany	craft	confusion	challenged
errands	creating	disempowerment	direction
evacuation	employment	emancipation	efforts
healing	functional	entrapped	energy
holiday	mastery	helplessness	exciting news
journey	output	illusions	fast-paced
leaving	perseverance	internal	focus
let go	process	intuitive	intensity
moving on	productive	isolation	keeping up
mysteries	progress	mentality	movement
pause	purpose	misguided	overcome
respite	repetition	negativity	overwhelmed
retreat	resourceful	oppression	powerful
sabbatical	routine	restriction	progress
self-care	servitude	seeking	quick change
self-respect	skilled	self-imprisonment	rapidly
travel	systematic	surrounded	speed
vacation	talented	uncertainty	stamina
walking away	tools	unclear	strike
wayward	working	victim	targeted

The **8 of Cups** invites you to put the needs of your Self above others at this time.

Minor Arcana
The Nines

 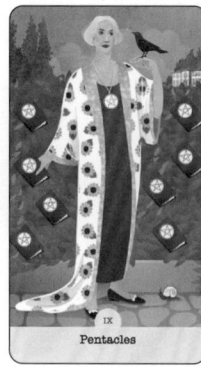  

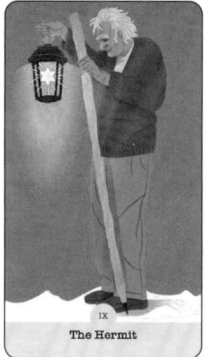

While the Eights launched the Minor Arcana into action and movement, the Nines take the reins and slow the energy, leading the writer toward the end of the numbered cards' stories. As such, the Nines are associated with The Hermit, who withdraws from the everyday goings-on and turns inward, seeking a spiritual awakening, knowledge, and self-fulfillment. When writing fiction, Nines can serve as guideposts for constructs such as attainment, contentment, completion, fruition, philanthropy, and protection.

Nine of Cups: Everyday Constructs

When the Nine of Cups appears on your writer's desk, its influence can feel a lot like the Six of Wands—success and achievement—but there's an additional layer of pride and even complacency here. The man in the card seems quite pleased with himself, what with his smug smile, puffed shoulders, and guarded arms. If this scene resonates with you, the writer, or one of your characters, congratulations! It looks like you're "sitting pretty," basking in the glow of your well-stocked trophy counter. You've won all the accolades and are displaying them proudly. You've developed important connections with people who have championed your success; therefore, you did not arrive at your position all on your own. Others assisted and even promoted your achievements, so it would be wise not to push everyone else away so that all you're left with are your possessions. Those won't keep you warm at night.

At its highest polarity, the Nine of Cups represents achievement, satisfaction, and self-esteem. At its lowest, it can indicate the self-serving pride, honor, and glory associated with winning and/or celebrity. The card's energy also reflects arrogance, being a braggart, self-righteousness, and putting all of one's eggs into the same basket.

Nine of Pentacles: Everyday Constructs

At its core, the Nine of Pentacles suggests material abundance and/or comforts, entrepreneurship, being "self-made," as well as financial and practical security. However, this type of success is not the result of luck, nor did it occur overnight.

If the woman in this card represents you, the writer, then you've invested a tremendous amount of time, effort, and hard work into your endeavors. Enjoy your successes and prosperity because you have arrived at a place where you are rich, not in materialism alone, but in wit and intellect. You have gained an abundance of wisdom and you have surrounded yourself with the fruits of your labors. As you savor your luxuries, however, you are not alone; you have a pet bird—or perhaps even a familiar—which symbolizes freedom, imagination, and spirit. In the *Mystic Storyteller Tarot*, the bird implies intellect and self-control (See Chapter 19 – *Symbolism in the Tarot / Bird(s))*, clearly mirrored by its Mistress. The Nine of Pentacles also represents the establishment of healthy boundaries, keeping negative energy at bay. If this resonates with you, then I'm certain the lesson wasn't learned easily. Nevertheless, you've made it—all of the persistence and consistency of the Eight of Pentacles has now paid off.

At its lower polarity, the Nine of Pentacles might indicate squandered affluence, materialism, self-indulgence, privileged circumstances, and even greed.

If you are writing a fictional character and are inspired by the Nine of Pentacles, then this muse might be a lovely woman, a duchess, a drag queen, an eccentric person, a gardener, an entrepreneur, the Lady of the house, a homemaker, a clothing designer or tailor, a model, or a proud pet owner.

Nine of Swords: Everyday Constructs

If the Nine of Swords resonates with you as a writer, the end or completion of a project might have you feeling overwhelmed or depressed. It was a tough, sometimes unrewarding journey, to be sure, but now the work is behind you. Now it's time to rest your mind and recover your sanity. At its highest polarity, when you are fighting through anxiety and/or depression, this card invites you to use those things to your advantage. How might what you've endured help inspire your next project, your next big move, or big event? How can you take back control from the nightmarish circumstances and channel the resultant haunting and conflicting thoughts into something therapeutic? A memoir, perhaps? Or what about a self-help book in which you can offer insights into your struggles in an effort to help others through their own?

At its lowest polarity, the Nine of Swords is overthinking and unhealthy rumination. Overthinking can be a treacherous cycle, a repetitive, hypothetical analysis of all the possibilities of what could go wrong. It's an anxious attempt at steering, controlling, and/or even protecting oneself from every possible negative outcome. Ruminating, on the other hand, involves stressing over the details of a situation that has already happened and about which one feels helpless in influencing or changing. Alternatively, the Nine of Swords can reveal the tendency of carrying the burden and conflicts of others, keeping secrets, and being haunted by past actions or pursuits gone terribly wrong.

Nine of Wands: Everyday Constructs

As a writer, it's natural to sometimes feel guarded of your work, creative ideas, and processes. And protecting one's energy and efforts is a good practice, for sometimes being a writer can feel like being on a stage, always performing, always chasing success—book sales, clicks, likes, reviews, subscriptions—whatever that looks like to the individual. The Nine of Wands is an invitation to keep and maintain your boundaries; try not to let negative reviews kill your spirit but use them as fuel for persistence. Unfortunately, not everyone is going to love your work as much as you. And sometimes people will even expect you to give away your work for free. This occurs especially for the self-published author. Protect your hard work and efforts; don't allow others to coerce you into giving away your work for free, especially friends and family. Defend your stance. If I've said this once, I've said it a thousand times: writing is hard. Your hard work is valuable.

Alternatively, if the Nine of Wands appears on your desk, and it resonates negatively, what are you afraid of? What or who is making you feel so defensive? Are you afraid of writing your truth? Do you fear Gran reading or learning about the risky scenes in your book? Are you afraid of bad reviews if you include controversial content in your writing? If the person in this card represents your fictional character, what happened to them? What caused their injury? Why have they built up a wall of protection and feel the need to stand guard? What or who has caused them to feel so paranoid and/or insecure?

Questions

- **Nine of Cups**: How can I enjoy my successes but still remain humbled? What achievements are worth celebrating and who helped me along the way?
- **Nine of Pentacles**: What does wealth, splendor, and prosperity look like to me? How can I be grateful for the non-material riches in my life?
- **Nine of Swords**: What is keeping me up at night? What is haunting me right now? How can I release the burden of carrying around the thoughts and opinions of others?
- **Nine of Wands:** What happened to me? How can I protect my energy from those who would harm me and/or see me fail?

Word List

cups	pentacles	swords	wands
abundance	affluence	anxiety	afraid
arrogance	boundaries	clarity	anxious
award	contentment	conflicted	apprehension
bragging	eccentric	cringing	boundaries
capitalism	endeavors	depression	challenges
celebration	enjoyment	despair	courage
complacency	extravagance	exhaustion	defensive
contentment	fortunate	fear	distrust
diva	freedom	grief	frightened
glory	hustle	guilt	guarded
greed	imagination	haunted	injury
haughty	independence	helplessness	insecurity
hoarding	intellect	humiliation	insulted
inflated	investments	isolation	opposition
materialism	lavish	nightmares	paranoia
overindulgence	luxury	obsessive	preparation
pompous	materialism	overthinking	protection
pride	opulence	overwhelmed	resilience
satisfaction	peace	regret	safeguard
self-righteous	prosperity	ruminating	self-defense
smug	satisfaction	sadness	stamina
sneering	self-sufficiency	secrets	struggle
success	splendor	terror	traumatized
triumph	successful	victim	walls
winning	wealthy	worry	warning

The 9 of Pentacles asks, "What does wealth and splendor look like to me?"

Minor Arcana
The Tens

Cups

Pentacles

Swords

Wands

Wheel of Fortune

The final numbered cards of the Minor Arcana, the Tens signify abundance, completion, coming full circle, the end of a cycle, final manifestations, overwhelming results, and preparing for new beginnings. In the Major Arcana, the Wheel of Fortune spins most diligently for the Tens, offering the support and drive they might need in order to move them toward their final destination. As such, when writing fiction, Tens reflect the hero (or The Fool) returning from their journey and/or returning to themselves, although changed from who they were at the start of their adventure. You will learn all about The Fool's journey in Chapter 32 – *Plot Development: The Hero and The Fool.*

Ten of Cups: Everyday Constructs

If ever there were a "happily ever after" card, it's the Ten of Cups. At first glance, it's easy to see harmony, happiness, and love illustrated in the scene. This is a card of pleasure, joy, and fellowship. All the stars are aligned, peace is restored, and dreams have come true. Happy days are here again, support is not only available but offered, and there are many reasons to celebrate. A rainbow stretches across the sky, an omen of new beginnings. And you know what Irish lore says can be found at the end of a rainbow, right? If this card resonates with you and/or your characters, consider it your pot of gold. But what is your idea of gold? What does "happily ever after" look like to you or the character you're writing? Remember, constructs such as happiness and success are relative, so what would it look like if all your dreams came true? What is your idea of a happy ending?

At its lowest polarity the Ten of Cups is not what it seems. Things might look, feel, and sound great on the surface, but what's the real story? When your gut is telling you that something seems too good to be true, it's probably a good idea to believe it. As such, the grass might be greener on the other side of the fence but at what cost?

Ten of Pentacles: Everyday Constructs

At its core, the Ten of Pentacles represents building solid foundations in which family, home, and fortune may grow and thrive. It's manifesting the wealth acquired by time and effort, with the intention of advancing one's family and future generations. Similarly, this card denotes gaining wealth in an ethical, selfless manner, and leaving behind a legacy to be proud of, celebrate, and share.

This card is a reminder that writing is a gift, and a magical one at that. Whether by genetic inheritance—perhaps your parent or grandparent was a creative, too—or honed by lots of practice, you have a gift of words, and this card calls for you to recognize your gift and not take it for granted. Additionally, the Ten of Pentacles invites you to look around you for all the riches and securities that you need, because even though you might not (yet) have financial fortune, your life can be rich in love, talent, dedication, and/or structure. The pattern in which the ten pentacles are arranged on this card is symbolic of the Kabbalistic Tree of Life. From creation to fulfillment, your bounty has come into fruition.

On a lower polarity, the Ten of Pentacles can convey the saying "more money, more problems." While it might look and feel great at the top, the only direction from the top is down. Wealth attained by greed, dishonesty, and other sinister means cannot make anyone truly happy. What's more, all the money in the world cannot buy integrity or peace of mind.

Ten of Swords: Everyday Constructs

If the Ten of Swords resonates with you, my fellow storyteller, then you've also known what it feels like to hit rock bottom. When this card crashes down onto your desk, it can feel like a harbinger of unfortunate endings. Whereas you thought the Nine of Swords was your very lowest, the Ten of Swords pulls that bed from beneath you and the swords come crashing down, a tenth sword adding insult to injury. In this card, the only direction is up. However, even though you might be at your wit's end, is what you're experiencing the end? Even when all the overthinking has resulted in an overkill, even when the walls you've worked so hard to build have surrounded and overwhelmed you, this card calls for you to look toward the sky. There's light on the horizon, and that light represents hope. That light is the promise of a new day.

Writers, when you feel like you have nothing else to give, you still have something else to say. You'll never lose your words. Even when words don't want to cooperate, and you can't seem to make them string together on paper, you still have them. And in those times you can use them on yourself. You can speak yourself up from rock bottom. Your old ways of thinking are dead. You have to move on from them or you will continuously feel defeated.

If this card resonates with your mental state, you might be feeling overwhelmed. Perhaps you have so much to do and so little time. Your projects, your characters, your family, social media, they're all requiring something from you right now and you've arrived at a point where you realize you can't satisfy everyone. Giving up is not the answer. Alternatively, perhaps you've received nothing but bad reviews or unfavorable feedback about a project, thus destroying your motivation. Giving up is never the answer. Instead, this card implores you to reframe your outlook. Ask yourself, What can I learn from all of this?

At its lowest polarity (as if things could get any lower for the poor soul in this card), the Ten of Swords is a reminder that you can't kill something that's already dead. As such, this card is the epitome of beating a dead horse. It's being stabbed in the back, experiencing backbreaking pain, or reaching a dead end.

Ten of Wands: Everyday Constructs

It's easy to associate this card with an exorbitant amount of back-breaking work. If this person resonates with a fictional character you are developing, what motivations are there for them to remain doing all that heavy lifting? Is this person being forced into servitude? As a stage card (See Chapter 19 – *Symbolism in the Tarot / Stage Cards*), are they made to perform or being paid for doing so? Alternatively, because wands symbolize fiery passion, and there are so many of them here, instead of this person being burdened beneath the weight of their work, perhaps they have reaped the fruits of their labor and are on the way home to share and enjoy them.

If the hardworking woman in this card represents you, the writer, you might often feel like you're carrying a heavy creative load, one that can overwhelm you if you aren't cautious. Are you anticipating a lot of writing ahead? A ton of edits, maybe? This card can be a reminder to work smarter and not harder at the work you love doing so much. However, when you have too many wands in the fire, so to speak, you are at risk of burnout. What is your motivation for working so hard on so many endeavors? Are you feeling the need to keep up with others on social media? If so, because the Ten of Wands is a stage card, all the writing, editing, engagement, videos, reviews, and so on can make you feel like you're on stage performing your hard work for all the world to see. It's okay to pause and rest. It's absolutely necessary to pause, set down your wand bundle, maybe even toss one or two that aren't serving you, and then reassess your plan on how you'll make it to that manifestation finish line.

At its lowest polarity, the Ten of Wands represents oppression, servitude, entertainment at the cost of someone else's burden and/or discomfort. It can indicate being weighed down with more responsibilities than one can safely manage. So much work can hinder the spirit and cause physical exhaustion and/or injury.

Questions

- **Ten of Cups**: What would it look like for all my wishes to come true? When I imagine my "happily ever after," who is there celebrating with me?
- **Ten of Pentacles**: How is what I'm writing serving my legacy? What good fortune can I share with those who have championed my success?
- **Ten of Swords**: What can I learn from this situation? When a new day dawns, how can I lift myself up and leave behind the circumstances that caused me so much pain?
- **Ten of Wands**: Are all of these creative endeavors serving my spirit or are they becoming a burden? Which project can I set aside in order to focus on and complete others?

Word List

cups	pentacles	swords	wands
alignment	abundance	aftermath	burden
celebration	ancestry	assaulted	carry
companionship	completion	betrayed	collection
completion	culmination	completion	completion
connection	estate	conclusion	culmination
contentment	excess	crisis	encumbered
culmination	family	culmination	excess
dream	fortune	dead	gather
excess	grateful	defeated	hard labor
happiness	homecoming	done	heavy
harmony	imbalance	endings	hoard
homecoming	inheritance	excess	imbalance
imagination	investment	imbalance	indentured
imbalance	legacy	loss	laborer
inspiration	life	obliterated	load
joy	longevity	overthinking	oppression
love	magic/k	overwhelmed	overwhelmed
nostalgia	opulence	perseverance	project
rainbow	prosperity	powerless	responsibility
relationships	reunion	ravished	schlepped
reunion	riches	resistance	service
success	security	rock bottom	servitude
support	success	the end	trudge
victorious	victory	turmoil	weighty
youth	wealth	wounded	workload

You might often feel like you're carrying a heavy creative load, like the 10 of Wands.

Practice Activity: Write In the Numbers

In the practice activity that followed Chapter 18, Section 1 – *A Suitable Story*, you drafted a story intuited from the Minor Arcana suit of your choice. This activity is similar, providing you with an opportunity for practicing mystic storytelling by considering only the numbered cards and how they might inspire you.

Part One:

1. Sort through your tarot deck and pull out all the numbered cards, setting aside the Major Arcana and the Court cards.
2. Next, organize the numbered cards into groups from the Aces through the Tens.
3. Sort through each numbered group and select your single favorite card from the group, and then arrange those cards in order Ace through Ten, as indicated on the spread. For example, were I to complete this activity, I would choose the Ace of Swords, Two of Wands, Three of Cups, and so on.
4. From left to right, Ace to Ten, what story can you imagine happening in these cards? Use your intuition and draft the story as it unfolds.

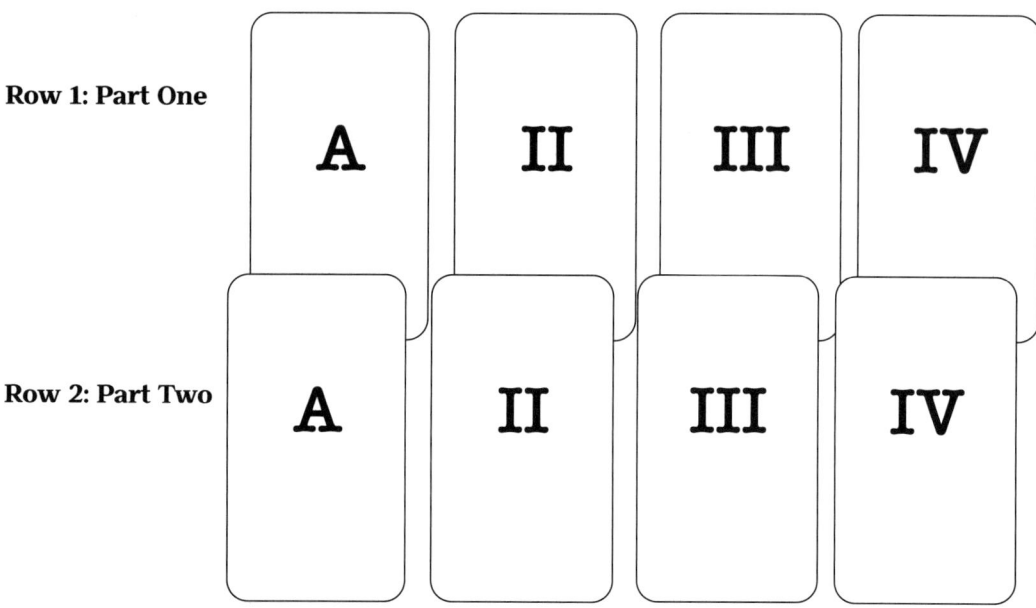

Row 1: Part One

A   II   III   IV

Row 2: Part Two

A   II   III   IV

Part Two:

5. Put your tarot deck back together in its entirety and reshuffle the cards.
6. When you are satisfied that the cards are shuffled well, turn the deck facedown as if you were about to deal them.
7. Turn cards over onto the space for the Ace until you arrive at the first Ace, laying it on top.
8. Move to the space for the Two and repeat the process, turning cards over until you arrive at your first Two.
9. Do the same for spaces Three through Ten. At any point, if you run out of cards simply collect the cards beneath the previous numbers and reshuffle your deck, repeating the process until you have a card turned over for each space.
10. From left to right, Ace to Ten, what story are these cards telling? How has the story changed from the first one you wrote in Part One? Use your intuition and draft a new story as it unfolds.

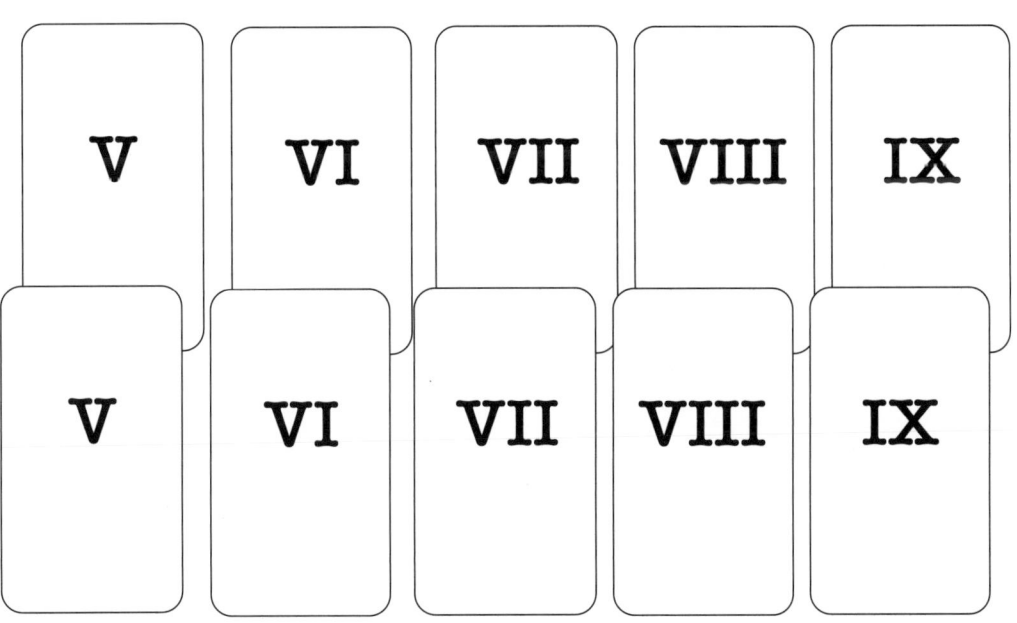

The Queen of Swords

Section 3 – The Court Cards

The Minor Arcana's 16 Court cards—also called "Courts" or "face cards"—are the personalities and actionable constructs of each suit. Similar to a standard deck of playing cards, which includes a King, Queen, and Jack face card for every suit, the tarot's Court is also comprised of face cards: Kings, Queens, Knights, and Pages, four per suit.

Although widely regarded as the most difficult cards to learn in the tarot, I interpret the Court cards as being rooted in service—to Self and to others. They are highly nuanced and full of personality, which from a writer's lens supports their relatability, and they also make the perfect avatars for fictional character development.

From the Page to the King, this section offers a deep dive into the Minor Arcana cards that have the most personality and relatable attributes in the entire tarot. Starting with the Pages and concluding with the Kings, I will cover the cards as a concept, with insights into how they might serve you and your storytelling practice. Additionally, each Court group includes a selection of questions you can ask if the cards' personalities and/or qualities resonate with you and/or the fictional character(s) you are developing. These questions are crafted to amplify intuition, helping you to discern your own muses associated with the cards. Finally, to conclude each Court group, I have provided a list of keywords that can help spark creativity and foster memorization of the cards' meaning(s). However, you are encouraged to build on the keyword lists, adding your own words.

Let's start this section with a review of the Pages.

Minor Arcana

The Pages

Page of Cups   Page of Pentacles   Page of Swords   Page of Wands

The youngest members of the tarot Court, the Pages are highly inspired and make excellent communicators. They are curious, interested, and eager to learn. Pages are scholarly, students of their corresponding elements—water, earth, air, and fire. They're hungry for knowledge and they share what they learn throughout the Minor Arcana. From the writer's perspective, the Page might resonate as one's inner child, and/or if you are a fiction writer conducting research to help pen your story, then you are demonstrating Page energy. You are the scholar, learning and gleaning inspiration for your writing endeavors. As characters, the Pages can be young people, including children and adolescents, who might be identified as apprentices, journalists, learners, messengers, novices, students, the town crier, gossips (in their lower polarities) and other people who share information. From news to helpful insights, the Pages are on the frontlines of receiving and sharing knowledge.

Page of Cups: The Emotional Communicator

Ruled by water, the Page of Cups is the most emotional communicator of the bunch. He feels very deeply and is excited to share what he's learned with whomever might listen. People and/or characters who exhibit Page of Cups energy tend to have vivid imaginations, and perhaps an imaginary (or paranormal) friend or two. The empath of his group, the Page of Cups is gentle, and he's sensitive to the feelings of others. As such, he can relate easily with other people and is probably also an animal lover. The Page of Cups is peculiar, unconventional, and naturally eccentric. He dresses in whatever he likes, whether others approve or not, and he's motivated by his own moral compass.

When his mood is low and/or his shadow Self surfaces, the Page of Cups can be vulnerable to negative influences, he can be awkward, flighty, hypersensitive, immature, and naïve. As such, he might not be taken seriously, and he can push others away. Unfavorable criticism might cause him to withdraw, becoming a wallflower or a recluse.

In pop culture, when I think of the Page of Cups, my mind always goes to Jon Cryer's character Duckie in *Pretty in Pink*. I also think of Luna Lovegood from the *Harry Potter* series and Penelope Featherington from *Bridgerton* (In case you haven't read or watched the series yet, this author won't say why...).

Page of Pentacles: The Practical Communicator

Ruled by the earth element, the Page of Pentacles conveys messages regarding tangible matters of the body, home, and work, to include finances and material possessions. Practical and sensible, they are the most pragmatic of the Pages, valuing honesty and integrity when sharing information and knowledge. These characteristics make them a reliable news source, forthright, and a trusted confidant. What you see is what you get. Forever curious about the world, the Page of Pentacles is always eager to learn. They're patient, not easily bored, dedicated to their mission to understand how things work, and they're thorough when sharing what they know. This Page aspires to become a corporate trainer, documentarian, gardener, postal worker, researcher, or scientist.

When their mood is low and/or their shadow Self surfaces, the Page of Pentacles can be a contradiction of their natural state. They can become quite boring, dull, impersonal, and withholding of important information. In financial matters, they can be fickle, vengeful, and they love a good game of tit for tat.

An example of someone who embodies the Page of Pentacles at their best is famed diarist and Holocaust victim, Anne Frank, renowned for documenting her everyday life while hiding from Nazi persecution during World War II. In fiction, Marvel Comics' Shuri—of the *Black Panther* series and sister to T'Challa, the Black Panther—is a brilliant young engineer, inventor, and scientist who demonstrates Page of Pentacles energy through skillful and dedicated mastery.

Page of Swords: The Intuitive Communicator

Ruled by air, which supports thought, intelligence, intuition, and, when necessary, conflict, the Page of Swords is dedicated to the swift and concise sharing of what she learns and knows. This Page doesn't have time to play around; she is serious and exacting. She says what she means, and she means what she says. As an intuitive communicator, she possesses keen instincts and is eager to speak the truth; however, she thinks before she speaks and does so in a thoughtful manner. The Page of Swords is a novice writer, philosopher, poet, lexophile, and a lover of linguistics. She is bold, brave, confident, precise, resilient, serious, and she demonstrates wisdom beyond her years. She's highly intuitive: she knows what's on your mind, what you're about to say next, and she's probably already sized you up when you first walked into the room.

When her mood is low and/or her shadow Self surfaces, the Page of Swords can become brash, competitive, harsh, impatient, and ruthless. She can swing her blade below the belt, aggressively undermining everyone and everything in her mission to learn and share her opinions, no matter how cutting they might be.

As a writer, Poet Laureate Amanda Gorman exudes Page of Swords energy in its most positive form. Jim Henson's character Sarah in *Labyrinth* is also an example, although in a much colder sense. I mean, she did give her baby brother to the Goblin King.

Page of Wands: The Inspired Communicator

Ruled by fire, the Page of Wands is the most passionate communicator of the group. Enthusiastic and compelling, this is a Page of unparalleled style and charisma. Unlike the Page of Cups, who relates emotionally to others and is therefore inspired by them, the Page of Wands finds motivation within. People and/or characters who demonstrate this Page's energy are highly artistic and creative. They're intoxicating to be around and their manner of communication and sharing information is thrilling and provocative. These individuals are innovators, risk-takers, and trailblazers. Driven by his fiery spirit, the Page of Wands is curious about what motivates others, and he knows the right thing to say with elegance and precise timing. He's adventurous, attractive, and spontaneous. A smooth-talker, he knows exactly what to say in order to steer and control volatile situations.

When his mood is low and/or his shadow Self surfaces, the Page of Wands is incorrigible, manipulative, sneaky, and vain. His risk-taking can get out of hand as he acts on impulse and makes rash decisions. When this side of his personality festers, he can be egotistical, demanding, and act like a spoiled brat.

An example of a fictional character who embodies the best of Page of Wands energy is Daniel Bae, one of the protagonists in the movie adaptation of Nicola Yoon's *The Sun is Also a Star*. Ever the inspired communicator, what with his poetry and impromptu karaoke make-out sessions, Daniel is passionately dedicated to helping the girl whose life serendipitously collided with his.

Questions

- **Page of Cups:** What do I have to learn from the unexpected and/or unconventional?
- **Page of Pentacles:** What practical information can I share that others might not know?
- **Page of Swords:** What gut instincts can I share that might help others? How can I deliver an uncomfortable message with grace and thoughtfulness?
- **Page of Wands:** What am I most passionate about sharing and how might that inspire others?

Word List

cups	pentacles	swords	wands
a proposal	advising	ambitious	charisma
connection	boring	bold	compelling
conversation	budgeting	brave	creativity
curiosity	curious	clarity	curious
eccentric	dependable	clever	demanding
emotional	documentarian	communication	flamboyance
feelings	dull	concise	immature
friend	fickle	confident	impulsive
friendship	focused	cutting	innovator
good news	honesty	enthusiastic	inspiration
immaturity	impersonal	exacting	learner
inspiration	integrity	focus	manipulative
learner	learner	gossip	messenger
learning	learning	instinctive	new project
messages	manifestation	intelligence	pompous
messenger	messenger	intuitive	potential
opportunities	opportunities	learning	precocious
peculiar	practical	messenger	risky
self-aware	pragmatic	philosopher	shallow
selflessness	progressive	poet	sneaky
sensitive	reliable	progress	style
surprises	researcher	scholar	tenacious
unconventional	scientific	student	trailblazer
unlikely	skillful	swift	vain
youth	trusted	truth	volatile

The Page of Cups is gentle, and he's sensitive to the feelings of others.

Minor Arcana
The Knights

Knight of Cups | Knight of Pentacles | Knight of Swords | Knight of Wands

When the Pages mature into adolescence, and their eagerness to communicate what they've learned evolves into taking action, they become Knights. Ranging from teens to young adults, the Knights are the seekers of the tarot. They receive messages from the Pages and put them into action, invoking movement and setting intentions for desirable outcomes as related to their suits, placement within a spread, and much more. Ever the initiators of stories that get moving and maintain the perfect pace, the Knights represent personalities that are motivated by and sustain the momentum of the heart, body, mind, and spirit. The Knights are also keen on romance and are always the first to make a move in relationships; however, they serve their Queens, whose instruction and demonstration about how others wish to be treated help guide their advancements.

When writing fictional characters, depending on the appropriate age range, Knight personalities can make ideal acrobats, athletes, chauffeurs, construction workers, cowboys, criminal investigators, detectives, doctors, explorers, firefighters, first responders, horse trainers, hunters, jockeys, laborers, law enforcement, locomotive engineers, martial artists, mercenaries, military personnel, pilots, racecar drivers, stunt performers, transporters, or any profession in which they can take action by working with their hands.

Knight of Cups: The Emotional Seeker

Ruled by water, the Knight of Cups is the most emotional Knight of the group. He's playful yet gentle, carefully guiding his horse so as not to spill his cup, which has his undivided attention. As such, this Knight is focused on, and motivated by, his relationships with others. He takes action but is mindful of momentum—he never wants to push or overcrowd another person. He's dedicated to seeking connections and he pays close attention to social cues. Like his Page counterpart, the Knight of Cups is an empath, and he can feel and relate deeply to the needs and desires of others, especially those who have captured his attention. The Knight of Cups' effort and action is strictly dictated by the pace others are going; he's not quick to rush in, and he doesn't typically leap into action. His methods and movements are controlled and deliberate, always cognizant of the heart and how tedious navigating feelings can be.

When his mood is low and/or his shadow Self surfaces, the Knight of Cups can be irritable, sulking, and just a whopping crybaby. When in his lower polarity, he can be down in the dumps, unmotivated, and/or he can refuse moving any faster than his own feelings dictate. This low-energy Knight is guarded—he doesn't trust what anyone else says or does, only how he is feeling in the moment. As such, he can easily succumb to addiction and obsession.

The movie *Hustle* provides an excellent example of a Knight of Cups in action. Without giving away spoilers, protagonist Bo Cruz's entire motivation for excelling at basketball perfectly demonstrates Knight of Cups energy. Other fictional characters who bring to mind Knight of Cups energy are Shakespeare's Romeo Montague, Patrick from *Schitt's Creek*, and Jamie from *Outlander*.

Knight of Pentacles: The Practical Seeker

Steady and grounded, the Knight of Pentacles is ruled by the element of earth. He's dependable, loyal, and trustworthy. He's set his eye on his goal, so you can bet he won't drop the ball (or, in this case, the book) until he's achieved it. This Knight works hard for his home and family, he's dedicated to his profession, and he takes calculated actions toward safety and completion. He maintains a steady focus on honing his skills, and he takes seriously how he manages his physical health and appearance. The Knight of Pentacles is generous with his time, money, and efforts. He rides coolly onto the scene bearing gifts, which are typically practical in nature. Have a felled tree in your yard? He's on the way with a chainsaw. Your car making sputtering sounds? He's underneath it replacing your fuel filter. This Knight is a reliable young lover or spouse, a son, a nephew, the person who mows the lawn, or the person walking from behind the counter before you can ask for help.

When writing fictional characters, the Knight of Pentacles makes a dependable muse for a carpenter, casino dealer, chef or baker, custodian, electrician, handyperson, homemaker, hustler, landscaper, massage therapist, mechanic, physical laborer, physical trainer, plumber, stylist, salesperson of practical goods, sign language interpreter, warehouse worker, or welder.

When his mood is low and/or his shadow Self surfaces, the Knight of Pentacles can become sloppy, careless, and aloof. He can blame others, expect more of others than he does himself, and he can leave those in need to "figure it out" for themselves.

As an example of a Knight of Pentacles character, I'm reminded of *The Office*'s super sensitive, goofy, calculated, and mischievous Jim Halpert. I mean, what better way of initiating both domestic and professional action than buying a house for your fiancé whom you also met at work? Other examples of this Knight are Joel from *The Last of Us* and Marmee in *Little Women*.

Knight of Swords: The Intuitive Seeker

The go-getter of the Knights, the Knight of Swords puts his thoughts into action, working diligently, precisely, and slicing through conflict. Ruled by the element of air, this Knight is resilience to the core. He is focused and determined. A seeker of intellect and truth, the Knight of Swords is highly perceptive and intuitive about courses of action, and he is incredibly insightful about the motivation of others. He moves in swiftly to bring an idea into fruition.

If this Knight resonates with you as a writer, perhaps a project you are currently working on is moving fast, with quick edits and speed-to-market needs. People need to read whatever this is you're writing, so this card encourages you to chase it with full force. Conquer inner-conflict by allowing your intuition to lead you in the direction you know in your gut is right for you and your project. Silence ideas that are counterintuitive and might snuff out your flame. Take immediate action on a new idea, for if you let your thoughts get away from you without capturing them, you could miss out on an opportunity to breathe new life into your writing practice or a particular project on which you're working.

When his mood is low and/or his shadow Self surfaces, the Knight of Swords can be cutthroat, unforgiving, and he can act without thinking. At his worst, he is cruel, thoughtless, selfish, and reckless with his words and actions. The low-energy Knight of Swords struggles against criticism, he overthinks, and he exhausts way too much time and energy on the hypothetical.

If you are penning a fictional character, the Knight of Swords makes a dynamic muse for the quick-witted. This Knight would make an ideal criminal investigator, detective, director, explorer, locomotive engineer, military leader, mercenary, oracle, psychic, seer, screenwriter, or writer. In fiction, there are so many examples of this Knight that it's difficult to choose which resonates most with me. As such, I will implement the process of elimination and choose Dev Patel's character Jamal Malik in *Slumdog Millionaire*. Final answer.

Knight of Wands: The Inspired Seeker

Rearing high on her zealous horse, the Knight of Wands rides into action in a fiery blaze of passion and purpose. The most enthusiastic of the entire Minor Arcana, this Knight is eager to be part of a movement, fervent about her cause, and ready to fight fire with fire at a moment's notice. She's young and inspired. Youth of any sort, whether in the form of a young adult like one of the Knights, a group, or reminiscing on one's own youth can inspire big, robust stories, especially if you're a writer of YA fiction. As such, the Knight of Wands sparks inspiration with vim and vigor, and she's capable of stirring profound change. Speaking of stirring and change, this Knight puts desire into action. The proverbial Knight in shining armor, she communicates through intense eye contact, followed by grand gestures. An artist, musician, scholar, or thespian, the Knight of Wands can be lustful, rebellious, and highly intoxicating, so when using her as a character muse, don't be shocked if you find yourself penning her into a secret tryst or torrid love affair.

When this card lands on your writer's desk, you are being called to take action on a creative project that fuels your inner fire. What moves your spirit? What makes you feel alive? What brings out your inner youth? The Knight of Wands is an advocate of rallying all your energy and charging full force in their direction. If this card resonates with you as a writer, you might find yourself in search of purpose, experimenting with a new story idea or writing project that's different than anything you've ever written before, or you might be on a path to entrepreneurship.

When her mood is low and/or her shadow Self surfaces, the Knight of Wands can be messy, spiteful, and vengeful. Overzealous and jealous, she can burn down everything she helped establish. The low-energy Knight of Wands is easily bored, frivolous, superficial, shallow, undermining, and unfaithful. She gathers no moss and puts down no roots, always on the prowl to woo and consume the next shiny person or thing.

Fictional examples of the Knight of Wands in full form include Starr Carter in *The Hate U Give*, Simon Basset, the Duke of Hastings in *Bridgerton*, and Oliver in *Call Me by Your Name*.

Questions

- **Knight of Cups:** How can I put my heart into what I'm doing while being careful to protect it?
- **Knight of Pentacles**: What practical methods can I put into action in order to make more time to do the things I enjoy?
- **Knight of Swords:** What are the thrills of acting on my thoughts? What are the consequences?
- **Knight of Wands:** What am I passionate about, and how can I use that desire to fuel my spirit?

Word List

cups	pentacles	swords	wands
addiction	boring	action-oriented	adventure
attention	calculated	aggressive	arrogance
careful	careful	conflict	brazen
charming	conservative	critical	charisma
companion	considerate	determined	cocky
connection	custodian	fast-talker	delightful
controlled	dedicated	fast-thinker	desire
creativity	dependable	focused	flamboyance
dedication	diligent	go-getter	frivolous
deliberate	faithful	hypothetical	hasty
desire	fidelity	impulsive	impulsiveness
dreaminess	grounded	intelligent	intense
empathic	handyperson	intuitive	intoxicating
fantasy	intentional	movement	jealous
feeling	investment	overthinking	lustful
heart	lazy	pursuant	overzealous
imagination	loyal	quick-witted	passion
intentional	perfectionist	restless	rebellious
mindful	physical	ruminating	spiteful
movement	practical	seeker	stirring
obsession	reliable	swift change	superficial
romance	routine	swiftly	vengeful
seeker	steady	thoughtful	vigor
slowly	stubborn	truth	vim
thoughtful	trustworthy	writer	virtuoso

The Knight of Pentacles is generous with his time, money, and efforts.

Minor Arcana

The Queens

Queen of Cups   Queen of Pentacles   Queen of Swords   Queen of Wands

Known for their nurturing, protective, and influential nature, the tarot's Queens serve as the conduits of the four suits. Employing their keen intuition, these individuals listen intently, carefully considering messaging received from the Pages, assessing the Knights' deployment, and then delegating expectations and guidance that directly influences and supports the Kings. The Queens harken back to The High Priestess and The Empress by fostering intuition and influencing character; they harness the elemental energies of their suits to cultivate effective change and encourage abundant outcomes. Through their respective suits, they galvanize relationships, opportunities, intellect, and purpose, helping to shape people and circumstances. The Queens are caregivers, counselors, mothers, nuns, nurses, planners, rehabilitation specialists, teachers, and trainers. They support community service, education, health and welfare, and progressive change. However, they aren't without their faults. The Queens' shadow sides can be the most infectious and manipulative of the entire tarot. After all, the hand that rocks the cradle is the hand that rules the world.

Queen of Cups: The Emotional Nurturer

Through her strong intuition and caring nature, the Queen of Cups is a nurturer of relationships. Ruled by the element of water, she is nourishing, kind, empathetic, trustworthy, and she sincerely cares about the dreams and goals of others. Ever the confidant and secret-keeper, this Queen is the first person called when sharing exciting achievements and clandestine events. In addition, she makes herself available when others are upset, in trouble, or simply in need of advice. The Queen of Cups is giving, nurturing connections by leading from the heart and responding rather than reacting. She teaches and demonstrates love, peace, and forgiveness, and she's the first responder in times of pain and loss. She champions causes that are near and dear to her heart.

When the Queen of Cups lands on your writer's desk, it's an invitation to nurture what's on your heart. You could be feeling unusually insightful and whatever project you're working on requires all of your energy and attention. Or, you might have fallen in love with the premise for a story and you won't feel settled until you've penned the first draft to see where it goes. The Queen of Cups calls for you to nurture this project, see it through to fruition, treating your characters and setting as you would your family and home. Conversely, if this card resonates with you as a person, it could serve as a reminder of the importance of nurturing your relationships, starting with yourself. The Queen of Cups champions self-care, prioritizing responsibilities—such as caring for family and pets—including setting aside time to nurture one's writing routine. Writers write, so it's important that we take every opportunity to do so in order to serve our own emotional wellbeing.

As a fictional character, the Queen of Cups makes the perfect supporting role. She might represent a mother, grandmother, favorite aunt, nurse, counselor, teacher, neighbor, friendly lunch lady, or closest friend. When using this card as a muse, consider how someone like this individual might help support your main character(s). What might the Queen of Cups say to the antagonist in your story to defend and/or protect your main character? Has this individual helped to mold your character(s) into someone your readers are destined to champion?

Considering the embodiment of the Queen of Cups as a character, my mind immediately turns to Sally Field as M'Lynn Eatenton in *Steel Magnolias*. Ever the Southern mama, M'Lynn fusses over her children (and at her goofball husband) in such a way that they know she loves them more than her friend Clairee loves her luggage.

When her mood is low and/or her shadow Self surfaces, the Queen of Cups turns inward, becoming selfish, uncaring, and she can demonstrate control disguised as "help." She might become abusive, anxious, attention-needy, nonchalant, and/or demonstrate hypochondriasis. She can become disinterested, helpless, and weak. The low-energy Queen of Cups can give up easily, making excuses, and displaying a negative attitude.

Queen of Pentacles: The Practical Nurturer

Ruled by the earth element, the Queen of Pentacles is grounded, solid, unwavering, and dependable. Like her Page and Knight counterparts, this Queen is steady, resolute, consistent, and persistent in her endeavors. She dedicates all of her time and effort to the supportive role she plays in her home and work environments—and work, she most certainly does. Although it might go unnoticed by those within her everyday circle, the work the Queen of Pentacles is doing starts beneath the surface, growing upward and outward. She channels her energy into planting seeds—people, activities, and initiatives—that will grow and thrive. This Queen believes in the Law of Attraction, and she subscribes to the thought that luck doesn't happen on its own. One manifests their achievements and wealth (whatever that looks like to them) not by chance or magic alone but by consistency, persistence, and adopting a positive yet realistic mindset. The Queen of Pentacles might attract abundance and fortune, but she is equally keen on self-preservation and protecting her home and work by establishing boundaries. She keeps her finances in check, and she is incredibly wise about growing and nurturing her economics, investments, and savings.

If this card resonates with you as a writer, you might enjoy working in your home and/or working from home. Therefore, work-life balance is a high priority. Similarly, writing-life balance is measured with equal importance. How can you set aside time apart from home and work to sow seeds that will grow your writing practice? What preparations can you make now in order to yield a thriving and practical writing routine down the road? Furthermore, if this card represents a fictional character muse, what hardships might they find themselves nurturing that others might not even see? How is making life easier for everyone else taxing for their own wellbeing?

When her mood is low and/or her shadow Self surfaces, the Queen of Pentacles can be firm, harsh, manipulative, rigid, and she can focus all her time and energy toward indulgent and self-serving endeavors. At her lowest, this Queen might demonstrate behaviors associated with agoraphobia, hoarding disorder, and/or Munchausen's syndrome.

As a character muse, the Queen of Pentacles might make an ideal accountant, archeologist, biologist, birth or death doula, college instructor, dietician or nutritionist, doctor, economist, farmer, financial officer, gynecologist, homemaker, homeschooling educator, homesteader, horticulturist, an ingénue, master gardener, matriarch, midwife, mother, nurse, teacher, volunteer coordinator, or a witch.

When I consider characters who personify the energy of this Queen, I'm drawn to Molly Weasley of the *Harry Potter* series. Who better to nurture (and conjure) matters of the home and material things (i.e. inanimate objects and Muggle treasures) than the ultimate homesteading witch? One of my favorite characters in the franchise, I want so badly for Mrs. Weasley to invite me to her table for a homecooked meal, listen to my writerly woes, and teach me how to get my dishes to wash themselves.

Queen of Swords: The Intuitive Nurturer

It's no secret that writers spend a great deal of time and energy thinking, pondering, ruminating, and sometimes even idealizing people, places, circumstances, and events. I know I do. Personally, I'm not as efficient at editing, managing internal conflicts, and establishing boundaries. While the former behaviors come quite easily and naturally, I find myself focusing more intention and energy toward the latter. As such, I'm learning to sharpen my intuition, leaning into thoughts and ideas rooted in my gut rather than pulled from the sky. When the Queen of Swords lands on your writer's desk, she may as well have arrived home. You are this Queen, I am this Queen, and we are each rulers of our own thoughts.

Ruled by the element of air, the Queen of Swords spends a lot of time inside her head. She is intelligent, highly intuitive, strategic, thorough, and she demonstrates mastery in self-protection. This Queen invites challenges so that she might overcome them. Armed with the sword of wisdom, she is prepared and ready to protect and defend her ideas, words, and work. A single critic looms, but from where this Queen is sitting, she's not moved. She's not powerless. She has freed herself from fear. The Queen of Swords faces and endures adversity with poise, strength, and resolve. Like her Page and Knight counterparts, she says what she means, she means what she says, and she can set her words into action at a moment's notice. If this card resonates with you as a writer, then you are already a mastermind at mastering your mind, or you are striving towards the goal. Keep your sword raised and your vision laser-focused. You will endure.

When her mood is low and/or her shadow Self surfaces, the Queen of Swords can be aloof, cold-hearted, cranky, and stoic. She is opinionated, yet at her worst rather than keeping her negative thoughts to herself, this Queen can volley insults like darts. Whomever originated the adage "Sticks and stones may break my bones, but words will never break me..." clearly never found themselves on the wrong side of the sharpest Queen in the tarot.

When writing fictional characters, the Queen of Swords makes an excellent muse for an adversary, a badass chick who gets shit done, a critical thinker, crone, cruel mother, dictator, a hustler, mother-in-law, a stern leader, or a shot-caller. She might be a college instructor, an editor, detective, philosopher, psychiatrist, researcher, therapist, widow, or writer.

As a fictional character, the Queen of Swords (in her cool stance and breezy regalia) is one such individual who, when allowed, can harness the power of influence to completely and totally change minds, if not control them entirely. An excellent example of allowing this Queen too much influence is the Grandmother in *Flowers in the Attic*. Decades have passed since I first watched the movie, and even longer since I first read V.C. Andrews' controversial book, but to this day a terrifying chill chases up my spine when I think of the matriarch of Foxworth Hall.

Queen of Wands: The Inspired Nurturer

The life of the party—and most likely the one hosting it—the Queen of Wands is one of the happiest, most creative, spirited, and eccentric personalities in the entire tarot. Leading the Queens in feistiness and wit, she is brave, outspoken, and quick to defend the oppressed, the underdog, and those who live and work on the fringe—whether by choice or force. This Queen is charming, clever, interesting, plucky, and she quickly attracts the support and comradery of strong, likeminded individuals. Ruled by fire, she's fiercely talented and she encourages others with her dazzling tenacity, her direct stance, and confident posture. Her strength and resolve is contagious, and she recognizes her power, directing it toward motivational endeavors that nurture excellence in others.

If this Queen resonates with you, then you are most likely drawn to people who are free-spirited, self-sufficient, vibrant, and dynamic... and whether or not you recognize these qualities in yourself, I'd venture a guess that you are a Queen of Wands. As such, when this Queen graces your writing workspace, you are encouraged to think outside of the box, consider stories about liminal spaces and the people who reside there, take risks, and write authentically.

In storytelling, the Queen of Wands character might make a brilliant adventurer, animator, art director, brand designer, creative director, deejay, event coordinator, fashion designer, film producer, fine artist, freelance writer, ghostwriter, graphic designer, illustrator, interior designer, jeweler, journalist, makeup artist, marketing director, musician, party planner, photographer, product designer, sex worker, social media specialist, stylist, tattoo artist, teacher, theater director, thespian, videographer, or the craftiest witch of any direction.

When the Queen of Wands' mood is low and/or her shadow Self surfaces, watch out. She is a force to be reckoned with. She can be irrational, merciless, unhinged, unstable, and ruthless. When she is irate, the Queen of Wands is capable of burning down everything in her path, no matter what the consequences or who might get in her way.

When considering fictional characters who resonate Queen of Wands energy, one who stands out in my mind is Mia Warren in the television of *Little Fires Everywhere*, by Celeste Ng. Creative, fiery, and manipulative when she has to be, she is willing to risk anything and everything for those she loves and protects

Questions

- **Queen of Cups:** What about my emotional wellbeing needs nurturing at this time?
- **Queen of Pentacles**: What seeds am I planting that will nurture my future growth?
- **Queen of Swords:** How can I silence my inner critic in order to sharpen my intuition?
- **Queen of Wands:** How can I nurture my authenticity?

Word List

cups	pentacles	swords	wands
advocate	consistent	apathetic	ambitious
aloof	dependable	boundaries	attractive
careful	economics	cold-hearted	authentic
caregiver	expansion	communicative	charming
compassionate	fertility	cranky	confident
confidant	financial	crone	courageous
counselor	growth	determined	cunning
emotional	farming	direct	dazzling
flighty	helpful	editor	determined
forgiving	homestead	focused	direct
friend	indulgence	independent	dynamic
intuitive	investments	intelligent	eccentric
love	manifest	intuitive	free-spirited
moody	nurturing	knower	independent
mothering	nutrition	opinionated	infectious
nursing	perseverance	self-protection	lucky
nurturing	persistent	sharp	magical
peace	planter	steely	partygoer
relationships	practical	stern	risk-taker
secret-keeper	prosperity	stoic	self-sufficient
self-care	realistic	strategic	stunning
selfish	savings	teacher	tenacity
sensitive	solid	thoughtful	vibrant
spiritual	thriving	unmoved	witch
teacher	unwavering	wise	witty

Minor Arcana

The Kings

King of Cups | King of Pentacles | King of Swords | King of Wands

The pinnacle of the Courts, the Kings rise to the top of the tarot's Minor Arcana hierarchy fully supported and enabled by their respective Queens, Knights, and Pages. Prioritizing guidance and protection, these personalities facilitate calculated decision-making, leading with confidence, strength, and the mastery of their suits and elements.

Proficient in matters relating to their respective suits, the Kings demonstrate expert skill in activities and professions associated with the heart (Cups), body (Pentacles), mind (Swords), and spirit (Wands). As such, they draw energy and lead from these sources. Therefore, when writing fictional characters, the Kings might represent one or more of the following roles: advisor, agent, boss, chief, coach, consultant, corporate manager, counselor, dictator, director, doctor, officer, organizational leader, overseer, pastor, president, principal, ruler, strategic planner, superintendent, or warden.

Like their Queen counterparts, the Kings are also informed by cards of the Major Arcana, especially The Emperor and The Hierophant. Like The Emperor, the Kings can represent fatherly, guardian archetypes, and like The Hierophant, these Court leaders advise, instruct, and mentor. They are also not without their faults—give a King too much authority and they may grow to believe they can rule the world.

King of Cups: The Emotional Leader

Ruled by water, the King of Cups is the most emotional leader in the tarot. Motivated by matters of the heart, this King is considerate, careful, and gentle in their leadership style. He is emotionally mature, encouraging, and kind. He sees the best in others and works tirelessly to lead by example, prioritizing people and their feelings and demonstrating patience and flexibility. At his best, the King of Cups is proficient in humanitarian efforts. As a servant leader, this King offers counsel and advises others to seek work that brings purpose and meaning to their lives. He shines at advocating for what's important to the people he serves and teaching them how to serve others. As such, he might excel as a chaplain, healthcare leader, hospice director, life coach, marriage counselor, relationship therapist, or social worker. Troubled by human suffering, the King of Cups makes the ultimate leader of movements to balance, change, and/or eradicate causes such as climate change, gender inequality, human trafficking, hunger, poverty, pollution, racial discrimination, socioeconomic disparity, sustainable agriculture, and water scarcity.

The King of Cups encourages you to harness adaptability, persistence, and resilience. The card might also be considered a direct invitation to write what's in your heart, mastering emotion and injecting more feeling into your article, essay, poem, or story.

When his mood is low and/or his shadow Self surfaces, the King of Cups is significantly weakened. He can succumb to addiction, obsession, and he might endure a crisis of confidence. At his lowest, this King can be disastrous, unstable, unpredictable, willy-nilly, and wishy-washy, causing those who look up to him to doubt their leadership and not take them seriously.

The muse for our *Mystic Storyteller Tarot* King of Cups is my late grandfather, a United States Marine who served proudly until a back injury sustained during service. Embodying the King of Cups energy, my grandfather never allowed being a wheelchair user to hinder his mobility or his compassionate spirit. He found immeasurable purpose as a disabled Veteran, spending the rest of his life writing about his experience and empowering others like him to do the most with what they had to offer: their hearts, relationships, and their stories.

In literature, one of my favorite examples of the King of Cups at his most compassionate and encouraging is Mr. Bennet of Jane Austen's *Pride and Prejudice*. "I could not have parted with you, my Lizzy, to anyone less worthy," he tells his daughter, Elizabeth, when Mr. Darcy has come to propose marriage. Although the practice of asking one's father for permission to marry his daughter was a social norm of the Regency period, Elizabeth Bennet's dad asked her what she wanted; he was more concerned about her feelings than how much money Darcy made (ten thousand a year). Mr. Bennet is the Dad every girl wishes she had. Kind, discerning, and patient (especially with his wife's nerves), this famous father perfectly demonstrates the King of Cups' emotional leadership style. I mean, how else could he have survived in a house bursting with such strong feminine personalities (and sensibilities)?

King of Pentacles: The Practical Leader

The most pragmatic and grounded of the Kings, the King of Pentacles has mastered what's physically and financially possible, and he leads the way in growing and sustaining wealth. Ruled by earth, he knows it well; from seed to root to surface, birth to death, this King is a master at understanding geology and physiology. As such, he is active yet sensible, teaching his constituents how to thrive within their physical regions, conditions, and limitations. The King of Pentacles collects the insights of his Page, Knight, and Queen to harvest what was learned, sown, and cultivated, respectively, to manifest and facilitate systems that perpetuate abundance and wealth. This King is a master facilitator of growth and prosperity, but rather than doing the work for others, he teaches, advises, and instructs how to obtain individual results and outcomes. Such a leadership method is conveyed by Chinese philosopher Lao Tzu: "Give a man a fish and you feed him for a day. Teach him how to fish and you feed him for a lifetime."

At his core, the King of Pentacles plans and practices, establishing systems that produce consistency and reliability with little to no waste. He sees potential and expects greatness, mentoring talent that will result in advancement and opportunity. He works hard and makes time to enjoy the fruits of his labor; however, because he demonstrates so much self-control, he encourages indulgence in moderation.

When his mood is low and/or his shadow Self surfaces, the King of Pentacles can be careless, greedy, prosaic, rigid, and unscrupulous. Systems fail and processes implode. His position can go to his head, resulting in tyrannical decision-making and authoritarian control.

In fiction writing, the King of Pentacles can wear many crowns. Ranging from skillful mastery of the physical body to understanding the land and leading agricultural efforts, this King could make a successful accountant, biologist, botanist, broker, dentist, doctor, environmental engineer, farmer, gynecologist, horticulturalist, investment planner, master gardener, obstetrician, pharmacist, physician, scientist, surgeon, or zoologist. In a corporate structure the King of Pentacles is either the chief executive officer (CEO), chief financial officer (CFO), or the chief operations officer (COO). He knows money, so he can lead the way in business, economics, finance, and investments.

Lounging comfortably on his earthy, obsidian throne, dressed in a tailored

Dionysian suit, the King of Pentacles is the Ruler of the Roost. When I think of this King, I'm reminded of domestic leadership, especially the industrious, salt-of-the-earth, down-home type. As such, sometimes this King can be stern, impatient, and in his lowest polarity he can be unkind. Albert Johnson, "Mister," from Alice Walker's *The Color Purple* embodies the sometimes harsh and brooding energy of this tarot personality.

King of Swords: The Intuitive Leader

Ruled by air, the King of Swords is one of the most intuitive thinkers in the Minor Arcana. Proficient in matters of the mind, this King is articulate, calculated, clever, curious, discerning, intelligent, and meticulous. He is an agile decision-maker, and he has a natural knack for analytics, learning, legal matters, logic, philosophy, and psychology. If this card shows up in your writer workspace, it calls for you to think with your head over your heart. Make calculated decisions about what you're writing and where you'll go with the process and/or the project. Plan, outline, and deploy a strategy for finishing a project before moving on to another. The King of Swords is a stickler for keeping one's word, fulfilling promises, and continually striving toward goals.

Although he is a critical thinker, the King of Swords' mind can have a tendency to wander, obsessively pondering hypothetical ideas and ruminating on what he could have, would have, should have said. He is especially prone to these negative thinking cycles when his mood is low and/or his shadow Self surfaces. He can be critical, harsh, inconsistent, and unforgiving, second-guessing the competence of others. This can lead to selfish, controlling, and impulsive behaviors. At his worst, this King succumbs to arrogance, condescension, narcissism, and shallowness.

At his core, the King of Swords is careful, exacting, and instinctive. He advocates for positive change, justice, fairness, and balance. Take a moment and compare him with the Justice card and it's easy to identify similarities such as arrow-straight posture and the brandishing of his sword in his right hand. This King's sword, however, tilts to the right, which indicates that he is thinking about the future. On the other hand, to the viewer (you and me), that sword is tilting toward the left, indicating that he is pondering the past.

As a fictional character muse, the King of Swords might represent an accountant, attorney, computer programmer, criminal investigator, counselor, detective, director, editor, engineer, forensic scientist, judge, mechanic, pilot, police officer, psychiatrist, psychologist, publisher, rocket scientist, therapist, statistician, or a writer. When considering fictional characters who exude King of Swords energy, I am immediately reminded of Randall Pierson of *This is Us.* Randall is a strong, determined, methodical, and intelligent partner, father, and leader. Like the King of Swords, he's always thinking, always calculating, and like the butterflies engraved on that sturdy throne, Randall is steady and solid on the exterior, yet soft and delicate on the inside.

King of Wands: The Inspired Leader

The King of Wands holds the highest standard of craftsmanship, creativity, enterprise, and passion in the entire Minor Arcana. Ruled by fire and leading by spirit, this charismatic King desires nothing more than to inspire others by helping them uncover and cultivate their own unique, innovative talents and skill sets. He's a flattering visionary, encouraging diligent effort and demanding excellence. Given this individual's captivating nature, he can't help but spark a passionate connection with nearly everyone who crosses his path. Fortunately, although this King's creative energy feels new and exciting, it's also lasting—it doesn't burn hot and fast before it fizzles out. The King of Wands ignites inspiration and then simmers, his ideas and creativity a smoldering resource within a vast and lasting desert of opportunities. This King is a master self-starter, and those guided by his tutelage tend to possess an entrepreneurial spirit and desire to create something remarkable from very little.

If the King of Wands represents you as a writer, there is a wildfire of possibilities just waiting to fly from your fingertips. Big results can come from small, conscious efforts; however, prepare to take necessary risks in order to write your story with passionate authenticity. You call the storytelling shots, so when this card blazes through a daily reading, or one of the tarot activities created for you in this book, you are being empowered to let your creativity spark the drive and motivation to pen a stellar Pulitzer Prize-worthy read.

When his mood is low and/or his shadow Self surfaces, the King of Wands responds on impulse, his ideas and actions feral and uncontained. He demonstrates risky behaviors and entertains hazardous conditions that might harm, and quite possibly destroy him and those who follow. At his lowest polarity, this King can be arrogant and demanding, abusing his power and exploiting others for his own gain. Flashy and conceited, he can stop caring and become hands-off, telling others what to do rather than showing them.

In its highest polarity, if this card represents your fictional character(s), there's a fiery individual on the rise in your story, and they're most likely smoking hot with an infectious personality. A force to be reckoned with, this character demonstrates strength and courage in the presence of adversity and danger, and their heroic efforts are motivated by those whom they love and/or desire the most. If the King of Wands is your antagonist, on the other hand, watch out! There's trouble ahead and your other characters will know it when they cross the threshold.

In the Mystic Storyteller Tarot, the muse for our King of Wands is another grandfather of mine (See also the *King of Cups*). A "self-made man," my Granddaddy was the hardest working person anyone had ever met, and he told the best stories with the funniest facial expressions. He had a fiery spirit, and he could always be found standing up for those less fortunate. For example, in the mid-20th century American South (and many other places as well), laws were established to keep people segregated by race. This meant different entrances to businesses: whites could enter through the front doors, but Black folks had to enter through the back doors. Not at my Granddaddy's smalltown business. The general manager of a local A&P supermarket, at his grocery store everyone was permitted to enter through the front doors, no matter what their appearance or class. He disputed local authorities about the absurdity of this law and was ultimately permitted to run his business as he saw fit. Shoppers were shoppers. People were people. That is King of Wands energy.

When I set out to decide which fictional character might embody the fiery, enthusiastic, entrepreneurial spirit of the King of Wands, the personality to step forward almost immediately was Christian Grey of the *Fifty Shades of Grey* franchise. Hot-tempered, fervent, and as suggested by the symbolism of the salamander at this King's feet, Mr. Grey is willing and able to walk on fire for his pursuits (See Chapter 19 – *Symbolism in the Tarot / Lizard*). On the outside, like the King of Wands, Christian Grey remains poised, dressed to the nines, his breathing measured and eye contact scorching with intensity. However, like the lions on the King of Wands' throne, at the slightest move Mr. Grey is ready to leap into action and/or conquer the object of his affection. All that heat can be dangerous, especially when trapped within small, enclosed spaces. Therefore, when Christian Grey steps into the opened elevator, if you know what's best for you, you'll probably want to wait for the next one. Or, if you share certain interests, maybe not.

Questions

- **King of Cups:** How can I lead with my heart? How can I guide and mentor others without allowing my emotions to get the best of me?
- **King of Pentacles:** What details and information can I glean from this situation that can help me make practical decisions?
- **King of Swords:** How can I quell my overthinking and master leading by my intuition? How can I use my words to master conflict?
- **King of Wands:** How can I employ my fiery spirit to inspire others? How can I demonstrate self-control so that I can lead with discernment?

Word List

cups	pentacles	swords	wands
adaptable	abundance	authority	abusive
advocate	achievement	conflicting	affectionate
compassionate	business	contemplative	arrogance
counselor	confident	critical	captivating
emotional	financial	decisive	charismatic
empathy	greedy	direct	conceited
fatherly	grounded	fair	controlled
feelings	indulgence	honor	demanding
flexible	industrious	hypothetical	desire
gift-giving	investments	impulsive	empowered
humanitarian	leader	insensitive	enterprise
kind	leadership	intellectual	enthusiastic
moody	moderation	intention	entrepreneur
patient	physical	intuitive	exploitative
persisting	practical	justice	flashy
prioritizing	pragmatic	leadership	flattering
resilient	prosperity	manipulative	innovative
sensational	provider	meticulous	inspiring
shallow	stable	mindful	magician
supportive	strategy	powerful	measured
tolerance	stubborn	standards	passionate
unpredictable	success	strategizing	sorcerer
unstable	uncaring	truth	smoldering
willy-nilly	wealth	unmoved	visionary
wishy-washy	wisdom	wisdom	wizard

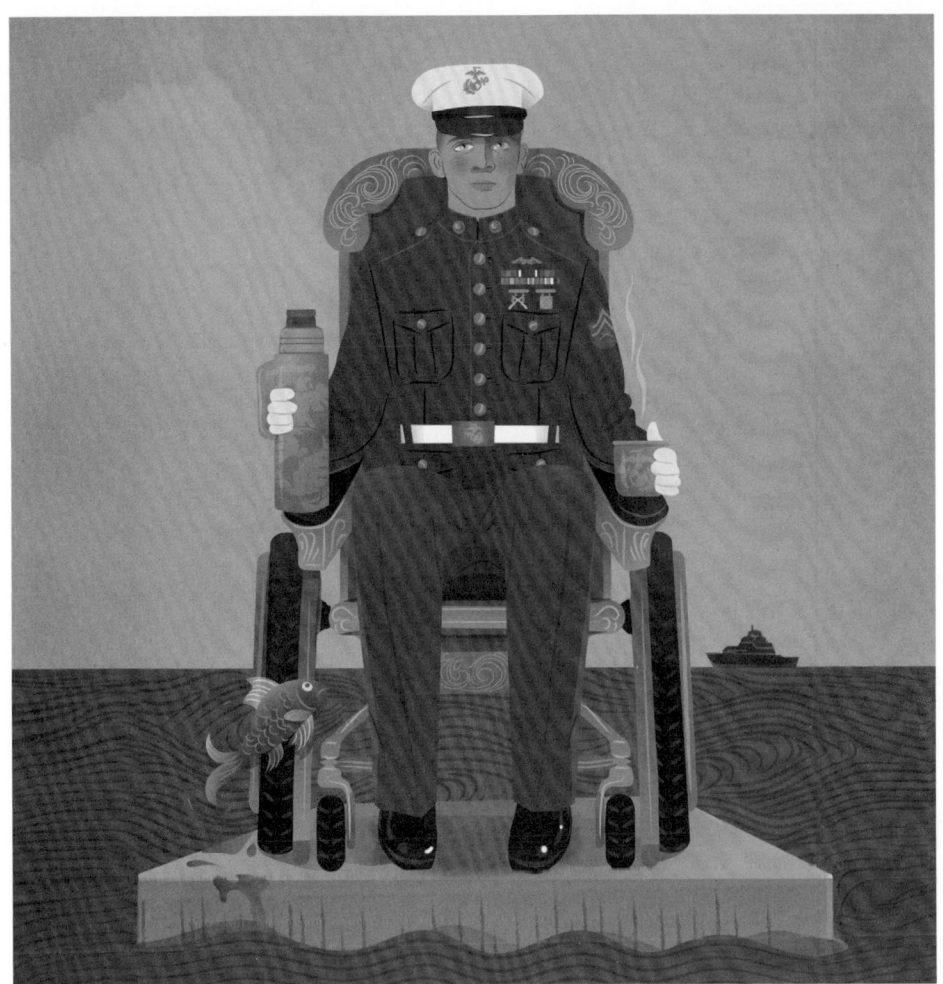

As a servant leader, the King of Cups offers counsel and advises others.

Practice Activity: Courts of Personality

As a writer of stories with elaborate plots and complex characters, the tarot has helped me with both plot and character design. One of my favorite methods of using the cards occurs during the writing process when I'm fleshing out each character's personality, determining how they will interact with one another and what role they will play in the storyline.

In that regard, I have designed this two-part practice activity to help with character development by imagining the Court cards as the cast of popular storylines. Doing so offers practice working with the tarot Court as character significators, which can in turn help you become more comfortable using them to inspire your own stories and cast of characters.

What you need for this activity:

- The Court cards from your Mystic Storyteller Tarot deck.
- Your favorite tools for notetaking.
- Your intuition.
- A favorite story, or one on which you are working.

To help inspire you, I have provided a list of six popular stories below:

The Color Purple
Harry Potter
The Office
Pride and Prejudice
Star Wars
The Wizard of Oz

On the opposite page, I've applied what I know about both the Court cards and the main characters from my favorite Jane Austen novel, *Pride and Prejudice*, and assigned a card for each.

Story Example: Jane Austen's *Pride and Prejudice*

The Pages

Page of Cups   Georgiana Darcy
Page of Pentacles   Charlotte Lucas
Page of Swords   Caroline Bingley
Page of Wands   Lydia Bennet

The Knights

Knight of Cups   Mr. Bingley
Knight of Pentacles   Mr. Collins
Knight of Swords   Mr. Wickham
Knight of Wands   Colonel Fitzwilliam

The Queens

Queen of Cups   Jane Bennet
Queen of Pentacles   Mrs. Bennet
Queen of Swords   Lady Catherine de Bourgh
Queen of Wands   Elizabeth Bennet

The Kings

King of Cups   Mr. Bennet
King of Pentacles   Sir William Lucas
King of Swords   Mr. Darcy *before* he falls in love with
                        Elizabeth Bennet
King of Wands   Mr. Darcy *after* falling in love with
                        Elizabeth Bennet

continued, following page...

Story Title: _____

The Pages

Page of Cups	
Page of Pentacles	
Page of Swords	
Page of Wands	

The Knights

Knight of Cups	
Knight of Pentacles	
Knight of Swords	
Knight of Wands	

The Queens

Queen of Cups	
Queen of Pentacles	
Queen of Swords	
Queen of Wands	

The Kings

King of Cups	
King of Pentacles	
King of Swords	
King of Wands	

What's next?

Next, get ready, because in Part Five of this book I will take you on a deep dive into the Tarot Code where you will learn how theory, archetypes, and symbolism amplify the cards, adding layers of inspirational information for storytelling. Be prepared to uncover profound ways of intuiting these symbols and applying them to your writing craft.

Part Five:

The Tarot Code

"Symbolism is the language of the Mysteries. By symbols men have ever sought to communicate to each other those thoughts which transcend the limitations of language."

Manly P. Hall
The Secret Teachings of All Ages

Chapter 19: Symbolism in the Tarot

. . . .

Whether writing fiction, memoir, poetry, or otherwise, symbolism is the spice rack of storytelling. A storm billowing over the distant, blustery horizon can mimic the emotional turmoil experienced by the main character. A pie cooling on a windowsill, birds prattling in the trees, and the silky crooning of Nat King Cole teasing the heady spring breeze can indicate that Aunt Sybil is preparing for a visit with your characters. Or is she preparing to eat them for dinner?

The house at the end of the street is overgrown with vines and rampant with ravens, its driveway hosting an old black sedan, the same car that has been following your character since chapter one. Could these details foreshadow death? Symbolism can add layers of meaning to your writing, and the symbols sprinkled throughout the tarot can help embellish language, plot decisions, character development, world-building, and so much more. After all, the tarot is a language of symbols. Animals, colors, directions, gestures, seasons, and structures can be interpreted as meaning various ideas and constructs, all of which can support creative processes.

As mentioned in Chapter 9, Pamela Colman Smith and A. E. Waite were both members of the Hermetic Order of the Golden Dawn, a secret society whose study and practice of symbology, numerology, and astrology heavily informed the development of the famed *Smith-Waite Tarot*. This very deck inspired our *Mystic Storyteller Tarot* and the symbols throughout. Furthermore, Christianity is deeply rooted in symbolism, the Bible almost entirely written in metaphor and allegory; the tarot reflects many of these very same stories. Simply put, storytelling that includes symbolic themes and references helps evoke an emotional response, connecting the reader with themes, settings, and characters. When executed effectively, symbolic references can mean the difference in merely telling or showing one's story.

The first time I read Dan Brown's *The DaVinci Code*,[68] the themes that resonated with me most were the artistic elements, especially the Old Masters, their paintings, and the virtual tour of the Louvre. Not long before writing this book, however, I watched the movie adaptation, and I felt like I was seeing an entirely different story unfold on the screen. My knowledge of religious symbolism and the occult was so much richer than back when I first discovered Brown's work. When the book was published in 2003, I was mostly curious to read it because of the Mona Lisa on the book's cover. When the movie was released, the book's cover was updated, to include a depiction of the painting peeling from its canvas and dissolving into symbols and iconography, several of which I now recognize as ancient Egyptian and alchemical in origin.

As you venture through this book, learning the traditional card meanings and deciding for yourself what ideas they represent, you will discover an elaborate network of symbols and iconography that adds layers of historical, mystical, and esoteric context to the cards. In addition to traditional meanings, however, if a particular symbol represents something unique to you, you are encouraged to honor and explore that meaning. For example, although the bird's traditional meaning is freedom, anytime I see a bird on a tarot card I am reminded of my grandmother, who was an avid birdwatcher. As such, I might associate birds with love and family. In this chapter, let's start exploring what I like to refer to as *The Tarot Code*.

Animals

Bat

A guardian of the night, the bat is symbolic of the transformation experienced after rising from a period of darkness. Although the bat is considered a lucky animal by some cultures, its lone appearance in the tarot occurs on The Devil card in the form of bat-like wings. In this regard, the meaning is not so lucky, as the wings suggest that the card's two figures are blindly following our Lady Devil, and that she is sucking the life out of her prey.[69] If The Devil card lands on your writer's desk, and those wings capture your attention, what stronghold is keeping you or your character(s) tethered to an unhealthy situation or practice?

Tarot card: The Devil (15 or XV).

Bird(s)

In the tarot, birds can symbolize freedom, inspiration, and they can sometimes serve as messengers from Spirit. Similarly, the dove is depicted as a divine messenger in the Bible, and in literature, it represents hope, love, peace, and purity. In The Star card, the ibis perching in the tree behind the woman is a sacred symbol to both Hermes and Thoth, the Egyptian god of wisdom, meaning higher thought.[70] See also Eagle and Falcon.

Tarot cards: Wheel of Fortune (10 or X), The Star (17 or XVII), The World (21 or XXI), Ace of Cups, Nine of Pentacles, Knight of Swords, and Queen of Swords.

Bull

The symbol of Taurus, the bull represents power, stability, strength, and stubbornness. Additionally, in art and literature the bull often symbolizes fertility and virility. If this animal catches your interest in a reading, about what are you or your character(s) being so stubborn? Alternatively, how and/or why are you or your character(s) being asked to step into your power?

Tarot cards: Wheel of Fortune (10 or X), The World (21 or XXI), and King of Pentacles.

Butterfly

Butterflies are a universal symbol for change and transformation. In the case of the petrified butterflies carved into the thrones of the Queen and King of Swords, these indicate a resistance to change. On the other hand, the butterflies that adorn the horse's bridle on the Knight of Swords convey facing change head-on.

Tarot cards: Knight, Queen, and King of Swords.

Cat

The cat is a symbol of independence and wit, and the ancient Egyptians considered the feline sacred. In some cultures, the cat is connected with femininity, the moon, and the power of transformation. As the Queen of Wands is considered by many to be the witch of the tarot, I think it's fitting that the only cat in the deck is also a black cat and serves as her familiar.

Tarot cards: Queen of Wands.

Crayfish

In The Moon card, this creature symbolizes emotions, water, and the writer's shadow voice. It can also indicate the ascension of consciousness at its earliest stage. If this animal catches your eye in a reading, what's your shadow whispering to you? Are these thoughts worth exploring?

Tarot card: The Moon (18 or XVIII).

Dog(s)

Dogs in the tarot can symbolize loyalty, faith, and one's conscious voice. In the Ten of Pentacles, an elder man pets one dog while a child plays with the other. According to author and psychotherapist Ellen Goldberg, the child and the elder indicate a beginning and an end.[71] On the other hand, in The Fool card, the little white dog represents the unconscious mind, barking a warning message as the person frolics dangerously close to a cliff.

Tarot cards: The Fool (0), The Chariot (7 or VII), The Moon (18 or XVIII), Six of Pentacles, and Ten of Pentacles.

Dragon

A common symbol in folklore and mythology, the dragon's significance is altogether opposite in Eastern and Western tradition. Whereas European lore often frames dragons as malefic, the mythical creatures are deemed benevolent and full of magic in the East. In the tarot, a dragon is seen perching inside one of the vessels on the Seven of Cups. Given its alternating meanings, you are encouraged to interpret the creature's significance depending on what resonates with you and/or the needs of your characters.

Tarot cards: Seven of Cups.

Eagle

In Indigenous American tradition, the eagle is a symbol of courage, freedom, honesty, independence, majesty, power, strength, success, truth, and wisdom. In the tarot, the eagle is often depicted as the symbol for Scorpio. If this animal catches your attention in a reading, it could be encouragement to seek freedom through expressing your truth.

Tarot cards: Wheel of Fortune (10 or X), The World (21 or XXI), and perhaps the Queen of Swords.

Fish

A common symbol in many cultures, especially lore, the fish's meaning runs as free and fluid as the water in which the animal lives. Directly associated with water, which represents change, feelings, and intuition, fish can also indicate the subconscious mind and thoughts. Around the world, many cultures view fish as good luck, a good omen, and symbolic of femininity, fertility, prosperity, and rebirth. In the zodiac, Pisces is represented by two fish, and in both the Christian religion and Egyptian deity worship, the fish symbol—also known as an ichthys (Greek word for fish) or ichthus—was used to identify believers and practitioners, respectively.[72]

Tarot cards: Page of Cups, Knight of Cups, and King of Cups.

Horse

Horses in the tarot signify companionship, direction, initiative, hard work, and momentum. The white horse upon which Death rides represents spirit, while the white horse in The Sun card symbolizes purity. In the Court cards, each of the Knights rides a horse, harnessing the energy of their suit in order to initiate action, movement, and progress. If one of the tarot's horses stands out for you during a reading, what actions are happening in the card and/or within those around it and how might they resonate with what you're working on right now?

Tarot cards: Death (13 or XIII), The Sun (19 or XIX), Six of Wands, Knight of Cups, Knight of Pentacles, Knight of Swords, and Knight of Wands.

Lion

In the tarot, the lion can symbolize courage, majesty, power, pride, protection, royalty, strength, and wisdom. However, the animal can also represent the beastly desires of the flesh. In the zodiac, the lion represents Leo and in the arts the "King of the Jungle" has made a lasting symbolic impact. Who doesn't remember the roar of MGM's Leo the Lion? And what about Aslan of *The Lion, the Witch, and the Wardrobe*? Anyone need a little courage? I know a Cowardly Lion who will show you where a certain Wizard is giving it away in exchange for a monologue on the subject.

Tarot cards: Strength (8 or VIII), Wheel of Fortune (10 or X), The World (21 or XXI), Two of Cups, Queen of Wands, and King of Wands.

Lizard

The lizard—sometimes referred to as a salamander—makes an appearance in the suit of Wands. Similar to life, the lizard suns itself in the fiery heat while gazing in the same direction as the King of Wands. In folklore the lizard is thought to enhance its sight by looking into the sun; such behavior indicates gaining perspective in the presence of immense force. The animal can also be found in a printed pattern on the Wands Court wardrobe, a symbol of vision in the midst of action, and a reminder that great results can be achieved by small, intentional efforts. If the lizard catches your eye in a reading, what small efforts are you being called to make to advance your craft?

Tarot cards: Page of Wands, Knight of Wands, and King of Wands.

Rabbit

Rabbits are impulsive, swift, and tentative creatures; however, in The Tortoise and the Hare fable, the hare represents impatience and haste. Perhaps the rabbit on the Queen of Pentacles card serves to remind you and/or your characters of the importance of grounding and exercising good judgement. Alternatively, in *The Hare and the Hound* fable, we are reminded that the strongest don't always win the day; sometimes luck favors the clever.

Tarot cards: Queen of Pentacles.

Ram

The ram is the symbol for Aries, the first sign of the zodiac and ruler of The Emperor card. Like its Major Arcana counterpart, this animal signifies determination, leadership, and responsibility. If the ram butts your interest in a reading, it could be preparing you or your character to stand up, get motivated, take action, and charge forward toward your goals.

Tarot cards: The Emperor (4 or IV) and Queen of Pentacles.

Raven

In the Nine of Pentacles, my favorite card of the Minor Arcana, the woman is making serious eye contact with a raven. In popular culture and folklore, the raven is considered a messenger from the gods. The bird often symbolizes curiosity, insight, prophesy, wisdom... and to a certain 19th century poet (Poe-t?), death.

Tarot cards: Nine of Pentacles.

Salamander (See lizard.)

Tarot cards: Page of Wands, Knight of Wands, and King of Wands.

Snail

Featured on the Nine of Pentacles, the snail can represent finding security and happiness within. After all, snails carry their homes upon their backs. Additionally, the snail is slow to move, what with being a pseudopod, meaning "false feet." Therefore, this animal might indicate that progress comes slow but steady and can sometimes unfold at a snail's pace. Because the woman in the card radiates prosperity, the slow and steady snail serves as a reminder that success is seldomly the result of luck, nor does it often occur overnight. A famous Theodore Roosevelt quote resonates this point: "Nothing worth having comes easy."

Tarot cards: Nine of Pentacles.

Snake or Serpent

In Rachel Pollack's Seventy-Eight Degrees of Wisdom, she writes that the snake is a magical creature representative of sexuality as "a force towards enlightenment."[73] As the snake sheds its skin during its growth cycles, the animal is symbolic of development, rebirth, and renewal. Additionally, snakes are adaptive and flexible. If this animal catches your attention in a reading, what aspect of yourself or your character needs shedding in order to facilitate growth? Or is your writing routine in need of an entire transformation?

Tarot cards: The Lovers, Wheel of Fortune (10 or X), and Seven of Cups.

Colors

Color has such an impact on emotions and mood that there is an entire branch of psychology dedicated to the subject. Understanding how and why color affects human perception can provide insight on motivation and behavior, two important considerations for the fiction writer. Across various cultures, different colors have diverse meanings and connotations, and personal preferences can also inform the significance of color. As you explore the tarot, whether pulling single cards or setting out multiple in a spread, pay attention to which colors catch your eye most prominently. How do the colors make you feel? Are they forming repetitive patterns? Which colors are your favorites? In this chapter, I will provide some insight around the most common colors in the tarot paired with their psychological and symbolic meanings.

Black

This color informs authority, beginnings, calmness, endings, fear, mystery, the occult, and seduction. Historically, the color has been associated with darkness, grief, and shadow; however, these negative connotations can be problematic and reductive. On a positive note, black is the color of power, protection, sophistication, and strength. In the tarot, the cards that include a large amount of this color call attention to what's unknown. If one of these cards lands on your writer's desk, how can you draw strength from its messaging?

Blue

One of the three primary colors, blue is the color of atmosphere, harmony, life, peace, spirituality, tranquility, and water. While lighter shades of blue promote calmness and trust, darker shades can evoke feelings of loneliness, despair, detachment, or solitude. On a lower polarity, blue directly relates to "having the blues" or "feeling blue." In the tarot, blue is predominantly featured on cards that lean towards imagination and inspiration. How does the color blue inspire you?

Brown

Because it's an earthy tone, the color brown is associated with comfort, dedication, endurance, loyalty, reliability, resilience, safety, security, simplicity, stability, and trust. The color is considered neutral and can therefore serve as a grounding influence, reminding one of the basics, their roots, and core values. In the tarot, brown is associated with material success and practicality. If this color stands out on a card in a reading, perhaps you or your character(s) are being called to ground yourselves and/or return to the basics.

Gray

The most neutral of all colors, gray is austere, conventional, even, moderate, monotonous, and standard. It can suggest depression, intellect, modesty, mystery, neutrality, sadness, and uncertainty. Fun fact: To see another color in its true, pure form, surround it with gray. For example, museum walls are painted variations of gray (most of which lean closer to white) because the color is best for showcasing artwork without any color influence or interference. In the tarot, gray leans toward mystery and/or uncertainty.

Green

Like the color brown, green is a dominant color in nature. Green influences balance, calm, endurance, harmony, hope, good luck, growth, happiness, optimism, peace, relaxation, stability, and tranquility. On a lower polarity, green can represent envy and sickness. In the tarot, green is a symbol of a fresh start, optimal health, money, and stability. If this color catches your attention in a card or reading, how does it make you feel?

Orange

A warm color, evoking thoughts of citrus fruit, fire, and summertime, orange can have a similar effect on mood and feeling. The color can represent optimism, energy, flamboyance, confidence. On a lower polarity, orange can represent aggression, arrogance, and caution. In the tarot, orange can convey healing powers and happiness. If this color resonates with you in a reading, consider it an invitation to turn up the volume, add more fuel to your fire, or any idiom related to injecting your writing practice with an extra dose of vivacity.

Pink

Warm and soothing, pink is a color that has been traditionally associated with innocence, femininity, love, and romance. Pink can also represent sweetness and optimism, hence the saying "seeing the world through rose-colored glasses." In the tarot, pink can indicate unconditional and nurturing love. If this color catches your eye in a card or a reading, how might you or your character(s) express love or compassion? Alternatively, have these sensations blinded you/them from seeing things clearly?

Purple / Violet

The color purple is associated with spirituality, enlightenment, and like Alice Walker's book of the same title, *The Color Purple* represents freedom. Additionally, because the earliest purple fabric dyes were costly, only the wealthy could afford them. Therefore, purple came to be associated with royalty, luxury, and opulence. In the tarot, this color informs deep-thinking and spiritual truth-seeking, and I would be remiss if I did not mention Prince in connection with this color. According to his family, purple was his favorite color because it was associated with royalty and made him feel "Princely."[74]

Red

Red is a color of extremes. One of the three primary colors, red symbolizes passion, love, anger, rage, desire, and power. In Renaissance era paintings, figures wearing the color red were meant to stand out in importance and significance. Similarly, in the tarot, the color red is prominently featured on cards that inform action, confidence, strength, and vitality. If this color pops out on a card or in a reading, consider your immediate feelings and thoughts about it. What messaging is the color trying to convey?

Yellow

One of the three primary colors, yellow is universally associated with the sun. This color highlights creativity, happiness, honor, hunger, intellect, and joy. Yellow is a color of clarity and positive energy, and in the tarot, the cards that feature a heavy amount of yellow are associated with intellect, positivity, and vitality. When this color resonates with you in a card or reading, you are encouraged to pause and reflect on how the energy and messaging it reflects or highlights.

White

Like black and gray, white is a neutral color. It symbolizes hope, peace, and purity. Historically, white has represented healing and protection, and in the tarot, it informs faith and innocence.

Elements & Suits

In the tarot, the elements—water, earth, air, and fire—can indicate several connections. They can mean the elements as they are expressed literally through the physical world (rain, dirt, wind, and light), in the human experience (heart, body, mind, and spirit), in their astrological associations (See Chapter 23), and as they relate to the tarot suits (cups, pentacles, swords, and wands).

Water (Cups)

Direction: West
In the physical world: creeks, dew, lakes, marsh, oceans, ponds, rain, rivers, streams, and swamp
In the human experience: Heart
Astrology: Cancer, Scorpio, and Pisces
Keywords: Change, emotions, feelings, intuition, and relationships
Tarot cards: The High Priestess (2 or II), The Chariot (7 or VII), The Hanged One (12 or XII), Death (13 or XIII), The Star (17 or XVII), The Moon (18 or XVIII), and the suit of Cups.

Earth (Pentacles)

Direction: North
In the physical world: dirt, flowers, ground, plants, and trees
In the human experience: Body
Astrology: Taurus, Virgo, and Capricorn
Keywords: Finances, home, material / physical, and work
Tarot cards: The Empress (3 or III), The Hierophant (5 or V), The Hermit (9 or IX), The Devil (15 or XV), The World (21 or XXI), and the suit of Pentacles.

Air (Swords)

Direction: East
In the physical world: breath, breeze, and wind
In the human experience: Mind
Astrology: Gemini, Libra, and Aquarius
Keywords: Conflict, curiosity, intellect, and thoughts
Tarot cards: The Fool (0), The Magician (1 or I), The Lovers (6 or VI), Justice (11 or XI), The Tower (16 or XVI), and the suit of Swords.

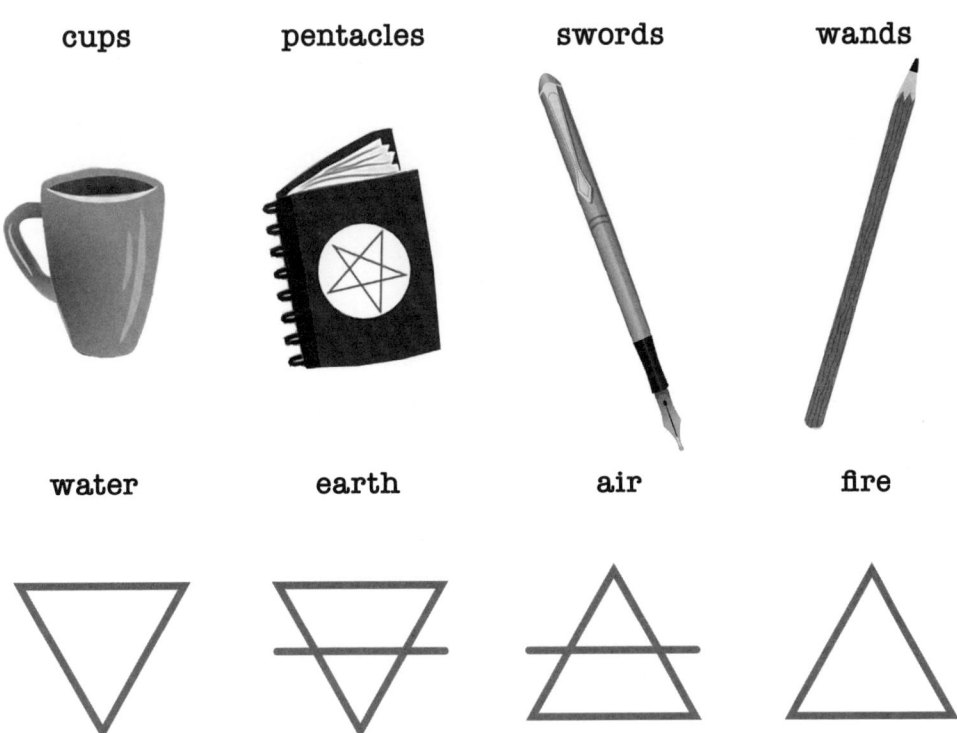

cups	pentacles	swords	wands
water	earth	air	fire

Fire (Wands)

Direction: South
In the physical world: fire, heat, light, sun, warmth
In the human experience: Spirit
Astrology: Aries, Leo, and Sagittarius
Keywords: Creativity, enterprise, inspiration, and passion
Tarot cards: The Emperor (4 or IV), Strength (8 or VIII), Wheel of Fortune (10 or X), Temperance (14 or XIV), The Sun (19 or XIX), Judgement (20 or XX), and the suit of Wands. In the case of The Tower card, fire represents cleansing through destruction. See also Fire in the Environment section.

Environment

Brick or Stone Wall

In the tarot, walls indicate safety and security. Pay attention to what's on both sides of the walls and you might be able to guess how you or your character(s) are being protected and/or kept safe.

Tarot cards: Justice (11 or XI), The Sun (19 or XIX), Three of Pentacles, Ten of Pentacles, and King of Pentacles.

Bridge

A bridge allows travel from one place to another; therefore, in the tarot, bridges are a symbol of movement, relocation, transition, and connecting one place to the next. If a bridge catches your eye in a card, perhaps you or your character(s) are moving from one moment to the next. Maybe a transition is in order.

Tarot cards: Five of Cups and Four of Wands.

Castle / Mansion

Because castles and mansions are associated with royalty and wealth, these structures in the tarot represent the achievement of goals, success, and living one's best life. If a castle or mansion resonates with you in a card or a reading, it could be a reminder to assess your goals. Similarly, it could mean remaining grateful for and proud of what you have achieved.

Tarot cards: Seven of Cups, Ten of Cups, Eight of Swords, Nine of Pentacles, Eight of Wands, Ten of Pentacles, Ace of Wands, Two of Wands, and Four of Wands.

City / Town / Village

In the tarot, cities and towns are representative of community, group achievement via teamwork, harmony, protection, security, and shelter.

Tarot cards: The Chariot (7 or VII), Five of Cups, Six of Cups, Ten of Cups, Seven of Swords, Four of Pentacles, Six of Pentacles, Eight of Pentacles, Ten of Cups, Ten of Pentacles, Eight of Swords, Four of Wands, Ten of Wands, and King of Pentacles.

Clouds

Clouds convey celestial messages and opportunities. They also indicate elevated thinking, growth, higher thought, and perspective. In some cases, I believe clouds symbolize mystery and hidden magic. Remember when you were a kid and you laid on the ground to look up at the clouds? Remember pointing up at the shapes they made? That's nephelomancy (cloud divination) at its finest. If a cloud or cloud system resonates with you in a card or reading, what do you see? What memories do the shapes evoke?

Tarot cards: The Lovers (6 or VI), Wheel of Fortune (10 or X), The Hanged One (12 or XII), The Tower (16 or XVI), The Star (17 or XVII), Judgement (20 or XX), The World (21 or XXI), Ace of Cups, Four of Cups, Five of Cups, Seven of Cups, Eight of Cups, Page of Cups, Ace of Pentacles, Nine of Pentacles, Ace of Swords, Three of Swords, Five of Swords, Seven of Swords, Eight of Swords, Ten of Swords, Page of Swords, Knight of Swords, Queen of Swords, King of Swords, and Ace of Wands.

Columns

Like pillars and herms, columns indicate balance, a beckoning, choice, decision, a gateway, safety, and security.

Tarot cards: The High Priestess (2 or II), The Hierophant (5 or V), and Justice (11 or XI).

Eclipse

In the tarot, an eclipse symbolizes an awakening, a shift in energy, and a transition. They inform change that is instinctual, subconscious, or under the surface. If you pull The Moon or the Eight of Cups in a reading and the eclipse stands out to you, it could mean an initiation into a major or minor transition, respectively.

Tarot cards: The Moon (18 or XVIII) and Eight of Cups.

Field / Grass

When exploring the tarot, don't forget to look at the background in each card, for there is symbolism and meaning hidden like Easter eggs. Fields, for example, have different meanings depending on their condition. A plowed field means you (or your characters) reap what you sow. Hard work and diligence can yield a plentiful harvest. On the other hand, a grassy terrain with flowers evokes an awakening, blossoming, growth, newness, and nurturing. In either case, when the Earth blooms, we are reminded of the passage "As above, so below."

Tarot cards: The Empress (3 or III), The Lovers (6 or VI), The Chariot (7 or VII), The Hanged One (12 or XII), Death (13 or XIII), Temperance (14 or XIV), The Star (17 or XVII), The Moon (18 or XVIII), Cups: Two, Three, Four, Five, Six, and Ten; Pentacles: Ace, Seven, Ten, Page, Knight, Queen, and King; Swords: Seven; Wands: Ace, Two, Five, Eight, and Queen.

Fire

In the tarot, a fire can denote various meanings, to include ambition, destruction, determination, energy, passion, power, renewal, a spark of inspiration, transformation, and will. Fire also has numerous historical, mythological, and religious contexts. According to Christianity, fire can symbolize divinity, illumination, knowledge, martyrdom, purification, and wisdom. In mythology, fire can bring spiritual renewal through baptism by fire or walking on fire, and the dying phoenix immolates itself in fire so it can rise again in youth, perpetuating an immortal cycle.[75]

Tarot cards: The Devil (15 or XV) and The Tower (16 or XVI).

Flower(s)

Popularized by the Victorians, the meaning of flowers is hidden throughout the tarot. In general, flowers mean beauty, joy, growth, love, and sensitivity, as indicated by the wildflowers in the Page of Cups, Page of Pentacles, and Queen of Pentacles, or the white flowers in the Six of Cups. However, lush foliage, like that in The Magician (1 or I), The High Priestess (2 or II), Three of Cups, Ten of Pentacles, and Four of Wands cards, can represent the manifestation of beautiful intent—magic blooming before one's eyes. On the other hand, many flowers yield individual meanings, depending on the card and/or other flowers in the vicinity. The following list includes specific flowers present in the tarot, along with their meanings and corresponding cards.

Iris—faith, hope, trust, valor, and wisdom; Temperance (14 or XIV).

Lotus—ascension, emergence, higher consciousness, rebirth, and renewal; Ace of Cups.

Red rose—beauty, hope, love, passion, and pleasure; The Magician (1 or I), The Hierophant (5 or V), Strength (8 or VIII), Nine of Swords, and Two of Wands.

Sunflower(s)—adoration, fame, fortune, happiness, and joy; The Sun (19 or XIX), Nine of Pentacles, and Queen of Wands.

White lily— death, majesty, modesty, and purity; The Magician (1 or I), Ace of Pentacles, and Two of Wands.

White rose—immortality, innocence, purity, transformation, silence, and youthfulness; The Fool (0), Death (13 or XIII), The World (21 or XXI), and Eight of Pentacles.

Grapes and Grapevines

Grapes and grapevines in the tarot symbolize abundance, blessings, bounty, celebration, fertility, inner transformation, prosperity, and redemption. In mythology, grapes are connected to the Greek deity Dionysus, god of fertility, merriment, pleasure, and wine.

Tarot cards: The Devil (15 or XV), Three of Cups, Ten of Pentacles, King of Pentacles, and Four of Wands.

Ice

When a card features ice or snow, these are indicators of contemplation, isolation, moving slowly, patience, postponement, and waiting. If you pull a card with a lot of ice or snow featured, perhaps you or your character(s) are being reminded to slow down and/or have patience.

Tarot cards: The Fool (0), The Hermit (5 or V), Judgement (20 or XX), and Five of Pentacles.

Lightning

In the tarot, lightning can indicate an epiphany, a sudden clarity of mind and the eradication of ignorance; in the Bible, lightning represents God's power or wrath.[76]

Tarot card: The Tower (16 or XVI).

Moon

The moon is representative of manifestation, the full moon reminding us to remain thankful for our many blessings. The crescent or sickle moon, on the other hand, represents psychic power, fertility, life and death, and in witchcraft it represents the divine feminine.

Tarot cards: The High Priestess (2 or II), The Chariot (7 or VII), Eight of Cups, and Two of Swords.

Mountains and Hills

In the tarot, mountains and hills can represent attainment, obstacles, protection, a steady foundation, security, and structure.

Tarot cards: The Fool (0), The High Priestess (2 or II), The Emperor (4 or IV), The Lovers (6 or VI), Strength (8 or VIII), The Hermit (9 or IX), Death (13 or XIII), Temperance (14 or XIV), The Star (17 or XVII), The Moon (18 or XVIII), Judgement (20 or XX), Cups: Four, Five, Eight, Ten, and Knight; Pentacles: Ace, Seven, Page, Knight, and Queen; Swords: Ace, Two, Five, Six, Seven, Eight, Page, and Knight; Wands: Ace, Two, Three, Five, Seven, Eight, Nine, Ten, Page, Knight, Queen, and King.

Path

A path in the tarot is a metaphor for a calling or taking a journey. If you pull a card with a path that stands out to you, what are you being called to do? Or where are you being called to go?

Tarot cards: Temperance (14 or XIV) and The Moon (18 or XVIII).

Pillar(s) or Herms

Like columns, pillars and herms indicate balance, a beckoning, choice, decision, a gateway, safety, and security.

Tarot cards: Death (13 or XIII) and The Moon (18 or XVIII).

Pomegranate(s)

In Greek mythology, Persephone is abducted from her parents, Zeus and Demeter, by Hades, Zeus' brother. While in the Underworld, she eats "the fruit of the dead," pomegranates. As such, the pomegranate is a symbol of life, death, and rebirth. Furthermore, the fruit's red juice can represent an elixir of youth, or perhaps even the blood of Jesus.[77] The pomegranate is often associated with bliss, luxury, and female sexuality.

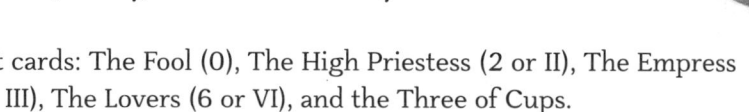

Tarot cards: The Fool (0), The High Priestess (2 or II), The Empress (3 or III), The Lovers (6 or VI), and the Three of Cups.

Rain

Historically, rain has been thought to represent clearing, inundation, restoration, and washing clean. Rain symbolizes the beginning and end of a storm, and it informs the irrigation and nourishment of fertile soil, both literally and figuratively. If you pull the Three of Swords in a reading and the rain stands out to you, what in your life or the life of your fictional character(s) is being washed away or needs to be cleansed?

Tarot cards: Three of Swords.

Rainbow

In Irish lore, the rainbow is a symbol of good luck, what with pots of gold being found where they end. Additionally, in the Biblical story of Noah and the Ark, the rainbow was cast in the sky as a promise from God that the torrential rains and flooding were over, and a new day was emerging. In this regard, rainbows represent new beginnings, hope, and peace. Rainbows are also an optical illusion, and in mythology they symbolize a bridge between mankind and the gods.[78]

Tarot cards: Ten of Cups.

Rocks

In the tarot, rocks can symbolize dangers and obstacles in one's path that should and can be avoided and/or overcome. Depending on their size, moving them might range from simple or seemingly impossible, but if they resonate with you, then perhaps you are being called to at least try. Alternatively, rocks could serve as a reminder to be still and strong like a rock.

Tarot cards: The Emperor (4 or IV), Temperance (14 or XIV), The Star (17 or XVII), The Moon (18 or XVIII), Eight of Cups, Two of Swords, and Eight of Swords.

Star

As long as history has been recorded—and even before—humans have looked to the stars and imagined meaning, possibilities, and lore. In that regard, a star's appearance in the tarot can mean direction, guidance, and illumination so that one might see clearly, both literally and figuratively. In particular, a six-pointed star (The Hermit card) represents the Jewish Star of David and/or Seal of Solomon, a symbol of guidance and wisdom. Additionally, the eight-pointed star, as featured eight times in The Star card, has several spiritual and esoteric meanings. In ancient Mesopotamia, for example, the eight-pointed star was a symbol of the goddess Ishtar, who was associated with Venus, and in Hinduism, Lakshmi, the goddess of wealth, was represented by a similar eight-pointed star.[79] For the five-pointed star, see Pentagram or Pentacle.

Tarot cards: The Empress (3 or III), The Chariot (7 or VII), The Hermit (9 or IX), The Star (17 or XVII), The Moon (18 or XVIII), Four of Swords, Two of Wands, and the suit of Pentacles.

Sun

In the tarot, the sun represents confidence, clarity, direction, energy, happiness, joy, life, peace, positivity, and warmth. If the sun or its rays stand out on a card or in a reading, consider how a particular situation is being illuminated.

Tarot cards: The Fool (0), The Lovers (6 or VI), Death (13 or XIII), Temperance (14 or XIV), and The Sun (19 or XIX).

Water (rivers, lakes, etc.)

Water is a symbol of intuition and the subconscious mind. In the tarot, water is often represented by the color light blue, which has calming effects. The High Priestess is the first card to feature this element, what with her garment flowing like water. This detail is thought to be the starting point of all the water found in the tarot. Every shower, stream, river, body of water flows from The High Priestess' robes.

Tarot cards: The High Priestess (2 or II), The Empress (3 or III), The Emperor (4 or IV), The Chariot (7 or VII), Death (13 or XIII), Temperance (14 or XIV), The Star (17 or XVII), The Moon (18 or XVIII), and Judgement (20 or XX); Cups: Ace, Five, Eight, Ten, Page, Knight, Queen, and King; Pentacles: Two and Queen; Swords: Two, Three, Five, Six, Eight, and Ten; Wands: Ace, Two, Three, Four, and Eight.

Wheat or Other Grains

In The Empress card, wheat indicates abundance, harvest, and manifestation. What are you manifesting in your pursuit of storytelling?

Angels in the tarot represent divine messengers.

Figures, Features, Hand Gestures, and Pose

Angels

Angels in the tarot represent divine messengers. The messages are specifically related to the card on which they appear, and to the writer, those messages might relate to you or your character(s). Alternatively, an angel can symbolize the Higher Self, higher thoughts, and divine inspiration, divine intervention, and divine wisdom.

Tarot cards: The Lovers (6 or VI), Wheel of Fortune (10 or X), Temperance (14 or XIV), Judgement (20 or XX), Seven of Cups, Queen of Cups, and Queen of Swords.

Child

In the tarot, children can represent innocence, naïveté, new beginnings, nostalgia, promise, purity, and youth. If a child resonates with you in a card or reading, it could also symbolize your inner child. In that case, consider what your inner child needs in this moment.

Tarot cards: Death (13 or XIII), The Sun (19 or XIX), Judgement (20 or XX), Six of Cups, Ten of Cups, Ten of Pentacles, Six of Swords, Seven of Swords, and the Pages, to some.

Crossed Legs

In both The Hanged One and The World cards, the figures' legs form a cross. In The Hanged One, the individual's crossed arms and head form a triangle shape. In alchemy, a cross above a triangle is the inversion of the symbol for sulfur, which means the completion of self-transmutation.[80]

Tarot cards: The Hanged One (12 or XII) and The World (21 or XXI).

Downward Pointing

In The Devil card, the lowered left arm indicates bringing light into darkness. In The Magician card, however, this gesture indicates "so below," as in the saying "As above, so below." Although The Magician holds a wand, his pointed finger also serves as a conduit for energy transfer.

Tarot cards: The Magician (1 or I) and The Devil (15 or XV).

Falling

Falling can indicate the loss of control, as in The Tower card. If the two people in this card stand out to you, consider their falling an invitation to explore what's falling from your own life. What's being ejected in order to serve your best interests?

Tarot cards: The Tower (16 or XVI).

Footing

In the Temperance and The Star cards, one figure's foot is in the water, symbolizing intuition, while the other rests on land, representing stability. Similarly, in The Moon card, the crayfish's claws are extended out on land, while its legs are still in the water.

Tarot cards: Temperance (14 or XIV), The Star (17 or XVII), and The Moon (18 or XVIII).

Footwear

There is an interesting occurrence on the Seven of Wands that is worth noting: the figure is wearing one laced shoe and one buckled boot. According to Marcus Katz and Tali Goodwin, authors of *Secrets of the Waite-Smith Tarot*, this detail is a nod from Pamela Colman Smith's theatrical days. The title character in Shakespeare's play *Petruchio* wears two different shoes, one laced and the other buckled. About the Seven of Wands, Katz and Goodwin further pose, "The card here carries the ideas of a war of words, battling down someone's position by belittling and even bullying them."[81]

Tarot cards: Seven of Wands.

Nakedness

According to A. E. Waite, a nude figure in the tarot symbolizes unveiled Truth.[82] Nakedness also denotes bravery, freedom, naïveté, opening oneself to the possibilities, success, spiritual graduation, and vulnerability. While the *Mystic Storyteller Tarot* does not feature fully nude figures, Pamela Colman Smith's original illustrations include several. Those cards are listed below.

Tarot cards: The Star (17 or XVII), The Sun (19 or XIX), Judgement (20 or XX), and The World (21 or XXI).

Pointing Up and Down

As seen in The Magician card, this gesture indicates "As above, so below," a popular saying credited to Hermes Trismegistus, author of the famed Emerald Tablet. The phrase indicates willing Earthly endeavors to match those of Heaven. See also Downward Pointing.

Tarot cards: The Magician (1 or I).

Prana Mudra

In the Prana Mudra, the thumb aligns with the extended pointer and middle fingers, while the ring and pinky fingers are folded into the palm. This hand gesture means life force and vitality. If you pull the Ten of Swords and this hand gesture stands out to you, how are you or your character(s) demonstrating strength in the midst of stringent rules or seemingly impossible obstacles?

Tarot cards: Ten of Swords.

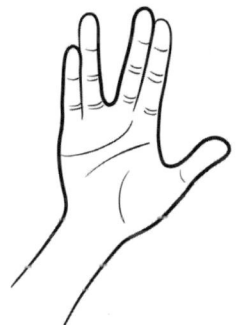

The Priestly Blessing Mudra

In the Priestly Blessing Mudra, the hand is extended, the thumb aligned with the length of the palm and the middle and ring fingers parted. This hand gesture denotes the Hebrew letter shin. Fun fact: Leonard Nimoy, famous for his role as Spock in the iconic Star Trek series and films, intentionally adapted the mudra to mean "live long and prosper," a gesture he'd learned from his own Jewish upbringing.[83]

Tarot card: The Devil (15 or XV).

Skeleton

The skeleton is a reminder of what we leave behind after death, our most enduring part, and our very own hidden treasure.

Tarot cards: Death (13 or XIII) and the Seven of Cups.

Other Symbols

Acorn

On the chalkboard in The Hierophant card, a pair of acorns represents oak knowledge and wisdom. As a seed, the acorn symbolizes growth and potential, as indicated in the proverb "Great oaks from little acorns grow." Perhaps the subjects before The Hierophant are seeking oak knowledge.

Tarot cards: The Hierophant (5 or V).

Ankh

Representing balance and eternal life, this ancient Egyptian symbol includes a circle or loop-like shape connected to the top of a cross. The circle symbolizes the sun rising above the horizon (the cross' lateral line), which the Egyptians connected to life and immortality.

Tarot cards: The Emperor (4 or IV) and The Hanged One (12 or XII).

Anubis

The original ancient Egyptian god of the dead (later replaced by Osiris), Anubis has the body of a man and the head of a jackal. The figure represents helplessness, death, and the afterlife.

Tarot cards: Wheel of Fortune (10 or X).

Arches

When you discover an arch in a tarot card, pay close attention to what's on both sides. The arch is a symbol for initiation, passage, and transition. Were you or your character(s) to walk beneath the arch, how might your lives and/or outlook change?

Tarot cards: Ten of Cups, Ace of Pentacles, Three of Pentacles, Ten of Pentacles, and Four of Wands.

Banner, Scarf, or Sash

In the tarot, banners and sashes symbolize the celebration of victory and success. However, when wrapped around the head, they indicate higher thinking and wisdom.

Tarot cards: Justice (11 or XI), The World (21 or XXI), Three of Cups, Nine of Cups, Four of Pentacles, Five of Pentacles, Six of Pentacles, Six of Swords, Ten of Swords, Queen of Swords, Three of Wands, Four of Wands, Nine of Wands, Ten of Wands, and Knight of Wands.

Blindfold

A blindfold is an apparatus that is used to keep someone from seeing. As such, the blindfold in the tarot represents being dishonest with oneself, a failure to face the facts, the inability to clearly see a situation, an unwillingness to accept the truth, and having something hidden or removed. On the other hand, if the individuals in the Two and/or Eight of Swords have deliberately blinded themselves, and this aspect of the card stands out to you, what is the intention?

Tarot cards: Two and Eight of Swords.

Boat

At face value, it's easy to presume that boats symbolize movement and travel. Drawing from the subconscious, however, these vessels can indicate deep thoughts churning into action. When you pull a card featuring a boat that resonates with you, what repressed thoughts need surfacing right now?

Tarot cards: Death (13 or XIII), King of Cups, Two of Pentacles, Six of Swords, and Three of Wands.

Caduceus

Two snakes wrap around the rod of Hermes, a symbol of balance, duality, healing, and wisdom.

Tarot cards: Two of Cups.

Cross

Although the cross predates the Christian religion, the symbol is most commonly linked with the crucifixion of Jesus Christ. It represents blessings, faith, love, prayer, and the promise of salvation. Furthermore, the equal-armed cross is symbolic of a crossroads, the four directions, the four elements, the four discernible life stages (birth, childhood, adulthood, and death), the four winds, Saint George's cross, and the Knights Templar.

Tarot cards: The High Priestess (2 or II), The Hierophant (5 or V), Death (13 or XIII), and Ace of Cups.

Crown

In the tarot, crowns can indicate authority, ego, higher thinking, intellect, royalty, and wisdom. A glowing crown means crowning achievement. A flowered crown denotes celebration, respect, and success.

Tarot cards: The High Priestess (2 or II), The Empress (3 or III), The Emperor (4 or IV), The Hierophant (5 or V), Justice (11 or XI), Death (13 or XIII), The Tower (16 or XVI), The Sun (19 or XIX), Two of Cups, Three of Cups, Seven of Cups, Queen of Cups, Four of Pentacles, Queen of Pentacles, Kings of Pentacles, Ace of Swords, King of Swords, Four of Wands, Six of Wands, Queen of Wands, and the King of Wands.

Feather

In the tarot, feathers represent air, free-thinking, justice, and truth.

Tarot cards: Four of Pentacles and Two of Swords.

Flag

A flag indicates an announcement of immediate change. It waves boldly and obviously so everyone in the vicinity can be made aware of the change.

Tarot card: Death (13 or XIII) and Seven of Swords.

Geometric Shapes

Square—On The Chariot, Justice, and Temperance, the square indicates Earthly desires and intentions, the shape's four points representing the "four corners of the world" and/or the four directions. However, in Freemasonry the square suggests morality and truth.[84]

Triangle inside a square—Temperance's amulet features this symbol. The triangle represents God, Sprit, and humanity, while the square denotes the physical world.[85]

Globe

In the tarot, the presence of a globe indicates totality.[86] The globe symbolizes achievement and having the world at one's fingertips. The globe's shape harkens back to the circle, which means completion and infinity.

Tarot cards: Two of Wands.

Heart

The heart is a universal symbol for love; however, it can also represent affection and happiness.

Tarot cards: The Empress (3 or III) and Three of Swords.

Jug (Vessel)

A container for water, which means intuition and feelings. In the case of Temperance, the dual vessels represent balance and harmony.

Tarot cards: Temperance (14 or XIV).

Keys

In the case of The Hierophant, two keys crossed represent the keys to heaven that are held by Saint Peter. Keys can also indicate intellect, hidden information, and knowledge. The key is the symbol of the Greek goddess Hecate, who can unlock the gates of death.

Tarot cards: The Hierophant (5 or V).

Lantern

In the tarot, the lantern represents devotion, faith, intelligence, internal light, remembrance, truth, vigilance, and virtue.

Tarot cards: The Hermit (9 or IX).

Lemniscate

The lemniscate is the symbol for balance, infinity, and simplicity. If this symbol resonates with you in a reading, what about your life needs balancing and/or simplifying right now?

Tarot cards: The Magician (1 or I), Strength (8 or VIII), The World (21 or XXI), and Two of Pentacles.

Lingam and Yoni

The lingam and yoni are Hindu symbols representing the union of the male and female principles and the totality of all existence. These symbols are featured on the front of The Chariot's carriage.

Tarot cards: The Chariot (7 or VII).

Ouroboros

Commonly depicted as a snake or lizard swallowing its own tail, the ouroboros symbolizes the cycle of life from birth to death to rebirth, wholeness, infinity, the ability to recreate oneself. The wreath in The World card is reminiscent of this symbol, and we also see it again on the Page, Knight, and King of Wands cards.

Tarot cards: The World (21 or XXI), Page of Wands, Knight of Wands, and King of Wands.

Pentagram and/or Pentacle

Upright—Contrary to popular misconceptions perpetuated by some religious organizations who believe the pentagram is "evil," and/or "Satanic," the symbol actually represents the five elements (air, earth, fire, water, and the fifth element, spirit... although Korben Dallas and Leeloo might beg to differ). This symbol's five-pointed star is encased within a circle, which represents eternity or Heaven.

Tarot cards: The Magician (1 or I), and the suit of Pentacles.

Inverted—Here is where the aforementioned misconceptions gain some footing. When inverted, the upside-down five-pointed star takes on the shape of a goat's head, which represents the darker aspects of occultism and is sometimes associated with dark magic. This inverted star can be seen on The Devil card, although there is no circle encasing it, as featured on a traditional pentacle.

Tarot cards: The Devil (15 or XV).

Scales

In the tarot, the scales mean balance, measuring, and making things level, even.

Tarot cards: Justice (11 or XI).

Sphinx

With the head of a human, the wings of an eagle, and the body and tail of a lion, the sphinx denotes nobility and divine opportunity. It can also represent the sun, life, and the soul.

Tarot cards: Wheel of Fortune (10 or X).

Stained Glass

Just like life, stained glass in the tarot indicates seeing something through a different lens. Our perception of what is represented by the card might be changing. If one of the tarot cards with stained glass lands on your writer's desk, perhaps you or your character(s) are being invited to pay closer attention to how you are seeing a situation.

Tarot cards: Five of Pentacles and Four of Swords.

Vesica Piscis

The shape made by the wreath on The World card is known as a Vesica Piscis, a geometric shape and sacred symbol formed by the intersection of two circles. Symbolically, this shape in The World card means the connecting of Heaven and Earth. Additionally, the Vesica Piscis represents divine femininity, fertility, the seed of life, and the Universal womb.[87]

Tarot cards: The World (21 or XXI).

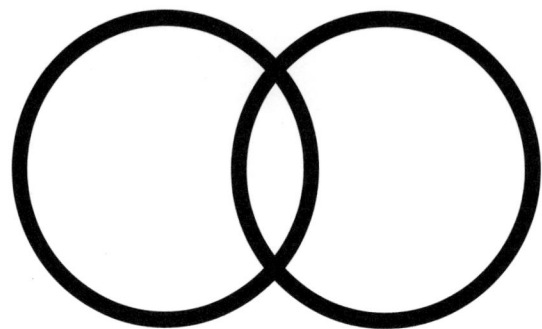

Wheel with Eight Spokes

In the tarot, the eight-spoked wheel can represent the Wheel of the Year, an annual cycle of eight Pagan festivals, or the Dharma Wheel, a traditional symbol in Buddhist teachings that advocates for moral order and enlightenment.[88]

Tarot cards: Wheel of Fortune (10 or X).

Wreath

A symbol of accomplishment, achievement, success, triumph, and victory; God's eternal love.

Tarot cards: Death (13 or XIII), The Sun (19 or XIX), The World (21 or XXI), Seven of Cups, Queen of Pentacles, and Six of Wands.

Stage Cards

There are several cards in the tarot in which the figure appears to be standing or moving on a stage-like platform. This stage is indicated by a set of parallel lines separating the background from a flat, solid surface in the foreground. This distinction is theorized in two ways. First, many believe the stage design is a nod to Pixie's background in theatre, and some tarot luminaries refer to the figures in a card(s) as "actors." As such, the stage card is considered an "Act," which might serve as a helpful guidepost for plotting and outlining purposes.

Tarot cards: Cups: Two, Eight, Ten, and Page; Pentacles: Two, Four, Six, Eight; Swords: Two, Five, Seven; Wands: Four, Nine, and Ten.

Zodiac

See Chapter 23 – Astrology and the Tarot.

Now that you have a reference bank for symbolism found in the tarot, including how you might glean inspiration from them, I'd like to introduce you to a formatting system that adds even more symbolic meaning to the cards. This diagram is often called the "3 x 7 Tarot Theory," and it directly overlaps with The Fool's Journey.

The Fool

The Magician

The High Priestess

The Empress

The Emperor

The Hierophant

The Lovers

The Chariot

Strength

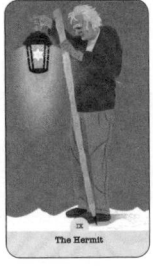

The Hermit

Wheel of Fortune

Justice

The Hanged One

Death

Temperance

The Devil

The Tower

The Star

The Moon

The Sun

Judgement

The World

Chapter 20: The 3x7 Tarot Diagram

. . . .

Although the origin of what tarot scholars refer to as "the 3 X 7 tarot diagram" and whom to credit for its development are unclear, many references list Lee Bursten, Philippe Camoin, Yves Levy, Rachel Pollack, and Van Rijnberk as either originators or contributors to the theory.

For consistency, I am referring to the model adapted by Rachel Pollack in her book *Seventy-Eight Degrees of Wisdom*. Her work has been a great influence in my own tarot journey, including the writing of this book. According to Pollack, the Major Arcana, or "key" cards, can be divided into three lines, each including a sequence of seven cards.[89] As you will learn in Chapter 22 – *Numerology: Tarot by the Numbers*, the numbers three and seven boast significant numerological symbolism, with three representative of the Holy Trinity or the Rule of Three, and seven a highly spiritual number and direct reference to the days of the week, continents, seas, and colors of the spectrum (Roy G. Biv).

Furthermore, if you are wondering how the Major Arcana fits into a 3 x 7 diagram when it contains 22 cards, it's important to note that the diagram is preceded by The Fool card, which exists independent of the rest and whose energy flows throughout.

You will learn more about The Fool's journey through the Major Arcana in Chapter 32 – *Plot Development: The Hero and The Fool*; however, by analyzing the keys in three rows of seven, you can see how The Fool's Journey starts to unfold.

Line 1

Line one represents The Fool's conscious interests and worries, such as love, education, leadership, and other external societal concerns. They are establishing boundaries, learning the framework and rules, setting benchmarks, and preparing for their venture.

Line 2

Line two denotes The Fool's withdrawal within, their concerns psychological and internally focused, including self-awareness, death, and rebirth. During this time, they endeavor a process of experimentation, practicing, nurturing, resistance, bargaining, unlearning, shedding, transitioning, uncovering, and realization.

Line 3

Finally, in line three The Fool applies what they've learned and is able to return to the conscious world having undergone a complete transformation. They have endured and/or embraced facilitation, manifestation, empowerment, settling, and acceptance.

Sound familiar? In fictional writing, almost every story arc has three major sections: a beginning, middle, and an end. The protagonist or hero—used here in a gender-neutral context—of such stories must navigate this arc, overcoming opposition and responding to obstacles along the way. This common narrative story template is known as the Hero's Journey. In the tarot, the Fool's Journey is quite similar, and in Chapter 32 you will learn how the two adventures overlap.

In summary, the 3 x 7 tarot diagram outlines the unfolding of the human experience, and it can be a helpful point of reference while outlining your own stories—whether personal or written. Next, let's examine a universal code especially familiar and insightful to fiction writers: archetypes.

Chapter 21: Archetypes

. . . .

First coined by the Greeks, the term "archetype" means "original pattern."[90] Such patterns are images or models of a person or a role. They include the mother, father, teacher, child, helper, and more, and they can represent similar meanings across various cultures and societies.

According to Swiss psychiatrist Carl Jung, an archetype is a collectively inherited subconscious idea, pattern of thought, or image universally spanning the collective consciousness.[91] In his work on the subject, Jung identified a dozen overarching archetypes that represent four main personality markers: the persona, the shadow, the anima or animus, and the self. These 12 archetypes are listed below, followed by a diagram (following page) of each with their prime motivators:

1. Ruler
2. Caregiver
3. Creator/Artist
4. Innocent
5. Sage
6. Explorer
7. Hero/Heroine
8. Wizard/Magician
9. Rebel
10. Everyman/Citizen
11. Jester
12. Lover

The tarot is full of archetypes, especially the Major Arcana and the Court cards, and these individuals are recognizable figures whom The Fool meets along their journey.

Interestingly, while it's unclear whether Carl Jung used the tarot, there is evidence that he knew about the cards. On March 1, 1933, the psychiatrist spoke about the tarot in a seminar he facilitated on active imagination. During the lecture, he described how the figures within the cards exemplified his archetypal theory. On the following page is a quote from the transcript of that lecture.[92]

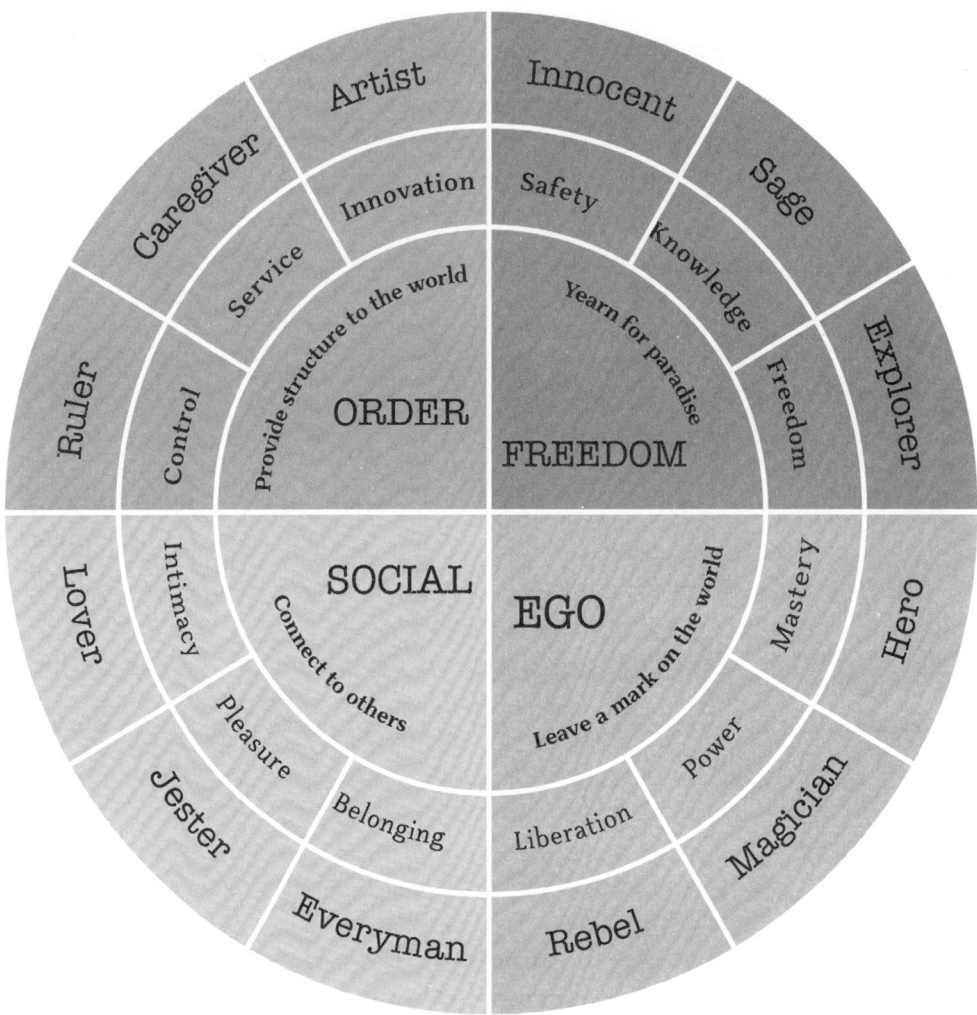

Carl Jung:

The original cards of the tarot consist of the ordinary cards, the king, the queen, the knight, the ace, etc.—only the figures are somewhat differ-ent—and besides, there are twenty-one cards upon which are symbols, or pictures of symbolic situations. For example, the symbol of the sun, or the symbol of the man hung up by the feet, or the tower struck by lightning, or the wheel of fortune, and so on. Those are sort of archetypal ideas, of a differentiated nature, which mingle with the ordinary constituents of the flow of the unconscious, and therefore it is applicable for an intuitive method that has the purpose of understanding the flow of life, possibly even predicting future events, at all events lending itself to the reading of the conditions of the present moment.

When considering the tarot and archetypes, many of the cards can be sorted into Carl Jung's 12 archetypal constructs; however, my interpretation of the tarot archetypes may differ from yours. As such, I recommend that you study both the tarot and the twelve archetypes and decide for yourself how they correspond.

Furthermore, it's helpful to note that several cards can be associated with the same archetype, as well as the same card can represent more than one archetype. As an example, I have identified possibilities for where I believe the cards correspond with Jung's 12 archetypes:

Ruler — The Empress, The Emperor, The Hierophant, The Chariot, The Tower, The Devil, the Queens, and the Kings

Caregiver—The Empress and the Queens

Artist—The Fool, Temperance, The Star

Innocent—The Sun and the Pages

Sage —The High Priestess, The Hierophant, The Hermit, The Moon, Pages

Explorer—The Fool and the Knights

Hero(ine) —The Chariot and the Courts

Magician —The Magician and the Kings

Rebel—The Devil and the Knights

Everyman—The Hanged One and the Courts

Jester —The Fool and the Pages

Lover—The Lovers, The Empress, The Devil, and the Knights

Not unlike the tarot, literature casts a wide net at capturing archetypal models and roles. In fact, I can ruminate on every fictional character I have ever written, spanning all of my work, and clearly identify the archetypes represented by each. If you have read my duology, *The Scars We Choose*, then you will immediately recognize protagonists Scarlett and Julian both as innocents and lovers, Pinkie

Perideaux as a sage and teacher, Zeke as a hero, and Ms. Blossom and Genevieve as caregivers, innocents, and victims. You might also say that Xavier McCobb is a villain... but so is Scarlett's mother, Faye Waverly. And if you've finished the series and read the bonus backstory, you might easily understand Faye's father, Fred Frye, as being a rebel.

Although Jung's 12 archetypes provide us with a place to begin our studies of the tarot's overlap, archetypes are not limited to a dozen. I have included an expanded list here; however, you are encouraged and invited to add your own archetypal discoveries to this list.

Archetype List

1. Addict
2. Advocate
3. Alchemist
4. Angel
5. Artist
6. Athlete
7. Avenger
8. Beggar
9. Bully
10. Caregiver
11. Child—magical
12. Child—orphan
13. Child—wounded
14. Clergy
15. Clown
16. Companion
17. Creator
18. Damsel
19. Detective
20. Engineer
21. Everyman/Citizen
22. Explorer
23. Father
24. Femme Fatale
25. Gambler
26. Goddess
27. Gossip
28. Guide

29. Healer

30. Hedonist

31. Hermit

32. Hero(ine)

33. Innocent

34. Influencer

35. Jester

36. Judge

37. King

38. Knight

39. Liberator

40. Lover

41. Luminary

42. Martyr

43. Mediator

44. Mentor

45. Miser

46. Mother

47. Mystic

48. Page

49. Pioneer

50. Poet

51. Priest

52. Prince

53. Princess

54. Prostitute

55. Queen

56. Rebel

57. Rescuer

58. Ruler

59. Sage

60. Scribe

61. Seeker

62. Servant

63. Scholar

64. Storyteller

65. Student

66. Teacher

67. Thief

68. Trickster

69. Vampire

70. Victim

71. Villain

72. Virgin

73. Visionary

74. Warrior

75. Witch /Wizard

add your own...

76.

77.

78.

79.

80.

81.

82.

83.

84.

85.

86.

87.

88.

89.

90.

91.

92.

93.

94.

95.

96.

97.

98.

99.

100.

101.

102.

103.

104.

105.

106.

107.

108.

109.

Chapter 22:
Numerology — Tarot bythe Numbers

. . . .

Numerology is the study of numbers and their energetic influence on the physical world. Every day, in every aspect of our lives, we are surrounded by numbers. Numerology seeks to uncover their meaning in order to understand how they might affect our experiences.

Subscribed to this understanding, early tarot deck designers intentionally assigned numbers to and within the cards. In most decks preceding the *Smith-Waite Tarot*, for example, the Minor Arcana cards were unillustrated pips, or "pip cards," with symbol correspondences assigned to each card. Much like the symbols featured on playing cards, the cups, pentacles, swords, and wands were featured on the pips—no figures, no settings, no other references other than the objects. To that point, understanding numerology was a must in order to discern the cards' full meanings. Even today, when working with decks such as the *Tarot de Marseille*, which includes unillustrated pips, you will likely feel more successful if you understand numerology.

The good news is that an awareness of numerology is not required in order to use the *Mystic Storyteller Tarot* for creative inspiration. However, the better news is having a point of reference around the significance of numbers can uncover additional aspects of the cards that can help amplify storytelling.

Although this chapter is not a comprehensive study of numerology as it informs the tarot, it can serve as an orientation to help you get started.

Easy Math

Let's be honest: math is hard for a lot of people, including me. If you are like me, and the thought of numbers and mathematics makes your palms sweaty and brings back memories of high school algebra, take a deep breath and then exhale. The math involved in numerology is simple addition and subtraction. No variables, no formulas... and no proofs, thank goodness.

In life and in the tarot, a common aspect of numerology is the reduction of large numbers and/or sequences of numbers (such as your date of birth) to a single-digit form, one (1) through nine (9). For example, your Life Path Number, which represents one's personality and talents in numerology,[93] is the number resulting from adding together the digits of your birth date and reducing them to their smallest figure. As an example of the easy math, *The Joy Luck Club* author Amy Tan's birthday is February 19, 1952, or 2/19/1952. I can perform simple math to determine her Life Path Number.

$$2 + 1 + 9 + 1 + 9 + 5 + 2 = 29$$

Now, let's reduce 29 to its simplest form:

$$2 + 9 = 11$$
$$1 + 1 = 2$$

Therefore, two (2) is Amy Tan's Life Path number, and in the tarot, that corresponds with her Soul Card, which is The High Priestess (2 or II).

There are several details to note when determining your personal tarot cards, like your Soul Card, and I cover them in Chapter 24 – *Your Tarot Code.* In this chapter, however, let's look at numbers, their numerological meanings, and their correspondences in the tarot.

Numbers in Tarot

As previously mentioned, the Minor Arcana consists of 10 pip cards and four Court cards for each of the four suits. That's 14 cards per suit. However, the numbered cards include the Aces through the Tens.

Although there is not a set rule that the Courts embody a particular number, for the purpose of numerology, a number can be assigned to them: Pages are number 11, Knights are 12, Queens are 13, and Kings are 14.

Because numbers one through 10 are the base numbers for working with numerology within the tarot, many cards in the Major Arcana require some easy math in order to determine their correspondences. In some instances, you will need to add the numbers together and reduce them to their lowest term.

For example, both The Sun card (19 or XIX) and Wheel of Fortune (10 or X) possess a numerological connection to the number one. Here's the simple math:

The Sun (19):   **Wheel of Fortune (10):**
$1 + 9 = 10$ $1 + 0 = 1$

Therefore, the numerological value for bothof these cards is one (1).

The following list provides numerological insight into numbers zero through 10 as they appear in the tarot. However, it's important to note that not all cards with a particular number correspond with every meaning of that number. For example, the number three can mean caring, celebration, cooperation, expression, longing, and results. However, the Three of Swords is more likely to represent caring, longing, and results, whereas the Three of Cups aligns more appropriately with meaning celebration, cooperation, and expression.

Numbers Zero through Ten in the Tarot

Zero: 0

Zero is a non-number, yet it is every number. It's infinite and present in everything and everywhere. Zero is the cosmic egg from which everything in the universe is born. In numerology and in the tarot, the number can represent ether, God, life, Spirit, Source, and Universe.

Tarot card: The Fool (0)

One: The Aces

In numerology, the number one can indicate birth, bravery, ego, gifts, inspiration, initiative, identity, independence, initiation, new beginnings, novel ideas, offers, opportunity, potential, and self-confidence. In the tarot, The Magician is the first numbered card of the Major Arcana, and the Aces are the first cards of the Minor Arcana.

Tarot cards: The Magician (1 or I), Wheel of Fortune (10 or X), The Sun (19 or XIX), and the Aces (all four suits)

Two: 2 or II

The number two can represent agreement, a duo, a pair, balance, choice, compromise, contract, cooperation, decisions, diplomacy, duality, harmony, opposition, partnership, tranquility, and union. In the tarot, many cards feature two animals, figures, and/or structures, such as pillars and columns.

Tarot cards: The High Priestess (2 or II), Justice (11 or XI), Judgement (20 or XX), and the Twos (all four suits)

Three: 3 or III

In numerology, the number three can convey celebration, collaboration, communication, compassion, cooperation, creativity, drive, expansion, expression, growth, longing, mystery, results, teamwork, and transition.

Tarot cards: The Empress (3 or III), The Hanged One (12 or XII), The World (21 or XXI), and the Threes (all four suits)

Four: 4 or IV

In numerology, the number four can represent focus, pause, planning, practicality, preparation, rigidity, stability, security, a steady foundation, and structure. Fun fact: In the English language, the word four is the only number word that has the same number of letters as the numeric value.

Tarot cards: The Emperor (4 or IV), Death (13 or XIII), and the Fours (all four suits)

Five: 5 or V

The number five is the first imbalanced number, meaning there is one additional facet that has thrown off the balance of the one, two, three, and four that came before it. Therefore, in numerology, five can inform adaptability, challenges, change, conflict, flexibility, grief, instability, liberation, and loss.

Tarot cards: The Hierophant (5 or V), Temperance (14 or XIV), and the Fives (all four suits)

Six: 6 or VI

In numerology, six can convey action to achieve harmony, adjustment, assistance, alignment, balance, compassion, empathy, healing, karma, love, and support.

Tarot cards: The Lovers (6 or VI), The Devil (15 or XV), and the Sixes (all for suits)

Seven: 7 or VII

The number seven can represent analysis, assessment, burden, challenges, conflict, faith, investigation, lessons, mystery, reflection, spirituality, struggles, and wisdom.

Tarot cards: The Chariot (7 or VII), The Tower (16 or XVI), and the Sevens (all four suits)

Eight: 8 or VIII

In numerology, the number eight can indicate accomplishment, achievement, action, control, goals, manifestation, mastery, movement, organization, power, strength, success, and work. The number relates to the eight spokes on the Wheel of the Year, with the corresponding eight Pagan Sabbats. Tip the number eight onto its side and it forms the lemniscate, the infinity symbol.

Tarot cards: Strength (8 or VIII), The Star (17 or XVII), and the Eights (all four suits)

Nine: 9 or IX

The final single-digit number in numerology, nine can represent attainment, contentment, an ending, completion, fruition, fulfilment, leadership, philanthropy, protection, a spiritual awakening, and Universal energy.

Tarot cards: The Hermit (9 or IX), The Moon (18 or XVIII), and the Nines (all four suits)

Ten: 10 or X

In the tarot, the number 10 can represent abundance, a completion, coming full circle, end of cycle, final manifestations, moving on, a new beginning, renewal, results, and a return to center.

Tarot cards: The Magician (1 or I), Wheel of Fortune (10 or X), the Aces (all four suits), and the Tens (all four suits)

Other Numbers in the Tarot

Eleven: 11 or XI

Eleven is a master number, meaning they carry more powerful positives and negatives than most numbers. As such, 11 informs incredible strength in trying times and helping one to cope during times of chaos and crisis. It can also represent enlightenment, charisma, and receptivity. The number 11 is also a psychic number, a gateway to the subconscious, just like the pillars on both the Justice and The High Priestess cards. Speaking of The High Priestess, 1 + 1 = 2, which informs balance, duality, partnership, and all the other previously mentioned two correspondences.

Tarot cards: The High Priestess (2 or II), Justice (11 or XI), the Twos (all four suits), and the Pages (all four suits)

Twelve: 12 or XII

In numerology, the number 12 can represent the cycle of life, a common example being the Gregorian calendar. Twelve can be reduced to the number three, as 1 + 2 = 3. In numerology, three can indicate cooperation, creativity, longing, and the other correspondences mentioned above.

Tarot cards: The Empress (3 or III), The Hanged One (12 or XII), the Threes (all four suits), and the Knights (all four suits)

Thirteen: 13 or XIII

In numerology, the number 13 is considered karmic and associated with Spirit. Thirteen can be reduced to the number four, which conveys focus, foundation, security, and the rest of the previously mentioned correspondences. In the tarot, however, these attributes occur after a significant change or transformation, which you can read more about in the Death card profile (Chapter 17, Key 13).

Tarot cards: The Emperor (4 or IV), Death (13 or XIII), the Fours (all four suits), and the Queens (all four suits)

Fourteen: 14 or XIV

In numerology, the number 14 can represent the expression of personal freedom, independence, lingering curiosity, and self-determination. When adding 1 + 4, we get five (5), a number that informs change, conflict, and instability. In the case of Temperance, number 14 in the Major Arcana, we can conclude that the figure in the card is working to counteract those constructs, promoting balance and harmony (See Chapter 17, Key 14 – Temperance).

Tarot cards: The Hierophant (5 or V), Temperance (14 or XIV), the Fives (all four suits), and the Kings (all four suits)

Fifteen: 15 or XV

The number 15 is both sacred and magical. It's sacred in that the number is featured throughout the Bible as meaning deliverance, freedom, and rest.[94] Fifteen is magic because it's the number of the Magic Square. In mathematics, there are ways to assign numbers one through nine to a grid of three columns and three rows where the sum of every column and every row is 15. In numerology, when adding 1 + 5, we get six (6). Six is the number of balance, karma, healing, and the other previously mentioned correspondences.

Tarot cards: The Lovers (6 or VI), The Devil (15 or XV), and the Sixes (all four suits)

Sixteen: 16 or XVI

In numerology, the number 16 can convey confidence, inner wisdom, and intuitive power. Sixteen can indicate perfectionism, debate, and philosophy.[95] On the other hand, when we reduce the number by adding 1 + 6, we get seven (7), the number of struggles, challenges, and lessons learned.

Tarot cards: The Chariot (7 or VII), The Tower (16 or XVI), and the Sevens (all four suits)

Seventeen: 17 or XVII

The number 17 can represent being on the right track spiritually and working hard to make one's dreams a reality.[96] When combined, 1 + 7 = 8, which is the number of achievement and manifestation, and when flipped on its side, eight becomes the lemniscate (infinity symbol; See Chapter 19 – Symbolism in the Tarot).

Tarot cards: Strength (8 or VIII), The Star (17 or XVII), and the Eights (all four suits)

Eighteen: 18 or XVII

In numerology, the number 18 is formed by the numbers one and eight, one representing new beginnings and new ideas and eight representing achievement and manifestation. When adding 1 + 8, we get nine (9), which can mean completions and endings.

Tarot cards: The Hermit (9 or IX), The Moon (18 or XVIII), and the Nines

Nineteen: 19 or XIX

The number 19 in numerology is associated with completions, happiness, honor, joy, and success. When combined, 1 + 9 = 10. In the tarot, 10 can represent finality and/or a return to center. And when reduced again, 1 + 0 = 1, the number of new beginnings and new ideas.

Tarot cards: The Magician (1 or I), Wheel of Fortune (10 or X), The Sun (19 or XIX), the Aces (all four suits), and the Tens (all four suits)

Twenty: 20 or XX

In numerology, the number 20 denotes the preparation for a spiritual journey.[97]Twenty is a reminder to take care of your whole self: mind, body, energy, and spirit. When doing the math, 2 + 0 = 2, the number of choice, decision, and union.

Tarot cards: The High Priestess (2 or II), Judgement (20 or XX), and the Twos

Twenty-One: 21 or XXI

The number 21 in numerology denotes fulfillment and manifestation. The number 21 reduces to three, which can represent creativity, expression, growth, celebration, and longing.

Tarot cards: The Empress (3 or III), The World (21 or XXI), and the Threes (all four suits)

Twenty-Two: 22 in Tarot

There are 22 cards in the Major Arcana. Additionally, the number 22 is significant in numerology because, like 11, it is a master number.

The Courts and Numerology

As mentioned in the opening of this chapter, although the Court cards are not numbered, for numerological purposes they can be assigned a consecutive number following the number 10.

The Pages—11

The Knights—12

The Queens—13

The Kings—14

Now that the Courts have been assigned a number, you can calculate their numerological correspondences within the tarot.

The Pages—The High Priestess (2 or II), Justice (11 or XI), the Twos (all four suits)
The Knights—The Empress (3 or III), The Hanged One (12 or XII), the Threes (all four suits)
The Queens—The Emperor (4 or IV), Death (13 or XIII), the Fours (all four suits). Additionally, even though the Queens align with The Emperor numerologically, they also align energetically with The Empress.
The Kings—The Hierophant (5 or V), Temperance (14 or XIV), the Fives (all four suits). Furthermore, just as the Queens correspond to the energy of The Empress, the Kings align with the energy of The Emperor.

As you can see, numerology casts an intricate, intertwined web of unique associations across the 78 tarot cards, and similar occurrences can be discovered when layering on astrological associations. In the next chapter, you will explore how astrology can offer robust meaning to the tarot.

Chapter 23:
Astrology and the Tarot

· · · · · · · · · · · · · · · · · · ·

The tarot and astrology go hand in hand. In fact, when A. E. Waite and Pamela Colman Smith were designing their deck in the early twentieth century, and later when Aleister Crowley and Lady Frieda Harris (AKA Jesus Chutney) created the Book of Thoth, astrology helped serve as a map for designating each card's placement in the deck as well as navigating their meanings.

In similar fashion, I have designed this chapter to read as a map for uncovering the tarot's astrological correspondences. From individual celestial bodies to the collective signs of the zodiac, I believe knowing the cards' historical, folkloric, and esoteric connections to the stars can deepen self-exploration and enrich your storytelling efforts.

Should you wish to learn more about astrology, specifically as it relates to the tarot, I recommend reading *Twist Your Fate: Manifest Success with Astrology & Tarot*, by Theresa Reed, The Tarot Lady.

Celestial Luminaries

Astrologers believe each celestial body within our solar system embodies individual characteristics, both benevolent and malevolent, that influence human temperament and energies, as well as lifetime events. From the sun to Pluto, each luminary is listed below, along with its corresponding tarot cards which take on one or more of the key associations. The list is organized by those viewable with the naked eye, or Chaldean Order, followed by the outer planets, which are only viewable with binoculars or a telescope.

☉ ☽ ☿ ♀ ♂ ♃ ♄

sun   moon   mercury   venus   mars   jupiter   saturn

The Sun

Linked to Divine power, origin energy, and one's inner spark, all life is nurtured by the sun. In the zodiac, the sun is associated with Leo, and in the physical body, the sun rules the heart and circulation. It is thought to foster action, growth, happiness, integrity, joy, life, nurturing, power, self-discovery, and warmth. As for days of the week, the sun is connected to Sunday.

Tarot cards: Strength (8 or VIII), The Sun (19 or XIX), Six of Cups, Four of Pentacles, Eight of Pentacles, Ten of Swords, and Three of Wands.

The Moon

While the sun has a direct influence on all life on Earth, the moon's influence is indirect, connected with biological rhythms and psychological processes. Earth's only natural satellite, the moon directly affects the tides, and its cycles represent the cycle of life, death, and rebirth. Associated with Cancer, the moon is associated with childhood, emotions, imagination, instinct, reflection, and unconscious desires. In days of the week, the moon is connected to Monday.

Tarot cards: The High Priestess (2 or II), The Chariot (7 or VII), Four of Cups, Six of Pentacles, Two of Swords, Seven of Swords, and Nine of Wands.

Mercury

In Greek mythology, Mercury was the messenger to the gods. As such, this planet is associated with communication, comprehension, humor, language, learning, logic, movement, organization, reason, and self-awareness. Linked to Gemini and Virgo, Mercury influences cooperation and discernment, which can affect how we associate ourselves and others with the rest of the world. With such a profound connection to communication and organization, it's easy to see why technology has a tendency to go awry when the planet is in retrograde. As for days of the week, Mercury is connected to Wednesday. Finally, Mercury is the mystic storyteller's planet, aligning with Hermes, Greek god of messengers, and The Magician card.

Tarot cards: The Magician (1 or I), The Lovers (6 or VI), The Hermit (9 or IX), Three of Cups, Five of Pentacles, Ten of Pentacles, Six of Swords, and Eight of Wands.

Venus

As the goddess of love, Venus is directly linked with relationships and stability. Ruler of both Taurus and Libra, Venus represents the duality of physical needs and balance, especially with regard to material and emotional security. Venus influences beauty, choice, connection, diplomacy, femininity, manifestation, manners, nurturing, strength, and wealth. In days of the week, Venus is connected to Friday.

Tarot cards: The Empress (3 or III), The Hierophant (5 or V), Justice (11 or XI), Two of Cups, Seven of Cups, Nine of Pentacles, Five of Swords, and Four of Wands.

Mars

Popularly known as the "red planet," Mars is directly connected with assertion, conquest, control, destruction, drive, masculinity, precision, and warfare. Linked to Aries, the Roman god of war, Mars can influence anger, competition, courage, decisiveness, dishonesty, oppression, and the misuse of strength. In days of the week, Mars is connected to Tuesday.

Tarot cards: The Emperor (4 or IV), The Tower (16 or XVI), Five of Cups, Ten of Cups, Three of Pentacles, Nine of Swords, and Two of Wands.

Jupiter

Named after the Roman king of the gods, Jupiter is known as the bringer of good fortunes.[98] Associated with Sagittarius, Jupiter is thought to foster expansion, hope, justice, knowledge, optimism, protection, self-confidence, success, truth, and wisdom. Because of these connections, Jupiter serves as a guide for educators, healers, and the judicial system. As for days of the week, Jupiter is connected to Thursday.

Tarot cards: Wheel of Fortune (10 or X), Temperance (14 or XIV), Nine of Cups, Two of Pentacles, Four of Swords, Eight of Swords, and Six of Wands.

Saturn

In Roman mythology, Saturn is known as the god of sowing or seed.[99] The planet is associated with conscience, form, honesty, order, responsibility, security, and structure. Saturn is also linked with control, fear, conflict, hardship, repression, and self-discipline. In days of the week, Saturn is connected to Saturday.

Tarot cards: The Devil (15 or XV), The World (21 or XXI), Eight of Cups, Seven of Pentacles, Three of Swords, Five of Wands, and Ten of Wands.

Outer Planets

Uranus

Because the planet was discovered in 1781, just before the French Revolution, Uranus is associated with discovery, non-conformity, revolution, and unexpected events. The planet is also thought to foster change, disruption, idealism, the inner voice, and unpredictable circumstances. Uranus is the ruler of Aquarius, and it represents independence, inventiveness, and originality.

Tarot cards: The Fool (0) and The Star (17 or XVII)

Neptune

Named after the Roman god of water and the sea, Neptune is thought to connect with illusion, inspiration, mystery, things unseen, and the unconscious mind. The planet informs human ideals and can provoke the urge to escape from reality. As such, Neptune inspires artists, humanitarians, musicians, mystics, and poets. It is attributed to compassion, imagination, empathy, psychism, sensitivity, and spirituality.

Tarot cards: The Hanged One (12 or XII) and The Moon (18 or XVIII)

Pluto

Downgraded to "dwarf planet" status in August 2006, Pluto is the smallest, most dense, and farthest planet from the sun. Named for the Roman god of the underworld, Pluto is linked to birth, death, and resurrection. The small-but-mighty planet also fosters a connection to one's inner darkness, promoting psychological development and transformation. Ruler of Scorpio, Pluto is associated with passion and sexuality.

Tarot cards: Death (13 or XIII) and Judgement (20 or XX)

The Zodiac

From Aries to Pisces, the zodiac is a collection of twelve signs, each formed by connecting specific stars into a familiar and relatable pattern. These signs create such patterns because of the way they appear in the night sky from here on Earth. Zodiac signs are based on how the sun passes through the patterns throughout a 12-month period. As such, your date of birth informs your "sun sign."

As you discovered in the previous assessment of celestial bodies and their connection to the tarot, the 12 sun signs each link to cards in both the Major and Minor Arcana. Below, you will find tables and summaries for the zodiac signs to include their associated timeframes, qualities, elements, ruling luminaries, keywords, and tarot cards.

Zodiac Signs

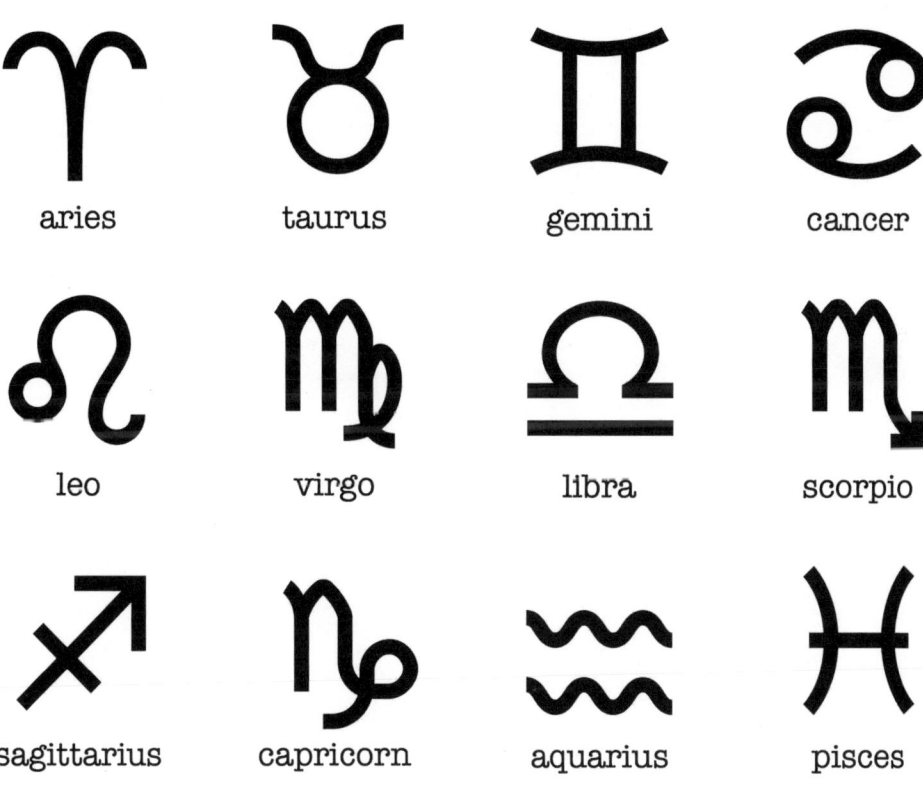

aries	taurus	gemini	cancer
leo	virgo	libra	scorpio
sagittarius	capricorn	aquarius	pisces

Elements, Suits, and Astrology

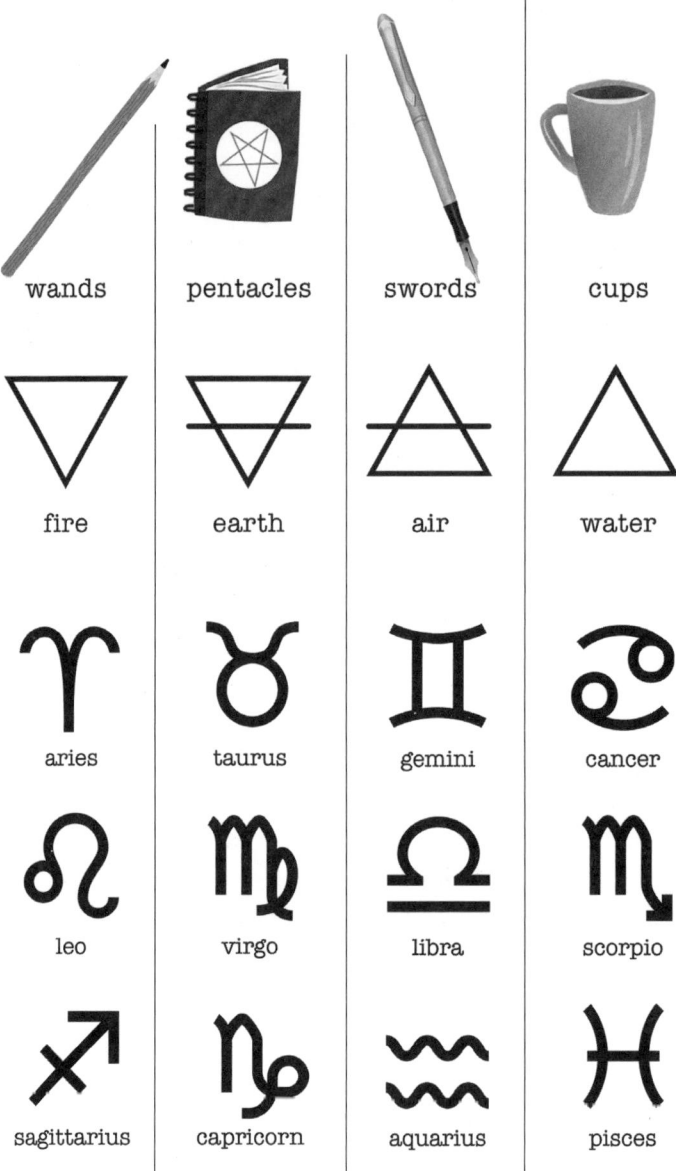

wands	pentacles	swords	cups
fire	earth	air	water
aries	taurus	gemini	cancer
leo	virgo	libra	scorpio
sagittarius	capricorn	aquarius	pisces

Quality

As for a sign's quality, this represents the changing stages of each season. Cardinal signs begin a season (e.g., Aries starts spring), fixed signs fully embody each season (e.g., Scorpio occurs in the middle of autumn), and mutable signs conclude the seasons, helping usher in the next (e.g., Pisces transitions us out of winter).

Aries

Timeframe: March 21 – April 19
Symbol: The ram
Quality: Cardinal—Aries initiates spring on the equinox
Element: Fire
Luminary: Mars
Keywords: Agile, childish, enthusiastic, impulsive, leader, and vivacious.
Tarot cards: The Emperor (4 or IV), Two, Three, and Four of Wands

Taurus

Timeframe: April 20 – May 20
Symbol: The bull
Quality: Fixed—Taurus is fixed in spring
Element: Earth
Luminary: Venus
Keywords: Elegant, determined, grounded, sophisticated, stubborn, and subdued
Tarot cards: The Hierophant (5 or V), Five, Six, and Seven of Pentacles

Gemini

Timeframe: May 21 – June 20
Symbol: The twins
Quality: Mutable—Gemini transitions spring to summer
Element: Air
Luminary: Mercury
Keywords: Communicative, discerning, flippant, intelligent, restless, and witty
Tarot cards: The Lovers (6 or VI), Eight, Nine, and Ten of Swords

Cancer

Timeframe: June 21 – July 22
Symbol: The crab
Quality: Cardinal—Cancer initiates summer on the solstice
Element: Water
Luminary: The moon
Keywords: Compassionate, emotional, intuitive, nurturing, psychic, and moody
Tarot cards: The Chariot (7 or VII), Tow, Three,, and Four of Cups

Leo

Timeframe: July 23 – August 22
Symbol: The lion
Quality: Fixed—Leo is fixed in summer
Element: Fire
Luminary: The sun
Keywords: Audacious, boisterous, bold, joyful, passionate, and warm
Tarot cards: Strength (8 or VIII), Five, Six, and Seven of Wands

Virgo

Timeframe: August 23 – September 22
Symbol: The virgin
Quality: Mutable—Virgo transitions summer to fall
Element: Earth
Luminary: Mercury
Keywords: Adaptable, candid, dependable, detailed, fidgety, and meticulous
Tarot cards: The Hermit (9 or IX), Eight, Nine, and Ten of Pentacles

Libra

Timeframe: September 23 – October 22
Symbol: The scales
Quality: Cardinal—Libra initiates fall on the equinox
Element: Air
Luminary: Venus
Keywords: Committed, evaluating, fair, indecisive, leader, and partner
Tarot cards: Justice (11 or XI), Two, Three, and Four of Swords

Scorpio

Timeframe: October 23 – November 21
Symbol: The scorpion
Quality: Fixed—Scorpio is fixed in fall
Element: Water
Luminary: Mars and Pluto
Keywords: Deep, fearless, fierce, secretive, sensual, and transformative
Tarot cards: Death (13 or XIII), Five, Six, and Seven of Cups

Sagittarius

Timeframe: November 22 – December 21
Symbol: The archer
Quality: Mutable—Sagittarius transitions fall to winter
Element: Fire
Luminary: Jupiter
Keywords: Adventurous, creative, excessive, intense, lucky, and mischievous
Tarot cards: Temperance (14 or XIV), Eight, Nine, and Ten of Wands

Capricorn

Timeframe: December 22 – January 19
Symbol: The goat
Quality: Cardinal—Capricorn initiates winter on the solstice
Element: Earth
Luminary: Saturn
Keywords: Dedicated, goal-oriented, tenacious, persevering, reliable, and stoic
Tarot cards: The Devil (15 or XV), Two, Three, and Four of Pentacles

Aquarius

Timeframe: January 20 – February 18
Symbol: The water bearer
Quality: Fixed—Aquarius is fixed in winter
Element: Air
Luminaries: Saturn and Uranus
Keywords: Friendly, empathetic, individual, selective, quirky, and unique
Tarot cards: The Star (17 or XVII), Five, Six, and Seven of Swords

Pisces

Timeframe: February 19 – March 20
Symbol: The fish
Quality: Mutable—Pisces transitions winter to spring
Element: Water
Luminaries: Jupiter and Neptune
Keywords: Concerned, dreamy, eclectic, intuitive, mysterious, and psychic
Tarot cards: The Moon (18 or XVIII), Eight, Nine, and Ten of Cups

Major Arcana and Astrology

#	Tarot Card	Element	Astrology	
0	The Fool	Air		Uranus
1	The Magician	Air		Mercury
2	High Priestess	Water		Moon
3	The Empress	Earth		Venus
4	The Emperor	Fire	Mar 21 – Apr 19	Aries
5	The Hierophant	Earth	Apr 20 – May 20	Taurus
6	The Lovers	Air	May 21 – Jun 20	Gemini
7	The Chariot	Water	Jun 21 – Jul 22	Cancer
8	Strength	Fire	Jul 23 – Aug 22	Leo
9	The Hermit	Earth	Aug 23 – Sep 22	Virgo
10	Wheel of Fortune	Fire		Jupiter
11	Justice	Air	Sep 23 – Oct 22	Libra
12	The Hanged One	Water		Neptune
13	Death	Water	Oct 23 – Nov 21	Scorpio
14	Temperance	Fire	Nov 22 – Dec 21	Sagittarius
15	The Devil	Earth	Dec 22 – Jan 19	Capricorn
16	The Tower	Air		Mars
17	The Star	Water	Jan 20 – Feb 18	Aquarius

18	The Moon	Water	Feb 19 – Mar 20	Pisces
19	The Sun	Fire		Sun
20	Judgement	Fire		Pluto
21	The World	Earth		Saturn

Minor Arcana and Astrology

Quality	Minor Arcana	Cups	Pentacles	Swords	Wands
		(Water)	(Earth)	(Air)	(Fire)
Cardinal	Twos, Threes, Fours	Cancer	Capricorn	Libra	Aries
Fixed	Fives, Sixes, Sevens	Scorpio	Taurus	Aquarius	Leo
Mutable	Eights, Nines, Tens	Pisces	Virgo	Gemini	Sagittarius

Minor Arcana and Astrology, expanded

#	Cups	Pentacles
Ace	Cancer, Scorpio, Pisces	Capricorn, Taurus, Virgo
2	Venus in Cancer	Jupiter in Capricorn
3	Mercury in Cancer	Mars in Capricorn
4	Moon in Cancer	Sun in Capricorn
5	Mars in Scorpio	Mercury in Taurus
6	Sun in Scorpio	Moon in Taurus
7	Venus in Scorpio	Saturn in Taurus
8	Saturn in Pisces	Sun in Virgo
9	Jupiter in Pisces	Venus in Virgo
10	Mars in Pisces	Mercury in Virgo

Swords	Wands
Libra, Aquarius, Gemini	Aries, Leo, Sagittarius
Moon in Libra	Mars in Aries
Saturn in Libra	Sun in Aries
Jupiter in Libra	Venus in Aries
Venus in Aquarius	Saturn in Leo
Mercury in Aquarius	Jupiter in Leo
Moon in Aquarius	Mars in Leo
Jupiter in Gemini	Mercury in Sagittarius
Mars in Gemini	Moon in Sagittarius
Sun in Gemini	Saturn in Sagittarius

Putting it All Together: Tarot and Astrology Wheel

The Tarot and Astrology Wheel features the alignment of Minor Arcana, planets, zodiac, and elements.

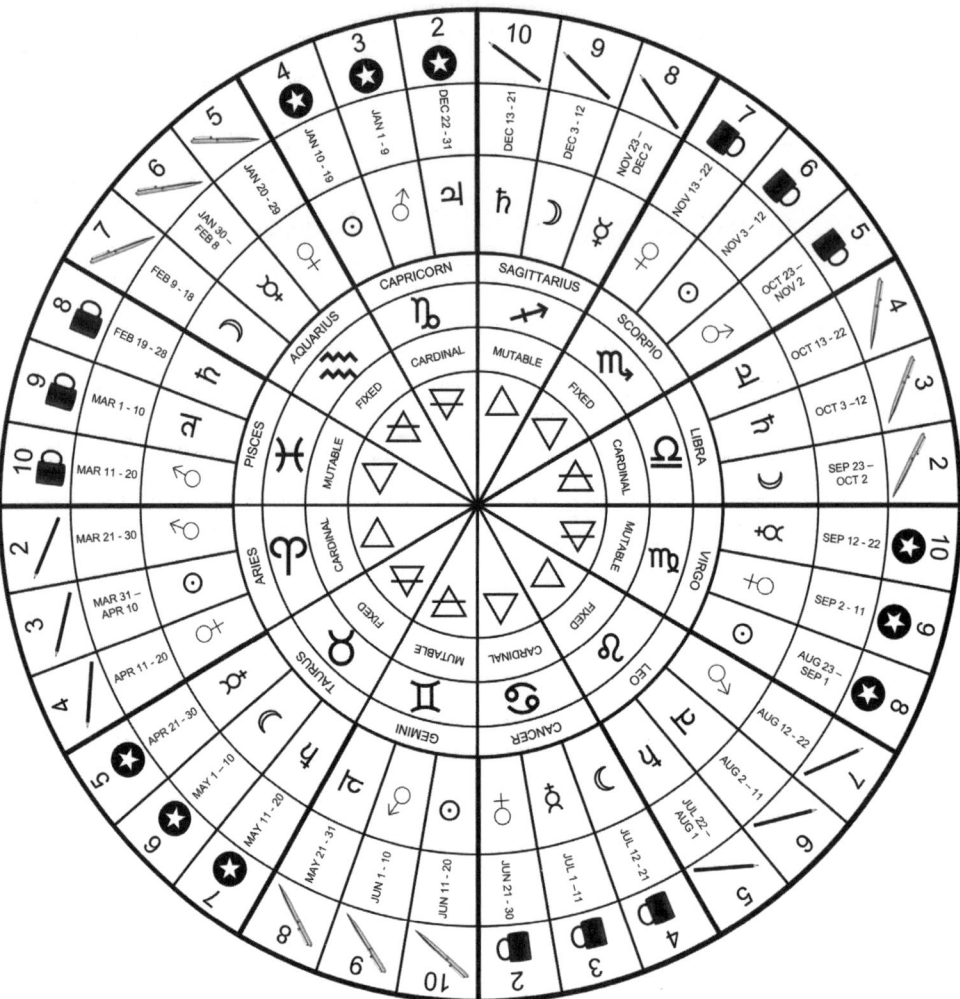

Although you learned the basics of astrology and the tarot in this chapter, if you are interested in learning more about astrology, I highly recommend picking up a book or two dedicated to the subject. There are also podcasts and YouTube channels which can help you increase your knowledge, and when sourcing information from astrology websites, be sure they are reputable sites, such as Astrology. com and Café Astrology. Up next, you will pair numerology and astrology to determine your "tarot code."

Chapter 24:
Your Tarot Code

. . . .

In your first activity of this book, you selected your favorite cards from the deck—your tarot guideposts. If you are like me and you enjoy self-discovery, personal introspection, and/or cultivating spiritual connections and routines, then get ready for a little interesting insight and (hopefully) a lot of fun. In this chapter, I will share with you my favorite methods for uncovering your "tarot code."

Your tarot code is a collection of cards that have been assigned to you from birth, annually, monthly, and even daily, if you so choose to honor a consistent routine. Self-discovery practices are often popular among writers like you and me. From journaling to blogging, fiction writing to poetry, many writers find connection and creative inspiration through reflection and rumination. The cards you will uncover in your tarot code can provide additional points of reference to your personal, creative, and even spiritual journey.

What you need for this chapter:

- Your *Mystic Storyteller Tarot* deck.
- Tools for notetaking.
- A computer with internet access.

In Chapter 22 – *Numerology: Tarot by the Numbers*, you learned how to calculate your Life Path number, which correlates to your Soul Card in the tarot. As a refresher, the following easy math example uncovers the Life Path number and Soul Card for one of my favorite fictional characters, Michael Scott from *The Office*. According to several fandom sites, Michael Gary Scott was born in Scranton, Pennsylvania on March 15, 1965.

$$3 + 1 + 5 + 1 + 9 + 6 + 5 = 30$$

Now, let's reduce 30 to its simplest form: $3 + 0 =$ **3**

Therefore, three (3) is Michael Scott's Life Path number, which in numerology represents his personality and talents.[100] In the tarot, the number three corresponds with The Empress (3 or III), which is his Soul Card. Use the following table to discover the Life Path numbers and Soul Cards for yourself, your friends, your family, and even your fictional characters.

Life Path Numbers and Soul Cards

Life Path #	Soul Card	Honorary Title
1	The Magician	The Magician
2	The High Priestess	The Intuitive
3	The Empress	The Creator
4	The Emperor	The Leader
5	The Hierophant	The Teacher
6	The Lovers	The Lovers
7	The Chariot	The Trailblazer
8	Strength	Strength
9	The Hermit	The Scholar

Birth Year is another easy card to turn over. Simply add the digits of the year you were born. This number corresponds to your Birth Year Card.

Here's Michael Scott's: $1 + 9 + 6 + 5 = 21$

$2 + 1 = 3$

Therefore, Michael Scott's Birth Year Card is also The Empress (3 or III).

Your Birth Year Card

Birth Year	Birth Year Card
1927, 1936, 1945, 1954, 1963, 1972, 1981, 1990, 1999, 2008, 2017, 2026	The Magician
1928, 1937, 1946, 1955, 1964, 1973, 1982, 1991, 2000, 2009, 2018, 2027	The High Priestess
1929, 1938, 1947, 1956, 1965, 1974, 1983, 1992, 2001, 2010, 2019, 2028	The Empress
1930, 1939, 1948, 1957, 1966, 1975, 1984, 1993, 2002, 2011, 2020, 2029	The Emperor
1931, 1940, 1949, 1958, 1967, 1976, 1985, 1994, 2003, 2012, 2021, 2030	The Hierophant
1923, 1932, 1941, 1950, 1959, 1968, 1977, 1986, 1995, 2004, 2022	The Lovers
1924, 1933, 1942, 1951, 1960, 1969, 1978, 1987, 1996, 2005, 2014, 2023	The Chariot
1925, 1934, 1943, 1952, 1961, 1970, 1979, 1988, 1997, 2006, 2015, 2024	Strength
1926, 1935, 1944, 1953, 1962, 1971, 1980, 1989, 1998, 2007, 2016, 2025	The Hermit

Use this table to discover the Birth Year Cards for yourself, your friends, your family, and even your characters. Next up: your Age Card.

Your Age Card

Apply the same easy math to determine your Age Card. This is a card you can lean into until your next birthday. As an example, at the time of writing this book, the year is 2023. Therefore, Michael Scott would be 58. Here's the easy math:

$$5 + 8 = 13$$

$$1 + 3 = \mathbf{4}$$

Therefore, Michael Scott's Age Card from March 15, 2023, to March 14, 2024, would be The Emperor (4 or IV).

Your Age	Your Age Card
1, 10, 19, 28, 37, 46, 55, 64, 73, 82, 91, 100	The Magician
2, 11, 20, 29, 38, 47, 56, 65, 74, 83, 92, 101	The High Priestess
3, 12, 21, 30, 39, 48, 57, 66, 75, 84, 93, 102	The Empress
4, 13, 22, 31, 40, 49, 58, 67, 76, 85, 94, 103	The Emperor
5, 14, 23, 32, 41, 50, 59, 68, 77, 86, 95, 104	The Hierophant
6, 15, 24, 33, 42, 51, 60, 69, 78, 87, 96, 105	The Lovers
7, 16, 25, 34, 43, 52, 61, 70, 79, 88, 97, 106	The Chariot
8, 17, 26, 35, 44, 53, 62, 71, 80, 89, 98, 107	Strength
9, 18, 27, 36, 45, 54, 63, 72, 81, 90, 99, 108	The Hermit

If you're old enough to know the song *I'm Henry VIII I Am*, by Herman's Hermits, and/or you've watched the movie *Ghost*, you will probably remember the line, "Second verse, same as the first!" ... That's the line these repetitive math exercises reminds me of. Next up: Year Cards.

Your Year Card

To calculate your Year Card, which is the card of the collective—everyone's card for this year—you simply add the numbers in the current year. Again, (cue the song) at the time of this book's writing, it's 2024; therefore, the Year Card is Strength (8 or VIII).

The following table includes years past, present, and future. You can use it to reflect and/or discover the corresponding tarot cards.

Year	Year Card
1927, 1936, 1945, 1954, 1963, 1972, 1981, 1990, 1999, 2008, 2017, 2026	The Magician
1928, 1937, 1946, 1955, 1964, 1973, 1982, 1991, 2000, 2009, 2018, 2027	The High Priestess
1929, 1938, 1947, 1956, 1965, 1974, 1983, 1992, 2001, 2010, 2019, 2028	The Empress
1930, 1939, 1948, 1957, 1966, 1975, 1984, 1993, 2002, 2011, 2020, 2029	The Emperor
1931, 1940, 1949, 1958, 1967, 1976, 1985, 1994, 2003, 2012, 2021, 2030	The Hierophant
1923, 1932, 1941, 1950, 1959, 1968, 1977, 1986, 1995, 2004, 2022	The Lovers
1924, 1933, 1942, 1951, 1960, 1969, 1978, 1987, 1996, 2005, 2014, 2023	The Chariot
1925, 1934, 1943, 1952, 1961, 1970, 1979, 1988, 1997, 2006, 2015, 2024	Strength
1926, 1935, 1944, 1953, 1962, 1971, 1980, 1989, 1998, 2007, 2016, 2025	The Hermit

Your Zodiac Cards

Here's where the repetitive math stops, and the calculations become more interesting. Your Zodiac Cards are those Major and Minor Arcana tarot cards that correspond with the signs of the zodiac. In this exercise, I will share with you how to determine four specific signs and cards that are relevant to you both as an individual and as a writer. They are your Big Three (Sun, Moon, and Rising signs/cards) and your Destiny Card. The Destiny Card reflects the Minor Arcana card associated with the day of your birth, which you might recall from Chapter 23 – *Astrology and the Tarot.*

Your Big Three

Determining your Big Three signs of the zodiac will require you to know the following information:

- Your date of birth
- Your time of birth—If this information is unavailable, use 12:00 pm
- Your location of birth (city and state)

Once you have this information handy, you can retrieve your natal chart, also known as a birth chart. A natal chart is a report that details the exact location of the sun, moon, planets, and other celestial bodies in the sky at the exact moment and location of your birth. This report is available free on many online websites, and it will reflect your Big Three. Simply look for your sun sign, moon sign, and your rising or ascendant sign, often depicted by the acronym ASC. My favorite free natal chart resource is the website Café Astrology. The web address for the free report is https://astro.cafeastrology.com/natal.php

Returning to *The Office*, the following example reflects the hypothetical Big Three for Michael Scott.[101]

- Pisces Sun
- Virgo Moon
- Cancer Rising

According to these coordinates, the following list reveals Michael Scott's Big Three tarot cards:

Pisces Sun: The Moon (18 or XVIII)
Virgo Moon: The Hermit (9 or IX)
Cancer Rising: The Chariot (7 or VII)

The Zodiac and the Major Arcana

Zodiac Sign	Date Range	Tarot Card
Aries	March 21 – April 19	The Emperor
Taurus	April 20 – May 20	The Hierophant
Gemini	May 21 – June 20	The Lovers
Cancer	June 21 – July 22	The Chariot
Leo	July 23 – August 22	Strength
Virgo	August 23 – September 22	The Hermit
Libra	September 23 – October 22	Justice
Scorpio	October 23 – November 21	Death
Sagittarius	November 22 – December 21	Temperance
Capricorn	December 22 – January 19	The Devil
Aquarius	January 20 – February 18	The Star
Pisces	February 19 – March 20	The Moon

Your Destiny Card

In her book *Tarot for Your Self*, tarot scholar and consultant Mary K. Greer describes the Destiny Card as the Minor Arcana card that corresponds with one's birth date.[102] As such, I have created a decan wheel that organizes the cards of the Minor Arcana and their zodiac correspondences in groups of 10. In reviewing the wheel, you can determine your Destiny Card for yourself, your friends, your family, and even your fictional characters.

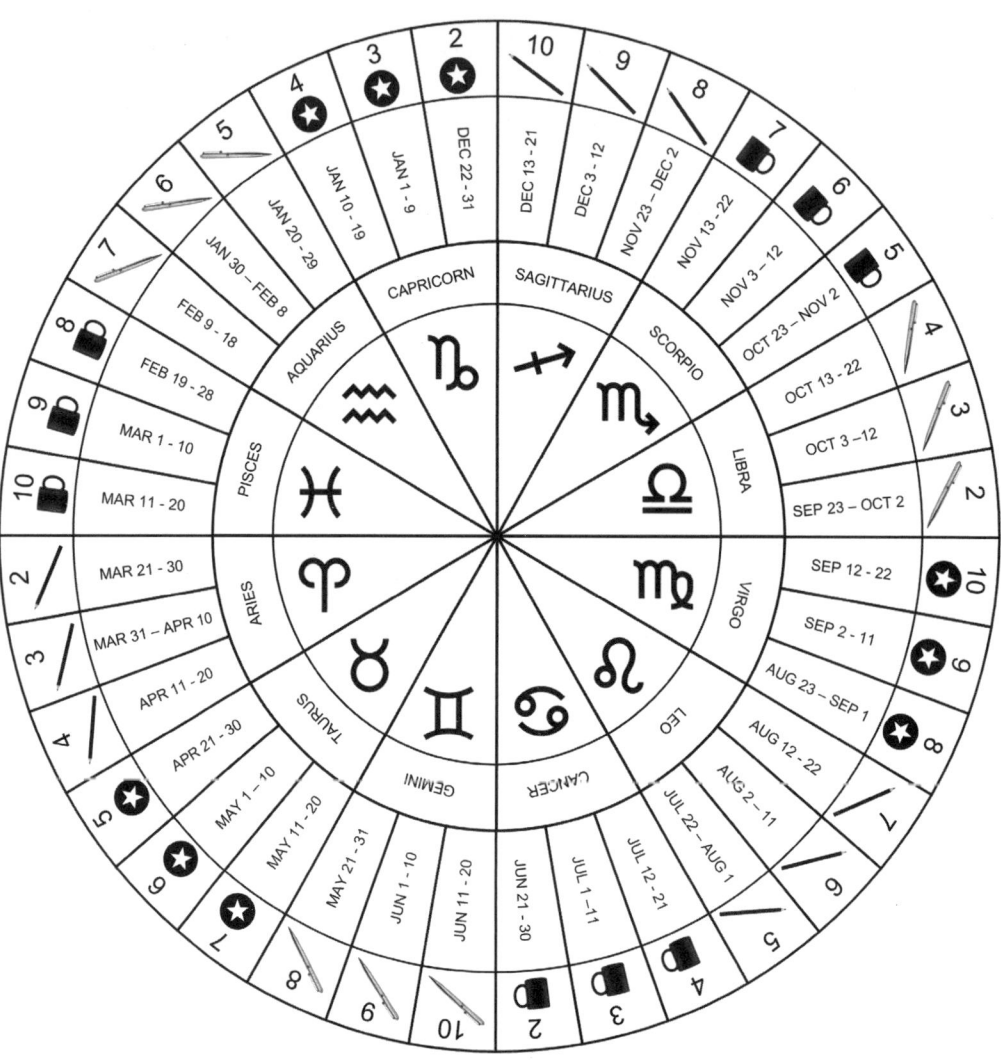

Your Daily Cards

A daily tarot practice can deepen your knowledge of the cards and enrich your storytelling craft. Each morning, before starting your day, or each day before beginning your writing routine, you can shuffle your deck and pull a single card to guide your day and/or your session. When I am pressed for time, but still want to stay connected to my intuition and tap into ideas that might inspire my work, I draw one card. On the days when I have more time to dedicate to my tarot practice, I draw three cards for my favorite daily spread: Theme / Obstacle or Opportunity / Blessing.[103]

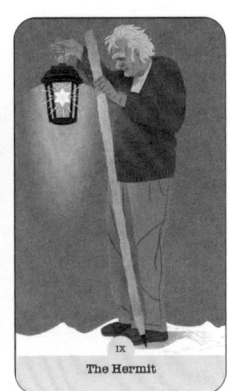

Position	Card	Interpretation
Theme	The Sun	Gratitude and joy are all around today.
Obstacle	Knight of Swords	A racing mind can be difficult to settle.
Blessing	The Hermit	I have something important to learn from a credible instructor.

From the moment I began learning the tarot many years ago, I journaled my thoughts about the cards. Over the years, with continuous practice and a steady routine, my creativity, imagination, and intuition flourished and sharpened, and I learned so much about myself through insights gleaned from the cards—my favorites and the ones associated with my natal chart.

While working with the tarot, whether for personal introspection or for creative inspiration, I highly recommend journaling your thoughts. Doing so can help you create a catalogue of tarot interpretations, refining your intuition and facilitating a consistent writing routine.

During your exploration, remember to lean into the cards assigned as your tarot code. As you have learned from this chapter, these cards have been available to inspire you even before you realized you were a creative writer.

For now, as you move ahead in this book, keep these cards handy for a fun practice activity: Similarities and Synchronicities.

Practice Activity: Similarities and Synchronicities

Self-discovery through the tarot is one of the most popular methods of using the cards. By exercising self-awareness and elevating intentional thinking, I believe this practice can help writers improve in their craft.

To conclude your exploration of *The Tarot Code*, gather the cards you selected as your tarot guideposts (Part One Practice Activity), along with the cards you identified as your tarot code (Chapter 24), because you are going to use them for this three-part practice activity.

What you need for this activity:

- 20+ minutes.
- *Mystic Storyteller Tarot* cards from *Your Tarot Guideposts Practice Activity* and Chapter 24 – *Your Tarot Code*.
- A clear, flat space on which to work: a desk, bed, countertop, table, etc.
- Your favorite tools for notetaking.
- Your insights, feelings, and thoughts.

Part One:

Let's get organized. Use the following table to organize and log your tarot guideposts and your tarot code. If you have more cards for the spaces provided, select your six favorite Major Arcana cards (two from each line of the 3 x 7 Diagram in Chapter 20), along with two of your favorite cards from each Minor Arcana suit.

(Worksheet, following pages.)

Practice Activity: Similarities and Synchronicities

Your Tarot Guideposts	
Favorite Cards from 3 x 7 Line One	
Favorite Cards from 3 x 7 Line Two	
Favorite Cards from 3 x 7 Line Three	
Favorite Cups cards	
Favorite Pentacles cards	
Favorite Swords cards	
Favorite Wands cards	

Your Tarot Code	
Your Life Path Number	
Your Soul Card	
Your Birth Year Card	
Your Age Card	
Your Year Card	
Your Sun Card	
Your Moon Card	
Your Rising Card	
Your Destiny Card	

Part Two:

Lay out your tarot guideposts cards in a row. If the row becomes too long for your working space, then only use the cards from the table in Part One.

Next, start a new row beneath the top row and lay your cards from Your Tarot Code. Where the cards are the same, simply set the single card in the middle of the two rows. Here's an example of my own cards:

Part Three: Activity Debrief

Using what you've learned about tarot symbolism, archetypes, numerology, and astrology, journal your discoveries by answering the following questions:

- Are any of the cards you chose as your tarot guideposts the same as those in your tarot code? If yes, which were they?

- What is a common theme unfolding in your cards?

- Which card stands out to you more than the others?

- When comparing your tarot guideposts with your tarot code cards, what are the color similarities?

- Which recurring symbols do you notice showing up in your cards?

- Which types of animals or figures appear throughout your cards?

- What interesting synchronicities can you uncover throughout the cards?

- Are there any overlapping astrological correspondences? For example, my favorite card in the tarot is The Hermit, so I was delighted when I first discovered that The Hermit is also my birth card.

What's next?

In Part Six: *Writing from Within*, you will bring together everything you've learned about using the tarot to amplify your creativity and apply that knowledge to the most common—and a few uncommon—writing traditions and practices.

Part 6:
Writing from Within

"Learn from everything, see everything, and above all feel everything! And make other people when they look at your drawing feel it too!"

Pamela "Pixie" Coleman Smith
Artist, Illustrator, and Author

Chapter 25: Intuitive Writing

· · · · · · · · · · · · · · · · · · · ·

For a moment, I'd like you to imagine Leonardo DaVinci's painting *Mona Lisa*. A replica of the famous portrait hangs in my office, a daily reminder of its intrigue. It's a painting of hidden secrets, and I particularly love the mystery around Mona Lisa's smile. I love pondering that legendary smirk and what DaVinci must have been thinking throughout the painting process. Who was this person? What sparked that curious smile? And why is the background uneven?

How does *Mona Lisa* relate to the tarot? Both are art. Both implore emotional and intuitive assessment and interpretation. Not everyone's analysis of Mona Lisa's smile is the same. Not everyone's ideas around art are the same. As such, the same can be said of the tarot.

Years ago, I added pulling cards to my morning routine. I studied the images, journaled about what I saw, and then researched the card interpretations, symbols, and descriptions for myself. In adapting a daily practice, I soon realized that my immediate, intuitive analysis of the cards didn't always align with what I had learned—they were unique to me. And that was more than okay. In fact, intuitive interpretation is the most important aspect of working with the cards as a creative tool.

Writing intuitively is a similar practice. It's trusting your immediate instincts about a story and allowing your mind, heart, and spirit to filter the details through your hands. Intuitive writing is what happens when an idea comes to you—in waking moments or in your dreams—and in the depths of your gut you know you must write about it. As a storyteller, I have leaned on my intuition—those gut instincts—for writing my novels, especially when the characters come to me from the depths of my unconscious mind, appearing as if a memory of someone real, someone I've known and even loved. Others may have written similar stories, but mine are intrinsically unique to me. And your stories are yours.

Therefore, as you continue working through this book, with the tarot, and in your future writing endeavors, pay close attention to your ideas, especially the nagging ones that won't relent. Listen to them, for they might prove to be a lot more than mere thoughts. They could be intuitive hits, waiting to be brought to life through a story.

In Part Six, you will learn how to pair the tarot with intuitive writing methods like sensory writing, which can add layers of depth to your stories.

Chapter 26:
Sensory Writing with the Tarot

. . . .

The best stories make us feel like we are part of them. Whether an article, book, movie, or stage play, a good story starts in the writer's mind, and then spills out onto the page—literal or digital. While reading your favorite books or watching your favorite movies, you're most likely imagining yourself as the character and/ or placing yourself in their world. You can see, hear, smell, feel, and taste what they are experiencing, if only in your imagination.

If you are a fiction writer, you will most likely recognize the statement "Show your story, don't tell it." Although this advice can be redundant, it's important. While writing, showing your story—which includes using descriptive language, metaphor, and dialogue—offers the reader an experience, rather than simply telling the story and expecting readers to take your word at face value.

Sensory writing—using words and phrases that make a connection to the five senses—can enrich one's storytelling with depth and nuance, offering the reader a virtually immersive experience. The table at right provides some examples of telling a story compared with showing it.

Immersive Practice

While writing fiction, I enjoy sharpening my skills through immersive practice. First and foremost, I mull over the ideas, characters, and stories that seem to appear out of the ether. Next, I pay close attention to my intuitive sensory responses: what I see, smell, hear, taste, and feel as the details unfold. I make lots of notes, capturing my ideas so I might recall them later.

Because I never know what or who is going to inspire me, or when inspiration might occur, I pay close attention to specifics. No matter where I am, I examine my surroundings thoroughly, listening intently, and acknowledging how people, places, or situations make me feel. Like a tourist in a new town, I look up, down, and around, homing in with granular interest. Airports are terrific places for putting sensory awareness into practice—they are a kaleidoscope of things to see, smell, feel, hear, and taste. Malls, sporting events, parks, any place where people gather, also work well.

Sensory Writing		
Senses	**Telling**	**Showing**
Sight / See	The girl cried.	Tears carved rivulets down the girl's blushed cheeks.
Sound / Hear	The song was beautiful.	My skin erupted with chills as his fingertips tickled the piano keys.
Smell	The food smelled delicious.	When the server brought out the fajitas, my mind wafted with memories of eating chopped steak and onion hoagies at the autumn carnival.
Touch / Feel	It felt great to be hugged.	She melted in her lover's embrace.
Taste	The coffee tasted so good.	As the latte warmed her belly, a ribbon of sweet foam lingered on her lips.

The tarot can be used in the same vein, serving as anchors for activating the senses. The table on the following page includes examples of sensory story-showing as inspired by a selection of tarot cards.

Sensory Writing		
Card	**Senses**	**Showing**
	Sight / See	From where she stood on the hill, Olivia had a clear view of the boat race. Defying the odds, and baffling those who wagered against the vessel, the Joan of Arc glided past the larger boats, winning first place.
	Sound / Hear	Although the instructor was a small man, his voice boomed from behind the podium, sailing around the auditorium and spilling out into the corridor.
	Smell	I could tell the storm was brewing. As the clouds billowed overhead, my nose prickled, my lungs filling with a warm and earthy petrichor.
	Touch / Feel	My migraine was no match for the sting of snow against my cheeks, or the chill settling into my throbbing, fractured ankle.
	Taste	Marco's throat scorched with rising bile. He didn't care how many of his friends loved his neighbor's craft beer. He wasn't falling for another rancid ale.

Practice Activity: Sensory Story-Showing with the Tarot

Now it's your turn. For this two-part practice activity, I have crafted a template and a selection of questions to help you glean sensory details from your tarot cards. You are invited to use these insights for more profound story-showing.

What you need for this activity:

*   Your *Mystic Storyteller Tarot* deck.
*   Your favorite tools for notetaking.
*   Your intuition.
*   Your five senses.

Sensory Story-Showing		
Tarot	**Senses**	**Show the card's story**
	Sight / See	
	Sound / Hear	
	Smell	
	Touch / Feel	
	Taste	

Part One:

Shuffle your tarot deck until you are satisfied that the cards are ready, then turn the deck facedown as if you were about to deal the cards.

Using the above template as a spread, turn over the first five cards from the top of your tarot deck, laying them upright onto the spaces for Cards 1 through 5. There should be one card for each of the five senses.

Ask yourself the following questions, using your intuition and five senses to consider the sensory details for each card.

Sight Questions:

- What do I imagine the person or animal in this card was doing that led them to this point?
- What colors stand out in this card and what influence do they have on the figure(s) and/or animal(s)?
- In what direction is the person, animal, or object(s) facing and why?

Sound Questions:

- What sounds are associated with the weather conditions in this card?
- If there is a person in this card, what sounds are they making or might they make in response to what's unfolding in the scene around or behind them?
- If there are two or more people in the scene, what are they saying to one another? What do they need to discuss?

Smell Questions:

- Depending on what the person in this card is doing, what do they smell like?
- What scents or odors linger in the air throughout this card?
- What is this card's season and what types of aromas are associated with it?

Touch Questions:

- If my fictional character or I were physically in the scene, what would the textures feel like to the touch?
- How is the person, place, or situation portrayed in the scene physically affected by the elements—water, earth, air, and fire—present in and/or represented by the card?
- If there is a person in the card, how would I imagine their clothing and/ or uniform feels against their skin?

Taste Questions:

- If there is a person in the card, and they were to invite me to their home for a meal, who is cooking, what would they serve, and how would it taste?
- If this card contains a cup, what's in it and what happens when I take a swallow?
- After examining the scene in this card, if I were stranded here, what would I eat to survive? How would I prepare it and what would it taste like?

Part Two:

For each of the five cards, use the sensory details collected from answering the questions and draft a story that shows what's happening in the card.

What's next?

How can you practice sensory writing, world-building, and other types of creative channeling without overthinking and getting stuck inside your head? Freewriting.

Chapter 27:
Freewriting Using the Tarot

. . . .

If you have ever brainstormed ideas, either before organizing an outline for your project or in lieu of an outline altogether, then you have most likely practiced the technique of freewriting. There is no structure or formula associated with the method; it's simply allowing one's thoughts to flow freely onto the page without interruption, overthinking, or editing. Freewriting is the epitome of writing intuitively because the technique captures one's immediate thoughts—the ones that linger beneath the surface, either subconsciously or entirely unconscious. By writing on impulse, without concern for grammar, punctuation, and spelling, storytellers can uncover ideas that can become long-term themes, we can tackle writer's block, and even relieve the anxiety of not writing, or not knowing what to write.

Freewriting is similar to stream of consciousness, a writing technique that explores the thoughts and feelings of a fictional character or narrator in order to provide the reader with greater detail than what is possible by description alone. Stream of consciousness was made popular by writers like Virginia Woolf, William Faulkner, Flannery O'Connor, and James Joyce who coined the phrase in the late nineteenth century.[104]

The tarot can serve as anchors for freewriting. After all, the cards are individual invitations for conjuring instinctive responses to their illustrations. In fact, if you have completed any of the activities in this book that ask you to capture your immediate thoughts about a card or spread, you have already attempted freewriting. Additionally, the cards can be used for sorting your ideas into topics. Although you don't have to know any of the details or even have an outline for your next writing project, establishing guides to inspire your freewriting can be a tremendous help. Likewise, you can use the cards for simply getting started.

Sometimes, the stress and anxiety of not knowing what to write can prevent us from getting started in the first place. Draw a tarot card and start writing. What flows onto the page doesn't have to make sense; eventually something will come through that will spark a creative flame.

Moving forward, as you venture into the start of a new writing project, or as you work through struggles caused by anxiety and/or writer's block, you are encouraged to pull one or more tarot cards and employ freewriting. Who knows? You might even uncover a stellar bestseller idea. Let's practice with a simple activity.

Practice Activity: Freewriting with the Cards

Before moving on to the next chapter, the following activity is an opportunity for you to put freewriting with the tarot into practice. The instructions are simple:

- Examine the tarot spread.
- Use one or more of the following questions to activate your intuition.
- Freewrite.

Questions:

1. What are your immediate thoughts about the following card spread?
2. When reading them left to right, what story comes to mind?
3. When reading them right to left, what story comes to mind?

Queen of Cups · The Emperor · Ace of Pentacles · VI Wands

What's next?

Are you a poet and you don't know it, but your feet show it... because they're long fellows? If this question made you cringe, don't worry, the next chapter is NOT about how to use the tarot to write bad dad jokes. If, however, the question earned a laugh, yay! Now, I don't know whether the poet Longfellow worked with the tarot, but many bards first used the cards for the purpose of inspiring poetry. In the next chapter, I'll share a story and a fun, easy practice activity that can help you do the same.

Chapter 28: Cards for Bards

. . . .

My introduction to poetry was early on, when I was a toddler. Gran stocked my shelves with Mother Goose, Dr. Seuss, and classic French and British nursery rhymes like *Frère Jacques*, *Old King Cole*, and *Humpty Dumpty*. Rhyming stories that danced from my grandmother's lacquered lips sparked a buzzing blissfulness in my belly. The experience was joy I could hear with my ears, see with my imagination, and feel with my heart.

Writing poetry, on the other hand, felt like an initiation, as if I were being invited to harness all that joy and cast spells onto my wide-ruled pages.

The schoolyear was 1984-85, and I was in the third grade. Our teacher would read to us after lunch, and one day she selected a new book we hadn't yet seen. From where I was sitting, I could tell that the book's jacket was pearly white with thin black line drawings and chunky slanted font. The book featured a spine much thicker than the spectrum of adapted American classics the teacher had traditionally chosen from our reading shelf.

"I have a treat for you," the teacher declared, "a new book of poetry..."

"Poetry?" a boy in the class interjected. The classroom trembled with soft snickering.

"Yes, poetry," she answered, matter-of-factly, resting the book on her lap and smoothing its cover with her palms. "Because that's our next writing lesson: poetry."

The class looked around at one another, many students with expressions twisted in confusion, others sighing with dread. A few of us, however, clung to the edges of our seats and desks, our brows hiked so high in anticipation that our foreheads must've stretched an entire inch.

"This book is called *Where the Sidewalk Ends*, by Shel Silverstein."

Other students may have nodded off in digestive drowsiness, but I sat wide awake, my eyes glazed over and my imagination cranking through the poems' scenes like a View-Master. A snail that lived in your nose and bit off your finger if you picked boogers, a girl who ate an entire whale, and a deserted home overrun with ferns and birds and bats and gnomes.

That day in third grade was the moment I fell in love with poetry.

While rhyming limericks and acrostic poems with lines that spelled out the seasons came easy for me to write, the style of poetry I most enjoyed proved more challenging: haiku.

Discovering that some of the wildest, most thrilling stories could be told in only three lines blew my seven-year-old mind. The challenge of choosing and arranging words that added up to only five, seven, and five syllables, respectively, became a storytelling task at which I excelled.

During one assignment, in particular, our class was paired together in teams and instructed to write and illustrate a haiku. Once we were finished, we would have to stand in front of the classroom, one of our pair holding our drawings while the other read our poem aloud. I was partnered with a girl named Brooke, who was an artist like me but who was painfully shy. We agreed that she would sketch and present our illustration, and I would write and read our haiku. Sadly, although I can see the illustration in my mind, I don't have it to share with you; however, I do remember our haiku.

> The ant's feet were stuck.
> He couldn't believe his luck.
> One drop of honey.

Since the third grade, I've written and saved enough poetry to publish several collections. When I started working with the tarot many years ago, poetry seemed an obvious exercise in creativity, and when I learned that the cards had been originally used as a poetry game (See Chapter 5 – *A Brief History of Tarot*), I began pulling cards and using them to inspire poems.

Haiku came easily, as three-card spreads provided convenient containers that encouraged syllable arrangement. Combine that structure with inspirational illustrations and the poetry felt like it was writing itself.

If you are a poet, the practice activity that follows is sure to help you learn to seek inspiration in the cards. On the other hand, if you've never attempted poetry or you haven't felt successful writing it, you are encouraged to give the activity a try. Who knows? You might find you're a bard with the cards after all.

Practice Activity: Intuit a Haiku

As mentioned in the previous chapter, haiku is an unrhymed short-form poetry standard, written across three lines. The words in the first line contain five syllables, the second line has seven syllables, and the third line concludes with five. These simple poems are meant to convey a larger picture with fewer words. In this activity, you can use your tarot cards for both structure and inspiration when writing haiku.

What you need for this activity:

- Your Mystic Storyteller Tarot deck.
- Your favorite tools for writing.
- Your intuition and imagination.

Instructions:

1. Shuffle your tarot deck until you are satisfied that the cards are ready, and then cut the deck into three piles.
2. Turn over the card from the top of each pile.
3. For Card 1, use your imagination and what you've learned about the tarot and its symbolism to intuit a 5-syllable phrase inspired by the card's illustration.
4. For Card 2, intuit a 7-syllable phrase that is related to the first one. Don't worry about your thoughts rhyming, as haiku doesn't have to rhyme.
5. Repeat for Card 3, intuiting another 5-syllable phrase that relates to the story unfolding across the lines.

Continued, following page.

Here's an example:

When I engaged in this activity, I drew the following cards: Temperance, Ten of Wands, and Seven of Cups.

Considering each card's illustration and symbolism, and applying the rules of haiku, here's the poem that came to mind:

> Sagittarius
> In my spirit, encumbered
> By my magpie heart.

Did you count out the syllables on your fingers, too? They're all there: 5-7-5. And together, the three lines tell a story about little ol' me.

Here's the story:

Ever the Sagittarian, I'm adventurous and I love to travel... however, I'm a "collector" and I need to have as many baubles and doodads and whatnots around me to help ignite inspiration. This means I don't travel light, and as you might imagine, my home is a maximalist's haven.

See? The haiku conveyed that entire story about me in only 17 syllables.

Here's how the haiku connects to the story:

Temperance – This card represents Sagittarius in the zodiac (See Chapter 23 – *Astrology and the Tarot*).
Ten of Wands – Wands are symbolic of passion and spirit, and the figure clearly looks encumbered with all those pencils.
Seven of Cups – Cups are the suit that represents heart and this fellow clearly has a collection of cups to rival a magpie's.

Alternative Version

Shake off the haiku rules, pull as many cards as you wish, and write a poem of any style.

What's next?

Throughout this book you've been encouraged to capture your thoughts about the tarot in a notebook or journal. Writers and journaling seem to go hand in hand. Show me a writer who doesn't have a hoard of notebooks, and I'll show you someone with self-control. If you are like me and enjoy keeping a journal (or a dozen), the following chapter just might feel like cracking open a shiny new notebook.

Chapter 29:
Journaling with the Tarot

. . . .

When I was eight, my mother finally took me to a particular store at our local mall. The place was called "Spoiled Rotten," and I had been begging Mama to take me since we'd moved to Montgomery, Alabama, a couple of years prior. She finally relented, and when we arrived my eyes widened, my head swirling with wisps of sweet vanilla seeping from the front entrance. Before I could tear away from her and pillage the pastel trove, she wagged her finger and said, "You can pick out three things. Three." She raised three fingers. "That's all."

The pressure was on. How in the world could I possibly choose just three measly things out of a place bursting with such colorful treasures? I pored over the narrow, packed aisles, again and again, until I finally laid my three items onto the blush laminate sales counter: a pink toothbrush and toothpaste set (I wanted to know how the toothpaste tasted... like cotton candy), a pack of miniature colored pencils (for the tooth fairy to answer the questions I'd left for her under on my nightstand), and a Hello Kitty Diary.

Since that day back in the summer of 1985, I have kept a diary and/or journal, and sometimes several at once. From lockable, secret-keeping diaries to journals with specific themes—art, birdwatching, dreams, gratitude, reading, and tarot—I have been capturing my thoughts and memories on blank pages for almost four decades.

If you are not already several stacks into a collection of notebooks and journals, journaling is a practice that can help writers in a myriad of ways, and pairing the tarot with this practice can amplify both the method and the outcome. In fact, one of the most effective ways to become acquainted with the tarot is by making the cards a part of your daily writing routine, exploring the images, focusing on the ideas that most immediately and intuitively stand out, asking questions, and then journaling your experiences. As such, journaling with the tarot can have a number of benefits to one's writing craft. It can help strengthen vocabulary, increase tenacity, power through writer's block, and a regular routine can also supercharge both intuition and imagination.

The Benefits of Journaling with the Tarot

Tarot and journaling are quite similar in that they both can be effective in helping to improve mental health. Additionally, as you've learned throughout this book, the tarot can be used as a tool for self-reflection and as guides for self-care. Journaling checks those boxes as well, so the benefits of combining both can magnify the process and potential outcomes. These benefits may include the following:

Coping with anxiety and/or depression—While journaling offers an outlet for safely expressing thoughts and feelings, the tarot can help identify triggers, provide direction, and inspire resolutions.

Managing stress—Pulling tarot cards can help prioritize challenges, concerns, and fears. Journaling about them can help track symptoms so that you can discover healthy ways of handling them.

Improving mood and quality of life—Journaling provides an opportunity for positive self-reflection and motivation, while the tarot can serve as anchors for processing negative thoughts and behaviors.

Meditation and relaxation—By including intuitive tarot journaling in your regular self-care routine, you are uncovering daily opportunities for meditation, quieting the mind, and relaxing the body.

Self-discovery and reflection—Journaling with the tarot can provide a conduit for reconnecting with ourselves and rediscovering who we are or revealing who we endeavor to become. Pulling cards can help with understanding our desires and dreams, naming our stressors, establishing healthy boundaries, and ruminating on aspects of our lives for which we are most grateful.

How to Get Started

Getting started journaling with the tarot is as easy as 1-2-3.

1. Invest in a journal—Whether a notebook or bullet journal, tarot-themed journal or traditional notebook, keep something handy on which to jot and track your thoughts. If you've never journaled, or if it's been a while since you practiced journaling, you can simply start out with an everyday lined notebook.

2. Use the tarot cards as journal prompts, referring to the word lists and questions throughout this book for topic ideas and reflection.

3. Plan your tarot journaling practice:

Daily—Pull a single tarot card at the start of the day for guidance or at the end of the day for reflection. Whichever you choose, journal your thoughts about the card each day.

Weekly—At the start of each week, pull a single card and journal your ideas for approaching the week, or pull seven cards and journal about your overall outlook.

Monthly—Similar to pulling cards daily and/or weekly, you might also pull cards as the months change on your calendar. You can do this by the month, or annually by pulling twelve cards for a year-ahead spread.

Annually—Remember what you learned in Chapter 24 – Your Tarot Code regarding your year card? At the end of the calendar year, calculate the numerology for the year ahead and journal your thoughts around personal goals, plans, and dreams.

The longer you practice journaling, the greater the opportunity for collecting and storing core memories. You might even use these recollections to pen a memoir. In the next chapter, I cover using the tarot for memoir writing.

· · ·  · · ·

Practice Activity: Journaling for Joy

In The World card profile, you learned that writing can provide storytellers like you and me with access to joy despite conflict. Journaling is one such vehicle for writing in spite of circumstances unfolding around us. What might that look like? How can you share your stories to inspire others? These questions can be answered by recalling the lessons you learned along The Fool's Journey through the Major Arcana.

What you need for this activity:

- Your Mystic Storyteller Tarot deck.
- A notebook, journal, or notes app.
- Your intuition.

Instructions:

1. Sort through your tarot deck and pull out all the Major Arcana cards and then set aside the rest of your deck.
2. Next, select a card, either by shuffling and drawing at random or by starting with The Fool.
3. While considering each card, ask yourself the following questions, journaling your answers.

The Fool—For what or whom are you searching? What are your greatest desires, your hopes and dreams, your Bucket List goals? Make a list and write about what your life might look like after attaining them.

The Magician—Who are The Magicians in your life? How are they responding to what's going on in the world? How are they surviving? How are they thriving? Study these individuals and make notes about them, because they could inspire a character or two in a future story.

The High Priestess—What ideas are lingering in your subconscious mind that you can shape into stories? What's pushing through the veil that wants to be written?

The Empress—Take a look around you. What's available in abundance? What ideas, influences, or people are immediately available for you to study and learn? Do you have old notes that you might spin into a fresh story? Have you written a story that you haven't done anything with that you might revisit and repurpose? The Emperor—What about your experiences are you rebelling against? Write about all the ways in which you feel great resolve and/or conviction to stand firm and fight what's happening to you or around you. How will you respond... or refuse to not respond?

The Hierophant—How can you shake off the writing rules that don't resonate with your creativity and develop your own unique writing style? Remember my advice to start simple, quiet your inner critic, and lean into your intuitive thoughts.

The Lovers—What's the story behind the story in your favorite songs? Your favorite movie or TV show characters? When the world around you feels uninspiring or out of control, you can always connect to music and story. Listen to your favorite songs on repeat, watch your favorite movies, re-read your favorite books, and then imagine a back story for the characters. Romance writers can especially find inspiration by imagining what might happen if a song or movie or book started or ended differently. Some of the best fanfiction has been inspired by stories and songs written before them.

The Chariot—How can you be a storytelling trailblazer? What ideas do you have that nobody else has written? What direction might your writing take if you were to write about how events in your home, community, and/or world are affecting you?

Strength—What if you focused on how much bigger your strength is than your fear? Just what can you endure? How can you write fearlessly?

The Hermit—In response to what's happening around you, what if you did nothing? What if you simply retreated and rested, giving yourself space and time to explore your innermost thoughts and feelings about your circumstances?

Wheel of Fortune—In what ways have your experiences changed you? Write about who you used to be before life intervened, write about who you are right now, and then write about who you aspire to become. Are these three the same person? If so, how has Lady Luck been on your side in spite of life's ebb and flow?

Justice—What if Justice isn't given but obtained? What if you are in control of the scales and don't have to wait around for other forces to balance them for you? What would your writing practice look like if you actively seized every day? What does "Carpe Diem" mean for you?

The Hanged One—You have the autonomy to intentionally change the way you interpret things that are happening around you. You can choose to look at events and situations from a different perspective. As such, how can you reframe negative emotions and intentionally seek joy within your circumstances?

Death—What if you started writing without regard for anyone else's opinion but your own? How might that fearlessness and freedom completely transform your writing practice and your storytelling voice?

Temperance—Creativity doesn't wait around on life to get out of the way before it steps in; it's always there, soaking up the events and storing memories that can be stitched into future stories. While life is happening to and around you, how can you moderate and/or lean into your feelings so that you can inject them into your stories at a later date?

The Devil—What or who are your demons? Write about them. No matter how ugly or heinous or shocking the words you might choose to describe them, put your thoughts to words and your words on paper. Get them out of your system. How might you use your demons to write (and then kill off) a deplorable, oppressive, or miserable fictional character? On the other hand, how might you write a swarthy, lustful, and irresistible antagonist?

The Tower— What if your greatest idea yet is simply waiting to strike? And what if that inspiration can be found right where you are? To stay inspired, you have to stay curious. Be a tourist, even in your own hometown. Look up, follow your intuition, take in every detail, ask questions, and discover meaning in the things you find most interesting. How can you access joy by being a tourist in your life right now?

The Star—After experiencing a swift, profound change, in what ways are you different? What does self-care look like for you and how were you able to recover, rejuvenate, and/or restore joy following the fallout? Write a story about your experience.

The Moon—Look around and inside you. What's calling for your attention right now? What obvious stories are beckoning for you to write them? Which stories are showing up in your dreams or when you're doing other things like showering or driving or working? What is your shadow voice saying to you that you might spin into a story?

The Sun—Despite what is happening in the world and/or your community, what are the best and most dazzling aspects of your life right now? Who shines brightest and warmest on your days? What or who can you always depend on to bring you unbridled joy?

Judgement—How are you being called to write something different than you've ever written? How can what's happening in your life help you foster a sense of purpose? Write a story about it.

The World—In your life right now, what's worth fighting for, living for, and writing for?

Chapter 30:
Memoir Writing with the Tarot

. . . .

I was a weird little girl. While other kids would meet one another and want to know what cartoons they were watching, which breakfast cereal was their favorite, and which Corey was coolest, Haim or Feldman (my vote: Haim), I met potential new friends and wanted to know the meaning behind their names, whether they believed in magic, and what day they were born.

Ever the curious kid who always wanted to know the story behind the story, I would learn someone's birthday and never forget it. After all, it was the first day of their very own story, and that was important to me. Although birthdays were my favorite dates to commit to memory, I also remembered other days: the day I got my ears pierced for the first time (1/7/85), the day the Space Shuttle Challenger exploded (1/28/86), the day my drive shaft fell out into the parking lot of Junkman's Daughter in Little Five Points (2/22/10), the day both of my grandfathers died (it was the same day: March 15), the day my mother and I first walked to the Alabama Shakespeare Festival for exercise. It was our hundredth new diet. The date was 8/8/88.

Like dates, I've also developed a pretty healthy obsession with movies. And when I first saw *Rain Man* (sadly, I don't recall the date), I was okay—excited, even—with being compared to a savant whose memory was also pretty specific and complex. "Rain Mandy" soon became one of my nicer nicknames.

During the months in 2019 when I was traveling a lot (See Chapter 17, *Key 20 – Judgement*), I spent a great deal of time reminiscing on my life to that point. In January of that year, I began compiling notes on my memories, which reached as far back as my circus-themed playpen and a yellow footed terrycloth sleeper. To stay organized, I created a spreadsheet, lining the first column with dates, 365 rows, into which I plugged a core memory of each day's significance. After my memory entries started turning into short stories, the cells growing wider and rows expanding, I titled the spreadsheet A Story for Every Day.[105]

And then, poof! The idea popped to mind that I would one day write a memoir with the same title.

Exploring the notion of memoir writing, a venture I had yet to endeavor, I started a blog, *A Story for Every Week*, and committed to writing just that—52 stories centered around dates I remembered and the details that made them stick. To summon inspiration, and spark memories for the blank rows on my spreadsheet for which I had yet to assign a memory, I pulled tarot cards. Each card inspired a situation, event, experience, person, or other memory for which I was able to assign a date.

In the previous chapter, *Journaling with the Tarot*, I shared a story about my very first diary. While writing that chapter, I kept the diary right beside my keyboard—for invoking memories of that Sanrio store shopping experience decades ago. Because I was able to look at Hello Kitty on the diary's cover and thumb through its pastel pages, I could more adequately recall the day, and I even remembered the other two items my mother bought me and why I'd selected them. The tarot works in the very same way as my diary; you can hold the cards in your hands, displaying them at your workspace for help with conjuring memory.

Using the Tarot for Conjuring Memory

When drawing cards for memory recollection, I recommend asking yourself one or more of the following who, what, when, where, and how questions:

- Who can the person in this card represent? For example, every time I pull the King of Cups and the King of Wands, they remind me of my two grandfathers, and I immediately recall my most fond memories of spending time with them.

- What theme can this card represent? Search this book for the card's word list and then scan the words until one ignites a memory you can draft into a story.

- When in your life does this card remind you? When asking this question, check your immediate thoughts. A person, object, or symbol might remind you of a specific memory. Even if you don't understand why, jot all the details you can recall. They can spark a story.

- Where can this card represent? Survey the background of the card(s) you pull. Is the setting by water? Is it dry and arid? Is there a vast, open sky? Are there lush trees and/or vegetation? Whichever resonates, you can write a story about a place or event that reminds you of this card's setting.

- How do you feel about the card and what memory do you associate with that feeling? Similar to what I've recommended in the When question above, capture your immediate thoughts around how a card makes you feel and then attach a memory to those feelings until a story comes forth.

Why? The question Why? is unique to you. Just be sure to answer the question honestly for the most authentic results.

Using the Tarot to Structure Your Memoir

There are a myriad of ways to structure your memoir, but when using the tarot, my recommendations are the following:

Chronological—This method follows a timeline; however, a memoir doesn't have to span one's entire lifetime. Rather, it might highlight an era, a personal theme, or a specific situation. For the latter, you would begin your story with a past event or situation, and then share the details in chronological order. Whichever timeline you choose, draw tarot cards—specifically or at random—and assign them a point on your timeline. The practice activity that follows this chapter offers an example.

Reverse Chronological—Start with the conclusion or result of a past event or situation, and then work backwards until you arrive at the starting point. Use the tarot cards in the same way as above but backwards in time.

Three-Act Structure—The classic three-act story structure includes the Setup, Confrontation, and Resolution, respectively. In Part Seven: *The Tarot Games,* I've included a practice spread that follows this familiar structure. For memoir writing, you can pull cards consciously or at random and assign them a point on the three-act storyline to help conjure memories.

The Fool's Journey—In Chapter 32 – *Plot Development: The Hero and Fool's Journeys*, I go into depth about another classic storytelling method, the Hero's Journey. The Fool's Journey is quite similar to both the Hero's Journey and the three-act story structure; however, its main sections are the Departure, Initiation, and Return. In the tarot, these three sections overlap the 3 x 7 tarot diagram you learned about in Chapter 20. You can use the Major Arcana cards as anchors for your own memories.

Thematic—When writing your memoir, you might decide that you don't want to follow a structure at all. As such, you can base your memories on various events, moving the reader back and forth in time based on thematic occurrences until they arrive at your conclusion, or "lightbulb moment." However, if you choose a thematic structure (or lack thereof, as it were...), just be sure the memory jumps relate in some way; you don't want to confuse your reader.

In the practice activity that follows, you can use your tarot cards, along with a bank of memory prompts, to develop a chronological structure for mapping your memoir.

Practice Activity: Map Your Memoir

Should you decide to structure your memoir around a particular situation, or even a specific period of time, this activity can help you mine for inspiration and map the details. You can approach this activity in one of two ways: mapping by topic or mapping by tarot.

What you need for this activity:

- Your *Mystic Storyteller Tarot* deck.
- Your favorite tools for notetaking.
- Your intuition.
- Your memories.

Mapping by Topic

To start, review the Memoir Prompts table (following pages) and select a prompt that most immediately sparks a personal story.

Next, sort through your tarot deck and select the cards that resonate with this story. Lay them in a row.

While considering the prompt and the cards, answer the following questions:

1. What memories come to mind most vividly?
2. Who were the people involved?
3. What sounds can you hear inside your mind?
4. What other sensory details can you recall? Smells? Tastes?
5. Use your notes to draft your personal story.
6. After you are finished, repeat this exercise until you've collected several stories on your memoir map. Then, organize them in a way that will keep the reader intrigued.

Mapping by Tarot

Sort through your tarot deck and select a card that most immediately sparks a personal story. You can do this randomly by shuffling your cards and then turning them over, or you can turn your deck right-side up and deliberately thumb through the cards until one evokes a vivid memory. Review the Memoir Prompts table and make a list of the prompts that supports your story.

Memoir Prompts Table		
Beliefs & Feelings	house	joining the military
a spiritual experience	job	landing your dream job
a time of embarrassment	movie	receiving a bonus
afraid to do something	person	water cooler gossip
an addiction	pet	
anger	song	**Firsts**
being ashamed	subject in school	best friend
being disappointed	teacher / mentor	big disappointment
being fearful	vacation	big move
cultural beliefs		car
feeling vulnerable	**Obstacles**	crush
grieving a loss	a dangerous situation	death experience
having fun	a death that changed you	house
in love	a time of oppression	job
intimacy	an accident	kiss
it still haunts you	discrimination	love
joy and excitement	challenges you faced	major trip
loneliness	criticism that cut deep	pet
pride	effects of war	pregnancy
regrets	fighting aging	relationship
resentment aches	regretting an action	sexual intimacy
sadness	self-image	significant loss
something funny	significant loss	spiritual experience
the happiest you've been	supreme disappointment	
worrying	the grieving process	**People**
your heritage		a boss who helped/hurt you
	Career	a celebrity
Favorites	a career achievement	a coworker
animal	a layoff	a memorable teacher
artwork	a promotion	an adversary
band	being terminated	best friends
book	best / worst boss	grandparents
car	challenges at work	influencers
city / town	memorable coworkers	leaders who made a difference
event	demotions	loathsome enemy
food	getting a new job	mentors who changed you

Memoir Prompts Table		
military comrades	hiking a trail	a move or relocation
nosy or helpful neighbors	hunting in the woods	a surprise
sibling rivalry	learning something new	a wedding
that one uncle	listening to music	adoption
your aunts	metaphysical	an accident
your closest cousin	painting a room	an argument
your club members	playing team sports	anniversary
your parents	reading a book	being promoted
	travelling abroad	camping trip
Eras	water sports	divorce and the aftermath
adolescence	writing something important	experiencing a lawsuit
adulthood	your book club	graduation
aging later in life	your gaming friends	historical event
being a young adult		major achievement
getting older	**Relationships**	new baby
leaving home	adversaries	new car
your childhood	connections	new house
your teen years	coworkers / comrades	new job
	dating	retirement
Hobbies & Interests	enemies	significant loss
a camping trip	familial	someone died
a photograph you took	friendships	the best trip
a road trip	intimacy	a breakup
an unusual talent	marriage	changing schools
animals you love	parenthood	
cooking a delicious meal	platonic relationships	**Holidays**
creative arts	religious connections	calendar celebrations
dance competition	spiritual connection	cultural holidays
drawing contest		landmark birthdays
field sports competition	**Events**	observances
fishing with someone special	a big win	religious holidays
fun or strange collections	a funeral or memorial	trips
getting healthy	a major transition	vacations
growing a garden	a mistake	days off school

Memoir Prompts Table		
School Days	**Add Your Own**	
after school shenanigans		
awards ceremony		
band room		
beginning / end of school		
bullies who sucked		
college / university		
elementary school		
extracurricular activities		
favorite classes		
friends		
graduation		
high school		
lunchtime		
middle school		
P.E.		
school trips		
social groups / cliques		
playing sports		
school play		
teachers / mentors		
the school bus		

What's next?

I've never met a writer who didn't experience a time when the words were simply not there. Writer's block can happen to every storyteller, the hurdles of which are unique and solutions seemingly elusive. The tarot has helped a great deal in my experience with writer's block. In the next chapter, I will show you how I've used the cards to launch me over those pesky creative and/or energetic hurdles.

Chapter 31:
Shuffling Through Writer's Block

. . . .

If you're reading this book, then you know that writer's block is no secret—it's one of a writer's most notorious enemies. Whether you've floundered on getting started with a project, wrestled with what two characters should say during a dialogue-heavy scene, grappled with what to write in an article or essay, or even struggled with what to say in a social media post, you've more than likely been stung by writer's block.

For many, overcoming this common dilemma can be achieved through implementing habits like mediation, setting aside time to write, eliminating distractions, brainstorming exercises, and progress tracking. On the other hand, these habits might seem easier read than done. From an energetic standpoint, writer's block is a lack of surrender, a misalignment with one's project. As such, the tarot can help, especially during brainstorming sessions.

Tarot Spreads for Shuffling Through Writer's Block

To help you climb out of your creative slumps, I've designed a selection of easy and accessible tarot spreads and activities. From sparking inspiration to making decisions, one or more of these activities might help.

What you need for these activities:

- Your *Mystic Storyteller Tarot* deck.
- Your favorite tools for notetaking.
- Your intuition.

Start, Stop, Continue

When you hit a block, this three-card spread can be a quick way of assessing what you need to start, stop, and continue doing in order to move forward.

1. Shuffle your deck until you are satisfied that the cards are ready, and then turn the deck facedown as if you were about to deal them.
2. Starting with the space for Card 1, pull three cards and lay them in the three spaces.
3. Ask yourself the following questions, using your intuition to consider the answers.

Card 1: What do I need to START doing in order to get over this block?
Card 2: What do I need to STOP doing in order to remove this block?
Card 3: What do I need to CONTINUE doing in order to move forward?

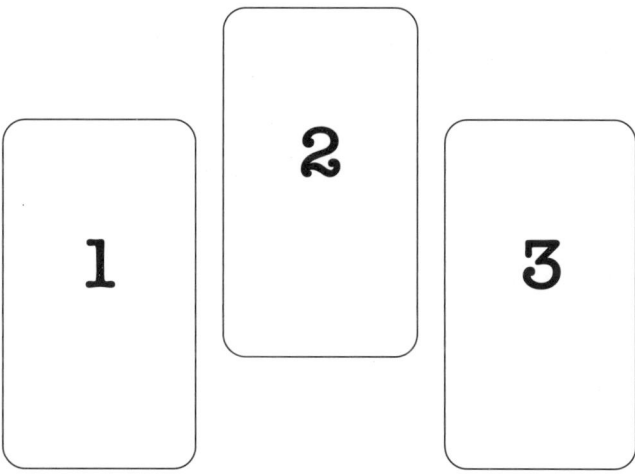

Advice Bridge Spreads

More three-card spreads! Since the tarot's mysterious origins, people have used the cards for divining advice. What should I do to attract a mate? How do I find a better-paying job? Which move should I make? The cards can even offer advice around writer's block. Now, you don't have to believe in supernatural forces guiding the cards—you can simply use your own intuition to mine ideas from the card illustrations.

As such, when you find yourself at a creative impasse, you might try the following three-card Advice Bridge spreads:

1. Shuffle your deck until you are satisfied that the cards are ready, and then turn the deck facedown as if you were about to deal them.
2. Starting with the space for Card 1, pull three cards and lay them in the three spaces.
3. Ask yourself the following questions, using your intuition to consider the answers.

Energy Block / Advice / Solution

Card 1: What's causing my energy block right now?
Card 2: What advice can help me work through it?
Card 3: What solution awaits?

Hurdle / Advice / Outcome

Card 1: What hurdle is blocking my creative energy right now?
Card 2: What advice can I use to leap over it?
Card 3: What does the outcome look like?

Problem / Advice / Goal

Card 1: What problem is affecting my creativity right now?
Card 2: What advice can help me move past it?
Card 3: What goal can I set in order to move forward?

Stuck at a Crossroads Spread

While this exercise was designed with fiction writers in mind, it can help with any kind of writer's block-related dilemma.

1. First, think of where you are in writing your story or project. Where is your character? What is the plot? What is the scene? Write what's happening right now—the issues and the concerns. Set aside your notes.
2. Next, search your tarot deck for the card that best represents you or your fictional character right now at this moment. Place the card in the center of the spread for Card 1.
3. Shuffle your deck and pull four additional cards, laying them around your character in the following order: north, east, south, and west. These cards represent considerations and decisions.
4. Ask yourself the following questions, using your intuition to consider the answers and move that writer's block out of your way.

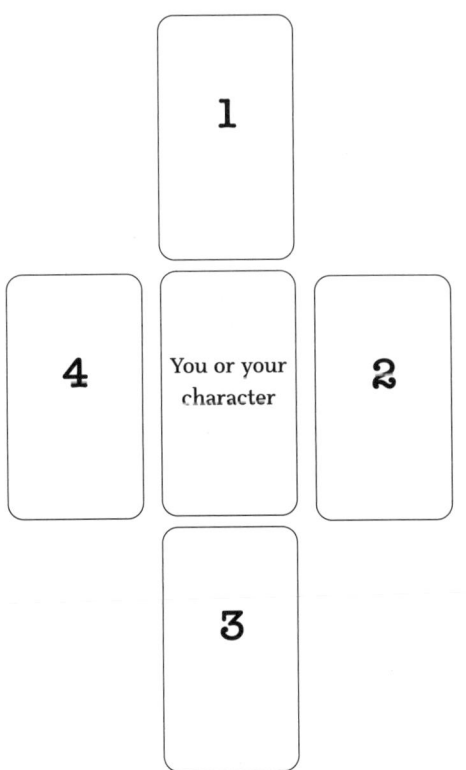

Card 1: (North) If my character or I keep pressing forward, what are the possibilities?

Card 2: (East) What can I uncover if I work with the direction of this card?

Card 3: (South) If my character or I turn around and go back in time, what might I change?

Card 4: (West) What can I uncover if I work with the direction of this card?

The Foolish Trip

Don't know what to write? Unclear about where in the world your main character is headed? Or are you feeling uninspired? Try jogging your creativity by taking a Foolish trip.

1. Shuffle your deck until you are satisfied that the cards are ready.
2. Find The Fool, which represents you or your character(s) in this dilemma. Lay the card in front of you, as far left as your space will allow.
3. Next, lay every card that follows The Fool in a line until you arrive at The World, which represents a conclusion. If you run out of cards before finding The World, continue with the cards that were ahead of The Fool.
4. From The Fool to The World, study the cards and then write the story that unfolds.

For a practice run, when considering this spread from left to right, what story comes to you?

The Fool

Ace of Cups

II
Pentacles

VIII
Wands

What's next?

The rest of Part Six was designed with the fiction writer in mind. In the chapters that follow, through my own intuitive insights, paired with credible research and guided activities, you will uncover methods for plotting your stories and writing relatable characters that jump off the page and into the hearts of your readers.

Chapter 32: Plot Development
The Hero and the Fool

· · · · · · · · · · · · · · · · · · · ·

In fiction writing, every story has an arc—a path leading readers from the beginning, through the middle, and to the end. A common story arc features the main plot, typically divided into seven sections, starting with the set-up and ending with the resolution. Meanwhile, other individual arcs, also known as subplots, unfold throughout. These might include an action sequence or an individual character's side story.

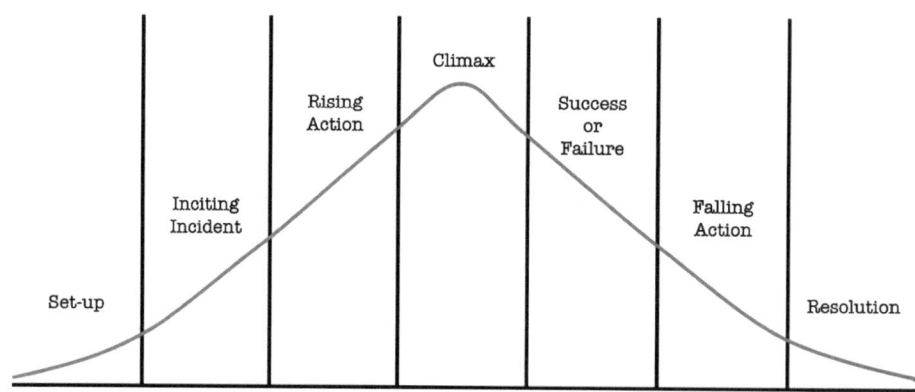

In Chapter 35, the Raiders of the Lost Story Arc practice activity utilizes the story arc for plot development practice and/or plot hole filling. For now, however, I'd like to introduce you to another narrative structure.

The Hero's Journey

In many fiction stories, the main character, sometimes referred to as the "hero," must navigate a similar path as the traditional story arc. Along their way, they meeting various archetypes, overcoming opposition, responding to obstacles, and eventually learning a major life lesson, if not several. In 1949, Joseph Campbell first coined this "hero's journey" in his work *The Hero With a Thousand Faces*.[106] Also called a "monomyth," Campbell's model outlines common phases, assigning them to a template storytellers have been using long before the mid-twentieth century.

When examining the hero's journey template, Campbell identified 17 different stages that can be summarized into three main parts:

1. **The Departure**—This is the embarking upon an adventure that separates the hero from their existing or ordinary world (what is known) and drives them onto a path of discovery (what is unknown).
2. **The Initiation**—The main part of a story, the hero is challenged with navigating various trials, during which their character is tested and cultivated.
3. **The Return**—This marks the hero's return to where they started —both literally and figuratively—renewed and/or changed, having discovered new ideas about the world and themselves.

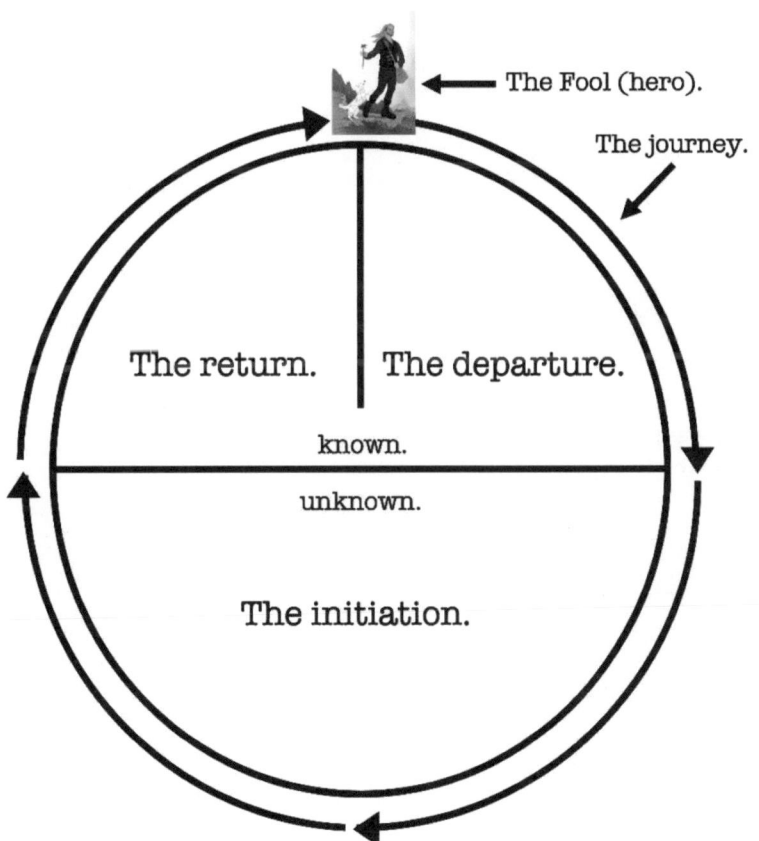

The Fool (hero).

The journey.

The return.   The departure.

known.

unknown.

The initiation.

When considering the hero's journey, many popular stories come to mind, including *Star Wars, Harry Potter,* and *The Hunger Games.* Using Harry Potter as an example, *The Boy Who Lived* not only navigates each of Campbell's 17 stages throughout the individual books, but the young wizard also encounters them throughout the overarching seven-story book series.

In my own writing, I've used this monomyth structure when writing nearly all of my books. In *The Missing Lamb,* for example, my main character, Lucky James, leaves her home in Florida and sets out for college at Emory University in Atlanta, Georgia. Early on, she is redirected from her path by serendipitous circumstances which introduce her to several new people and an entirely different place than the one she was originally headed. By the book's end, Lucky is a changed girl, her outlook on both her own life and the concept of family completely transformed by her experiences.

In the tarot, the Fool's journey is quite similar to the hero's, and through the following examination I will show you how the two adventure models overlap.

The Fool's Journey

When considering The Fool along a similar journey as Harry Potter or Lucky James, the cards can advance in a myriad of ways. In the illustration that follows, I have framed the Major Arcana along a path that mimics the hero's journey, labeling the three main stages. Please note: The Fool's journey does not have to follow the Major Arcana cards in order. It must, however, start with The Fool and end with The World. Depending on the individual story, the various cards between The Fool and The World can be placed in differing spots along the way. For the sake of showing The Fool's journey in its original order, I have arranged them around the template from zero to 21.

Following the Fool

To illustrate how The Fool's journey overlaps the hero's, I will tell you The Fool's story as I perceive it. Remember, this story is unique to me, and your interpretation might be completely different.

In this story, The Fool is our main character—they could even be you or me—and they are setting out on an adventure. They have their bag packed with everything they need, their furry familiar, and a nonchalant outlook that shouts ahead of them, "Carpe diem!"

As The Fool prepares for their trip, they must first consult with those who can help them get started. First, they seek the skill and craft of a mystic craftsperson

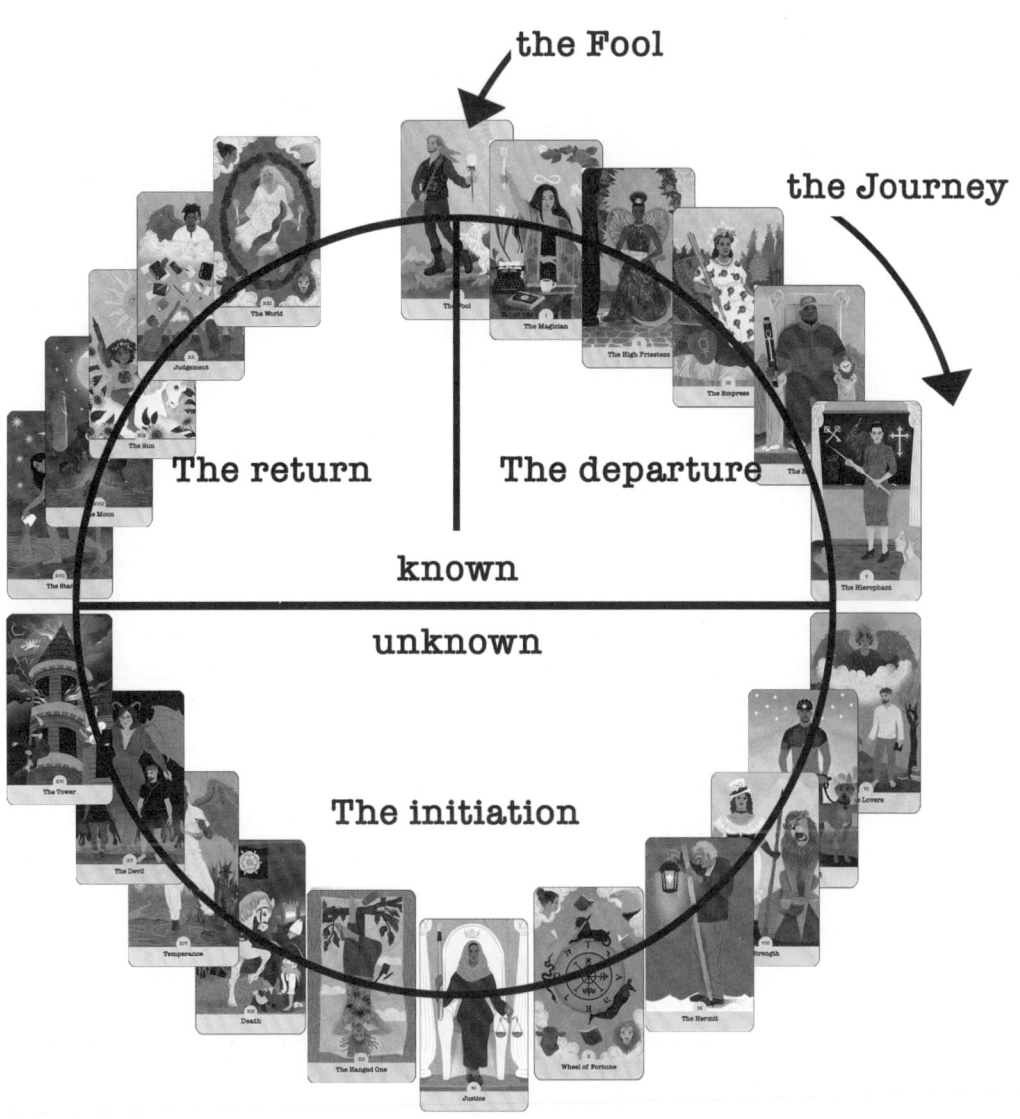

the Fool

the Journey

The return   The departure

known

unknown

The initiation

(The Magician), who offers a selection of tools and practical advice they will need along their way.

Next, The Fool meets with a wise visionary (The High Priestess) who reminds them of the importance of paying close attention to one's intuition—those gut feelings that will (almost) never lead them astray. "Consider what is both known and unknown," the oracle advises.

After consulting with these two individuals, The Fool says goodbye to the aspects of home which have provided nurturing love, security, structure, and instruction (The Empress, Emperor, and Hierophant, respectively). While The Fool is equal parts excited and nervous about this new trip, at first they feel like a fish out of water. Like the biblical story of Adam and Eve, The Fool is aware of their freedom and their responsibility for making the journey (The Lovers). Additionally, they feel supported and courageous, capable of overcoming any task that comes their way (The Chariot and Strength).

Without warning, The Fool happens upon a lone teacher (The Hermit), who has a wealth of knowledge and who warns them of pending ups and downs, helping to prepare them for inevitable turns of luck (Wheel of Fortune) and reminding them of the importance of maintaining balance of thinking, feeling, and action (Justice).

As The Fool endures their first series of mishaps, they recall the wise teacher's messaging, pausing to reflect on their journey with the hopes of gaining a different perspective (The Hanged One). They are enlightened by how profoundly changed they feel to this point in their travels, and they realize these circumstances have transformed them (Death). While they are still the same individual who set out on this adventure, The Fool must acclimate to the person they are becoming (Temperance). Again, they feel strong and focused.

Swooping in like a nighthawk, The Fool is faced with a situation that, at first glance, is tempting beyond reason (The Devil). Seduced by this encounter, they momentarily forget everything they've learned to this point, imbibing succulent deceit and engaging in risky behavior, when a sudden and terrifying incident blasts them off their feet, rocking their foundation and quaking their core (The Tower). Shaken, battered, and bruised, The Fool refuses to be defeated, and resolves to view what has happened as an epiphany, conquering those who would mean them harm.

Recalling the teachings of the visionary, the structure of home, and the wise insight of the reclusive teacher, The Fool has no choice but to pause, retreat, rest, and reflect (The Star), if they are to complete their journey and return home. During this respite, they learn of mysteries related to what has happened to them, and after pondering whether to set out on the next adventure or stay the current course (The Moon), they realize that true joy and happiness was theirs all along (The Sun), and they can survive a thousand more quests, if required, no matter the timing or setting.

In the end, The Fool heeds a calling to share what they have learned in order to benefit others (Judgement) in a profound way. Alas, after everything they've experienced, they arrive back home in a state of gratitude, wonder, and accomplishment (The World).

Now it's your turn. In the activity that follows, you can use the *Plotting The Fool's Journey* spread to flesh out your own hero's journey.

Practice Activity: Plotting The Fool's Journey

This practice activity can be helpful for planning and outlining a novel. However, the accompanying spread will require a little more space than is likely available around your writer's desk. Therefore, if you are able to clear a space on your bed, your bedroom floor, the kitchen countertop, or wherever you can spread out, you will have more room to work with the cards. Furthermore, there are two ways of pulling cards for this spread: deliberately or at random.

Deliberately Assigning Cards

If you already have an idea of the major characters and events in your timeline, you can sort through the cards and intentionally pull them as they resonate with you. For example, you might choose the King of Swords as your main character (Card 1) and the Eight of Wands as a situation that occurs abruptly without warning (Card 17).

Randomly Pulling Cards

On the other hand, if you are unclear about what you want to write and/or how you want your plot to unfold, try shuffling your deck and pulling cards at random, reflecting on the ideas that come to you as you intuit their placement around the spread.

What you need for this activity:

- Your *Mystic Storyteller Tarot* deck.
- Your favorite tools for notetaking.
- Your intuition.
- As much of your fictional story as you have to this point.

Review the archetypes/themes assigned to the spaces on the spread, and then place the cards in a circular layout, following the diagram on the rpreceding page. You can pull them deliberately (for the characters and/or events you already have planned) and/or at random.

For the spaces filled at random, use your intuition to consider how the card relates to the theme/archetype.

Make notes for each card, and then use them to plot your story.

First six cards: The departure (known):

Card 1: Your main character (MC).
Card 2: A person or place with tools to help the MC's purpose.
Card 3: A psychic person or a hidden secret.
Card 4: A motherly, nurturing person who wants what's best for the MC.
Card 5: A fatherly, dependable person who wants what's best for the MC.
Card 6: A teacher or institution with guidance, knowledge, and/or rules.

Cards 7–17: The unknown

Card 7: A relationship or a significant connection made with others.
Card 8: A leader, a new initiative, or a new direction.
Card 9: A person, place, or thing that demonstrates strength.
Card 10: A wise person, such as a mentor or guru.
Card 11: A minor change or turn of luck.
Card 12: Weighing options or justice being served.
Card 13: A different perspective or a turning point.
Card 14: A transformation, or gradual but major shift.
Card 15: Finding balance or an activity that fills the MC's cup.
Card 16: An adversary, enemy, or an oppressive situation.
Card 17: A situation that occurs without warning, changing everything.

Last 5 cards: The return (to the known)

Card 18: A period of recovery, or a person to help rescue the MC.
Card 19: Mysterious happenings or unanswered questions.
Card 20: A new idea or an exciting announcement.
Card 21: A call to action.
Card 22: A resolution or conclusive ending.

Chapter 33: Character Development with the Tarot

. . . .

Back in high school art class, I read a quote by the famous Italian sculptor, Michelangelo, that has stayed with me all these many years. He said, "I saw an angel in the marble, and I carved until I set him free." Like Michelangelo's sculptures, my characters have always come to me, even before a story's plot or setting. With each book I've written, I made it my mission to set them free, chipping away at their individual details and then building a world around them based on how I imagine they might move through it.

When my novel *Only the Rocks That Float* started taking shape, the initial idea that stepped forward was a set of fraternal twins, a boy and a girl named Lucas and Dolly. I'd known for many years that I wanted to write a book inspired by my grandmother's experience growing up on a small farm in rural Depression-era Alabama, but until those twins came to mind, I hadn't known how I might weave a similar story. My grandmother had lived on the farm with her cousin, who was also a girl and not much older than she. As I started plotting my novel, I simply replaced the idea of two girls with Lucas and Dolly. As I began exploring these twins, carving away at my mind's vision of them, I exposed shocking, even controversial details that would affect the entire storyline.

Like Michelangelo releasing his sculpture from the marble, as you write your own characters, you are freeing them from the imagination and giving them a life that, when written well, feels so real that your readers might reach out and touch them. What's more, well-written characters can maneuver a plot. YA author Nicola Yoon comes to mind—her stories entirely shaped by their relatable yet complex characters. Everything, Everything is character driven, and what a bittersweet story they made it. Another example is Stephen King, many of whose characters are so believable that they've become their own unique archetypes. John Coffey, Annie Wilkes, and Andy Dufresne are among my favorites.

When writing fiction, the tarot can be the instrument used to carve your own characters. From the archetype-rich Major Arcana to the personified Court cards, you can glean inspiration for your characters by imagining how they might relate to the themes represented in the cards. The practice activity *Courts of Personality* provided a hands-on example. Another way of getting to know your characters is by interviewing them, imagining them as real people (because they're real to us, right?), and asking them questions related to their personality, preferences, desires, goals, and even their past. To aid in this process, I have designed a 78-question character interview that employs every card in the tarot to help you create a detailed character profile.

78-Question Character Interview

The Fool   Tell me about a time when you took a leap of faith.

The Magician Who is the most resourceful person in your world and how have they helped you?

High Priestess Tell me something about yourself that no other person knows.

The Empress Have you ever created something meaningful? If so, what was it and how has it affected your life?

The Emperor Who can you lean on for stability and security?

Hierophant   What lesson or tradition have you carried with you since childhood?

The Lovers   What is your current relationship status? If you have a partner, tell me about them. If you're single, how has that shaped you?

The Chariot   What is your greatest motivator?

Strength   Tell me about a time when you had to be strong in the face of fear.

The Hermit   Have you ever purposely spent time alone to think? Why? What did you learn?

The Wheel   Tell me about a time when you experienced a change of direction.

Justice   Tell me about a time when you got what you deserved.

Hanged One   When have you had to surrender to something new and/or different? How has your perspective changed between then and now?

Death	What person, place, or thing has transformed you the most?
Temperance	When have you had to deliberately seek balance in your life?
The Devil	Who are your enemies? What oppresses you? What or who is your weakest temptation?
The Tower	Tell me about a time that you experienced a profound shift in thinking.
The Star	After a difficult experience, how do you restore your energy?
The Moon	What is something you struggle with letting others know about you?
The Sun	Who or what is the source for your greatest joy?
Judgement	Tell me about a time when you were called to do something completely outside of your comfort zone.
The World	Tell me about your most memorable conclusion or ending.

The Cups

Ace	What is the happiest news you've ever received?
Two	Who fills your cup? Alternatively, who is always trying to take from you but never gives anything back?
Three	You're throwing a party. Who are you inviting and why are you celebrating?
Four	When was a time when you didn't get what you wanted?
Five	Tell me about a time when losing something or someone resulted in you not appreciating what you still had.
Six	What is your favorite memory from childhood?

Seven	Have you ever struggled to make a decision of the heart? What were the circumstances and outcome?
Eight	Tell me about a time when you walked away from someone or something of significance.
Nine	What accomplishment are you most proud of and why?
Ten	What would your life be like if you were perfectly happy and content? Who would be there to enjoy it with you?
Page	Have you ever formed a friendship with someone unexpected? Tell me about them.
Knight	Tell me about a time when you had to demonstrate patience for something for someone else.
Queen	Who is/was the most nurturing person in your life? Tell me about them.
King	Who is/ was someone in your life who demonstrated servant leadership?

The Pentacles

Ace	If you won the lottery, what would you do?
Two	How do you manage work-life balance?
Three	Tell me about a time when you had to work on a project or complete a task as part of a group.
Four	What is your experience with saving money? Are you good at it? Or are you a spender?
Five	Have you ever been sick and/or destitute? If so, what was your experience?
Six	Has anyone ever offered you charity? Did you accept? If so, what

were the circumstances?

Seven   Tell me about a time when you had to wait on something to which you'd invested a lot of time, money, and/or attention.

Eight   What's your job? What do you do in order to make money?

Nine   If money and time weren't an issue, how would you live your best life?

Ten   If you died today, what legacy would you leave behind?

Page   What was your first job? What did you learn from it?

Knight   Tell me about a time when you had to bail someone out of a situation at home or at work.

Queen   Did you know or live with your mother? What are your memories of her? What stories have others shared about her?

King   Did you know or live with your father? What are your memories of him? What stories have others shared about him?

The Swords

Ace   What's the most brilliant idea you've ever had?

Two   Have you ever had to make a difficult decision? Tell me about the situation and the outcome.

Three   Who betrayed you? How did it happen?

Four   What's your relationship with sleep? Do you get enough? Do you take naps?

Five   Tell me about a time when you felt defeated.

Six   Have you ever had to move or seek asylum somewhere far away from home? If so, what was your experience?

Seven	Has anyone ever stolen something from you? If yes, what was taken? Did you ever get it back?
Eight	How do you silence your mind and/or prevent yourself from overthinking?
Nine	What is your worst nightmare?
Ten	Tell me about a time when you felt like you had hit rock bottom?
Page	What kind of a student were you in school? What's your highest level of education?
Knight	Tell me about a time when you had to think and act fast.
Queen	Besides yourself, who is your biggest critic?
King	Name a thought leader who has made a difference in your life.

The Wands

Ace	Tell me about a time when you had a spark of creativity or initiative that changed your life.
Two	What does success look and feel like to you?
Three	If you could travel anywhere in the world, where would you go?
Four	Tell me about a memorable celebration you attended. Who was there? What was the occasion?
Five	Have you ever experienced conflict with another person or group? If so, what was your experience?
Six	Have you ever been victorious at something and/or felt celebrated? What were the circumstances?
Seven	Tell me about a time when you had to defend yourself.

Eight	How do you respond when there are several tasks coming to you at once?
Nine	How effective are you at establishing boundaries?
Ten	What burdens you?
Page	How do you feel about your self-image? Do you have high self-esteem? Why or why not?
Knight	Who is your "knight in shining armor," the one person you can call for anything?
Queen	Imagine you are at a party. Are you mingling? Are you a wallflower? Are you the host?
King	If you started your own business, what would it be?

Additional Considerations for Character Development

In addition to interviewing your characters, you can explore a variety of methods for uncovering information about them that will help them resonate with the reader. These include using instruction from Chapter 24 – *Your Tarot Code* and the subsequent activity—specifically the Your Tarot Code portion—to uncover astrological correspondences. You might even decide on your character's date, time, and place of birth, and then run their information through a natal chart tool. My favorite free natal chart resource is the website Café Astrology. The web address for the free report is https://astro.cafeastrology.com/natal.php. Furthermore, you can pull tarot cards that reflect your character's personality and then search the accompanying word lists in Part Four of this book for additional details.

Practice Activity: Tarot Story Starters

While writing, or during periods when a writer cannot write—because of time, lack of tools, or writer's block—one often benefits from reading. Immersing oneself in the worlds and ideas of others can help a writer arrive at their own. Not only is it common for writers to seek inspiration through stories written by others, but it's quite necessary. To quote Stephen King, "If you want to be a writer, you must do two things above all others: read a lot and write a lot." Why read a lot? For inspiration on matters such as voice, style, dialogue, and world details so that you might refine your own craft.

As you have discovered throughout this book, the tarot is a highly intuitive tool for inspiring storytelling, in part because each card holds unlimited story potential. Start pairing the cards with others and the opportunities continue expanding. To that point, the tarot is a collection of at least 78 stories, and in the practice activity that follows, I've drafted a selection of tarot story starters to help inspire your creativity.

What you need for this activity:

- Your *Mystic Storyteller Tarot* deck.
- Your favorite tools for notetaking.
- Your intuition.
- Your creativity.

Instructions:

1. Read the following tarot story starters (next page) and then choose the one that resonates with you the most.
2. Search through your tarot deck and find the accompanying card. Display the card where you can see it while writing.
3. Finish the story. There are no rules—you can be as creative as you like.

Tarot Story Starters

The Tower

The day started like any other: filing books returned to the overnight drop and then registering new ones received by donation or directly from the publisher. Also like any other day, I had to figure out where I would live after I clocked out that afternoon. While pushing the book cart through the stacks, I cycled through my options. On Oliver's sofa, crawl back to Mom's place, under the walking trail bridge... And that's when I saw it. Lying on the floor between the stacks for Religion and Spirituality and Romance was an envelope. I stooped to pick it up, glancing around to check that I was still alone in the library. I opened the paper flap, emptying the contents into my palm. A key fell out, heavy and cold, a skeleton key, the bow of which had been engraved with three letters: T. O. R. My heart climbed to my throat. I looked up at the glowing EXIT sign over the library's back door. And that's when I knew...

Five of Cups

Our mother was never the same after Cedric and the twins disappeared. No matter what Alicia and I did to care for her, to remind her that we were still here and that we needed her, nothing seemed stronger than her grief. One day after school, the week before spring break, I busted open my piggy bank and used the coins to buy three bus tickets. Down at the station, Mr. Lowell said I only had enough money for one ticket. But he'd known our family's story, he'd said. "It's all anyone talks about 'round these parts." After accepting Mr. Lowell's condolences and listening to his theories about what had happened last summer, I walked back home with three tickets to...

Nine of Pentacles

Hidden at the end of a long and winding dirt road, just off Localita Montefalconi in beautiful Casaglia, you can find the Il Volo Del Falco Vineyard. Once a year, proprietor Claudia Ciccone, a jovial and eccentric recluse, hosts a contest, the winner of which receives an all-inclusive stay in the finest accommodations her sprawling villa has to offer. To enter the sweepstakes, all you have to do is...

Ace of Wands

The hand of Aodh, God of Fire, appeared as if a specter. From the clouds, he offered the Wand of Boudicca to eight-year-old Carson Callahan, the youngest person in the land to ever...

Nine of Pentacles

Ms. Finster (who was probably an old spinster) called me up to her desk. At the sound of my name, the class gasped. As I rose from my seat, I swallowed down bile climbing in my chest. Making eye contact with the terrifying teacher, she held what looked like my research paper, giving it a shake as she barked for me to hurry up. I glanced around, shrugging. What could she possibly want? I thought. I'd never scored lower than perfect marks on all my work in her class. I advanced down the aisle, hushed whispers volleying behind me, when the classroom door flew open, banging against the cinderblock wall. In walked...

Part Seven:

The Tarot Games

"Creativity is intelligence having fun."

Albert Einstein
Theoretical Physicist

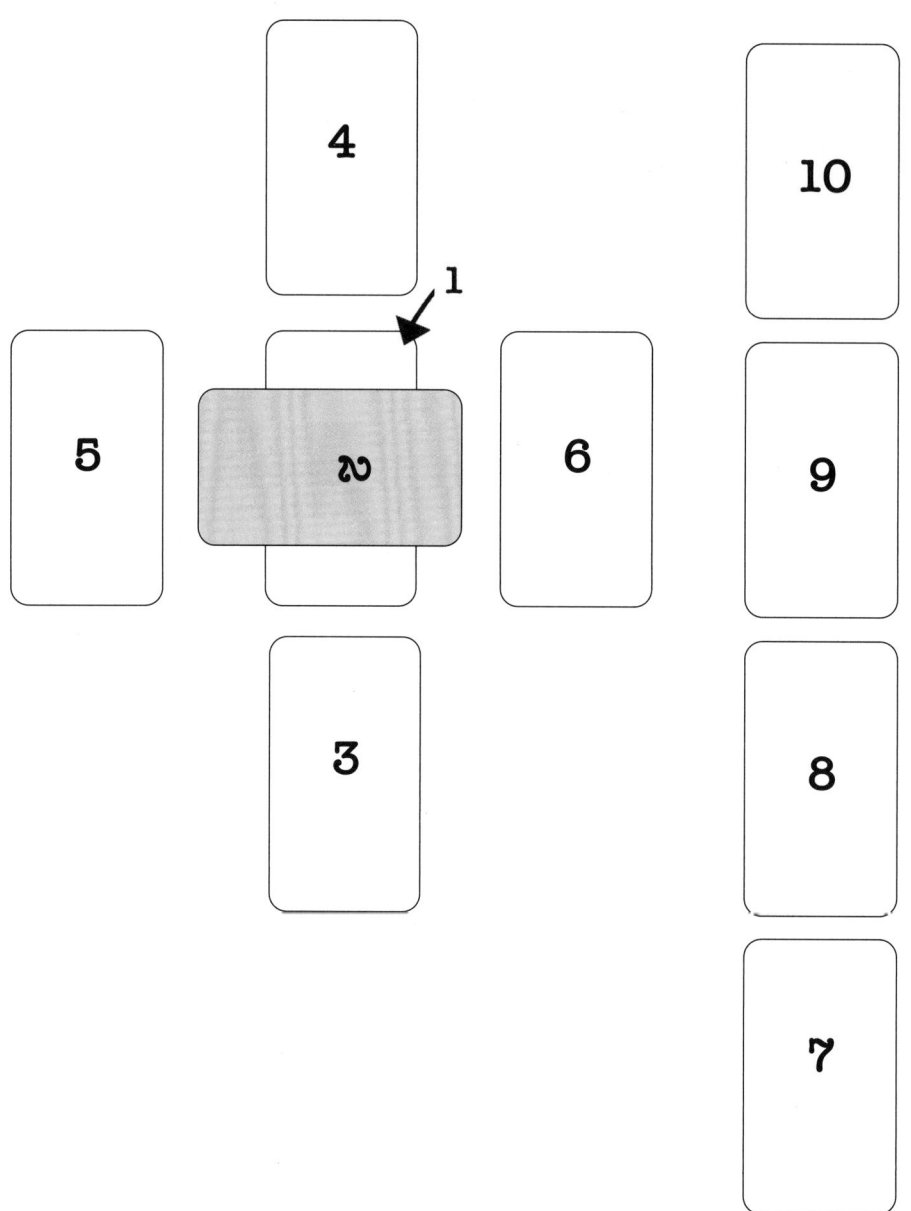

Chapter 34: The Writer's Cross

. . . .

Both learning and writing are more effective, and seem to come more naturally and easily, when the method and practice are both motivating and enjoyable. When we're having fun, dopamine, a feel-good neurotransmitter, is released in the brain, which can also stimulate memory retention. With these ideas in mind, I have developed a selection of writing-related activities that might help stimulate your writer's intuition and enhance your creativity. To start, I'd like to introduce you to my own version of the Celtic Cross spread, one of the most popular spreads in tarot practice.

Although the origins of the Celtic Cross spread are unknown, the first published reference occurred in 1910 when A. E. Waite published *A Pictorial Key to the Tarot*. The spread consists of 10 cards, each with a specific position and purpose, and can be used for everything from problem-solving to providing a life snapshot. For a comprehensive dive into the spread, I recommend *Seventy-Eight Degrees of Wisdom, A Tarot Journey to Self-Awareness*, by Rachel Pollack.

The Writer's Cross is my own version of the Celtic Cross. Like the original, it includes 10 cards; however, the positions are specific to the writer. I designed this spread for a creative and/or divinatory means of assessing a writing-related problem or situation in order to move forward with more insight and direction.

What you need for this activity:

- Your *Mystic Storyteller Tarot* deck.
- Your favorite tools for notetaking.
- Your intuition.

Instructions:

1. Think about a problem or situation you are facing in the writing project on which you are currently working.
2. While thinking about that issue, shuffle your tarot deck until you are satisfied that the cards are ready, and then turn the deck facedown as if you were about to deal them.

3. Starting with the space for Card 1, lay a card in each of the 10 spaces.
4. Capture your immediate thoughts about each card.
5. Once you've finished making notes, start at Card 1 and then move through the spread as if reading a story.

Card 1: You, the writer, in your everyday state.

Card 2: This card relates to what's "crossing" you, the problem or situation you're experiencing right now with what you're writing.

Card 3: This is what lingers in your subconscious mind around this writing-related problem or situation.

Card 4: What's at the forefront of your thoughts, your conscious mind? What's keeping you up at night?

Card 5: You in the past—how you dealt with similar circumstances.

Card 6: Your near future—something you can do to shake things up and make a difference in the outcome.

Card 7: You right now in this situation. Note the difference between this card and Card 1; this card is different because the problem or situation has had an effect on everyday-You.

Card 8: This card reflects your environment—the people around you, your support system, your messy (or clean) desk, your familiar, etc.

Card 9: This card uncovers your deepest hopes and fears related to the problem or situation with what you're writing.

Card 10: This is the outcome—what things might look like on the other side of this problem or situation.

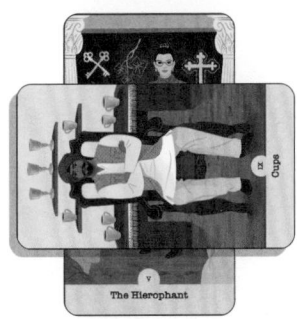

Chapter 35:
Raiders of the Lost Story Arc

. . . .

The Raiders of the Lost Story Arc exercise is a simple tarot spread you can use for practice developing a new story idea, or for working out specific details and/or filling in plot holes within a storyline you've already started writing.

What you need for this activity:

- Your *Mystic Storyteller Tarot* deck.
- Your favorite tools for notetaking.
- Your intuition.
- A story idea.

For practice developing a new story:

- Shuffle your tarot deck until you are satisfied that the cards are ready, and then turn the deck facedown and set it on your workspace.
- Cut the deck into seven small piles and place them, in any order of your choosing, on the seven spaces.
- Starting with Pile 1, flip the top card over and then move to the next pile.
- Once all piles feature a turned card, intuit the story that unfolds, from set-up to resolution.
- Draft the story and save it for a future project.

Use your intuition to decide what new ideas the plot hole cards bring to the story. Repeat from Step 3 until you are satisfied with the outcome.

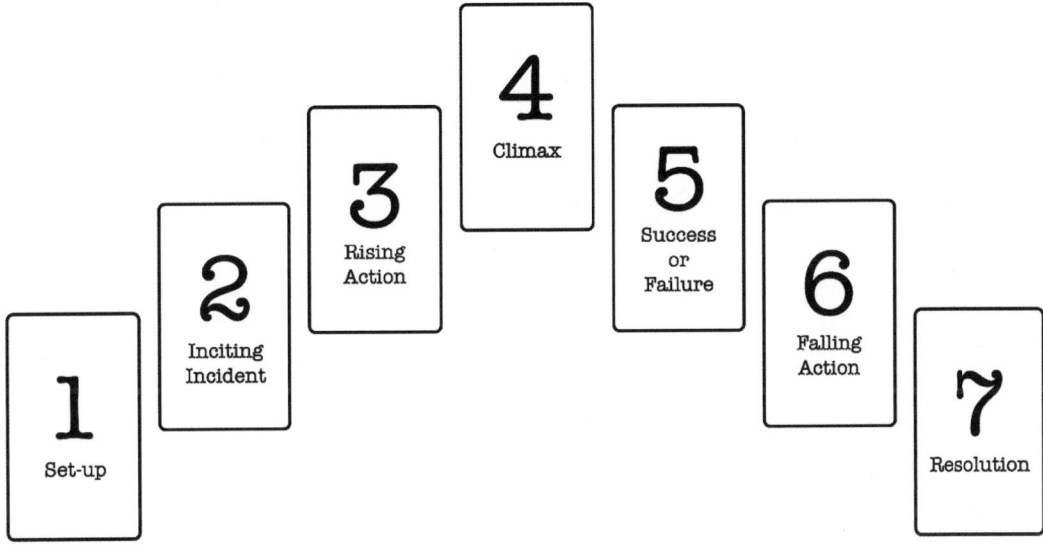

For filling plot holes within a story you've already started writing:

1. Sort through your tarot deck and pull cards that represent the parts of your storyline you are settled on or have already fleshed out.
2. Shuffle the remaining cards until you are satisfied that they are ready, and then turn the deck facedown as if you were about to deal them.
3. Start turning cards over onto the spaces that remain—your plot holes—and when all spaces are filled, examine the entire plotline from left to right.
4. Use your intuition to decide what new ideas the plot hole cards bring to the story.
5. Repeat from Step 3 until you are satisfied with the outcome.

Plot holes in my story. I know how the action builds, and how it all ends, but I haven't yet tackled the falling action.

Chapter 36:
The Road Less Traveled

. . . .

Back in Chapter 17, Key 7 you learned about The Chariot card and its many implications, including drive and motivation. If you are a writer of fiction, and you are faced with which direction to take your character(s), this spread can help.

1. Shuffle your tarot deck until you are satisfied that the cards are ready.
2. Find The Chariot card and place it in the space for Card 2.
3. The card before it (Card 1) is what might happen should your character choose the easiest route on their journey and the card after it (Card 3) is what might happen if your character chooses the road less traveled.
4. Ask yourself the following questions, using your intuition to consider the answers.

Card 1: What might happen should my character choose the easiest route?
Card 2: The Chariot, my character.
Card 3: What might happen if my character chooses the road less traveled?

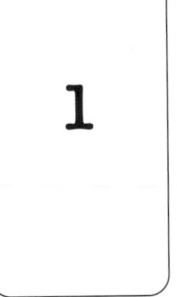

- Who are these people?
- How does their conversation start?
- What are they talking about?
- Are they arguing?
- Are they gossiping?
- Is there any flirting going on?
- Are they debating opposing sides of the same idea?
- What happens after they part ways?

Chapter 37: Royal Dialogue

. . . .

Writing dialogue can be tricky, and my initial advice is to read the work of others specifically so you can see—both from the lens of a writer and a reader—how the interchanges are crafted. Next, practice. Imagine two characters engaging in a conversation and write what they're saying. This can help you get the hang of all the mechanics involved. And, of course, you can use your tarot deck for inspiration. The following spread was designed with writing dialogue in mind.

What you need for this activity:

- Your Mystic Storyteller Tarot deck.
- Your favorite tools for notetaking.
- Your intuition.

Instructions:

1. Shuffle your tarot deck until you are satisfied that the cards are ready, and then split the deck into two piles.
2. Turn over the first card on each pile. Keep turning them until you arrive at two Court card figures facing one another.
3. First, look around at the two cards' surroundings.
4. Next, look at what the individuals are wearing, their age, posture, etc. Remember, gender, race, and age are completely up to your own discernment.
5. Ask yourself the questions under the spread at left, using your intuition to consider the answers.
6. Write their conversation.

Chapter 38: Growing a Family Tree

. . . .

Are you planning a fiction series? Is your storyline a saga that will include one or more large families or other connected groups of characters? There are a plethora of genealogy software programs you can use to build your fictional family trees; however, to get started, organized, and/or for an easily accessible planning tool, you can also use the tarot. Your tarot cards can help inspire and plan groups, families, platonic and/or romantic relationships, and even adversarial connections. As such, I have designed two family tree spreads. Please note, however, that although the spreads are templates, they're pliable. None of the positions are set, so feel free to adjust your card placements to suit your project.

What you need for this activity:

- Your *Mystic Storyteller Tarot* deck.
- Your favorite tools for notetaking.
- A story idea that includes a family or other group.
- Your intuition.

Instructions:

1. First, decide which template you'd like to use for inspiration,
2. Next, search through your tarot deck and select a card to represent each character in your fictional family tree.
3. Start with one character and lay the card that represents them on the space numbered 1.
4. Continue moving through your character cards until your entire tree is grown.
5. Take a picture of your spread and use it to fill in the spaces on the family tree program of your choice. *Hint: PowerPoint works well. You can use shapes for positions and lines for connectors. An alternative route is Insert > SmartArt > Hierarchy.*

Family Hierarchy Template

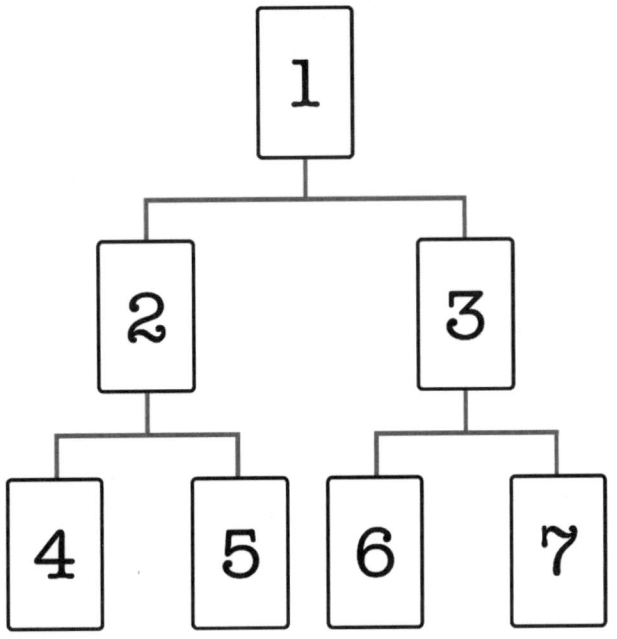

Family Saga Template

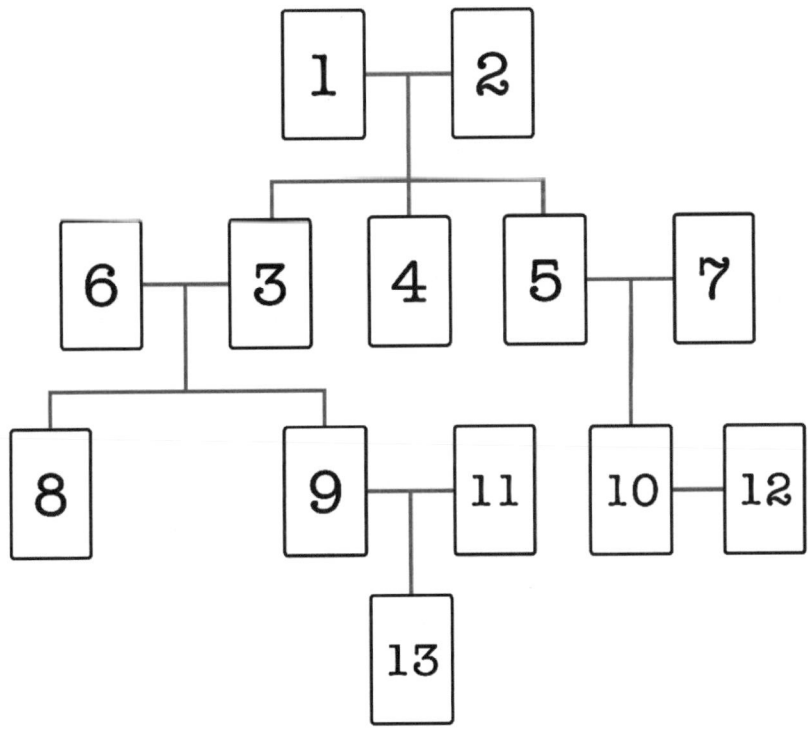

Family Drama Template

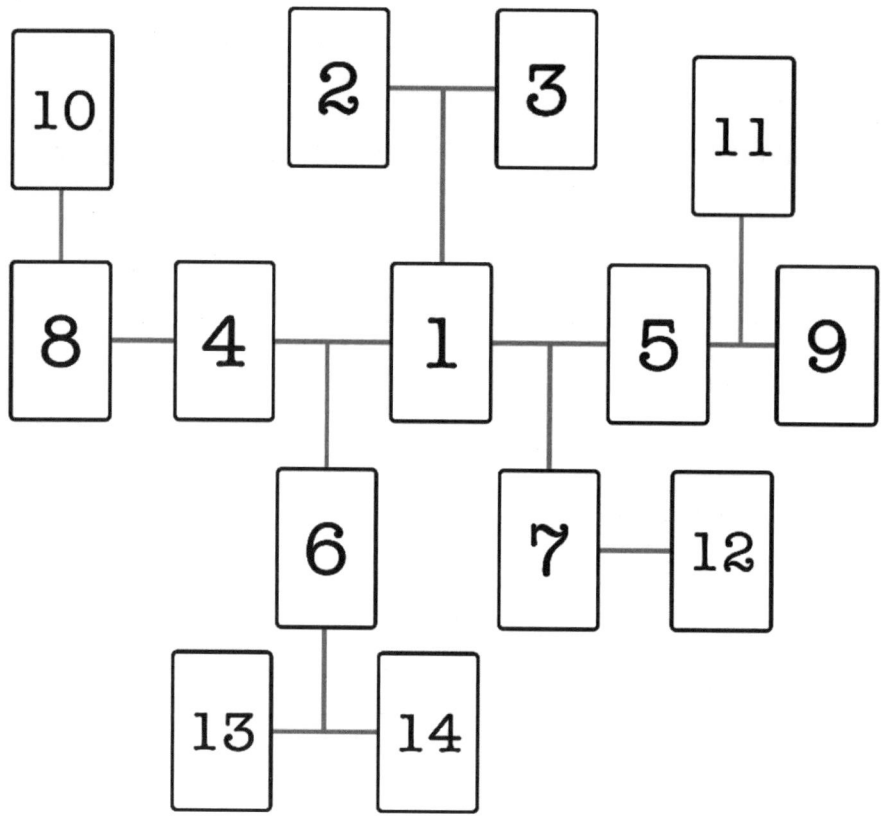

Chapter 39: Campfire Storytime

. . . .

In October of 1984, when my best friend Stacie was seven years old and in the first grade, a group of teachers chaperoned her class on a camping trip in Joshua Tree National Park. One evening before bed, Stacie and two other girls walked together to the nearby makeshift restrooms. Afterwards, they settled in their tents, too giddy to sleep. Half an hour later, the police arrived at their campsite, and although Stacie didn't understand what was going on, she knew something serious was happening because the adults had become frantic, checking every tent and gathering the kids together to be sure everyone was accounted for. Once Stacie's mother arrived to pick her up, she told her what had happened. About 30 minutes earlier, right around the same time as when Stacie and the other girls had gone to the restrooms, three-year-old Laura Bradbury disappeared. The toddler had been with her brother at the same restrooms. Although there is speculation around Laura's death—you are welcome to research but be forewarned the details are grim—the child's disappearance remains unsolved.

Many of the most memorable stories ever told can't be found in books, on a stage, or on any screen. They're shared orally—family anecdotes, legends, ghost stories, and first-hand accounts of remarkable events. The story I shared above is the latter. It's one my best friend says she'll never forget, and it's shared year after year in her family. These campfire-worthy tales are an important part of humanity's social fabric, and they're made so memorable because of the storyteller, where we are when we hear them, and how they make us feel.

The following Campfire Storytime activity is a game you can play with several folks while gathered around a table, the living room floor, or wherever there is occasion to share stories. It's especially fun for camping trips, holiday dinners, and team building.

Activity: Campfire Storytime

What you need for this activity:

- Your *Mystic Storyteller Tarot* deck.
- A clean, empty bowl.
- A pen or marker.
- Post-It notes or a notepad.
- At least six people.
- Everyone's intuition.

Instructions:

1. Using Post-It notes or slips of paper cut from a notepad, mark each with the numbers one through however many people are participating.
2. Fold the pieces of paper until the numbers cannot be seen and place them inside the bowl. For example, if you have eight people playing the game, then you should have eight folded numbers in the bowl.
3. One person scrambles the numbers well, draws a number, and then passes the bowl around the group.
4. Each person draws a number; however, DO NOT LOOK. Don't unfold the slips of paper. Set the numbers to the side without revealing who pulled what.
5. Decide who will shuffle the tarot deck and then shuffle the cards really well.
6. The shuffler deals one card facedown in front of each person, setting the rest of the deck facedown in the center of the group.
7. The group looks at their numbers.
8. Whoever has Number 1 turns over their card and starts a story The story can be whatever their card reminds them of, and if they are stuck or feel uninspired by their card, they can draw one additional card from the deck and pair it with the first to aid in inspiration. When Storyteller Number 1 gets to a stopping point, the Storyteller with Number 2 picks up where they left off in the story, drawing an additional card, if necessary. The max number of cards each person can have in their hands is two.
9. Repeat this process until everyone around the group has added to the campfire story, with the very last person closing the story.
10. For a Halloween version... same rules, but make it spooky!

Part 8:

Endnotes & Sources

Endnotes

1   *Mystic Storyteller Tarot* (La Panthère Studio, 2024) was inspired by Pamela Colman Smith's original illustrations.

2   *Tarot Mythology: The Surprising Origins of the World's Most Misunderstood Cards.* (n.d.). Collectors Weekly. Retrieved September 24, 2022, from https://www.collectorsweekly.com/articles/the-surprising-origins-of-tarot-most-misunderstood-cards/

3   James, B. (n.d.). *MPP38 Ellen Goldberg: Tarot & Palmistry.* Medicine Path with Brian James. In this episode, Goldberg explains the origin of the term "gypsy," which many believe to be a slur. Its occurrence in this book relates to the origin, not the slur.

4   *Definition and etymology of tarot.* (n.d.). Etymonline. Retrieved October 16, 2022, from https://www.etymonline.com/word/tarot

5   Goldberg, E. (n.d.). *School of Oracles.* School of Oracles. https://schooloforacles.com/

6   Many definitions in this list have been sourced from the *Merriam-Webster Dictionary*; however, not all iterations of the definitions are used for every word. Other definitions were sourced from the Dictionary.com website.

7   Definition of creativity. (n.d.). In *www.dictionary.com*. Retrieved September 25, 2022, from https://www.dictionary.com/browse/creativity

8   Kaufman, S. B. (2015, September 9). *Creative People Are...* Scientific American Blog Network. Retrieved October 16, 2022, from https://blogs.scientificamerican.com/beautiful-minds/creative-people-are/

9   *Definition and etymology of intuition.* (n.d.). Etymonline. Retrieved September 24, 2022, from https://www.etymonline.com/word/intuition

10   Stoker, B., A-E, A., & Berghorn, R. (2022, March 22). *Powers of Darkness: The Unique Version of Dracula.* Timaios Press.

11   *Interview with Stephenie Meyer.* (2009, November 13). [Television]. The Oprah Winfrey Show. Harpo Productions.

12   Colyard, K. W. (2016, October 6). *Where Does Stephen King Get His Ideas? Here Are The Creepy Origins Of 10 Terrifying Tales.* Bustle.

13   Jung, C. G., & Hull, R. (1981, August 1). *The Archetypes and The Collective Unconscious* (Collected Works of C.G. Jung Vol.9 Part 1) (Collected Works of C.G. Jung, 48) (2nd ed.). Princeton University Press.

14   Pierce, C. A. (2016, November 8). *"An O without a figure": The Fool and the Concept of Zero in King Lear.* Crossroadstarot. https://crossroadstarot.wordpress.com/2016/11/08/an-o-without-a-figure-the-fool-and-the-concept-of-zero-in-king-lear/#more-291

15   Kasparek, C. A. (1984). *Ethan's Quest Within : A Mythic Interpretation of John Steinbeck's The Winter of Our Discontent.* http://liblink.bsu.edu/catkey/225291

16   Auger, E. E. (2018). *Tarot and T.S. Eliot in Stephen King's Dark Tower Novels* [Article]. SWOSU Digital Commons. https://dc.swosu.edu/mythlore/vol36/iss2/22/

17   Pierce, C. A. (2015, August 8). *Don't Be Afraid of Virginia Woolf: Tarot Imagery in "The Searchlight."* Crossroadstarot. https://crossroadstarot.wordpress.com/2015/08/08/dont-be-afraid-of-virginia-woolf-tarot-imagery-in-the-searchlight/

18   Kaplan, S. R. (2018). *Pamela Colman Smith: The Untold Story.* U.S. Games Systems Inc.

19   Smith, P. C. (1899). *Annancy Stories.* R. H. Russell, New York.

20   Smith, P. C. (1905). *Chim-Chim: Folk Stories from Jamaica.* The Green Sheaf, London.

21   Kaplan, S. R. (2018). *Pamela Colman Smith: The Untold Story.* U.S. Games Systems Inc.

22   *Biography Pamela Colman Smith.* (n.d.). https://www.daneel.franken.de/tarot/Biography%20Pamela%20Colman%20Smith.html

23   Ransome, A. (1907). *Bohemia in London . . . With Illustrations by Fred Taylor.*

24   Wirsching, T. (2021, March 29). *Pamela Colman Smith: American.* The American Renaissance Tarot. Retrieved September 29, 2022, from https://www.americanrenaissancetarot.com/blog/2019/3/1/pamela-colman-smith-american

25   The card game called "52 Pickup" is a prank. When I was eight years old, my grandfather (*Mystic Storyteller Tarot's* King of Cups) asked me if I wanted to play a card game. When I eagerly agreed, he explained that he would first shuffle my Walt Disney World playing cards. In doing so, he released the cards all over the floor in front of me. "Now, pick 'em up!" he exclaimed, pleased with himself. I was not amused.

26   *arcana | Search Online Etymology Dictionary.* (n.d.). https://www.etymonline.com/search?q=arcana

27   Pollack, R. (2019). *Seventy-Eight Degrees of Wisdom: A Tarot Journey to Self-Awareness* (A New Edition of the Tarot Classic) (Third Edition, Revised). Weiser Books.

28   Lebo, K. (2021, April 14). *A Secret, Symbolic History of Pomegranates.* Literary Hub. https://lithub.com/a-secret-symbolic-history-of-pomegranates/

29   Reed, T. (2017, March 5). *The Empress* (episode 13). The Tarot Lady. https://www.stitcher.com/show/tarot-bytes/episode/the-empress-49627089

30   Katz, M. and Goodwin, T. (2015, April 8) *Secrets of the Waite-Smith Tarot: The True Story of the World's Most Popular Tarot.* Llewellyn Publications.

31   Powell, B. B. (2021). *Greek Poems to the Gods: Hymns from Homer to Proclus* (First). University of California Press.

32   The Editors of Encyclopedia Britannica. (2022, September 5). *Eleusinian Mysteries | Greek religion.* Encyclopedia Britannica. https://www.britannica.com/topic/Eleusinian-Mysteries

33   I'm a superfan of *The Office.* If you aren't a watcher, this is a reference to the show where my favorite character, Dwight Schrute, decides to print his own currency. If you are also a fan, what is the cash value of a Schrute Buck?

34   *Mystic Storyteller*, Amanda Hughes, and La Panthère Studio are not affiliated with, nor do we support, the nonprofit organization that uses the acronym *NaNoWriMo.* When referring to National Novel Writing Month by the same acronym, NaNoWriMo, we do not imply any connection to the organization.

35   Borrelli, C. (2020, December 25). *Debating Dan Fogelberg's 'Same Old Lang Syne': Beloved holiday classic, or worst thing to come out of Peoria?* Chicago

Tribune. https://www.chicagotribune.com/entertainment/ct-ent-dan-fogelberg-same-old-lang-syne-20201217-rzel3crk5rgwrb3jmp4x3cmrye-story.html

36 Katz, M. and Goodwin, T. (2015, April 8) *Secrets of the Waite-Smith Tarot: The True Story of the World's Most Popular Tarot*. Llewellyn Publications.

37 Pollack, R. (2019). *Seventy-Eight Degrees of Wisdom: A Tarot Journey to Self-Awareness* (A New Edition of the Tarot Classic) (Third Edition, Revised). Weiser Books.

38 The Editors of Encyclopedia Britannica. (1998b, July 20). *yoni | Hinduism*. Encyclopedia Britannica. https://www.britannica.com/topic/yoni

39 Mingren, W. (2018, November 22). *Understanding the Dharma Wheel: This Ancient Symbol Holds Secret Meanings*. Ancient Origins. https://www.ancient-origins.net/artifacts-other-artifacts/dharma-wheel-0011033

40 Hughes, A. (2022). How does scrolling through social media make you feel? [Data set]. Instagram. www.instagram.com/haintbluecreative

41 Definition of doomscrolling. (n.d.). In www.dictionary.com. Retrieved April 20, 2022, from https://www.dictionary.com/browse/doomscrolling

42 Howcast. (2018, November 12). *How to Read the Hanged Man Card | Tarot Cards*. YouTube. https://www.youtube.com/watch?v=cjlZE4slkPQ

43 Fellowes, J. (2015, January 11). *Downton Abbey* (season 5, episode 2) [Television]. BBC.

44 Pollack, R. (2019). *Seventy-Eight Degrees of Wisdom: A Tarot Journey to Self-Awareness* (A New Edition of the Tarot Classic) (Third Edition, Revised). Weiser Books.

45 Howcast. (2018, October 15). *How to Read the Death Card* | Tarot Cards [Video]. YouTube. Retrieved October 15, 2022, from https://www.youtube.com/watch?v=3Sa9ZlzczkI

46 The Writers College. (2019, October 16). *Best Writing Tip: Write as if Everyone You Know Is Dead*. The Writers College Times. Retrieved October 11, 2022, from https://www.writerscollegeblog.com/best-writing-tip-write-as-if-everyone-you-know-is-dead/

47   Davies, J. (2022b, April 22). *Writing What You Need to Read: One Quote Shared by Countless Authors.* BOOK RIOT. Retrieved October 11, 2022, from https://bookriot.com/who-said-writing-what-you-need-to-read/

48   Hazel, D. (2019, July 16). *Angels in the Tarot Cards with Donna Hazel. Biddy Tarot.* Retrieved October 23, 2022, from https://www.biddytarot.com/angels-in-tarot-cards/

49   This is a reference to the 1939 movie *The Wizard of Oz.* In the film, based on L. Frank Baum's 1900 novel *The Wonderful Wizard of Oz,* Dorothy Gale is searching for her way back home to Kansas, the Scarecrow is searching for intelligence, the Tin Man seeks a heart, and the Cowardly Lion wants nothing more than to be courageous.

50   Covey, S. R., Collins, J., & Covey, S. (2020, May 19). *The 7 Habits of Highly Effective People: 30th Anniversary Edition* (The Covey Habits Series) (Anniversary). Simon & Schuster.

51   Radford, B. (2016, March 24). *What is Alchemy?* livescience.com. Retrieved October 23, 2022, from https://www.livescience.com/39314-alchemy.html

52   Ouspensky, P. D. (1913). *The Symbolism of The TAROT.* The Trood Printing and Publishing Company, St. Petersburg. Translated by A. L. Pogossky.

53   Ohlheiser, A. (2015, February 27). *The Jewish roots of Leonard Nimoy and 'live long and prosper.'* Washington Post. https://www.washingtonpost.com/news/arts-and-entertainment/wp/2015/02/27/the-jewish-roots-of-leonard-nimoy-and-live-long-and-prosper/

54   Team Astroyogi. (2022, November 7). *The Devil.* Astroyogi.com. https://www.astroyogi.com/tarot/majorarcana/devil.aspx

55   *About LIGHTNING in the Bible* - WebBible Encyclopedia - ChristianAnswers. Net. (n.d.). https://christiananswers.net/dictionary/lightning.html

56   *Number 16 Meaning.* (n.d.). https://affinitynumerology.com/number-meanings/number-16-meaning.php

57   Rhys, D. (2022, September 27). *Meaning of the 8-Pointed Star (Octagram).* Symbol Sage. https://symbolsage.com/8-pointed-star/

58   Waite, A. E. (1966). *The Pictoral Key to the Tarot* (3rd Printing). University Books

59   Echols, S. E., Mueller, R., & Thomson, S. (1996). *Spiritual Tarot: Seventy-Eight Paths to Personal Development* (1st ed.). William Morrow Paperbacks.

60   Emma. (2022). *The Meaning & Symbolism Of Angel Number 17 - Numerology Nation.* Numerology Nation. https://numerologynation.com/angel-number-17/

61   Hunter, B. C. M. (2022, March 18). The world's happiest countries for 2022. CNN. https://edition.cnn.com/travel/article/worlds-happiest-countries-2022-wellness/index.html

62   Report, T. (2020, September 14). *"World's happiest man" says the secret to being happy takes just 15 minutes a day.* The Business Standard. https://www.tbsnews.net/feature/wellbeing/worlds-happiest-man-says-scret-being-happy-takes-just-15-minutes-day-132904

63   On page 64 of his memoir *On Writing,* Stephen King shares the story of receiving rejection letters and stabbing them onto a nail he'd hammered into his bedroom wall. You can read a synopsis of the anecdote in The Magician profile, Chapter 17, Key 1.

64   Hazel, D. (2019, July 16). *Angels in the Tarot Cards with Donna Hazel. Biddy Tarot.* Retrieved October 23, 2022, from https://www.biddytarot.com/angels-in-tarot-cards/

65   Emma. (2022, March 8). *7 Reasons Why You Are Seeing 20 – The Meaning Of 20.* Numerology Nation. https://numerologynation.com/angel-number-20/

66   Kirti, K. (2021, December 16). *The Fascinating Iconography of Vesica Piscis - The Collector.* Medium. https://medium.com/the-collector/the-fascinating-iconography-of-vesica-piscis-5674bd834dd7

67   Pollack, R. (2019). *Seventy-Eight Degrees of Wisdom: A Tarot Journey to Self-Awareness* (A New Edition of the Tarot Classic) (Third Edition, Revised). Weiser Books.

68   Brown, D. (2003). *The Da Vinci Code* (1st ed.). Doubleday.

69   Team Astroyogi. (2022, November 7). *The Devil.* Astroyogi.com. https://

www.astroyogi.com/tarot/majorarcana/devil.aspx

70   Echols, S. E., Mueller, R., & Thomson, S. (1996b). *Spiritual Tarot: Seventy-Eight Paths to Personal Development* (1st ed.). William Morrow Paperbacks.

71   Howcast. (2018c, December 19). *How to Read the Tens | Tarot Cards* [Video]. YouTube. https://www.youtube.com/watch?v=Q8fmPGFnp6A

72   Rhys, D. (2022b, October 6). *What Is Ichthys Symbol – History and Meaning.* *Symbol Sage.* https://symbolsage.com/ichthys-symbol/

73   Pollack, R. (2019). *Seventy-Eight Degrees of Wisdom: A Tarot Journey to Self-Awareness* (A New Edition of the Tarot Classic) (Third Edition, Revised). Weiser Books.

74   Associated Press. (2017, August 31). *Prince's Other Sister: Purple Was His Favorite Color, Not Orange.* Billboard. https://www.billboard.com/music/pop/ prince-purple-favorite-color-sharon-nelson-7949892/

75   The Editors of Encyclopedia Britannica. (2023, January 6). *Phoenix | mythological bird. Encyclopedia Britannica.* https://www.britannica.com/topic/ phoenix-mythological-bird

76   *About LIGHTNING in the Bible* - WebBible Encyclopedia - ChristianAnswers. Net. (n.d.). https://christiananswers.net/dictionary/lightning.html

77   Lebo, K. (2021, April 14). *A Secret, Symbolic History of Pomegranates.* Literary Hub. https://lithub.com/a-secret-symbolic-history-of-pomegranates/

78   Rhys, D. (2021, July 26). *Rainbow - Meaning and Symbolism.* Symbol Sage. https://symbolsage.com/rainbow-meaning-and-symbolism/

79   Beyer, C. (2019, January 21). *What You Should Know About Octagrams - Eight-Pointed Stars.* Learn Religions. https://www.learnreligions.com/ octagrams-eight-pointed-stars-96015

80   Howcast. (2018b, November 12). *How to Read the Hanged Man Card | Tarot Cards.* YouTube. https://www.youtube.com/watch?v=cjlZE4slkPQ

81   Katz, M., & Goodwin, T. (2015). *Secrets of the Waite-Smith Tarot: The True Story of the World's Most Popular Tarot* (Illustrated). Llewellyn Publications.

82   Waite, A. E. (1966). *The Pictoral Key to the Tarot* (3rd Printing). University Books.

83   Ohlheiser, A. (2015, February 27). *The Jewish roots of Leonard Nimoy and 'live long and prosper.'* Washington Post. https://www.washingtonpost.com/news/arts-and-entertainment/wp/2015/02/27/the-jewish-roots-of-leonard-nimoy-and-live-long-and-prosper/

84   Katz, M., & Goodwin, T. (2015). *Secrets of the Waite-Smith Tarot: The True Story of the World's Most Popular Tarot* (Illustrated). Llewellyn Publications.

85   Ouspensky, P. D. (1913). *The Symbolism of The TAROT.* The Trood Printing and Publishing Company, St. Petersburg. Translated by A. L. Pogossky.

86   Avia. (n.d.). Globes. *TarotTeachings.com.* https://www.tarotteachings.com/symbol-meanings-of-tarot-d-k.html

87   Kirti, K. (2021, December 16). *The Fascinating Iconography of Vesica Piscis - The Collector. Medium.* https://medium.com/the-collector/the-fascinating-iconography-of-vesica-piscis-5674bd834dd7

88   Mingren, W. (2018, November 22). *Understanding the Dharma Wheel: This Ancient Symbol Holds Secret Meanings. Ancient Origins.* https://www.ancient-origins.net/artifacts-other-artifacts/dharma-wheel-0011033

89   Pollack, R. (2019). *Seventy-Eight Degrees of Wisdom: A Tarot Journey to Self-Awareness* (A New Edition of the Tarot Classic) (Third Edition, Revised). Weiser Books.

90   Pollack, R. (2019). *Seventy-Eight Degrees of Wisdom: A Tarot Journey to Self-Awareness* (A New Edition of the Tarot Classic) (Third Edition, Revised). Weiser Books.

91   Jung, C. G., & Hull, R. (1981, August 1). *The Archetypes and The Collective Unconscious* (Collected Works of C.G. Jung Vol.9 Part 1) (Collected Works of C.G. Jung, 48) (2nd ed.). Princeton University Press.

92   Jung, C. G., & Douglas, C. (1997). *Visions: Notes of the Seminar given in 1930-1934.* Vol. 2. (Princeton NJ, Princeton University Press, Bollingen Series XCIX, 1997), p. 923.

93 Numerology.com Staff. (2022b, October 3). *Life Path Number Calculator*. Numerology.com. https://www.numerology.com/articles/your-numerology-chart/life-path-number-calculator/

94 *Meanings of Numbers in the Bible: The Number 15*. (n.d.). Bible Study. https://www.biblestudy.org/bibleref/meaning-of-numbers-in-bible/15.html

95 *Number 16 Meaning*. (n.d.-b). https://affinitynumerology.com/number-meanings/number-16-meaning.php

96 *The Meaning & Symbolism Of Angel Number 17*. (2022, January 14). Numerology Nation. https://numerologynation.com/angel-number-17/

97 Emma. (2022, March 8). *7 Reasons Why You Are Seeing 20 – The Meaning Of 20*. Numerology Nation. https://numerologynation.com/angel-number-20/

98 Christiane. (2019, August 5). *Tarot & Astrology: Planets*. Cosmic Spirit Tarot. https://www.cosmictarot.co.uk/tarot-astrology-planets/

99 The Editors of Encyclopedia Britannica. (1998, July 20). *Saturn | Roman god*. Encyclopedia Britannica. https://www.britannica.com/topic/Saturn-god

100 Numerology.com Staff. (2022b, October 3). *Life Path Number Calculator*. Numerology.com. https://www.numerology.com/articles/your-numerology-chart/life-path-number-calculator/

101 In Season 2, Episode 19 of *The Office*, Michael announces that he shares the same birthday as Eva Longoria (March 15), and Dwight Schrute makes an irreverent comment about the exact time of Michael's birth: 11:23 am. In another episode, Michael reveals his age, and with some research, I discovered his birth year as being 1965. Although the show never reveals the place where Michael was born, for the sake of this exercise, I used the city and state where the character lives: Scranton, Pennsylvania. With these details, I was able to retrieve Michael Scott's natal chart and determine his Big Three.

102 Greer, M. K. (2019). *Tarot for Your Self: A Workbook for the Inward Journey* (35th Anniversary Edition) (Anniversary, Workbook). Weiser Books.

103 The 3-card spread "Theme, Obstacle/Opportunity, Blessing" is one that I designed; however, you might find similar spreads in your tarot studies.

104 MasterClass. (2022, September 2). *Writing 101: What Is Stream of Consciousness Writing? Learn About Stream of Consciousness in Literature With Examples* - 2023 - MasterClass. https://www.masterclass.com/articles/writing-101-what-is-stream-of-consciousness-writing-learn-about-stream-of-consciousness-in-literature-with-examples

105 While titles are too short to be protected by copyright laws, *A Story for Every Day* and *A Story for Every Week* are titles of a memoir and blog, respectively, created by me, Amanda Hughes.

106 Campbell, J. (1973). *The Hero With A Thousand Faces* (21st ed.). Princeton University Press.

Acknowledgements

. . . .

All books start out as ideas, and most end up with one or two names on their covers, but the reality of bringing a book to shelves, hands, and hearts depends on a team of dedicated supporters. *Mystic Storyteller* would not have been possible without several Muggles and magickal folk.

My highest gratitude and lowest bow goes to my Backers. Your support is an honor, and I sincerely hope this book and cards inspire stories that enrich your life and the lives of others as you have so graciously done for mine.

To Shederal, the love of my life and my favorite Emperor, thank you for your listening ear and pointed feedback while I was crafting this book. Your unbiased nature and unconditional love and support not only make me a better writer but a much better person. Thank you, also, for changing the way I think about The Emperor, because before your warmup suit and sneakers, he felt like a stodgy old curmudgeon.

To Jalan and Devan, my Knights of Cups and Pentacles, you are my best work and my favorite gifts. I'll never create anything as beautiful and meaningful as you, but with your love and support, I'll never stop trying.

To Stacie, my Six of Pentacles, my closest friend and Sister, thank you for patiently and genuinely listening to me while I used our dinner tables and road trips as whiteboards for piecing together this book. Like your card, you are generous with your time and resources, and none of my books could have been written without you.

To Grisel, my Six of Wands, my editor and cherished Sister, you walked into my life the most incredible, magickal gift. Your fiery determination and spirit have ignited my world in ways I never imagined before the day we met. Thank you for lighting the path for this book and tarot deck to find their way.

To Stacey, our Queen of Wands, your work provided me exactly what I pray this book and these gorgeous cards do for others: a calling to create fearless, authentic stories that change hearts and minds. I am indebted to the Universe for its synchronous magick in crossing our paths.

To Shannon, our Queen of Pentacles, I'm grateful every day to have found your work. Your wisdom and insight nourished my soul while drafting this book, and I'm incredibly lucky to call you my friend.

To Weslyn, our Death Rider, and Roz, our illustrator, thank you both for your keen eyes and hands, along with your imbuing the *Mystic Storyteller* project with the highest intentions for creative transformation and abundance.

Enormous gratitude goes to Theresa Reed. Your words and chill energy were most instructive and appreciated while writing this book. And that you read and reviewed it? Wow! I'm honored and humbled. Thank you for making the tarot accessible in a way that resonates in every 'hood and on any street.

Many special thanks go to my Sisters, friends, peers, and fans who supported me during the writing and publishing of *Mystic Storyteller.* Maria, C-Mac, Debbie, Erika, Nancy, Thomas, Sonja, Mandi, Jillian, Lisa, Christiana, Connie, Mimi, Victoria, Cyndera, and many, many more.

And, finally, to Pixie, Pamela Colman Smith, for her tremendous contribution to tarot, and to Pinkie Perideaux, my very own High Priestess who brought her work to my imagination. Thank you.

· · ·  · · ·

About the Author

. . . .

In her more than thirty years as a storyteller and visual designer, Amanda "Mandy" Hughes has written and designed over a dozen works of literary, Southern Gothic, and women's fiction under pen names A. Lee Hughes and Mandy Lee.

Mandy is the founder of Haint Blue Creative®, a space for readers and storytellers to explore, learn, and create. She holds a Bachelor and Master of Science in Psychology, and she has worked as an instructional designer for over twenty years.

When she's not writing, Mandy enjoys the movies, theater, music, traveling, nature walks, birdwatching, and bingeing The Office. She is a tarot enthusiast who has spent over a decade using the cards to enhance creativity and foster wellness. Her book *Mystic Storyteller: A Writer's Guide to Using the Tarot for Creative Inspiration* is her first work of nonfiction.

Mandy lives in Georgia with her husband and four sons, two of whom are furrier than the others (but not by much). Visit her website at haintbluecreative. com and follow her on Instagram @HaintBlueCreative.